Keith J. Laidler

1980

Ottawa

Gary Werskey

The Visible College

Allen Lane

Allen Lane
Penguin Books Ltd,
17 Grosvenor Gardens, London SW1W 0BD

First published 1978

Copyright © Gary Werskey, 1978

ISBN 0 7139 08262

Set in 11/12 Bembo
Printed in Great Britain by
Ebenezer Baylis and Son, Ltd,
The Trinity Press, Worcester, and London

To John Wolfers, human agent *par excellence*

'One basis for life and another for science is *a priori* a lie.'
Karl Marx

Contents

List of Illustrations

Preface

In the ten years it has taken to bring this work to fruition, I have received help from literally hundreds of men and women. To mention them all would result in a rather meaningless and somewhat self-congratulatory list.

Nevertheless I must mention: Everett Mendelsohn, who introduced me to this subject and supervised my doctoral research; Joseph and Dorothy Needham, who generously shared with me their memories, their papers and their home during the summer of 1968; Bob Young, who inspired me (and many others) to ask more searching questions about my work; Michael Totton, who helped to put me in touch with a far larger number of socialists from the thirties than I would have ever been able to meet on my own; John Wolfers, whose faith in me and this book never faltered, even when I (and it) did; and Jennifer Hurstfield, who, as a socialist and feminist, was most responsible for my own radicalization – without which I could never have understood an earlier generation of socialists.

They and the others made this book possible. Unfortunately, I still had to write it. Whatever mistakes and errors of judgement remain are all my own.

G.W.
Highbury,
London,
September, 1977

Foreword

The 'Invisible College' [consists of] persons that endeavour to put narrow-mindedness out of countenance by the practice of so extensive a charity that it reaches unto everything called man, and nothing less than an universal good-will can content it. And indeed they are so apprehensive of the want of good employment that they take the whole body of mankind for their care.

But . . . there is not enough of them.

Robert Boyle, 1646/7[1]

The Visible College has five central characters, three themes and a single purpose. Each of these elements deserves a brief preview.

The men whose activities and ideas I am featuring are J. D. Bernal (1901–71), J. B. S. Haldane (1892–1964), Lancelot Hogben (1895–1975), Hyman Levy (1889–1975) and Joseph Needham (1900–   ). Although these five cannot be said to have formed a cohesive group in the inter-war period, they did hold a number of qualities in common. The first one is that their commitment to socialism predated the so-called 'Red Decade' of the 1930s, which is usually reckoned as the starting point for their generation's radicalization. Another attribute they shared was their participation at various times in party politics, whether on the left wing of the Labour Party or in the Communist Party of Great Britain. Finally, through their many books and articles, they were the authors of a large and distinctive body of socialist thought. Of course they were not the only outstanding 'progressive' scientists of their era. The names of P. M. S. Blackett, N. W. Pirie, W. A. Wooster and even C. H. Waddington come to mind here. But none of them combined in his own life all of the characteristics I have ascribed to Bernal, Haldane, Hogben, Levy and Needham. That is why I have grouped them together into the 'Visible College'.*

* My title plays upon the name of a London-based society of natural

I have written a collective biography – as opposed to a general and more abstract account of the scientists' movement in the thirties – because I believe that no significant social phenomenon can be understood apart from the motives and aspirations of the persons who shape it. (I also happen to find histories rooted in the lives of particular individuals much easier to read.) Yet while men and women can be said to make their own history, they seldom do so under conditions of their own choosing. That is one of Marx's insights which I have tried to apply both to the different circumstances of my five subjects and to the organizations they helped to set in motion. Hence I shall be continually moving about between the concrete details of a man's life and the broader political drama of his time and place.

Running throughout this interplay between biography and social history will be three major themes. One of these is a reassessment of the kinds of intellectuals who found their way into the pre-war Left. I do not share the view of many previous writers on this topic that the typical middle-class radical of the 1930s was a politically inexperienced poet who naïvely opted for communism only to find that his 'God' had failed him by the following decade. However well that hypothesis might work with a few individuals and however comforting it might be to some unreconstructed 'Cold Warriors', it simply breaks down when applied to the experiences of the great majority of this period's left-wingers, including the scientists. Hence there is a real need to determine why some parts of the intelligentsia were more prone to leftist ideas than others; and why some of the radicalized intellectuals eventually turned their backs on all varieties of socialism while others did not. That is one reason for taking a closer look at this generation of socialists.

---

philosophers, the 'Invisible College', which flourished briefly over three hundred years ago during the English Civil War. Whether or not this group was in any sense an important forerunner of the Royal Society, the desire of its members, as 'scientists', to 'take the whole body of mankind for their care' certainly did anticipate the aspirations and projects that would be later advanced by Bernal and his associates. Indeed, as we shall see, the left-wing scientists of the 1930s were very fond of drawing parallels between their 'revolutionary' situation and that of their counterparts from the 1640s.

For more information about the 'Invisible College' see M. Purver, *The Royal Society; Concept and Creation* (London, 1967). Cf. C. Webster, 'The Origins of the Royal Society', *History of Science*, vol. 6 (1967), pp. 106–38.

A second theme is the discovery of what a particular grouping within the Left was doing and saying at this time. Until recently there has been a tendency to trivialize the thought and experience of left-wing intellectuals from the thirties. Their 'theory' has commonly been regarded as little more than a collection of slogans handed down from the Soviet-dominated Third International, while their 'practice' was supposedly limited in the main to the production of pamphlets for the faithful. But such was not the case with a number of the scientific Left's leading spokesmen. They not only fashioned their own novel, coherent and contrasting interpretations of Marxism but closely linked their theoretical perspective to a set of highly effective political practices as well. Together these beliefs and actions constituted a form of politics whose nature and limits deserve the most careful scrutiny.

The final theme I want to tackle is the impact of the thirties' generation of socialists on my own. Once again the pre-war Left has been the victim of two very serious misconceptions. Either it has been said to have had little or no effect on British political developments since the Second World War; or, alternatively, its vision of socialism is supposed to have been categorically rejected by the New Left of the 1960s. In fact both propositions need to be modified, not least in the case of the old Left's scientific cadres. Many of their ideas did enter into mainstream politics in this country, first through the early wartime debates on the need to modernize Britain and later via the attempts of Harold Wilson and the Labour Party to launch a 'white-hot' technological revolution. Admittedly most younger socialists have long since abandoned the technocratic reformation of British capitalism as a worthy or workable goal. Yet their own socialism usually still retains the 'scientific' ethos which Bernal and his comrades had first evolved forty years ago. How significant a continuity this is and what it implies about the Left's future prospects is a third area to be explored.

There are of course many other themes – the left-wing scientists' contributions to various fields of biology and physics, their writings on the history and philosophy of science, the relationship between their private and public lives – that I might have chosen to high-light. While not altogether absent here, they only enter the text to the extent that they illuminate the main story line. In other words

I am principally concerned to describe and analyse what it meant for an intellectual to be an active socialist around the time of the Second World War.

This tale may therefore be of interest to socialists, intellectuals, academics, people who are politically engaged in this period and, more broadly still, anyone who finds biographies a good 'read'. In its telling I have tried to keep in mind the needs of these different but overlapping groups.* Ultimately, however, what they all require is a lively narrative that is faithful to its subject. I hope *The Visible College* successfully approximates that ideal. For, as a socialist, historically minded sociologist and avid reader myself, I believe that this story deserves to be more widely known.

* Perhaps the group which suffers most from the approach I have adopted here are my fellow academics. In *The Visible College* I have not directly and in detail engaged in any of the historiographical or sociological debates surrounding my subject. (Hence the references, which are used solely to document the source of a quotation or little known 'fact', have been relegated to the rear of the book.) Where I stand in these various wrangles should be reasonably clear to those who are most closely involved in them. But for a more explicit statement of my views see my: 'British Scientists and "Outsider" Politics, 1931–1945', *Science Studies*, vol. 1 (January, 1971), pp. 67–83 (reprinted in Barry Barnes (ed.), *Sociology of Science* (Harmondsworth, 1972), pp. 231–50); 'Making Socialists of Scientists: Whose Side Is History On?' *Radical Science Journal*, nos. 2/3 (1975), pp. 13–50; and 'The Visible College: A Study of British Left-wing Scientists, 1918–1939', unpublished Ph.D. thesis, Harvard University, 1974.

Part One

Before the Thirties

Chapter One

High Science and Low Politics

... the modern man of science knows that he is respected, and feels that he does not deserve respect. He approaches the established order apologetically. 'My predecessors', he says in effect, 'may have said harsh things about you because they were arrogant, and imagined that they possessed some knowledge. I am more humble, and do not claim to know anything that can controvert your dogma.' In return, the established order showers knighthoods and fortunes upon the men of science, who become more and more determined supporters of the injustice and obscurantism upon which our social system is based.

Bertrand Russell, 1931[1]

When we settle down to read about the lives of poets or politicians, we already feel that we know them. For all of us have some knowledge of the kind of domain in which these people move and the sort of work they do. In fact we have been encountering them, albeit at a great distance, ever since early childhood. At school, literature and politics were the bread and butter of literally thousands of English and history lessons. Now upon coming home from work we turn on the news, which usually turns out to consist of a series of political events. If we wish to escape from the reality projected in these broadcasts, we often turn to works of fiction, of history or possibly even of biography. Ironically, however, one reason why we can relax with our books in this way is that they tend to reflect back and reinforce our notion of what the world is like and who is important in it: hence our continuing love-hate relationship with artists and statesmen. We understand them too well.

Scientists, by contrast, are almost complete strangers to most of us, because we do not know where they come from or how they spend their time. Indeed, having been denied access to their history and culture, we are often tempted to regard them as pretty uninteresting people. Not even well written accounts of such scientific

'greats' as Darwin and Einstein have succeeded in removing this
stigma. The fault here has largely resided in the refusal of bio-
graphers to trace out the web of social relationships in which their
subjects' lives are deeply entangled. Until authors and readers alike
undertake that enterprise, we are likely to go on forsaking the world
of science for that of literature and politics.

Our need to understand how the scientific vocation is organized
and integrated with other social pursuits is especially great in a book
which is principally concerned with the careers of five highly
atypical academic scientists. They were 'deviants' in that, unlike the
vast majority of their peers, they were committed to the overthrow
of British capitalism and the creation of a socialist commonwealth.
Just how unusual they were in this respect, if not others, needs to be
established and explained. So the first thing we must do is describe
the environment in which, between 1901 and 1931, they came of age
as scientific workers. That means, for a start, discussing 'pure' or
what I prefer to call 'High Science' as it was practised at Cambridge
– a community that left a profound mark on all professional
researchers in this period. Thereafter we can identify what brand of
politics normally attracted the most 'scientific' approbation. We
should then be able to appreciate some of the important changes
that were made in the organization of British science around the time
of the First World War. Having specified the structure, outlook and
dynamics of their rarefied yet exciting milieu we can more easily
understand, and possibly even identify with, the struggle of its more
rebellious inhabitants.

1. Cambridge Science

'High Science' is research which academic scientists hold in the
greatest esteem. In the twentieth century High Science in Britain
has had the following characteristics. It is 'pure', i.e. undertaken for
purely intellectual as opposed to utilitarian reasons. It is 'hard' and
'experimental': which means, among other things, a bias towards
the techniques and problems of the physical sciences and an aversion
to speculative theorizing which runs far ahead of empirical
investigations. High Science is also 'fashionable', 'hot' science, a
research area of outstanding promise or continuing excitement. It is,
above all and at its best, the work of 'first-rate' practitioners.

The locus for pure, hard, experimental, fashionable and first-rate science was, and probably still is, Cambridge. Certainly in the inter-war period an affiliation, whether past or present, to Cambridge science was almost mandatory for anyone who looked forward to a bright future in academic research. No other university had such an abundance of human and physical resources to devote to 'disinter-ested' investigations. Its graduates were 'naturally' the big men in their chosen fields. By sitting on important government committees and controlling the major laboratories in and out of Cambridge, they were able to determine the style, the ethos and, not least, the direction of pure science in Britain. As might have been expected, the most fashionable of scientific enterprises were based in Cam-bridge itself. Between 1918 and 1939, for example, its Cavendish Laboratory and Dunn Institute were the homes of the two finest research schools in what were then the two hottest subjects, particle physics and biochemistry. Given the excellence of those institutions alone, it looked as if Cambridge's dominance of High Science would continue for at least another generation. So would the pressures on academic scientists to get themselves identified as 'Cambridge men'.

Yet there was far more to becoming a Cambridge man than merely learning and developing the branch of physics or biology that happened to interest you. Once admitted into this ancient university, your research interests were woven into a way of life and a set of attitudes which you were expected to uphold. The values generated from within this culture were unsurprisingly élitist and competitive. Among the most highly prized virtues were loyalty to your lab and dedication to your work. Political commitments were your own affair, as long as they did not impede your full participa-tion in the activities of your chosen research community. (But politics were thought to be such an irrational enterprise that any overt preoccupation with them was bound to cast some doubt on your 'soundness'.) Whatever else might be said about the life-style of Cambridge scientists, it was not one likely to inspire or sustain socialist convictions and practices. On the contrary: this unique community of High Scientists might be powerful enough to re-shape and assimilate the socialism, however revolutionary, of its most rebellious members. Of course this idea needs to be elaborated. For Cambridge science has long been associated with traditions of 'free' enquiry rather than intellectual constraint.

How then was it possible for the vast majority of its products to end up holding deeply hierarchical views of what science was like and how society worked? Consider the circumstances of a typical Cambridge scientist. *He* was recruited from a suitably aristocratic, bourgeois or professional family and often had the advantage of a private income. As an ex-Cambridge biochemist recently observed of his own lab in the 1920s: 'most, say seven out of ten of the staff and research workers had some inherited money . . . This gave them a feeling of security and independence.'[2] After receiving a public school education, he went up to Cambridge as an undergraduate and then stayed on to do a higher degree. Thus for a minimum of six years he was working in a town and university setting then notorious even by English standards for its ritualized observance of class distinctions. Indeed it was entirely possible for him to spend years at Cambridge without ever speaking to working-class people, other than a small army of deferential college servants and laboratory attendants. Apart from social class, he found that sex was the most important stratifying principle. Male domination, which typified the university as a whole, was especially obvious within the Cambridge scientific community, where there were ten times as many men as women. That imbalance grew even worse upon his promotion to a senior staff position. By this stage he was spending almost his entire working life with prosperous and 'clever' bourgeois males. As a member of an intellectual élite – entry to which was largely reserved for one class, one sex (and one race) only – it would be remarkable if he did not begin to think in élitist terms.

Inside his own lab the Cambridge scientist was exposed in numerous ways to views that corresponded with his daily practices. Naturally he was soon made aware of the norms and values of High Science. Hence any gravitation on his part towards industrial research was bound to be regarded as somehow both morally and intellectually suspect. It was widely known, for example, that Sir Ernest Rutherford – the Cavendish Professor and doyen of British physics – 'had no interest whatever in technology and technical problems. It even seemed that he nursed a prejudice against them, insofar as work in the area of applied science was concerned with money motives'. Rutherford's dictum in these matters was that 'God and Mammon' (Rutherford and big business?) were diametrically opposed masters. 'And', one of his ex-students has written, 'he was right of course.'[3] To our Cambridge man, however, an even more powerful objection to work done for extra-scientific ends was that it must, almost by definition, be intellectually less demanding than pure research. That view was reflected in the mathematician G. H. Hardy's estimate of war-work in science as 'essentially second-rate and dull'. However 'public-spirited and praiseworthy' such preoccupations might be, they were not worthy of 'a first-rate man with proper personal ambitions'.[4]

Who was and who was not a 'first-rate man' was yet another system of ranking that pervaded and defined the life of the Cambridge scientist. His main concern, inevitably, was whether he himself would be judged first-rate enough to merit the esteem of his colleagues. A young Cavendish student named Lancelot Law Whyte, after months of worrying about this very question, realized early one wintry morning in 1923 that he was not going to make the grade.

A wise old Cambridge man whom I had consulted some time earlier, had said to me, 'Only stay at Cambridge if you can be a star of the first magnitude. Otherwise clear out and have a more varied life.' I had hoped to be some kind of star, but now I knew I had no chance. I must follow this moment of clarity at all costs; it might never return. By 7 a.m. I was dressed; by 8 packed; . . . by 10 I had seen Rutherford . . .; by 11 I had caught a train . . . I never returned to Cambridge.[5]

At the top of this star system were the heads of major departments and laboratories. Their authority was rooted in scientific prestige, paternalistic in character and rarely if ever questioned by the research students whom they oversaw. Thus Rutherford personally supervised nearly all of the Cavendish post-graduates; 'his boys' as he liked to call them. Their counterparts at the Dunn Biochemical Institute saw their mentor, Sir Frederick Gowland Hopkins, as being *in loco parentis* to them. Obviously the work of these father-figures was seen as exemplary. That both of them held knighthoods was a feudal touch that helped to bring into focus the three main constituents of the Cambridge scientific community: a pre-industrial town, a pre-capitalist university and an aristocratic conception of science. In these circumstances it was an advantage to be something of an aristocrat yourself.

By now it should be clear that Cambridge scientists had a coherent sub-culture. Yet their social homogeneity and shared values were only partly responsible for their community's cohesiveness. Especially in the twenties and early thirties, their solidarity was mightily enhanced by their knowledge that, as they defined it, 'this is a golden age of science'. That was C. P. Snow writing as a physical chemist in 1933. He continued: 'Judged by the number of great scientists, this is by far the richest time there has ever been.'[6] Some of the 'greatest' of these, such as Hardy, Hopkins and Rutherford, were of course at Cambridge itself. Through their pioneering investigations and those of their colleagues and students, they were able to generate tremendous excitement and sustain their intellectual morale for years at a stretch. Such *esprit de corps* was essential in an era when primitive equipment obliged researchers to spend long hours, day and night, in the labs. Out of such enforced comradeship these men came to rely upon one another socially as well as professionally.

Soon the boundaries of their workplaces and homes began to blur rather badly. Not content with discussing physics from nine to five, young physicists from the Cavendish formed an after-hours discussion circle in the early twenties to keep themselves informed, stimulated and amused. Over at the Dunn Lab Cambridge bio-chemists were showing themselves to be equally obsessive about their own science (and each other). They even produced a humorous annual between 1923 and 1931. Called *Brighter Biochemistry*, it pro-vided the Dunn's inmates with a chance to prove that pure scientists were as susceptible to pure corn as lesser beings. ('Take Umbrage for Your Spleen', 'Spend your Holidays in High Dudgeon', etc.) Apart from inspiring these highly organized escapades, Cambridge labora-tories lent themselves to more private and personal uses, including sexual encounters. Some young male researchers, in particular, recognized the exotic charm of their futuristic surroundings. One of them, I have been told, even went to the trouble of harnessing an oscilloscope to a gramophone; a homemade device whose dancing images – especially those produced by American jazz recordings – were used to convince potential lovers of an artistic persuasion that art and science really were compatible. (Most, but not all, of these trysts were heterosexual affairs.) The significance of that episode, not to mention the physicists' club and *Brighter Biochemistry*, was its demonstration of how enveloped Cambridge men could become in the totalizing environment of High Science.

A final cause/consequence of these researchers' self-absorption and communality was their relative isolation from the cultures of non-scientists, notably those in the arts. C. P. Snow's combative 'two cultures' actually existed in Cambridge, if nowhere else; though the conflict between them is almost as difficult to document as the reasons for it. Occasionally there appeared in print a small salvo from an arts man like Julian Bell, complaining that 'the scientist . . . was innately incapable either of creating or appreciating art.'[7] Shortly afterwards, a disgruntled researcher would turn this complaint on its head by ridiculing the scientific illiteracy of Bell and his fellow 'arties'.[8] Snow has since recalled how the literati then arrogated to themselves the title of 'intellectual'.[9] His explanation for this refined form of adolescent name-calling is, roughly, that scientific intellectuals were at heart committed to and optimistic about the scientific-industrial evolution of British society. Poets, writers and artists generally, on the other hand, were at this time estranged from the advancing mass-civilization which threatened to overwhelm their minority culture. To the extent that natural scientists were identified with various forms of 'modernization', it is not surprising, Snow has concluded, that they became favourite targets for students and donnish aesthetes.

Up till now this portrait of Cambridge science has simplified a complex world so as to bring out the social structure and values which held it together and made it unique. It is, however, misleading – not quite a true likeness of the subject – in at least two respects. There were important variations in the ethos and operation of different laboratories. Thus the Dunn Lab had in its leader, Gowland Hopkins, a less dominating figure of authority than, say, Rutherford. Its organization was also less hierarchical and formalized than the Cavendish's, where post-graduates were clearly separated from the rest of the staff. Cambridge biochemistry was also associated with some applied work on human nutrition, although its emphasis was clearly on pure research. Yet possibly the most striking thing about the biochemists was that a respectable minority of them were women, quite a few of whom married male co-workers at the Dunn. Only the class composition of the institute marked it out as a Cambridge institution.

The other amendment is of course that some Cambridge scientists were not 'typical' at all. Indeed a few of the younger researchers were organizing around this time scientific counter-cultures, which dared to flaunt some of High Science's (and High Scientists') more staid conventions. Unfortunately, the entrance requirements into this marginal, quasi-bohemian world were even stiffer than those which obtained in the labs themselves. It was essential that you were: unconventional enough to break down both the internal margins of scientific disciplines and the external boundaries marking the sciences off from the arts; and talented enough to get away with it. Few men and women combined sufficient energy, wit, cleverness and iconoclasm to lead this sort of life and still keep up their research commitments. Nevertheless there have always been a handful of them resident in Cambridge. In the twenties, as we shall see, their names were J. D. Bernal and J. B. S. Haldane, each of whom had his own circle of friends and admirers drawn from both sexes and both cultures.

However, there were in the Cambridge of this era limits set on the diversity of its institutions and the idiosyncracies of its members. Hence the Dunn, for all its progressiveness, operated firmly within the traditions of High Science. Ex-Cambridge undergraduates were always favoured, first as post-graduates and later as staff members. Men were promoted far faster than women. Pure science was favoured over applied. And, to judge from the great efforts poured into *Brighter Biochemistry*, the lab was the most powerful force operating in the lives of all its members. As for the counter-culture, one can only note that its denizens – self-selected as an exceptionally clever élite within an élite – normally chose to stay on at Cambridge and uphold their professional obligations. Ironically, the energy they had to expend breaking free from some aspects of the culture of High Science was a striking confirmation of its strength.

2. The Open Conspiracy

If High Scientists were as a rule politically inactive, that hardly debarred them from having political opinions. Nor, given their social background and professional standing, should we be surprised to learn that their views were comfortably contained within the ruling class's ideological spectrum. They were also unlikely to have been ignorant of the many 'scientific' solutions to the nation's problems that were put forward from the Edwardian era onwards. Not only were these proposals reported and endorsed in *Nature*, Britain's (and the world's) leading journal of science, but they presented the scientific élite with new opportunities to advance their own studies as well. However, so great was the political inertia of this privileged grouping that it could not be stirred into action except in the most extraordinary circumstances; like total warfare.

As it happened the preconditions for such a crisis were readily apparent by 1914. Britain, the world's leading imperial power, was in a precarious state. Mainly as a consequence of the overwhelming strength of a banking sector that preoccupied itself with overseas trade and investment, the British domestic economy was enfeebled and uncompetitive. Manufacturing industry was in a particularly bad state. Compared with their German rivals, British firms were grossly undercapitalized, too small in scale and overly concentrated in declining craft-based industries, as opposed to the newer and more profitable science-based forms of production. Unfortunately for these industries they were unable to 'rationalize' their operations because private investors and the banks were not prepared to lend them the necessary capital. The only other way of enhancing their profitability was to increase the rate at which they exploited other resources, namely their work forces. Even that avenue was being slowly closed off, as the political and trade union arms of the labour movement grew in numbers, strength and militancy during this period. In fact a wave of big strikes between 1910 and 1914 provoked widespread doubts as to whether the workers could any longer be relied upon to fight for King and Country. At a time when Germany and other lesser powers were beginning to probe the weaknesses in Britain's Empire, the issue of military and indeed moral strength was an important one for the nation. A number of respectable reforming societies even went so far as to argue that large numbers of Britons would never be able to prepare themselves either morally or physically for combat, because they had become so sodden with alcohol, riddled with vice, prone to disease and inclined to crime. These were some of the reasons why for many observers the social and economic regeneration of Great Britain had grown into a political necessity.

One of the most interesting responses to this particular crisis came from a politically and professionally heterogeneous group of 'social-imperialists'. This is the term used by such historians as Geoffrey Searle[10] and Bernard Semmell[11] to designate individual Tories (Joseph Chamberlain), Liberals (Lord Haldane) and Fabian socialists (Sidney and Beatrice Webb), as well as particular organizations like the British Science Guild, that pressed for social reform designed to increase the working class's stake in the survival of imperialism. What these reforms were is less important for us than the means whereby they were supposed to have been achieved. For the necessary if not sufficient condition for social imperialism was that all sections of British society had to become more efficient in performance and more scientific in outlook. The appeal to science ran through all the writings and propaganda of the social imperialists, and it was not used merely as a rhetorical device to distinguish them from their old-fashioned, unscientific opponents. They recognized, for example, the need for greater state and private investment in research facilities, which, it was hoped, would eventually lead to substantial advances in medical, military, agricultural and of course industrial technologies. The attraction of this strategy for capitalists in science-based industries and High Scientists in universities, both of whom might wish to expand their enterprises, was obvious. But to workers on the receiving end of such 'progress', the benefits were not quite so straightforward. Some trade unionists were already becoming aware of the ways in which technical innovations, whether in the form of new machinery, assembly lines or time-motion studies, might be used to throw them out of work, take the skill out of their jobs and, in general, subject them more firmly to the will of their employers. Nevertheless rationalization was a difficult process to resist when, as the social imperialists insisted, it alone could bring the social and material benefits which the labour movement sought for its members. Capital and labour therefore had to collaborate more closely (and quickly) at the point of production. Otherwise both sides might be overwhelmed in the coming international struggle for power.

The call for cooperation between classes perennially in conflict with one another was bound to produce some programmatic inconsistencies, even among the eminently 'scientific' proponents of social imperialism. Their contradictory views on human biology nicely illustrate that point. United in their fears about 'racial decay' – the overproduction of dirty, licentious, diseased and unintelligent workers – they were internally divided about its causes and cures. Two schools of thought, the 'environmentalists' and the 'eugenists', contended with one another here. The environmentalists were convinced that poverty, slums and social despair were primarily to blame for the malnutrition, ill-health and alcoholism which, in their view, prevented those of proletarian parentage from performing well (or at least better) in schools, factories and on the battlefield. They therefore proposed to reform and widen the state's welfare services, especially those bearing on public health and medical care. To social imperialists of a eugenic persuasion, however, these proposals would hasten, not arrest, the deterioration of British 'stocks'. For they – and 'they' included a future Tory Prime Minister (Neville Chamberlain), Liberals like John Maynard Keynes and socialists such as Harold Laski – believed that the decrepitude and supposed 'stupidity' of slum dwellers was due essentially to their poor genetic constitution. Hence any environmental improvements brought about through increased public assistance would not only fail to increase the intelligence and physical stature of its recipients but actually encourage them to reproduce still more 'sub-standard' human beings as well. This would add to the state's welfare burdens, which of course would ultimately have to be shouldered by well-born or aspiring families. Since they were already limiting the size of their households, these additional taxes would depress still further the fertility rates of the nation's 'best', i.e. its fittest, most intelligent breeders.* The eugenists' plan to stave off racial suicide was simplicity itself. Spread the knowledge of birth control to the lower orders. (Marie Stopes' organization, which was designed to achieve this end, called itself the Society for Constructive Birth Control *and* Racial Progress.) Sterilize the feeble-minded, the criminally insane, the drunken 'unemployables' and other 'low-grade mental defectives'. Encourage financially the 'right' sort of

---

* J. M. Keynes in 1925: 'How can I adopt a creed [Marxism] which, preferring the mud to the fish, exalts the boorish proletariat above the bourgeois and the intelligentsia, who, with whatever faults, are the quality in life and surely carry the seeds of all human advancement?' From J. M. Keynes, *Essays in Persuasion* (New York, 1963), p. 300; also quoted in B. Easlea, *Liberation and the Aims of Science* (London, 1973), p. 118.

parents to have more children. At first sight this analysis and programme could not have been more different from that of the environmentalists. Yet both groups were merely relying upon two different forms of biological engineering, in order to produce a population fit and clever enough to preserve the existing social order.

These and other tenets of social imperialism were repeatedly endorsed in the leading articles, features and book reviews of *Nature* from 1914 to 1939.[12] One reason for the durability of this perspective was that for all but five of these twenty-five years this journal was run by one man, Sir Richard Gregory. His significance for our story is unusually great. For no single individual was then more closely in touch with the spectrum of activities pursued by Britain's natural scientists. Gregory was himself at various times an influential figure within the British Association for the Advancement of Science, the British Science Guild and the National Union of Scientific Workers. As the Editor of *School World* and, later, the *Journal of Education*, he kept a close eye on science education. He was also on top of developments in scientific publishing through his direction of Macmillan's Science Department. Apart from these positions Gregory forged a number of links between himself and key academic, industrial and governmental researchers, plus their employers, many of whom he met at his London club, the Athenaeum. Gregory even numbered among his associates a handful of trade unionists and Labour Party politicians. Out of all these contacts he and his chief 'leader' writer, an employee of the chemical giant I.C.I. named Rainald Brightman, were able to offer a broadly representative view of what the more important scientists were doing and thinking, and what that implied for the rest of British society. Their conclusions marked both them and their sources out as social imperialists.

What then was *Nature*'s attitude to the struggle between capital and labour as it developed during Gregory's long editorship? To Gregory the answer depended entirely on which of the two parties came closer to adopting a 'scientific attitude', especially with regard to the role science and scientists ought to play in industry. Brightman once summed up this scientific outlook as 'the willingness to accept change, the capacity to explore new situations, and to develop appropriate methods undeterred by prejudice or precon-

ceived ideas'. Other qualities that he saw clustering about this outlook included 'sincerity of purpose, loyalty to truth, patience, . . .
humility, unselfishness and the capacity to work with others'.[13]
Until about 1920 it was Gregory's opinion that the labour movement was more sympathetic to these scientific ideals than most
capitalists. 'If England does not lead in industrial development,'
Gregory had argued in his best-selling book of 1916, *Discovery, or
The Spirit and Service of Science,* 'it is not because of lack of new ideas,
but on account of want of scientific insight among her manufacturers, and want of faith in the ultimate value of organized
industrial research.'[14] By contrast, a *Nature* editorial of 7 August
1919 confidently asserted that 'the causes of scientific education and
scientific research . . . stand to profit enormously by the advent of
a Labour Government'.[15]

Yet only four years later Gregory was to be found bitterly
complaining that

> The Labour Party's recent manifesto says nothing of what science has
> done or may do to improve the world . . ., but asks, 'Can the method of
> Science be applied to nothing save the organization of men for war and their
> equipment with instruments of destruction?' We have here a paraphrase of
> Ruskin's assertion that 'The advance of science cannot be otherwise recorded
> than by the invention of instruments to kill and pull down noble life' – a
> view in which distorted vision is combined with the sin of ingratitude.[16]

Nor would *Nature* forgive these ingrates in the decade to come.
Gregory's disaffection from the labour movement was by then being
fuelled from several directions. None of Ramsay MacDonald's
governments, for instance, did anything notable to expand and
apply scientific research. Resentment was also expressed in *Nature*
about the resistance of Labour politicians to extending the influence
of scientific men in government. But what Gregory most abhorred
was the trade unions' use of the strike weapon, which he viewed as
'anti-social' and destructive of 'the nation's efforts to boost industrial
efficiency'.[17] It followed that such actions were clearly 'anti-
scientific'.

What could explain such irrational behaviour? Here was the
suggestion of one of *Nature*'s reviewers, who is quoting with deep
approval from one R. Austin Freeman's *Social Decay and
Regeneration.*

The manual workers are becoming frankly anti-social as well as anti-democratic. Their activities are directed, not against the employers, but against the community. 'The working man tends to be a bad citizen.' He plots 'to starve the country into submission; to treat his fellow citizens as a somewhat uncivilized invading army would treat an enemy population.' 'The profound lack of the most rudimentary ethical conceptions which underlies these anti-social actions becomes manifest when we contrast the implied standard of conduct with that of the more intelligent classes.' . . . The bulk of the men no doubt do not realize that they are committing a crime against their fellow-citizens; but this only proves the very low quality of their intelligence. 'The sub-man is usually a radically bad citizen.'[18]

This diatribe against the working class was a foretaste of the editorial support that Gregory extended to programmes of 'negative' eugenics, beginning in 1924. He had already decided many years earlier that at least a significant minority of workers would never reach 'that condition of intelligence upon which sound socialism must depend'.[19] Now he became a vice-president of the Society for Constructive Birth Control and Racial Progress. Thereafter, although the editor of Nature always gave space both to environmentalists[20] and to those eugenists who wished to stimulate the fertility of the 'intelligent classes',[21] he was in no doubt that these were not the most effective remedies for racial degeneration. For they did not touch at all the large numbers of proletarian 'mental defectives'. According to Nature, intelligence testers had already discovered that 'a large proportion of the slum populations consists of . . . "morons" – that is, of mental defectives of comparatively high grade. These people are lacking not only in intelligence but also in self-control, which is the basis of morality, and they reproduce recklessly'.[22] And yet, 'by our grandmotherly system of doles, maternity benefits, etc., we are doing our best to encourage' the overproduction of 'the lowest and least-skilled section of the population'.[23] The journal even outdid the Eugenics Society by calling not merely for 'voluntary' sterilization of hereditary mental and physical defectives,[24] but for compulsory sterilization as 'a punishment for the economic sin of producing more children than the parents can support'.[25] Moreover, as late as 1936, Gregory and his associates were not afraid to make explicit the connection between such scientific oppression and their hostility to 'troublesome' elements in the working class. 'Dock labourers and miners', ran one leading article, 'figure prominently in the overproduction of children, and it is worthy of note that in both groups there is a large proportion of the Iberian element in our population from Wales and Ireland.' It is 'the reproduction of this class that we wish to prevent.'[26] To those misguided 'do-gooders' who might take exception to such unalloyed 'social Darwinism', Nature issued this stern warning:

> Humanitarian sentiment acting in ignorance of the laws of biology is a most dangerous thing and produces devastating results. Compulsory birth control seems to us the only remedy capable of averting these results. Truly, though hardness of heart be given divine condemnation, Nature [read Nature] is equally severe on stupidity and wilful ignorance.[27]

Such were the laws of biology as laid down by science's most authoritative periodical.

Meanwhile, Nature's inner circle was able to console itself with the slow but steady conversion of industrialists into true believers in science. Gregory's earlier criticisms of the business community's scientific illiteracy faded out in the twenties. By 1932 Brightman was convinced that, although manufacturers had been insufficiently scientific in their outlook, this tendency was now passing.[28] Four years later he was able to conclude that 'everywhere in industry . . . the importance of applying . . . the help that science can afford is widely realized'.[29] One reason for this transformation of attitude, Brightman thought, was that large corporations were relying upon 'boards of directors which collectively combine the knowledge of finance, general organization, administrative problems, and the trend of scientific and technical developments requisite for wise and far-seeing decisions on general policy'.[30]

To Nature the paradigm of such business organization and the paragon of scientific virtue had to be the directorate of Imperial Chemical Industries, Limited. When I.C.I. was formed in 1928, its leading figures were immediately and favourably identified in a Nature editorial as H. G. Wells' 'open conspirators' come to life and ready to extend the writ of science.* This was high praise indeed.

---

* The comparison was ready-made, because these were the very men Wells had in mind to manage his 'open conspiracy'. The conspiracy was first mooted in his novel of 1926, The World of William Clissold, in which Wells looked forward to a world dominated by a network of multinational corporations.

2

We are prepared to believe that Sir Alfred Mond [I.C.I.'s founding father] is inspired by an idealism akin to this, that he realizes that the economic direction of world affairs must be based on the scientific study of all those factors fashioning the environment of man, that industry at its truest and best must be the prelude to man's highest expression. The men he has chosen to deal directly with these matters and to control certain factories and processes enjoy his confidence and inspire us with the same feeling.[31]

The anonymous author of this encomium to science-based mono-poly capital was a Labour M.P. called A. G. Church, of whom more later. In another editorial Rainald Brightman, an I.C.I. employee, strongly seconded a suggestion of Sir Harry McGowan, I.C.I.'s second managing director, that the chemical industry should in fact undergo still more centralization. In short, I.C.I. was urged to expand until it controlled directly or indirectly the entire chemical industry. 'The effective rationalization thus secured would', obser-ved Brightman, 'stabilize development and coordinate or expedite research.'[32] In *Nature*'s eyes the big chemical firms could do no wrong. One week a spate of serious accidents involving the storage and use of dangerous chemicals would be blamed upon inadequately trained personnel (workers), who would soon be put right by public-spirited industrial chemists and their employers.[33] The following week Gregory would praise 'the generous way in which successful industrialists have endowed the prosecution of scientific researches'.[34] Yet the most striking aspect of I.C.I.'s image, as pro-jected in *Nature*, was that here was a 'soulful' corporation devoted mainly to public service and scientific advance; profits were only a secondary consideration. To Church it was obvious that 'this gigantic industry is based on science, and modern science with its progressive dynamic outlook forces its disciples along hitherto

---

For, he argued there, it 'is only through a conscious, frank and world-wide cooperation of the man of science, the scientific worker, the man accustomed to the direction of productive industry, the man able to control the arterial supply of credit, the man who can control newspapers and politicians, that the great system of changes they have almost inadvertently got going can be brought to any hopeful order of development'. Wells himself quotes this passage on page 743 of his *Experiment in Autobiography* (London, 1969), where he also discusses more fully his long association with social imperialism, *Nature*, Sir Richard Gregory and, not least, the Mond dynasty that founded and ran I.C.I.

untrod paths in search of greater knowledge and', he added truth-
fully, 'towards greater power.'[35]

Despite the at times tremendous imbalance in the dedication of
capital and labour to scientific advancement Gregory and his
associates went on attempting to promote 'a spirit of unity among
all classes through the alliance of science, invention and labour
working as a single force for national development and common
welfare'.[36] Their main agency of reconciliation here was the British
Science Guild, which had been founded in 1905 by Gregory's
predecessor at *Nature*, Sir Norman Lockyer. In 1924 the guild even
staged a special conference on Science and Labour where, it was
hoped, the representatives of labouring men and women might
endorse 'the claims and progress of science and its applications'.[37]
A large number of industrialists, scientists and M.P.'s turned up for
the conference, but very few trade unionists. Perhaps it was just as
well, in view of the patronizing stance adopted by several of the
main speakers towards the labour movement.* Nevertheless the
workers' apathy here did not bode well for Gregory's dream of
'making the Empire strong and secure through science and the

---

* When the proceedings were published, they were roundly condemned by
one of the scientific élite's lone rebels, the Nobel Prize-winning physical
chemist, Frederick Soddy. 'It is assumed throughout *Science and Labour*', he
charged, 'that the Israelites ought to be grateful to the Egyptians for all the
employment they find them.'

'. . . the readers of this book are expected to assume that there is an established framework of society and government with which every change must
conform, the preservation of the framework as such being the object of all
true believers. The distressing symptoms of society's *malaise* are to be alleviated
and ameliorated piecemeal, but it is incredible that there should be any real
disease.'

'Sir Oliver Lodge handsomely admitted the workers as part of the living
population of this country, with whose improvement science is concerned.
Though apt to be unreasonable and misled by agitators, they are noble at
heart and sound at the core when the call comes, presumably to get blown up
with the plethora of stuff they make, for there is a limit to the consumptive
powers even of Ruskin's rats and worms.'

'In its manifold activities this conference seems to have searched diligently
in the dark for the black cat that is not there, and science, that can see through
a steel door and look into the inside of the atom, can be as blind as Nelson to
what it does not want to see.'

From F. Soddy, 'Science in Blinkers', *Scientific Worker*, vol. 5 (December
1924), pp. 86–7.

application of the scientific method'.[38] And if that hope failed to materialize, then might not Britain be faced with a further weakening of the economy, declining possibilities for investment and, most fearfully, growing demands for a social revolution? This was not a pleasing prospect to Gregory and his allies.

> In countries which have large untapped natural resources, revolutionary experiments may perhaps be indulged in without doing permanent irreparable damage, but in England it is a life-and-death matter to combat them... Our very existence depends on daring private enterprise, just as truly as did that of our Norse forefathers. . . It must therefore be our constant endeavour to encourage private enterprise in every possible way . . .[39]

In any event, *Nature*'s supporters were unlikely to support a revolution of any sort, having persuaded themselves with the magic words that 'nothing revolutionary can be proposed on any rational basis.'[40] The existing social order, on the other hand, suitably enlarged and retooled, was proving itself to be a most scientific and humane form of industrial and social organization. All it lacked was the wholehearted cooperation of the masses.*

Such was *Nature*'s outlook on politics and, by extension, that of the scientific élite as well. But that assertion needs to be qualified in two ways. First, it must be said that the opinions which found their way into Gregory's journal represented only one of a number of variations that could have been made on themes that were central to ruling class ideology. Some High Scientists, for example, many

---

* During the winter of 1928–9 there was a brief indication, in the form of the 'Mond-Turner' talks, that the labour movement might one day accept the scientific gospel as it was preached in *Nature*. These discussions brought together the General Council of the Trades Union Congress, led by Ben Turner, and a group of mainly 'big' businessmen, headed by Sir Alfred Mond. At a time when trade unionists were still suffering from their collective defeat in the General Strike, it was perhaps not surprising that the T.U.C. representatives were ready to express in public their willingness to 'use their power to promote and guide the scientific reorganization of industry, as well as to obtain material advantages from this reorganization'. While nothing came of this new alliance, largely because of opposition from the employers' main confederations, it was a foretaste of concessions that were to be made quite often after the Second World War. For two complementary analyses of the Mond-Turner talks, see: E. Hobsbawm, *Labouring Men* (London, 1964), esp. pp. 325–6; and M. Jacques, 'Consequences of the General Strike', in J. Skelley (ed.), *The General Strike, 1926* (London, 1976), esp. pp. 389–93.

have objected to the eugenic strain in *Nature*'s leading articles (although there is no record that any such objections were received). Many more of them were undoubtedly so persuaded of the historical importance and moral worth of their own work that they probably found it difficult to muster *Nature*'s enthusiasm for the industrial feats of various scientifically enlightened businessmen. (As we shall soon discover, however, Gregory's values were really not all that different from theirs in this respect.) Otherwise their conservatism, whether of the progressive, moderate or reactionary variety, was almost a foregone conclusion. Certainly that was the opinion of those few High Scientists, notably Bertrand Russell and Frederick Soddy, who did not subscribe to their colleagues' complacency about class-based inequalities and injustices. If we choose to adopt their perspective here, then it is probably all to the good that Britain's scientific élite was generally content to leave politics to its publicists.

3. Scientific Imperialism

In our somewhat static presentation of the professional practices and political outlook of High Scientists, we have overlooked some of the ways in which their relationships both to the state and to other kinds of scientific workers were changing, especially around the time of the First World War. These developments would prove to be significant at two levels. On the one hand they would demonstrate and reinforce the scientific élite's power and authority within the community of science. On the other they would bestow upon that domain an explicitly political dimension that had previously been lacking. Both processes conspired, in the short run at least, to increase the odds against our finding a High Scientist who was also a socialist.

Between 1911 and 1920 a number of state institutions were founded to encourage medical, military, agricultural and industrial research. The most ambitious of these ventures was the Department of Scientific and Industrial Research. Its main duties were to administer: the state's own civilian research facilities; post-graduate grants for academic investigations; and the industrial research associations, which were to be jointly financed by private firms and public money. In these endeavours the D.S.I.R.'s administrators were supposed to be guided by an advisory council. As with the Medical and Agricultural Research Councils, this body was free to ignore the short-run requirements of particular government departments. More importantly for our purposes, it was also dominated by a relatively small coterie of High Scientists as well. Their position in the state apparatus accordingly allowed them (through their parliamentary champions, notably Arthur Balfour and Richard Burdon Haldane) to redefine a mandate oriented to the solution of pressing social and industrial problems as one that emphasized the need to enlarge the opportunities for practising pure science in their laboratories. This argument, the quintessence of common sense if one were an academic researcher, was to govern much of the country's scientific affairs for the next fifty years.

The scientific élite's pre-eminence here rested upon a long-standing 'commonplace article of British belief "that there is one Science" and the University was its teacher'.[41] Certainly that was a perspective which Sir Richard Gregory's *Nature* regularly elaborated and defended. To Gregory science was essentially a pursuit of truth for its own sake, an enterprise whose sole object was to understand nature better. Indeed so exalted a venture was this that it regularly required the services of 'the divine afflatus* which inspires and enables the highest work in science'.[42] Engineering and industrial research were, by contrast, devoted to the control of nature for material ends. Although these activities were crucially dependent upon scientific advances, Gregory nevertheless regarded them as 'the province of the inventor rather than that of the man of science'.[43] On the basis of that apparently innocuous distinction he concluded that, as the font of all scientific knowledge, High Scientists had to serve as the state's leading makers of science policy. Only they sufficiently understood the 'inner logic' of their disciplines to know where the next scientific breakthrough might be made. Without their guidance science would cease to advance and so eventually, argued Gregory, would technology and industry. Therefore High Scientists had to exercise their hegemony over all forms of research: absolute

* An 'afflatus' is defined by the Oxford English Dictionary as either 'hissing'; 'the inspiration of supernatural knowledge'; 'an overmastering influence, poetic or other'; or 'a local febrile disease accompanied by diffused inflammation of the skin'. Such apparently are the occupational hazards of scientific life.

control over their own studies was already a self-evident necessity. Gregory would not, however, allow industrial or governmental researchers anything like that measure of autonomy. As one of *Nature*'s leading articles asserted, 'though they may regret the gradual encroachment of bureaucracy on the freedom of scientific investigations, [applied scientists] have to recognize that they are primarily public servants whose first duty is to perform their allocated tasks in the social machine'.[44] Such an imposition in the domain of High Science would of course in Gregory's view 'be repugnant to the best research workers'.[45] They had to stay on top.

Yet the writ of High Scientists was neither unlimited nor un-challenged in this period. Their influence on the development of government strategies and policies, apart from those specifically directed at scientific institutions, was at best rather slight.[46] Even within the D.S.I.R. they were unable to impose their will upon some of the more recalcitrant directors of state laboratories and industrial research associations.[47] One reason for this indiscipline, according to a group of 'up and coming' Cambridge researchers in 1919, was that the elders who manned the advisory councils were often too remote from contemporary laboratories to command the respect of those immediately below them.[48] That charge took on some force when in the early thirties the scientific élite could not prevent a temporary cutback in funds available for university research. But by this date senior academics had at least managed to lay the material and ideological foundations for Snow's 'golden age' of High Science. They had, in other words, succeeded in looking after themselves and their progeny.

Their relationship with rank and file scientific workers employed in government and industrial labs was not nearly so satisfactory; as is evident from a brief look at the short history of the National Union of Scientific Workers. Founded in 1918 and officially registered as a trade union, the N.U.S.W. hoped to represent the economic interests of a large and growing body of applied scientists. The union was determined to secure for its members higher salaries, greater security of tenure and more control over their jobs. It was also 'opposed to differentiation between the sexes for the purpose of depressing the economic conditions of either'.[49] Though the N.U.S.W. specifically eschewed the strike weapon, its militancy was unmistakable and made possible a number of pioneering negotiations with state agencies and other employers. By the early twenties it had attracted over a thousand members and had established branches at, among other places, the National Physical Laboratory, the Royal Aircraft Establishment and Woolwich Arsenal, as well as Siemens and the General Electric Corporation. Included in its membership was a smattering of left-wing socialists who were active trade unionists and belonged either to the National Guilds League or to the young Communist Party of Great Britain. Theirs, however, was a distinctly minority view. Indeed the N.U.S.W. was not even willing to affiliate to the Trades Union Congress, let alone the Labour Party. Nevertheless, through its concentration upon the status of its members as professional employees, it was potentially a promising 'school for socialists', the first of its type to spring up inside Britain's scientific community. The union was also a base from which a challenge to the hegenomy of High Science might be launched.

Yet by the time of the world slump the National Union of Scientific Workers had virtually collapsed. Two obstacles had been put in its way. One of these was a complex of events – Britain's economic decline in the early 1920s, the formation of company-dominated staff associations, the rivalry of other professional organizations – all of which frustrated the N.U.S.W.'s growth in the public and private sectors. Those developments might not have proved so disastrous had the union not contained within its ranks such a sizable contingent of academics. In fact the N.U.S.W. had first been proposed by a group of Cambridge scientists (ubiquitous as ever), who wanted to see 'scientific workers . . . exercise in the political and industrial world an influence commensurate with their importance'.[50] This remained the outstanding goal of the union's university members, many of whom were uncomfortable from the start with their organization's activities as a registered trade union. Their unease stemmed mainly from a desire to separate science off from the irrational struggle of capital and labour. However meritorious in other respects, this perspective debarred the N.U.S.W. from vigorously prosecuting the claims of its indus-trial branches, at precisely the moment when they were most vulnerable. Membership declined accordingly. In a bid to reverse this trend, the union launched in 1927 an appeal for new recruits, who were told that, in the wake of the General Strike of 1926, the organization was going to de-register as a trade union and change its name to the Association of Scientific Workers. This initiative was supported by *Nature*[51] and a bevy of distinguished professors.[52] Six hundred scientists, mainly academics, joined the new A.Sc.W. Yet, stripped of its old bargaining powers, it was not at all clear what this revamped body could do for its members. By 1930 a large number of its adherents, new and old, had left the A.Sc.W., which was now close to bankruptcy. Whether or not by design, a university-based scientific establishment had thus succeeded in denying to rank and file researchers in the 'outside world' an organization that might have ably represented their interests.*

Here was one more example not only of High Scientists' power within the scientific community but of their tendency to shy away from endeavours that smacked in any way of trade unions and socialism as well. Such an outcome was to be expected from a social grouping that was drawn from a variety of privileged milieus, educated at public schools, indoctrinated with an aristocratic conception of science, based in élitist institutions of higher learning and, finally, coopted as special counsellors to the capitalist state. They were, in short, a part, albeit a rather minor and discrete part, of the British ruling class, and they behaved as such; not least on those rare occasions when they made their political views explicit. Though

---

* The N.U.S.W.–A.Sc.W.'s general secretary throughout the 1920s was Major A. G. Church. This is the same Major Church whose fulsome praise of Imperial Chemical Industries we quoted earlier. So enamoured of I.C.I. was Church that he invited its first Chairman, Sir Alfred Mond, to become a member of the National Union of Scientific Workers. Mond accepted and then in 1927 publicly backed the N.U.S.W.'s move to de-register as a trade union. One year later Mond (later Lord Melchett) established a short-lived monthly, aptly named *The Realist*, with Church as its editor. Nor was Church's relationship with Britain's leading monopoly capitalist the only example of his conformity to the politics expressed in *Nature*. He very reluctantly joined the Labour Party and became an M.P. in 1924 (see below, pp. 122–3). When the labour movement proved itself to be incapable of undergoing an instant scientific conversion, he attacked (anonymously) both trade unions and the Labour Party in the leader columns of *Nature*. Later Church would introduce into Parliament the Eugenics Society's bill for the sterilization of mental defectives. After this brief review of Church's loyalties, we cannot be surprised to learn that his closest friend in the House of Commons was William Ormsby-Gore, a 'progressive' Tory. We have not heard the last of Major Church.

their social system allowed for quite a lot of ideological variation (within certain limits) and a small measure of rebellion, it was remarkably closed. What changes did take place between 1900 and 1930, inside and outside the domain of High Science, tended to reinforce both the conservatism and authority of its leading practitioners. Their protégés were in turn all the more likely to reproduce correct attitudes and fit the life that had already been prepared for them. The main exceptions to this rule at that time are the principal subjects of our inquiry.

By way of summary, we can quickly trace the early career of one of their more 'normal' contemporaries, Julian Huxley, who operated safely and typically within the boundaries of High Science. Like J. B. S. Haldane, Huxley derived from and was bound for the scientific élite of his day. Unlike some of his elders, he was not afraid to popularize scientific discoveries or enter into 'semi-scientific' public controversies. Yet in spite of his widespread and long-lived reputation as a free-thinking 'liberal', Huxley was from the outset of his career a scientist who seemed to take all of his political cues from Nature. For instance, he assumed the presidency of the National Union of Scientific Workers after it had ceased to function as a trade union. He also subscribed to a number of Sir Richard Gregory's eugenical beliefs. To be fair, Huxley did not want to sterilize en masse various sections of the Welsh and the Irish, or most coal miners and dockers for that matter. But he did believe that the inherited potentialities of slum dwellers were below average, and that this was 'almost certainly not due to the effect of living generation after generation in the slums, but to the fact that a considerable proportion of types that have inherited poor qualities have gradually drifted into slum conditions of living'.[53] Huxley went on to warn in 1931 of the tendency 'for the stupid to inherit the earth, and the shiftless, and the imprudent, and the dull. And this is a prospect neither scriptural nor attractive'.[54] As a measure to hold down the birth rate of the working class, Huxley advocated (during the worst phase of the world depression) that the continuance of unemployment relief be made conditional upon a man's agreement to father no more children. 'Infringement of this order could probably be met by a short period of segregation in a labour camp. After three or six months' separation from his wife he would be likely to be more careful the next time.'[55] If that kind of thinking were typical of a politically 'moderate' High Scientist, we at last may be able to appreciate how exceptional were some of the socialist beliefs – and actions – of J. D. Bernal, J. B. S. Haldane, Lancelot Hogben, Hyman Levy and Joseph Needham.

Chapter Two

Worker, Warrior, Citizen, Socialist

Already, in 1918, we knew that politics had a lot to do with science.
Lancelot Hogben, 1968[1]

The pre-1914 crisis of British capitalism transpired during the early adulthood of J. B. S. Haldane, Lancelot Hogben and Hyman Levy; and was succeeded, in the late adolescence of J. D. Bernal and Joseph Needham, by a period of post-war political disenchantment. How these changing conditions affected each man's life obviously depended upon his own unique circumstances. Yet the net effect on their social outlook was strikingly similar. For by the war's end the foundations of their Edwardian world – family, friends, religion – had generally, though not entirely, been destroyed or seriously shaken. What now came to unify their existence was a devotion to scientific research and to its humane extension into the lives of working people. However, such apparent unity could easily break down upon a closer examination of their scientific sensibilities. The arbiter of these differences in fact turned out to be whether they first encountered 'science' as workers, warriors, citizens or social idealists.

1. Hyman Levy: The Scientist as Worker

On 7 March 1889, in Edinburgh, Hyman Levy was born into poverty, on the periphery of the Scottish working class. His father, an exile from Tsarist Russia, was a self-employed picture-framer whose workshop could be found in the damp, 'built-to-last-forever' slums of the Old Town. The business was supposed to support his wife, the daughter of a German Rabbi, and their seven children. But the resources of the Levy family were stretched so thinly that some of the offspring, Hyman included, were forced to sleep in the shop, which was just across the street from a particularly rowdy public house. Late into the night young Levy would listen to 'the cursing and quarrelling' of the pub's more drunken customers. 'I heard their bodies and their fists', he would later write, 'smash against the wooden door within a yard of where I lay, while I prayed and entreated God to send them home.' That experience alone would have been enough to have confirmed his retrospective judgement that Edinburgh was 'a terrifying city'.[2] A further misery was the intermittent persecution to which young ruffians subjected him as a Jew of foreign parentage.

Anti-semitism was not a new experience for Levy's mother and father, who nevertheless persisted in the practice of their religion and sent their children to a Hebrew school. At home the parents mingled their slightly different Yiddish dialects, when they talked to Hyman's brothers and sisters, or played host to a meeting of local Zionists. A third 'tongue' Hyman Levy acquired, along with the social world that sustained it, was that of the streets – a thick Scots brogue that coloured his speech for the rest of his life. However, inside the elementary school rooms packed with forty or fifty underclad and underfed children, the only accent tolerated was the precisely rolled English of the Edinburgh bourgeoisie. This daily interplay between such a diversity of cultures was bound to stimulate Levy's social awareness and might even, in the right circumstances, provoke him into political action.

One connection with politics has already been mentioned: the Zionist discussion group, where Levy could learn about the history of the pogroms in Eastern Europe. Through this same coterie he was also introduced to the Victorian rationalist's approach to natural and social knowledge, as well as to a rather vague and idealistic species of socialism.[3] Yet in terms of true working-class consciousness it was Levy's mother who was the more direct source of her son's later political orientation. Thus while her husband and his friends were busy philosophizing, she would wander down to 'The Mound' – Edinburgh's Hyde Park Corner – to listen to socialist orators like Keir Hardie. Soon her son was doing the same. On some of these occasions he would buy

. . . with a copper I could ill afford, . . . a penny pamphlet with a picture on the outer cover of a heavily bearded gentleman called Karl Marx. This I took to the public library where there was at least heat and light, and read slowly and carefully; but it beat me. I could not understand the language in which it was written . . . [For example] I knew the 'proletariat' only too well, but the word was not in my vocabulary.[4]

Mrs Levy's ideological exhortations to her son were more direct and more personal: 'never become a wage-slave!'[5]

That was easier said than done. The Levy children were made to understand very early in their lives how important it was to apply themselves to their studies. (Young Hyman internalized this message so successfully that he once won a school prize for New Testament history.) But despite his evident quickness at mathematics and most other subjects, it looked late in 1902 as if the thirteen-year old Levy was headed for a career as a skilled worker. An interview for a five-year engineering apprenticeship with the firm of Redpath-Brown had even been arranged. At this point Levy's schoolteacher intervened and forbade his charge to take up any manual job. Levy was instructed instead to wait a few months, obtain a bursary from the local fee-paying high school (Heriot's) and then prepare himself for entering the University of Edinburgh. He did as he was told. After securing a scholarship through competitive examination, Levy entered Heriot's in the autumn of 1903. As it happened, the school's curriculum had been drastically reformed in 1886, with far more ample provision allotted to scientific and technological fields. Levy later felt that 'Heriot's was probably the most scientific and most technically advanced [school] in the country at the time, teaching mathematics to a high standard, with excellent physics and chemical laboratories, the beginning of a biology lab, and an engineering and woodwork shop'.[6] The main drawback of this environment was extra-educational: Levy's financial inability to participate in the sports programme was a constant reminder of the gulf between his social rank and that of the fee-payers.* The subsequent discovery of kindred spirits in the school only partially compensated this poor yet proud Jewish Scot for the hidden injuries arising from his class position.

* A possible indication of the social pressure exerted on young Levy as he first walked through Heriot's gloomy, imposing courtyard is the inflated description of his father's occupation – 'art dealer' – that is found on his school registration card. As the only Jewish boy then at Heriot's he had enough prejudice to overcome without having to contend simultaneously with the stigma of poverty.

The social climate of Edinburgh University, which Levy entered with the aid of a Heriot Scholarship in 1908, was, if anything, worse. The world-famous medical school was essentially a ruling-class preserve, as were the more esoteric arts subjects such as Classics. To the extent that those further down the social scale found their way into the university's precincts, the preferred route for them was through 'modern' subjects, pre-eminently the natural sciences. That did not of course necessarily mean a great degree of working-class consciousness on the part of either staff or students in these fields. On the contrary, the lecturers and professors were making every effort, it appeared to Levy, to consider their physics, chemistry and maths as 'useless' and as effete as the more aesthetic side of bourgeois culture. Years later, Levy remained dumbstruck by such escapism.

When, as a student, I heard it argued that one's life should be devoted to science or art *for its own sake*, and that nothing else mattered, I could only gasp in astonishment. These people seemed to be speaking a different language from me ... Not that I underestimated those cultural pursuits. On the contrary, I valued them so deeply that I felt that they could not be enjoyed unless they had been fought for, not merely accepted; otherwise they are mocked by the hateful reality underneath.[7]

So apparently uninvolved with the rest of the world (and so conservative) was the university that it boasted no political society of the Left until 1910, when a small number of undergraduates, among them Levy, founded a branch of the Fabian Society there. The one advantage of Edinburgh's quietism – remember, this was one of the bitterest periods in British social history – was that it threw up few distractions from the business of mastering one's studies. Levy graduated in 1911 with a distinguished First Class Honours degree in mathematics and physics.

Levy's performance at university would seem to have indicated his suitability for postgraduate research; his simultaneous attainment of a Fergusson Scholarship (won in open competition between representatives of the four Scottish universities), a Carnegie Research Fellowship and an '1851 Exhibition' award gave him the financial wherewithal to realize that ambition. He was advised to continue his studies of theoretical physics at Cambridge. Yet Levy found it difficult not to regard that move as a betrayal of his social background and political ideals. Not only did Cambridge represent the educational apogee of Britain's class system but it also sustained and promoted the ideology of High Science which Levy had already found quite abhorrent. In Levy's own retrospective words: 'at that time Cambridge held a "class grip" in maths and physics, and I felt it would be treachery to play up to that'. So Levy refused to go to Cambridge 'on class grounds'.[8] Instead he went on to the University of Göttingen in Germany, which in any event probably offered more scope for a theoretically inclined physicist than Cambridge. Among Göttingen's exceptionally brilliant staff could be found Max Born, David Hilbert, Felix Klein and Edmund Landau. They revealed to Levy much of the excitement and significance of the intellectual revolution then taking place in the physical and mathematical sciences.

While the young Scot appreciated and was stimulated by those developments, he found himself becoming more strongly attracted to the work of Professor Adolf von Karman on hydro- and aerodynamics. What Levy saw in von Karman's work was the possibility of extending abstract theories of mathematics, via arithmetic, to solve practical engineering problems. Perhaps Levy fancied such a union of theory and experiment, in part, so that he might have a convincingly practical rationale for pursuing his abstruse researches. Whatever the reason, his interest in statistics and arithmetical calculators was shared by another expatriate at Göttingen, an American named Norbert Wiener, who later became a founding father of cybernetics. Levy's friendship with Wiener and other Anglo-American students repeated his earlier pattern of associations restricted to social outsiders like himself. The German undergraduates, by comparison, often filled Levy with revulsion. Again, he saw them as the irresponsible representatives of an imperious ruling class, particularly those who bore the 'civilized' marks of duelling upon their scarred faces.

When war was declared on the Continent, Levy returned to Britain, determined to continue his aerodynamical studies. Unfortunately, the country's leading theoretician in this area was based at Oxford, not a notably less aristocratic environment than Cambridge. Levy accordingly reined in his anti-establishment feelings; but only momentarily. After a few months in Oxford he gave way to his strong anti-German feelings and then succumbed in due course to the propaganda of 'King and Country'. Perhaps, he thought, the Royal Flying Corps might be interested in someone with his expertise. After inquiring about the possibility of a commission, Levy was invited to a large Whitehall office for an interview, which turned out to be something of a fiasco. Some of the assembled officers had clearly never heard of aerodynamics; others were simply puzzled by this plucky Scots 'laddie'. 'Can you ride a horse?' one of them asked Levy.

I looked up, rather surprised [Levy was to recollect fifty years later] . . . Riding a horse in England, at that time at any rate, was the prerogative of a person who lived in a higher class than mine . . . I said, 'Well, I don't know, I have never tried.'
So there was a long silence again. After one or two other questions of no consequence, the chairman then said to me: 'Now, are there questions you wish to ask?' I replied: 'Well, I would like to know why I must be able to ride a horse.' He looked at me, rather surprised, and said: 'That's obvious. Any person who can ride a horse can fly a plane.'[9]

(In view of the mode of aerial warfare practised at the war's beginning the officer's reply is not quite so absurd as it sounds.) Despite that exchange, Levy received his commission and was posted to Salisbury Plain. There, by his own admission, he failed to get along with his fellow flyers, whom he was not afraid to take to task for their unscientific ways. His behaviour was possibly responsible for the local commanding officer's inspired suggestion that Levy be seconded to the aerodynamics department of the National Physical Laboratory at Teddington (on the outskirts of London). His troublesome subordinate readily agreed to go during the spring of 1916.

Levy's subsequent four-year sojourn at the N.P.L. played a crucial role in his later estimation of what science's social significance was and what its social destiny ought to be. His job was to develop mathematical theory useful for improving the 'flyability' of aeroplanes designed to kill people and level cities with unprecedented efficiency. At Teddington Levy had all the capital he required to embody his theoretical models into small-scale physical ones that could then be tested in a number of simulated conditions. (Such support would not be available to him when he later took up a university post.) On the other hand, strategic and bureaucratic requirements conspired to prevent his publishing all aspects of his research.[10] He also encountered, as a technical expert in the Civil

Service, considerable discrimination against scientifically, as opposed to classically, trained personnel. There were often petty, sometimes destructive inhibitions placed in the way of staff who had good ideas they wanted to develop in their own way. And the pay was derisory, unscaled and seemingly non-negotiable. The historical basis of the entire operation was that, in the wake of twenty years' agitation to expand Britain's scientific resources, the men and the plant had finally become available. What had not been foreseen was how this new work force would react to a highly bureau-cratized life where 'the divine afflatus which inspires and enables the highest work in science' rarely made an appearance. Nor had the N.P.L.'s Director, Sir Richard Glazebrook, reckoned in 1916 on the rather different and more disquieting afflatus that was about to visit his staff in the shape of Hyman Levy's socialism.

During his first eighteen months at Teddington Levy capitalized on or created a series of incidents that would eventually lead to the staff's demand for trade union representation. (He was simul-taneously developing his agitational powers as a street speaker for the local Labour Party.) The low status of these trained scientists was brought home to them when they were asked to take part in a national labour census by registering themselves and their occupa-tions down at the local Labour Exchange. But on the forms they were to fill out there was no job category even remotely related to that of scientific researcher. Levy therefore asked the clerk in charge what he and his fellow 'research workers' should do. 'Research workers?' repeated the clerk. 'Oh well, put yourselves under the heading of "general labourers"!' At this point Levy insisted on his co-workers' reflecting on the significance of their new designation.[11]

Meanwhile the men were experiencing inside the N.P.L. some attempted regimentation commonly associated with 'general labour'. Perhaps Glazebrook had come under the influence of F. W. Taylor's principles of 'scientific management', which were just then coming into vogue in Britain. For one morning the staff found on their desks a questionnaire inquiring as to what each man was doing at every hour of the working day. Levy, by this time something of an informal shop steward, quickly arranged a meeting to discuss what an appropriate, collective response to the circular should be. The group decided to complete it by writing beside each hour:

Time	Activity
8.30– 9.30	Thinking
9.30–10.30	Thinking
10.30–11.30	Thinking
11.30–12.30	Thinking
12.30– 1.30	Thinking
1.30– 2.30	Thinking
2.30– 3.30	Thinking
3.30– 4.30	Thinking
4.30– 5.30	Thinking

The forms were returned and never seen again; not, however, before Levy and others were able to stir up general resentment about the extent to which employees were unable to control their own working conditions.

The final straw was low pay, the absence of salary scales and the secrecy of wage negotiations. Each of these taboo subjects was raised when Levy, then unmarried, discovered that he and a workmate with a family and several years of research experience behind him were both earning the same money: £2 6s. per week. Yet the rumour, widely believed within the N.P.L., was that Glazebrook had a standing offer for anyone seeking a pay rise: either the Director would mercifully forget the whole incident; or he would arrange for the claimant's transfer into the army. Levy, with considerable courage, challenged this myth very soon after his arrival by walking into Sir Richard's office and threatening to go back into the Royal Flying Corps unless his salary was increased. Levy's audacity was shortly rewarded with a boost in his weekly earnings.[12] And on the basis of that experience Levy urged his fellow workers to demand from the Department of Scientific and Industrial Research a minimum annual salary of £200, a proper scale of salaries, guaranteed paid holidays, etc. To his credit Glazebrook supported his employees' petition, but the D.S.I.R.'s top man, Sir Frank Heath, claimed in 1917 that his hands were tied – unless the N.P.L. scientists were prepared to form themselves into a trade union. Then, Heath explained, it would be perfectly appropriate for his department to set up the appropriate machinery and get down to the serious business of negotiation.

The thought of professionally qualified individuals becoming unionized was still a fairly radical one in 1917. On the other hand, the N.P.L. was not the only place where government researchers were growing militant.[13] So were those employed at the Royal Aircraft Establishment in Farnborough and at the Woolwich Arsenal, to name but two. Hence when the memorandum of Cambridge academics proposing a National Union of Scientific Workers was released early in 1918, the response from state-managed laboratories was both stronger and more coherent than anything elicited from the universities. Levy, for example, led an eighty-seven strong delegation from Teddington into the N.U.S.W. Between 1918 and 1920 he was also one of his union branch's two main negotiators. And, most importantly, he was able to play a leading role in establishing a salary scale for his scientific 'brothers'.

Yet these undeniable accomplishments, the very prototype of the effective action a scientists' trade union could have undertaken in the twenties, were not to be followed up. Instead an academically-oriented national executive would de-unionize the organization as part of its campaign to raise the professional status of science. Levy of course was to oppose this trend, because his own experience had taught him that a scientist might be one of many things: an academic, a bureaucrat or something much more like a shop-floor worker. Science, he knew, was no longer an indivisible enterprise. But he would fail to deflect the university men from a course that reflected both their own self-interests and, Levy would have added, their limited knowledge of the wider world. Perhaps the N.U.S.W.'s difficulties went even deeper, to differences in the class background and social role of its various constituencies. What, after all, could a Scottish Jew born into poverty expect from an association originating – even in part – from the aristocratic preoccupations of the University of Cambridge?

2. J. B. S. Haldane: The Scientist as Warrior

On the morning of 9 August 1904, an eleven-year-old public schoolboy accompanied his father on a stroll through Edinburgh's Old Town. They inspected the Grassmarket and the Cowgate, as well as the filthy, overcrowded tenements just off the High Street. That night – possibly in the comfort of his family's spacious 'New Town' flat – the boy observed: 'The Old Town contains the Edinburgh slums which are the worst I know. I was glad to see one place', he added magnanimously, 'where new houses had been built where there had been a dirty close.'[14] Such were young John Burdon Sanderson Haldane's thoughts on Hyman Levy's neighbourhood.

At that moment the social worlds of Haldane and Levy could not have diverged more sharply. Yet forty years later they would be comrades in the Communist Party of Great Britain. Unlike Levy, however, Haldane would have to repudiate a thoroughly bourgeois background before he could affirm communism. His severance of the lines that bound him to the political conventions of his class was a long and tortuous process: partly because it would not be clear for many years where, socially and politically, he ought to re-attach himself; and partly because the pain of breaking with his past was to surprise J.B.S. by its depth and duration. Why he eventually opted for a variety of militant Marxism in the 1930s is not a question to be answered by surveying the details of his pre-adult life in isolation from what was happening in Britain and the rest of the world, either then or later. What can be pinpointed are the elements in Haldane's youth that initially undermined and eventually negated his loyalty to the ultimately conservative and imperialist ideology of his peer group. For J.B.S. turns out to have been a most exceptional child of a most unusual family.

In at least one respect Professor John Scott Haldane and his wife Louisa were typical representatives of their social stratum: they had the financial and familial resources to assure their children, Naomi and Jack (J.B.S.), of a healthy, comfortable and stimulating life. Besides a succession of roomy houses in Oxford, where Professor Haldane was a celebrated physiologist, the family had access to numerous residences scattered about the country. During the summer holidays J.B.S. and his younger sister (the writer Naomi Mitchison) were taken as far west as the Cornish coast and as far north as the Scottish Highlands. There they indulged in the pastimes then deemed appropriate for 'well-born' children. In young Jack's case this meant, among other things, learning to shoot, box and ride (although he apparently made no attempt to fly a plane!). Needless to say, until his departure for boarding school the boy's daily life was structured by the ritualistic separation of two sorts of persons – his parents' equals and his parents' servants.

For good measure not only did J.B.S. experience his social place, he was taught it as well, mainly in a series of private educational establishments. His preparatory school was the Dragon in Oxford, where he, along with the sons and daughters of dons and others of comparable status, were instructed to a high standard.* (It was thanks to the school's requirement of a vacation-time diary that J.B.S.'s youthful observations have survived to this day.) Then came Eton. After a slow start Haldane took the measure of England's most famous public school and proceeded to become Captain of the School, which also assured his entry into the prestigious Pop Society. Now he was prepared for an absolutely stunning under-graduate career at New College, Oxford. That was how he managed, according to Naomi Mitchison, to sail 'triumphantly through all his exams, spreading himself in friendships and light and the golden air of the pre-war years for the upper classes. His friendships were very wide, with young men of completely varied interests.'[15] Among his closest confidants were Aldous and Julian Huxley, Lewis and John Gielgud and his sister's future husband Dick Mitchison (later made a Labour peer). And if his social success was noteworthy, his academic record was even more so. By 1914 he had achieved the unusual feat of First Class Honours in both Mathematics and Classics. Combined with the high social standing of his family, Haldane's repeated demonstrations of intellectual brilliance guaranteed him a favourable position – somewhere – within the ruling class.

One side-effect of J.B.S.'s completely conventional élite education was to lay bare the uniqueness of his own home. What was especially notable about his schools was that they were geared

---

* Shortly after Haldane left the Dragon, the eugenist Cyril Burt gave the school's students an alphabet test on which they did considerably better than their counterparts in an Oxford elementary school, who in turn excelled the performance of a group of slum children in Liverpool. 'It would be difficult to explain these results', crowed one eugenical enthusiast, 'on any other theory than that mental capacity is inherited. Whatever are the innate differences between university professors, small tradesmen and the denizens of the Liver-pool slums, by the time they reach adult life there is little question that the order in which they would be placed with regard to their intellectual qualities is the same as that in which they are here written.' From Edgar Schuster's *Eugenics* (London, n.d. [1913]), p. 155. Haldane, the Dragon alumnus, started off his career with similar ideas, which are described below on pp. 96–7.

primarily to the needs of English gentlemen, reared in the Church of England and destined either for idleness or for governing. The Haldanes, on the other hand, sprang from a somewhat different mould. They were Scottish, not English, and agnostics rather than Anglicans. Most importantly, the clan as a whole embodied the liberal virtues of the intellectual aristocracy instead of the more reactionary attitudes associated with the landed gentry and established entrepreneurs. The Wayneflete Professor of Physiology at Oxford, for example, was John Burdon Sanderson, J.B.S.'s namesake and uncle. Another uncle was Richard Burdon, Viscount Haldane of Cloan: a distinguished Liberal and later Labour cabinet member; an outstanding champion of university expansion; and the first Chairman of the British Science Guild. John Scott Haldane himself was a gifted physiologist, a redoubtable philosopher of science, a Fellow of the Royal Society, and, as we shall see, a humanitarian who was not afraid to use his learning to relieve the suffering of 'ordinary' men and women. In retrospect, these political and cultural differences between the Haldanes and other 'fractions' of the dominant class might appear slight. Yet they were then substantial enough to strike a persistently dissonant note in young Jack's upbringing.

Even in the context of his own home he was aware of the coexistence of two subtly conflicting life-styles, two ways of viewing the world politically. For his mother, née Louisa Kathleen Trotter, did not conform to the traditional Haldane image. Descended from a long line of military men and leisured country gentlemen, she was in fact an uncompromising Tory and fervent supporter of Joseph Chamberlain's brand of social imperialism. This was the conservative philosophy that Mrs Haldane hoped to instill in her son, on whom she lavished intense adoration and equally intense demands. Her efforts were initially well rewarded. By the time of his eleventh birthday J.B.S. was already echoing and amplifying his mother's ideology. 'My mater and I', runs his diary entry for 18 September 1903, 'are very sorry to hear of Mr Chamberlain's resignation, but hope he will get into office again soon.' That the boy had become a social imperialist at such a tender age was not surprising in view of Louisa Haldane's vigorous activities on behalf of the Victoria League, Children of the Empire, etc. She particularly enjoyed school holidays when she could easily second her children for one imperial purpose or another. Thus on 29 July 1902 mother and son set out for a small village near Edinburgh in order to lecture to an assemblage of adolescents on Children of the Empire. 'Mother told us very much what is put in the papers,' recorded the dutiful J.B.S.: 'that it is a society for making people more able to fight for their country, and to be useful if they emigrate to the colonies . . . That the Empire isn't a lot of little countries but one big one. In fact, to teach them to be good citizens of the Empire. We enrolled about ten and will, we think, soon start a local branch.' Along with an all too eager readiness to shoulder the white woman's burden, Mrs Haldane combined an aristocratic humanitarianism with contempt for the urban proletariat and any one in trade. Only those in pre-industrial circumstances seemed capable of winning her respect. Such activities conflicted, often sharply, with the Liberal outlook of her husband and in-laws.

In the face of numerous political disagreements within his family, J.B.S. adhered to a generally conservative world-view up to and including his undergraduate days at Oxford. But his conservatism was flexible enough to accommodate many of his elders' more progressive actions. He became especially adept at placing an imperialist gloss on Richard Burdon Haldane's politics – no mean feat considering how strongly his mother detested his uncle's views. Consider this entry in J.B.S.'s diary for 28 August 1902.

Uncle Richard went away to London. He is going to see about the site of the new London University [the Imperial College of Science and Technology] which is going not to teach you General Chemistry, Classics, and so on, only, but also Engineering or whatever special profession you are going to take up. For instance, if you are going to be a brewer, they'd teach you the Chemistry you'd want to know about fermenting, etc. – have a teaching brewery with all the newest apparatus which one can really see working instead of only models and diagrams. And where you can experiment a bit. They have that kind of thing in Germany and if we don't keep up with them in our education we shall lose our 'supremacy in trade' which hasn't got to happen and *isn't* going to either.

One could not imagine a neater pairing of his uncle's respect for Germany's intellectual traditions with his mother's hostility towards any rival to British imperialism.

Liberal ideals were also communicated to J.B.S. through his father's investigations into mining diseases and colliery explosions.

From about 1900 onwards John Scott Haldane made a point of taking his son down with him into the mines. On one such occasion the pair were determining the amount of fire-damp in a shaft. Haldane senior asked J.B.S. to stand up near the roof and say something. 'He recited "Friends, Romans . . . countrymen", but before he got to "the evil that men do", he passed out. "That", as he said later, "taught me a lot about fire-damp." '* Young Haldane probably also learned a good deal about the hardy virtues of miners, the obduracy of mine owners and the ineffectualness of Home Office civil servants. Nevertheless, it is more than likely that, even as a boy, he regarded the welfare of such workers as one of the many responsibilities that had to be borne for them by their social and intellectual betters. That sentiment went deep and was later to be reflected in his undergraduate endorsement of a eugenics movement then bent on curbing the reproduction of the allegedly unintelligent lower orders.[16] Once again, the Liberal heritage of Haldane's father was being reinterpreted to the advantage of his mother's Toryism.

Having considered the degree to which J.B.S. had absorbed Louisa Haldane's ideological principles, his subsequent conversion to socialism at the end of the First World War seems almost bizarre: certainly it struck his mother as perverse. In fact, the story of his slow political transformation is surprisingly straightforward. It begins within the family setting, where the distribution of power worked inexorably against the maintenance of Mrs Haldane's 'hold' over J.B.S. (She always referred to her husband as 'S.P.', which stood for the 'Senior Partner'.)[17] It continues with his brief emergence as a true Haldanian Liberal. It culminates with a rejection of that Liberalism which, by 1918, he regards as morally bankrupt. Needless to say, his mother's more reactionary views are still more vehemently rejected.

How then did J.B.S. become a 'real' Haldane? He was a male child, and, as such, he was from birth more a member of his clan

---

* As quoted in 'The Cuddly Cactus', New Statesman Profiles (London, 1958), p. 188. When J.B.S. joined the Communist Party in 1942, his boyhood adventures in the mines were naturally well publicized: 'So, thousands of feet beneath the earth, with pit props blown away and roof falls threatening, he learned the scientist's detachment and dispassionate regard for facts, unheedful of personal dangers, which has since marked his life.' From Peter Phillips's Daily Worker League Pamphlet Prof. J.B.S. Haldane, F.R.S. (London, n.d. [c. 1942]), p. 3.

than Mrs Haldane could ever have been.* More importantly, Jack had unusual intellectual gifts; he could, for example, read English at three, German at the age of five. Such high abilities were soon being channelled in the direction of J. S. Haldane's scientific interests. Even before his years at Eton J.B.S. was being treated by his father as a fellow scientist – a distinction which was ultimately withheld from his younger sister. The first paper of the father-and-son duo was published in 1912. In addition to this most important collaboration, J.B.S.'s identification with the Edwardian 'man's world' was extended through educational institutions and recreational activities explicitly reserved for men. Fortunately, he was physically and intellectually tough enough to prove himself capable of being such a man. He also had before him the splendidly active and important careers pursued by his male relations, who inevitably came to serve as models of what he might become. Their political credibility was thereby enhanced considerably in J.B.S.'s eyes. His mother, by contrast, was associated with the unproductive roles of wife, hostess and overseer of children. In the long run her lack of involvement with the world was bound to cast doubt on her opinions of it. That was how, politically speaking, she lost her son to the Haldanes.

Apart from the influence of a strong maternal presence, the only potentially serious obstacle to J.B.S.'s emergence as a Haldane was Eton. His initiation into the family was, however, already well advanced when he first entered the school in 1905. On that occasion he arrived with his arm broken and trussed up in a sling. That made him a natural target for some of the older boys, who in any event would have resented his arrogance, brilliance and intensely Scottish pride. For eighteen months he was mercilessly harassed. He begged his parents, without success, to have him removed from this brutalizing environment. (In one of his letters to them during this period, he admitted: 'I am rather sick with people and things in general. Goodbye.')[18] Afterwards J.B.S. masterfully came to terms with Etonian life, but his experience as a persecuted minority of one left its mark on him. His disaffection from the mainstream values of

* Naomi Mitchison records in her autobiography (*Small Talk . . . ; Memories of an Edwardian Childhood* (London, 1973)) how Louisa Haldane was excluded at Cloan from prayer meetings, at which only blood relations of the Haldanes (and occasionally their servants) were allowed to attend. Her children of course were permitted to be present.

upper class life was now complete enough to assure both his social and political alignment with the more progressive side of the Haldane line. Thus later at Oxford he found himself joining not only the University Liberal Club but the local Cooperative Society as well.

Haldane had only just settled into his new political affiliations when war was declared between Britain and the central powers. He immediately enlisted as an officer in a crack Scottish regiment, the Black Watch. Early in 1915, at the age of twenty-two, J.B.S. went over to the front lines, where he witnessed the first use of chlorine gas in combat. Since the chlorine's primary effect was to inhibit respiration, it was not long before his father – at the invitation of Uncle Richard, then Lord Chancellor – was also in France carrying out physiological experiments upon himself and his son. Their findings suggested the need for a respirator more efficient than the army had at its disposal. To their dismay the General Staff did not immediately implement that recommendation; the result of their failure, according to J.B.S., was disastrous British losses at Loos in September 1915.[19] In the interim the younger Haldane had been posted back to Scotland to take up responsibilities as head of a bombing school at Nigg. His later assignments included service in the Middle East, where he was wounded by a British shell in the summer of 1917. After several months' convalescence in India, he returned to Britain and was released from active duty.

Many stories could be related about Haldane's exploits on the battlefield. (He was a courageous soldier who discovered to his great horror, that he actually enjoyed killing.) But what interests us here is how his wartime experience helped to alter his political outlook still further to the Left. Like many veterans he very early decided that the 'Great War', for all its death and destruction, was not being waged in the service of any praiseworthy values. Yet officers and enlisted men alike, in ever increasing numbers, were being asked to sacrifice their livelihoods, if not their lives. These were Haldane's comrades in the trenches. There, for the first time in his life, he associated closely and constantly with labouring men. From them he learned, as he put it in the late twenties, 'to appreciate sides of human character with which the ordinary intellectual is not brought into contact'.[20] That contact undoubtedly helped to dispel some of his eugenical prejudices about the abilities of working-class people. As for his many close pre-war associates, most of them were killed in action. Thereafter, his sister has since recounted, J.B.S. 'never made friends in the same spacious way . . . His [later] friends were men and women in his own discipline, work friends. The play world was gone forever.'[21]

With his personal links to the governing class so wastefully severed, Haldane grew even more resentful of a political system that was to renege on its promises of 'homes fit for heroes'. Asquith and Lloyd George were especially anathema to him, partly because they had connived with the Tories to oust R. B. Haldane from high office. Yet to J.B.S. they were merely symbols of the moral decline and ideological obsolescence of traditional Liberalism. In the post-war era great social changes for the benefit of working people would have to be carried out quickly – and scientifically. But the Liberals had already proved to Haldane's satisfaction that they were incapable of taking such action. Within a few years he would be publicly condemning both their gross mismanagement of the war and, more generally, the pride Britain's governors took in their ignorance of science.

J.B.S. now stood on the brink of proclaiming himself to be a self-made 'scientific' socialist. It would be many years, though, before he defined more clearly what he meant by socialism and how he might help to achieve its realization. That did not prevent his parents from concluding far earlier that their son had permanently lost his inherited political senses. Louisa Haldane, of course, suffered most from an ideological estrangement which also entailed J.B.S.'s more general disaffection from her as a mother. Yet, as the gulf between their politics widened and deepened over the years, the lasting influence Mrs Haldane had exercised over her boy would become ever more apparent. For, like her, he would have to find the strength to voice political convictions utterly alien to his social milieu.

3. Lancelot Hogben: The Scientist as Citizen

Like Hyman Levy, Lancelot Hogben grew up in a social environment where the affluence of a J. B. S. Haldane was unknown. In Hogben's own words, he was from birth well acquainted with 'the discomforts of rubbing shoulders with a large family on a small parental income'.[22] Another parallel with Levy's childhood was the centrality of an unconventional religious creed to the formation of Hogben's social identity. As the son of a Plymouth Brethren evangelist, Hogben was to share with Levy the pain of being ostracized because of his parents' religion. Indeed, of the two, Hogben's isolation from his contemporaries was probably the more pronounced.

His involuntary identification with the family faith began on 9 December 1895, when he was born in Portsmouth, two months ahead of schedule. The miraculous circumstances of his birth inspired his fundamentalist mother to vow that her son would become a medical missionary. As if to seal her pledge to God, Mrs Hogben christened her boy with the name – 'Lancelot' – of a Plymouth Brother noted for his work in foreign missions.

With his fate already determined for him, young Hogben was expected to participate fully in numerous religious observances both in and out of his home. Sometimes Lancelot would work in the mission run by his father for down-and-out sailors. A special feature of Rev. Hogben's ministry were the Saturday night and Sunday morning services he conducted down on the Portsmouth beach. Under a banner which proclaimed that 'GOD IS LOVE', Hogben's father preached long and hard to the assembled about the eternal punishment that awaited them after death. Although Lancelot would later repress the content of these sermons, he would always remember that banner as, 'in its way, a work of art'.

On the foreground were displayed the theatre, racecourse, public house, dancing saloon and gaming tables along the edge of a precipice over which poor folk in a semi-incandescent condition were tumbling into a lake of brimstone and fire. It invariably drew a large crowd.[23]

Apart from the beach and the mission, the locus of daily religious observance was to be found in the Hogbens' home. Lancelot thus found it difficult to bring friends there from school without involving them in some elaborate piece of ritual. On one such occasion a new-found schoolmate was lambasted – during an hour-long family prayer – as a presumptive unbeliever who, together with his parents, was headed for everlasting disaster. In later life Hogben would bitterly recount how this episode 'earned me my martyr's crown when the story got round the school'.[24]

Through such practices, the beliefs of the Brethren were drummed into Hogben at an early age. The Bible was said to be an infallible and a living book. Services were often self-managed by the congregation without the aid of a pastor: whoever was moved to speak did so. (Women, however, were not allowed this privilege.) Another anti-authoritarian aspect of a Brethren's faith was his duty to disobey 'the powers that be . . . when the civil government interferes with his conscience in obedience to God's command'. But the likelihood that such disobedience might become common was considerably reduced by the sect's dismissal of politics and social reform generally as 'but the whitewashing of a house built on sand'.[25]

The otherworldly cast of the Plymouth fellowship's beliefs, together with the isolation forced upon Hogben by his family's strict religious regimen, ought to have rendered him an orthodox recluse ready to accept whatever task the church had in store for him. What inhibited and eventually negated that process was Hogben's introduction to science. It followed from his mother's pledge that, if her son was to become a physician in the service of the Lord, then he would have to study medicine and the sciences that underlay that field. Hence Lancelot was allowed and even encouraged to read secular texts on botany and zoology. By the age of nine he was already making excursions into the Hampshire countryside to identify and collect local flora and fauna. His interest in scientific pursuits was also quite unintentionally enhanced by his father's sermons, which portrayed science as a worldly pleasure akin to 'Sunday travelling, whist and dramatic entertainment'.[26] Soon young Hogben was viewing the scientific life as an alternative to rather than as the complement of religious endeavours.

With the closure of his father's mission in 1905, Hogben and his family went to London. In such a vast and cosmopolitan city it became easier to break free from parental scrutiny. He attended Tottenham County School, where he was able not only to deepen his knowledge of biology but to strike up friendships with a group of largely working-class boys as well. In this godless environment Lancelot developed quickly and covertly into both a rationalist and a socialist. Trinity College, Cambridge, however, was not aware of these developments when it awarded Hogben – just before his seventeenth birthday – an open scholarship. (He was the first student from a London County Council secondary school to earn this distinction.) Hogben had sat for the Trinity exam because the college offered the largest cash prizes. Yet his father's income was so low that Lancelot was obliged to obtain a supplementary grant from the L.C.C.'s maintenance scheme for poor boys at university.*

Once at Trinity Hogben found himself liberated from only some of the constraints of his early life. The college was intellectually stimulating if you happened to be, like Hogben, a medical student with a lively and inquiring mind. He benefited considerably from the teaching of Trinity's trio of eminent physiologists: Walter Morley Fletcher (first Chairman of the Medical Research Council), A. V. Hill (winner of the 1922 Nobel Prize for medicine) and the young and gifted Keith Lucas (who was killed in the First World War). Bertrand Russell was also to be found in the college, giving lectures on the philosophy of science which resonated strongly with Hogben's own rationalism. Having spent his adolescence trying 'to offload beliefs which are not susceptible to rational proof',[27] Hogben was now prepared to become, as had Russell in his Trinity undergraduate days, an avowed and confirmed atheist. Perhaps just as significant a departure from the pre-natal projections of his mother was Lancelot's new desire to dedicate his life to scientific research rather than medical practice.

But life at Trinity was far from limited to sporadic interchanges between teachers and students. Equally if not more important were the extra-curricular activities – sports, discussion circles and social clubs – which the privileged products of the English public school system inevitably dominated. Once again Hogben was being treated as an outsider. 'Naturally,' he related in 1968, 'I associated with those

* The L.C.C.'s efforts in this area were naturally thought by eugenists to be a colossal waste of time and money: 'the London County Council sets up educational ladders in all parts of the metropolis, but finds it difficult to get boys to go up them. The number of children in the schools maintained by the rates who are bright enough to make it worth while to give them the scholarships provided by the London ratepayers is hardly enough to fill them. No difficulty is experienced in filling those at the public schools or university with boys of a very respectable level of intelligence, whose fathers belong mostly to the professional classes. This is a rough and vague method of comparison which', wrote Edgar Schuster (*Eugenics*, p. 226) in a rare moment of humility, 'though not in itself very convincing, is put forward as deserving of thought.' It was just this sort of 'rough and vague' eugenic propaganda that Hogben set out to demolish in the late 1920s.

who were [similarly] estranged from the Establishment.'[28] The most important expression of Hogben's estrangement was political. In his first year at Cambridge he joined the university's Fabian Society.

Like most university-based Fabian branches at this time, the Cambridge society was considerably to the Left of older members, including the Webbs. In this respect at least Hogben was a typical undergraduate. He felt that the central feature of British society was the exploitation of workers by their employers. If socialism were ever to be achieved here, it would have to be through (probably violent) class warfare. The primary goals of a socialist Britain would be the creation of socialist men and women who could live simply and harmoniously together on terms of true social equality. From these very general statements it might be deduced that Hogben had already encountered some of Marx and Engels' most basic works. This, in fact, had happened. However, the effect of their writings on Hogben's politics was limited. What most fascinated this underprivileged Trinity medical student about Marxism was its emphasis on the interrelationship between social needs and scientific advances. While that theme was to become central to Hogben's later writings, it played no role in his political thought and practice at this time. Who did figure very strongly in the shaping of his socialist ideals was William Morris, one of the Fabians' earliest and most determined opponents. Hence it was not surprising that, when Hogben assumed the secretaryship of Cambridge's Fabian Society in 1914, he was determined to 'de-Fabianize' it. Within nine months the organization had swung so far from Fabianism that it was prepared to change its name, at Hogben's suggestion, to that of the Cambridge University Socialist Society.

One factor behind the radicalization of Hogben and his contemporaries was the outbreak of the First World War. Yet until the introduction of conscription in 1916, their response to what they saw as an ignoble imperialist venture was diffuse and uncertain. Hogben, for example, decided immediately after obtaining his Cambridge degree in July, 1915, to offer his services to the Red Cross. For the next six months he worked in Belgium and France as a member of an ambulance unit. But when compulsory military service was introduced in Britain, Hogben returned to Cambridge in order 'to join my socialist friends who had decided to be conscientious objectors'.[29] That Hogben now chose to oppose a law from whose provisions he, as a medical student, was legally exempt, was clear testimony of the strength of his anti-war and socialist convictions. His refusal to serve King and Country accordingly led to a court conviction and his removal to Wormwood Scrubs prison.*

After five months' imprisonment Hogben was freed early in 1917, because his health had 'given way'. Later he would tell a young zoology student named Ivor Montagu 'scarifying tales . . . of brutal treatment' meted out at Wormwood Scrubs, 'including water torture, recalcitrant men in detention fixed motionless under a perpetual drip from a holed bucket suspended above their heads'.[30] How Hogben's own physical constitution was broken is not certain. But he was forced to spend the better part of a year recuperating in London from his ordeal.

During this period of recovery Hogben tried to express his political experiences and beliefs through poetry. His poems were gathered together and published in 1918 under the title *Exiles of the Snow, and Other Poems*. In this volume Hogben's diction is surprisingly romantic, even Swinburnean.† The content of the verses, however, is uniformly brooding and bitter. Thus in 'Shades of the Prison House' Hogben conjures up his hatred of the tyranny to which he has been subjected.

---

* Hogben's resolve to challenge the draft was strengthened by Bertrand Russell's public statements on this issue. When Russell himself was imprisoned in 1918 for his anti-conscription activities, he received the following letter: 'Dear Mr Russell, I am only writing a little note to tell you how splendid I think your stand has been. Being an ex-convict I understand a little at what cost you have been true. It is inspiring to us who are younger men and who see so many of our friends succumbing to cynical indifference or academic preoccupation to know that there is at least one of the Intellectuals of Europe who have not allowed the life of the mind to kill the life of the spirit . . . This is rather ineffective, but well, Good Luck. Yours very sincerely, Lancelot Hogben.' As quoted in Bertrand Russell, *The Autobiography of Bertrand Russell*, vol. 2 (London, 1968), p. 83. Ironically, Hogben's decision to disobey 'the powers that be' echoed one of the tenets of the childhood religion, which he had already consciously rejected.

† Hogben soon regretted this public display of romanticism. In 1921 he went to the publishers and 'bought up every copy . . . to consign to the flames'. L. Hogben, letter to the author, 21 January 1974.

3

A world of sextons! Not a thankless task
For hire: the doctor starched, the chaplain too
Who wears upon his face the hangman's mask,
Warders and governors, men with crooked hearts
Like the gnarled roots of an old churchyard yew –
These to the soul's internment bring their arts.[31]

Other poems attack Christianity as a 'faith that feeds on the fear of men who walk alone in the night'.[32] One verse even disavows science as a self-sufficient guide to human happiness and progress. Indeed the only hope Hogben allows for his countrymen is the possibility that Britian might become a socialist commonwealth. Significantly, the title poem, 'Exiles of the Snow', was a paean to the recent Bolshevik Revolution.

As Hogben's health slowly revived, he began to involve himself in London's left-wing *demi-monde*, the informal headquarters of which was a seedy Soho establishment called the 1917 Club. His main political activity was workers' education. Apart from the biology classes he taught at Birkbeck College, Hogben's efforts were concentrated upon the Plebs League. 'The Plebs' had been founded as part of an effort to align the intellectual training of labouring men and women more closely with militant forms of politics. Hogben worked hard for the league both as a part-time lecturer at the Central Labour College and as a writer for the *Plebs Magazine*. His chief contribution to the organization was his insistence that working-class socialists required scientific as well as economic knowledge to wage the class war successfully.

Another issue then of great importance to many young socialists was feminism. Hogben was forced to confront this question with great seriousness. For by 1918 he was married to Enid Charles, who was not only a committed feminist but an accomplished mathematician as well. Like Hogben, Ms Charles grew up in a family headed by a strict man of the cloth. She also resembled her husband in terms of scientific brilliance, which she had previously demonstrated at Cambridge by excelling all the male senior wranglers of her year in the 'maths tripos' examinations. But, as a woman, she was then debarred from receiving a university degree.

In the context of their married life Hogben and Charles attempted to live along feminist lines. (This venture was warmly supported by their East End neighbour and close friend, Sylvia Pankhurst, whose

newspaper – *The Workers' Dreadnought* – sometimes featured articles by both Charles and Hogben.) She was to pursue her intended career as a statistician; she also wanted to retain her own name.*
They were, however, equally keen to have children – four in all – and it was this desire that was soon to complicate their anti-sexist compact. Nevertheless, husband and wife had found a degree of happiness and companionship with each other at a critical time in their lives. One can scarcely imagine the positive effect this must have had on Hogben's morale after his long years of suffering.

4. J. D. Bernal and Joseph Needham: Scientists as Social Idealists

J. D. Bernal and Joseph Needham were too young to have their lives 'mucked up' directly by the First World War. But that is not the only reason they have been paired together here. Both went up to Cambridge at a time when the intellectual atmosphere of the university was peculiarly intense. By the end of the twenties they were intimate friends. Their affinities with each other then strengthened over the years. They were attracted to similar philosophical problems concerning scientific theory and practice. To their professional (and political) discussions each was able to bring an extraordinary erudition in the history of science. In later years Bernal's devotion to the Soviet Union as a model for socialist development would be matched by Needham's championing of post-revolutionary China. Finally, despite an apparent cleavage between the militant atheism of Bernal and the devout Anglo-Catholicism of Needham, the two men recognized that they shared

* In later life many of Hogben's colleagues would bridle at his insistence that they not refer to Enid Charles as 'Mrs Hogben'. There are other examples to hand of his lifelong adherence to feminist ideals. For instance: 'Before I went to Sweden I thought of Scandinavia as a symbol of women's emancipation. The unvarnished truth is that the Swedes – like the Germans – share with the Scots the conviction that cooking is the natural and exclusive daytime function of the female sex. The chief difference between Swedish and Scottish women is that the former have something to show for it. In Uppsala I visited one laboratory where the director is a radical. All the lady assistants curtsied when they came into his presence. I had the self-control to restrain from giggling the first time I saw them do it. In my laboratory, all my staff call me Lancelot or uncle. If one of my coeds curtsied, I would chew gum at her.' Lancelot Hogben, *Author in Transit* (New York, 1940), pp. 54–5.

a common religious, even mystical sensibility. Yet their temperaments could not have been more different: Bernal was a wiry, redhaired, audacious Irishman with a quicksilvery brilliance; Needham, a tall, lumbering, bookish Englishman given to introspective ruminations. Hence their underlying similarities were all the more remarkable.

Why Bernal and Needham came to have so much in common can be partly explained by parallel experiences in their youth. Let us begin with Needham, who was born in London on 9 December 1900. He was the only child of a misalliance between Dr Joseph Needham – a Harley Street physician noted for his pioneering work in anaesthesiology – and Mrs Alicia Needham, better known to the public as Alicia Adelaide Montgomery, a composer of salon music and popular songs. Having parents with such divergent talents ought to have been an enriching experience for their son, and, in some ways, it was. From his father, young Joseph derived a keen interest in science, as well as a precocious taste for nineteenth-century philosophy. His mother encouraged him to appreciate the subtlety and depth of classical music. Unfortunately, when the two parents joined forces, they found themselves perpetually at cross purposes. In fact, their son 'grew up . . . in the midst of a battlefield; or, in what might be perhaps a better image, ferrying between two pieces of land separated by an arm of the sea'.[33] Unable to reconcile the antagonisms between a sober scientist-father and a rather feckless artist-mother, young Needham withdrew from the family quarrels and came increasingly under his father's influence. Shortly before his removal to boarding-school he decided on a career in medicine.

If Bernal's home life was no less complicated than Needham's, it was at least more harmonious. He was born on 10 May 1901 in a small village (Nenagh) in County Tipperary, Ireland. His father, Samuel Bernal, was an Irish Catholic who, in his youth, had run away to sea and even sheepfarmed in Australia before returning to Nenagh to become a gentleman farmer. He also brought back an American-born bride, Elizabeth Miller. To the rough and ready life of rural Ireland, Mrs Bernal brought a most unusual blend of Protestantism, enlightenment and female emancipation. She had been one of the first graduates of Stanford University in California and had at one time been a journalist. According to C. P. Snow, she was 'a little like a character out of Henry James – expatriate, literary, cultivated'.[34] Needless to say, Mrs Bernal found few connections between her past history and new circumstances, and this hiatus undoubtedly contributed to the careful oversight she exercised over the education of her highly intelligent first-born son, Desmond. Nothing was to stand in the way of his intellectual growth. Thus when Bernal's aptitude for and love of science began to manifest itself, mother and son began to plot out his transfer to an English school, where scientific facilities were presumed to be superior to those available in Ireland. Against such a formidable duo Bernal's father had no choice but to acquiesce.

The scientific proclivities of Bernal and Needham, each spurred on by his favourite parent, were now to be catered for by two similar institutions. Bernal was sent to Bedford School in 1914; Needham was to be found that year at near-by Oundle School in Northamptonshire. Of the two public schools, Oundle was the more progressive. Its Headmaster, F. W. Sanderson, was an energetic apostle of 'learning through doing', not least in the area of scientific studies. His greatest reform at Oundle had been the introduction of engineering workshops allied to courses in applied science, which were themselves designed to make young Oundelians hunger after more theoretical subjects. In this context the advent of the First World War was almost a godsend to Sanderson. For Britain's deficiencies in industrial production allowed him to transform the school into a munitions factory. Once a term, each form of boys would spend a week turning out bullets and shells, thereby learning simultaneously the values of science, teamwork and patriotism. Not far behind Oundle on the industrial front was Bedford, where the students managed to fulfil contracts for ammunition and submarine valves (for a firm run by Alfred Yarrow, an old Bedfordian).[35] Such a practical introduction to scientific and engineering subjects, while undoubtedly beneficial to Bernal and Needham, did not precisely meet their well-defined scholastic requirements. Both were already drawn to more esoteric studies – geometry and theoretical physics in Bernal's case, zoology and philosophical biology in Needham's. What advancement they made in these areas therefore had to take place outside the formal curriculum. Another factor that probably contributed to their dissatisfaction with such education was the martial atmosphere of the times. Neither of them was enamoured of military discipline, drilling and display (although Needham was to serve very briefly in 1918 as a surgeon sub-lieutenant in the navy). In Oundle's Officer Training Corps Needham could not summon up the degree of 'enthusiasm' that Sanderson demanded from his charges. And when, fifty years later, I asked Bernal for a comment about Bedford, he would only say that it was 'an army-type English public school'.[36]

Bernal's and Needham's lukewarm response to the call of King and Country signified the presence of other radical sentiments.* From a very early age Needham regarded himself as a socialist in the manner of H. G. Wells, whose scientific romances and utopian novels he devoured, despite his parents' disapproval. Yet for many years he rarely expressed his political beliefs, save in a strained argument or two with his High Tory father. Bernal's ideological commitments were, by contrast, far more exposed. For, as an Irish Catholic at an English public school, he was forced to discover how strongly he felt about Britain's oppression of his country. In the wake of the Easter Rising of 1916 in Dublin and other parts of Ireland, Bernal – at the age of fifteen – became convinced that violent means would have to be employed if the cause of national liberation were to succeed.[37]

As schoolboys, Needham's socialism and Bernal's nationalism were both intimately connected with their scientific aspirations and religious convictions. Needham, the young Wellsian, naturally saw the advance of science and socialism as virtual synonyms for the same process. Such enlightened 'scientism' was amplified still further in Oundle's history classes, where Sanderson (who was a close friend of Wells) would assign his pupils a historical period and then order them to 'find out between you what contribution that period has made to progress'.[38] For Bernal the Irish nationalist, on the other

* There is a danger here, of course, of overstressing the radicalism of these bourgeois adolescents. In Needham's case, for example, vaguely socialist ideas could still easily and contradictorily coexist with more orthodox ones. Thus, in the reports of the Oundle Debating Society carried in the school's paper (*The Laxtonian*) between 1916 and 1918, one can read of Needham's support for such motions as: 'Games in public schools are beneficial to the nation as a whole'; 'Boys come to school to develop their characters and not to learn'; and 'Corporal punishment justifies its existence by its long standing'. However, in one of his last debates, Needham did strenuously oppose the resolution that 'the education of the British working man is adequate.'

hand, the link between scientific and social progress was considerably more down-to-earth. Because he had been able to witness in his travels between home and school the enormous contrasts between pre-industrial Ireland and industrialized Britain, Bernal came to realize – before his tenth birthday, he once claimed – that his people would have to win their economic as well as their political independence from their oppressors. In other words, the nation's productive capacities would have to be revolutionized, and for that enterprise a large measure of scientific expertise would be required.

It seemed to me [then], [Bernal would later write in an autobiographical fragment] that these two things, the relief of the sufferings of the country and the possibilities of science, could in some sense be united. Science offered the means, perhaps the only means, by which the people of Ireland could liberate themselves. I saw it narrowly in a purely nationalist sense, but it led me to an interest in science which grew to be a dominating interest in my life.[39]

Like Hyman Levy, Bernal required his scientific life to be infused with social purpose.

Bernal and Needham also experienced a need to situate their science and politics within religious frameworks. This was especially true of Needham, who saw himself from adolescence onwards as 'a person who absolutely could not do without a "world-view"'.[40] Here he was strongly influenced by his father. During his adult life, the elder Joseph had passed through the Anglo-Catholicism of the Oxford movement, the mysticism of the Quakers, ending up with the rationality of Christian modernism. The final tendency was ably expressed every Sunday morning at the Temple Church in London, where Bishop E. W. Barnes presided. For many years the two male members of the Needham family would faithfully attend these services, thereby enabling the son to listen to 'discourses on the pre-Socratic philosophers and medieval scholasticism and all kinds of things which would not ordinarily come into sermons'.[41] At home young Needham could follow up any points he didn't understand with the aid of his father's large and erudite collection of philosophical and religious works. But his religion was not only learned; it was deeply felt as well. Needham's piety and idealism, in conjunction with his political leanings, thus rendered him a devout Christian socialist. His ethos comes through clearly in the following hymn-like stanza from a poem he wrote at Oundle about his hopes for post-war reconstruction:

> And when we proceed to the work of rebuilding
>   The Civilization of Europe again
> We will cast off the trammels of ponderous ages
>   And start right afresh letting no wrong remain.
> We will make a clean sweep of all errors and littleness
>   Chase from our planet the spirit of Gain.
> We will make a new start – Which shall not be in vain.[42]

What direction the 'new start' would take in practice, however, remained a mystery to the idealistic Needham.

Until he entered Cambridge University, Bernal practised his Catholicism with a zeal that matched Needham's observance of Anglican rites. Indeed, before his enrolment at Bedford Bernal had distinguished himself at a Jesuit-run prep school in Lancashire by founding a Society for Perpetual Adoration. Through this organization he was able to organize night-long prayer vigils on the part of his dormitory companions and himself. (The Jesuit authorities, perhaps because they sensed that the project was inspired as much by mischief as by devotion, soon put a stop to it.) A good part of Bernal's spiritual ardour inevitably stemmed from his earnest nationalism. The church was an integral component of Irish culture and, as such, Bernal was able to view it in his schooldays as a bulwark against the anglicization of himself and his native land. But the longer he remained isolated, through his education, from the context which gave political meaning to his religious practices, the more difficult it became for him to sustain his faith.

Bernal's arrival at Emmanuel College, Cambridge, in 1919 was – no other phrase will do – an intellectual, political and religious turning point in his life: Needham's undergraduate period was not nearly so significant for his development. Having seen numerous parallels between their earlier lives, their divergence at the moment when they finally came together in the same community might seem a bit odd. But this apparent paradox can be easily dispelled by emphasizing the content rather than the structure of their childhoods. For as an Irishman Bernal was obliged to look at Britain through 'alien eyes'; Needham, the favoured Englishman, was not. Hence the stability and future prospects of *British* institutions – the economy, the church, the schools, the scientific community and the Empire, including Ireland – became problematic for Bernal, at a very early age, to a degree that Needham would not be able to appreciate until much later.* Yet it was only in the peculiar atmosphere of post-war Cambridge that this difference would be manifested with Bernal's emergence as a social rebel.

What needs stressing here is how much political and intellectual energy animated the university just after the First World War. The colleges were filled not just with young men like Bernal and Needham but also with hundreds of ex-soldiers, whose presence moderated the often frivolous unreality of undergraduate society. Politics played a more prominent part in their lives than was the case with their pre-war counterparts. In particular, a far higher proportion of those who were politically active were toying with one variety or another of socialism. One of the chief beneficiaries of this ultimately short-lived trend was the Cambridge University Socialist Society. Apart from this greater concern for the 'outside' world, there was also a more serious orientation taken to course work. This was especially true of the veterans, whether students or dons, who had been forced to interrupt their studies because of the war. As it happened, the university was sufficiently well staffed with teachers gifted enough to satisfy such high aspirations, notably in the natural sciences. For while Frederick Gowland Hopkins had already established the excellence of his Dunn Biochemical Institute, Sir Ernest Rutherford was about to oversee the development of a brilliant school of young physicists at the Cavendish Laboratory.

The impact of such an environment on Bernal was immense. He threw himself completely into the course, the politics and whatever

* Patricia Cockburn attributes the notion of the 'alien eye' and its connection with political radicalism to the British Communist Party's leading theoretician, R. Palme Dutt: 'Dutt remarked [c. 1933] on the fact that of all the British intellectuals showing some sympathy with communist ideas and aims, an astonishingly small number had lived wholly in England. For such sympathies to be aroused, it seemed to be almost de rigueur for a person to have had a chance to look at England from the outside.' Patricia Cockburn, *The Years of the Week* (Harmondsworth, 1971), p. 42.

Within the Visible College, one not only encounters the Irish Bernal but the Scottish Levy and Haldane. And for all the abuse that he suffered up to the end of the First World War, Hogben could well be regarded as a 'naturalized' alien. That leaves Needham – the least political of the group until the early 1930s.

forms of avant-garde social life Cambridge had to offer. His scholastic performance was brilliant, including an original crystallographic paper that caught the eye of Sir William Bragg, who promptly offered Bernal a post-graduate position at the Davy-Faraday Laboratory in London. That Bernal preferred crystal to particle physics was, in part, a reflection of a clash between his speculative temperament as a theorist and the no-nonsense experimental bias of Rutherford's research school. Nor was Bernal able to limit his fields of inquiry to those deemed appropriate for a physics student. Indeed he was more likely to be found in a library than a laboratory, delving into works on ancient history, Chinese ceramics, economic theory or modern art. His memory was photographic, his knowledge encyclopedic. (In an interview with one of his close associates, I was told that Bernal once literally read a hefty encyclopedia from cover to cover.) But what made him such a remarkable figure for his age was his ability to structure his wide knowledge into arresting and novel patterns of thought. That was how he picked up, while still an undergraduate, the nickname by which his friends would refer to him for the rest of his life: Bernal became, in their eyes, the 'Sage'.

The 'Sage', however, had much to learn from the men and women who came to befriend him. They told him, among other things, that the nationalistic foundations of his political beliefs were altogether too narrow. One of his friends, H. D. Dickinson – a future professor of economics at Bristol University – began taking Bernal to meetings of the Socialist Society. Bernal's introduction to socialism was quickly succeeded by a thorough study of the Marxist classics, which were lent to him by Allen Hutt (who was already a communist). For the next six months Bernal methodically covered most of the available writings of Marx, Engels and Lenin, including *Capital* and *State and Revolution*. He emerged from this period intellectually committed to revolutionary socialism; shortly after leaving Cambridge he was to join the Communist Party of Great Britain.

Now that he was a Marxian socialist as well as an Irish patriot, Bernal had to re-evaluate his previous compact between politics, religion and science. With the aid of his new socialist perspective, Bernal could see that Roman Catholicism was both reactionary and anti-scientific. Marx and his followers, by contrast, not only urged a social revolution but also, and this was crucial for Bernal, placed a high value upon having a scientific world-view. At this point science – then for Bernal the only sound, 'objective' method for discovering valid knowledge about nature and society – began to vie with Marxism as his political pole-star. For he believed at this stage that science 'held the key to the future', and he supported the forces of socialism precisely because they alone 'were gathering to turn it'.* Meanwhile his observance of and belief in the Catholic faith became progressively more attenuated.

Needham's undergraduate career was not nearly so stormy. Far from overthrowing his earlier religious beliefs and practices, he extended them as a member of the Confraternity of the Holy Trinity (S.T.C.) and as Secretary of an Anglican society for medical students called the Guild of St Luke. The guild was important to Needham for the evening lectures it sponsored on the historical, philosophical and scientific facets of Christianity. On the basis of such meetings he was able to further his erudite explorations of ancient and medieval learning. A more up-to-date interest was undergraduate discussions within his own college (Caius) about such sexual radicals as Edward Carpenter, Havelock Ellis and, above all, Sigmund Freud. But the shy Needham rarely revealed the results of all this intellectual effort to others. He was equally quiet about the progress of his scientific studies, which were leading him out of medicine into the stimulating milieu of Hopkins' biochemical lab. There was, however, one area of endeavour where Needham failed to advance his earlier opinions, and that was politics. Indeed it would take a decade of important changes both within himself and his society before he could reconstruct his political views in the decisive manner of his contemporary, Bernal.

* From J. Bernal, 'Verantwortung und Verbflichtung der Wissenschaft', in Elga Kern (ed.), *Wegweisser in der Zeitwende; Selbstzeugnisse bedeutender Menschen lesansgeleben* (Munich/Basel, 1955). Bernal's obsession with the scientific foundations of social development struck his undergraduate friends as a very significant and somewhat worrying dimension of his politics. For example, when in 1939 Allen Hutt reviewed Bernal's classic work on *The Social Function of Science*, he discovered that many of its passages 'vividly recalled youthful Cambridge conversations between Bernal and the present reviewer'. Hutt went on to note that Bernal still had a tendency twenty years on 'to idealize science as a revolutionary factor in itself and of itself'. Allen Hutt, 'Science and Society', *Labour Monthly*, vol. 21 (June, 1939), pp. 319–20.

By the early post-war period Levy, Haldane, Hogben, Bernal and Needham had, in their own distinctive ways, conjoined the causes of science and socialism. But of these, only Levy and Hogben – our two most 'disadvantaged' subjects – had attempted to give substance to their convictions through, respectively, trade union agitation and opposition to the First World War. Bernal and Haldane, on the other hand, had just begun to find themselves politically estranged from the privileged worlds that had nurtured them. Needham alone remained loosely attached to the bourgeois conventions of his youth, and even his loyalties were suspect because of his covert Wellsian tendencies. However, whether any of them would lean still further leftwards in the 1920s was unclear. For while they knew what they wanted to achieve for themselves in science, they were uncertain what they could do for others through politics. Nevertheless, they were, as Lancelot Hogben recently observed, different in one respect from the older generation of High Scientists: 'already in 1918 we knew that politics had a lot to do with science'.

Chapter Three

Cambridge Men

As the practical possibilities of any kind of political decision receded (in the twenties), . . . I turned with greater concern to the other side of the process of social transformation, that represented by science.

J. D. Bernal, 1955[1]

In the 1920s all of these young socialists, save Hyman Levy, put their scientific careers well ahead of their political commitments. High Science proved to be an absorbing pursuit when it was uninterrupted by several years of warfare and amply fuelled with new injections of money, ideas and people. Meanwhile a decade which witnessed one of the working class's greatest defeats (the General Strike), together with the subsequent demoralization of the Labour Party and near-demise of the Communist Party, was bound to be a testing one for all adherents of socialism, whatever their vocation. You had to be highly militant and sufficiently experienced in various forms of class struggle to keep on fighting for what in the short run was a losing cause. Hyman Levy, the most class-conscious of our subjects, was just that sort of person.

In the cases of Bernal, Haldane and Needham we have, by contrast, been dealing with younger men whose socialism was far more tentative, abstract and untested. Indeed, apart from their failure to put their beliefs to work, their most outstanding political characteristic was a readiness to equate the causes of science and socialism. That allowed them to regard their scientific work as a special type of politics. But the science that the three of them embraced was, even they would have admitted, pretty far removed from the central antagonisms of capital and labour. Furthermore they practised their research within the most rarified and powerful of scientific communities, Cambridge. And as Cambridge men, they were exposed to a set of attitudes and conventions that coloured their views of science and therefore, it followed, of socialism. In the next two chapters we shall be observing how they interacted with this unique environment, in order to contrast their experiences with those of Levy. For such 'non-political' differences between scientists who were socialists will help greatly to illuminate the two forms of politics that then divided them. One of their number who refused to settle easily into either scientific culture was the elusive, idiosyncratic Lancelot Hogben.

1. The Counter-culture

Prominent among the figures who never quite fitted into the mainstream of Cambridge scientific life were Bernal, Haldane and Needham. But certainly Needham came very close. His poetic essay of 1932, 'Cambridge Summer',[2] was to reveal an unsurpassed love for the university and its environs. An even more striking testimonial to Needham's devotion was (and continues to be) his unbroken association with one college, Caius, and one laboratory, the Dunn Biochemical Institute. He revered Gowland Hopkins, who appointed his admiring young protégé to a succession of posts, capped in 1932 by the Sir William Dunn Readership in Biochemistry. Needham was then only thirty-one years old.

Yet his claims to biochemical fame rested largely on the publication of a rather unconventional study called *Chemical Embryology*.[3] This work, which was inspired by 'a vision of the developing egg as a most wonderful factory of changes and synthesis',[4] was unusual both in form and in content. Rather than limit himself to a recitation of which chemicals were produced at what stage of embryonic development, Needham unfurled an enormous speculative canvas. In three weighty volumes he discussed at length: the history of embryology; the philosophical implications of treating morphogenesis biochemically; the genetic and evolutionary significance of the embryo's chemical productions; and the future course which embryological research should take. It was a staggering achievement; but was it good science?* For Needham was violating all

---

* Years afterwards the boyish-looking Needham would be approached at scientific conferences and congratulated on the work of his famous father, the author of *Chemical Embryology*!

In the Dunn Lab itself, Needham's encyclopedism was definitely seen as 'off-

kinds of normal scientific practices. He was rendering 'hard', 'experimental' facts 'soft' by exposing the historical and philosophical conventions that sustained them. In his desire always to connect different biological levels – without reducing one to the other – he found himself moving in the opposite direction from most of his colleagues in biochemistry. For these reasons Needham's peers were rarely able to resolve how his work should be evaluated.

Such ambivalence might have disheartened Needham had he relied solely upon biochemists for intellectual support. Yet it was abundantly clear from nearly every page of *Chemical Embryology* that he had been keeping some very odd company outside laboratory hours. Philosophers, artists and theologians were among Needham's favoured sources. They comprised in turn a good part of the audience for his own learned essays, two collections of which had been published by 1931.[5] Needham's work interested them chiefly because of its celebration of the integrity and autonomy of the 'great forms' of human experience, including religious mysticism. As a practising scientist and devout Anglican, Needham was expected to have experienced personally the psychological difficulties of crossing and recrossing the boundaries between religion and science. It was also possible that he was unusually well positioned to estimate the extent of scientific domination over society. These at any rate were the messages that came across to such unlikely readers as T. S. Eliot and F. R. Leavis, who allowed Needham to grace the pages of *Scrutiny* and *The Criterion* – publications not often noted for their rapturous support of modern science.

It would be wrong, however, to imply that Needham was totally isolated within the scientific community. *Chemical Embryology* was generally well received in the professional journals. In Cambridge itself he received support from philosophically minded young scientists in the counter-culture like Bernal and the embryologist

---

beat', even before the publication of *Chemical Embryology*. Thus in the fifth issue of *Brighter Biochemistry* (1927, p. 14) a 'reviewer' praised a 'new work' by Needham, entitled '*Eggs; From Aristotle to the Present* (in 27 volumes)'. The 'review' goes on to recommend the study to millionaires who wish to fill their library shelves. Among the items singled out for special praise was the fourteenth appendix – 'On the Appearance of Eggs in Music Hall Jokes (with a discussion of music hall jokes in general and eggs in general)'.

C. H. Waddington. Along with J. H. Woodger, a philosopher of science based in London, they would form the nucleus of the Theoretical Biology Club, one of the most important underground scientific enterprises of the 1930s. Another important future member of the T.B.C. was Dorothy Moyle, whom Needham married in 1924. Her classical work in the biochemistry of muscle contraction was much more in the mainstream of her discipline than chemical embryology. Though a firm believer in and scrupulous critic of her husband's research, even she had to admit that her Joseph was operating at a tangent, albeit a fascinating one, to the main pre-occupations of Cambridge biochemistry.

More tangential still was Bernal's relationship to the Cavendish and for that matter to the entire Cambridge scene. As an under-graduate he had already discovered that his special love of form and geometry 'was best expressed in the new atomic knowledge of the structure of matter'.[6] This meant X-ray crystallography, a subject very much to the side of Rutherford's preoccupations with particle physics. But in London Bernal was able to study at the Royal Institution under a leading crystallographer, Sir W. H. Bragg. Between 1923 and 1927, in the company of Sir William and a brilliant coterie of students, including Kathleen Yardley (Lonsdale) and William Astbury, Bernal was a happy man. 'I do not think', he reflected in later life, 'that any of those who were in their twenties would ever have wished to work anywhere else. As Dame Kathleen Lonsdale has said, we had to be kicked out!'[7]

Fortunately for Bernal, the Cavendish authorities had meanwhile decided to establish a special sub-department in his field. He was of course, with his Cambridge background and already outstanding scientific credentials, a strong candidate for this job. Yet the atmo-sphere surrounding his subsequent interview was apparently cool and tense on both sides.[8] Naturally Bernal wanted the appointment; he also recognized how traumatic and ambivalent his previous time in Cambridge had been. On the other side of the table, not a few of the more senior interviewers probably regarded this young Irish-man with his long, unruly and very red hair as not quite 'sound'. But when asked what he wanted to do with the sub-department, Bernal unleashed a forty-five minute monologue stuffed with ideas about what the future of X-ray crystallography would be and how he and his assistants might shape it. Such a staggering display of intellectual prowess finally secured him the job. He was back in Cambridge.

This did not, however, signify that Bernal had won either scientific or social respectability. So long as he was at Cambridge (and Rutherford remained alive), resources for X-ray crystallography remained limited. The sub-department, recalls one of Bernal's ex-students, was 'housed in a few ill-lit and dirty rooms on the ground floor of a stark, dilapidated grey brick building'.[9] To the difficulties of doing research under these conditions were added a paucity of studentships and a lack of technicians. Nevertheless, Bernal made the Crystallographic Laboratory into an exciting centre of excellence. His own work encompassed structural analyses of liquids and metals, as well as of a wide range of organic and biological molecules. These studies were, it would seem, good solid, orthodox work that ought to have impressed his elders. But Rutherford noted with some dissatisfaction Bernal's tendency to hand over many of his own projects to research students and associates. His failure to follow up earlier investigations was linked to other 'deviant' forms of behaviour. Bernal was not a good enough experimentalist for the rough and ready conditions at the Cavendish. Even at the Royal Institution he appears to have been decidedly unlucky with apparatus and research materials. If a charwoman did not inadvertently destroy one of his experiments, then Bernal himself was perfectly capable of undoing eighteen months of labour by dropping an infinitesimally small crystal onto the lab floor. This pattern of misfortunes undoubtedly reinforced another quality unprized by Bernal's scientific elders, namely his inveterate and highly speculative theorizing about his own, and even worse, other people's disciplines. This time the beneficiaries of his peculiar gifts included not only his own post-graduates but also his peers in neighbouring fields, notably biochemistry and embryology. To these men and women Bernal was a compelling and inspiring scientist. To C. P. Snow he was, in retrospect, 'perhaps the last of whom it will be said, with meaning, that he knew science'.[10] As awesome as that very Snow-like tribute might sound and however true it may have been, this did not mean that Bernal would ever find favour with the managers of High Science at Cambridge. Between him and them ran a vague but very real fault line. On one side stood, in their eyes, an undisciplined 'young Turk'; on the other was assembled what he would call and criticize in later life as the 'scientific gerontocracy'.

Bernal was of course much less acceptable to official Cambridge society. His undergraduate college, Emmanuel, did not offer him a Fellowship. Nor did Bernal seek out a similar niche elsewhere. He was an 'undesirable'. His professional eccentricities did not help him here, but they were of secondary importance. What hurt Bernal was, first, his politics and, second, his unconventional marriage. Although not an active Communist in the 1920s, he was nonetheless a 'Red' and that in itself was a subversively odd thing for a don to be.

Yet it was probably Bernal's manners and morals that gave the greatest offence. By the time he had returned to Cambridge Bernal was married to Eileen Sprague, a Newnham graduate by whom he was to have two children. Theirs was a strong if very stormy marriage. For Bernal, though he loved his wife very much, was not a monogamous spirit. His liaisons were legendary. More striking still were his attempts to make explicit, smooth over, reconcile and even transcend the jealousies and other emotional conflicts that resulted from his amorousness. Opinion was divided among Bernal's friends as to how empathetic he was to his lovers' needs and feelings. In Snow's first major novel, *The Search* of 1934, Constantine – the polymathic crystallographer for whom Bernal served as the model[11] – certainly came across as very indifferent to the women with whom he slept. More recently, though, Needham has argued how deeply Bernal cared about all of his friends, whatever their sex. Even if Needham has misjudged his friend in this respect, it is the case that the Bernal household was always the vital link in a lively network of young and gifted individuals who had not succumbed to the settled routines of Cambridge life. Bernal was hardly the 'leader' of this sub-culture; but through his intellectual brilliance and real *joie de vivre* he managed to shape and hold it together. This comradeship naturally helped him in all of those projects where he was going against the established grain. As he never tired of saying to one of his closest friends, 'no love affair . . . will ever work where there isn't a community of social feeling'.[12] Bernal might have said the same thing about his science and his politics.

Cambridge, sadly, offered no commune into which J. B. S. Haldane could comfortably settle. For a start his selection as the first Dunn Reader in Biochemistry was rather surprising. Although he had already shown himself at Oxford to be an outstanding physiologist with a burgeoning interest in genetics, his biochemical qualifications were not at all evident. Haldane did manage to confirm, but only partially, Hopkins's support of his candidacy by publishing a pioneering study in the kinetics of enzyme action. Even then J.B.S.'s career was veering off very sharply towards the new highly mathematical and non-experimental field of population genetics. In a crucial set of papers published between 1924 and 1932, he set out to account for evolutionary change by mathematicizing Darwin's metaphor of natural selection. Haldane's work, statistically ingenious yet very much in the orthodox Darwinian tradition, established beyond doubt his reputation as a scientist of the first order. As early as 1926 he was asked to head the Genetics Department of the John Innes Horticultural Institution. This part-time appointment, along with another – a research professorship in physiology at the Royal Institution – were indicative of Haldane's drift from Cambridge biochemistry. Hence his decision in 1933 to take up the full-time post of Professor of Genetics at University College, London, came as no great shock. He was by then forty years old, a Fellow of the Royal Society and at the height of his considerable scientific powers. Cambridge, which was unprepared to support on a large scale the as yet low-prestige field of genetics, could hardly have expected to hold on to Britain's most illustrious geneticist.

From the standpoint of not a few of his more elderly colleagues, Haldane's departure probably came as something of a relief. For his digressions from Cambridge norms had not been limited to his choice of scientific interests. To put it bluntly: J.B.S. proved to be no gentleman. Many thought his behaviour outside the laboratory was scandalous and disgraceful. Haldane did, in fact, enjoy publicly mocking many social conventions, not least those that governed what people might say and do about 'sex'. Thus in the embarrassing silences of a Cambridge dinner party he might, Ivor Montagu has since recalled, throw off 'some such sentence as: "I have never gone in really seriously for bestial sodomy." '[13] Such antics were of course almost intolerable within the confines of a don's drawing-room. Unfortunately, J.B.S. had a gift for self-advertisement that was to spread his fame – or infamy, some would have said – far beyond the university's environs.

Take the furore surrounding Haldane's marriage to Charlotte Burghes in 1925. Mrs Burghes was a newswoman and novelist who had sought J.B.S.'s advice the previous year about some of her science fiction. That meeting engendered others, and they were soon devoted to one another. But with Charlotte already married (and the mother of one son), their future as a couple was uncertain unless they staged the kind of adulterous situation then required to secure a divorce. This action led not merely to highly publicized divorce proceedings, but also to Haldane's dismissal from his readership for acts of 'gross immorality'. (The university body responsible for this action consisted of six men and was called, to outsiders' delight, the 'Sex Viri'. Since then one man has been added so that it could be renamed the 'Septem Viri'.) With the support of the liberal Hopkins and the National Union of Scientific Workers, J.B.S. took the matter before a private tribunal which eventually overruled the inevitably renamed 'Sex-Weary'. It was an important victory in that it gave academics a greater degree of autonomy in the conduct of their private lives. Yet it also meant that Haldane's name was now firmly placed in the vanguard of sexual emancipation.

This was not the first time that J.B.S. had with great fanfare strayed from the moral pathways marked out for 'real' Cambridge scientists. In 1923 he had spectacularly broken the unwritten rule that first-rate researchers should not 'sensationalize' their science before 'lay' audiences.* Haldane's little book *Daedalus, or Science and the Future* did all that and more. It epigrammatically and glee-fully broached a host of unthinkable subjects, including the potential benefits of manufacturing to any specification test-tube babies. 'I can', he mused, 'foresee the election placards of 300 years hence . . ., "Vote for O'Leary and more girls", or perhaps finally, "Vote for MacPherson and a prehensile tail for your great grandchildren".'[14] This clever, naughty combination of sex, science and social affairs was to become the hallmark of J.B.S.'s popular writings in the twenties. In later essays he would open out still further the private world of the laboratory. One of the most delightful of these, 'On Being One's Own Rabbit', described the risks which some scientists

---

* Haldane was well aware of this convention, and had himself tried to enforce it earlier on Julian Huxley, one of whose experiments had been mis-reported in, of all places, the *Daily Mail*. See Julian Huxley, *Memories* (London, 1970), p. 126.

took in experimenting on themselves.[15] (Haldane himself was a regular imbiber of bizarre liquids such as dilute hydrochloric acid.) Others delved non-committally into the possibilities of life on other planets, the existence of a supra-individual reality called the 'Great Being' and the applicability of Kantian idealism to modern physics. Occasionally J.B.S.'s speculations would grow more serious and profound. In his 'The Origin of Life' of 1929 he set out a thoroughly 'materialistic' explanation as to how living organisms might have arisen out of a 'dilute soup' of sugars and other simple organic substances. This was an exciting conception in its own time, and it was, along with the work of Soviet physicist A. I. Oparin, to inspire a research tradition that has been sustained to this day.[16]

The main animus behind this article and most of Haldane's public entertainments was to show that the 'universe is not only queerer than we suppose, but queerer than we *can* suppose'.[17] Armed with this rationalization for unlimited philosophical licence, J.B.S. was determined, above all else, to amuse himself and others. Thus when the idealist astronomer Sir Arthur Eddington once remarked that all (male) materialists must think of their wives as differential equations, Haldane's audience would start grinning in anticipation of what their hero might say in return.

I recently put this point to a happily married physicist of my acquaintance. He replied that he would not love his wife if he did not believe that she was a differential equation, or rather that her conduct obeyed one. He loves her because she has a definite character which renders her conduct intelligible even when it is surprising. And in this she certainly resembles a differential equation. There are dull differential equations just as there are dull wives. There are others, such as Schrodinger's wave equation, which is at the bottom of a great deal of modern physics, that lead to the most odd and beautiful results. Men have fallen in love with statues and pictures. I find it far easier to imagine a man falling in love with a differential equation, and I am inclined to think that some mathematicians have done so. Even in a non-mathematician like myself, some differential equations evoke fairly violent physical sensations similar to those described by Sappho and Catullus when viewing their mistresses. Personally, however, I obtain an even greater 'kick' from finite difference equations, which are perhaps more like those which an up-to-date materialist would use to describe human behaviour.[18]

(One wonders what sort of 'kick' the physicist's wife derived as the object of this extraordinary piece of objectification.) Putting all of Haldane's popular *œuvre* together, it would be difficult not to sympathize a bit with older scientists who thought him to be more than a little 'unsound'.

But to well-educated, mainly young people of 'advanced' views, J.B.S. became a true cultural hero. He was, along with Aldous Huxley, 'one of our major intellectual emancipators', recalls Isaiah Berlin, one of his schoolboy admirers from the twenties.[19] Haldane's books sold well. Leading articles in newspapers were devoted to them, as were two book-length replies to *Daedalus* by Bertrand Russell and Robert Graves.[20] As a public figure, his arrival can be precisely dated. For between 1923 and 1924 he was to crop up as a major protagonist in not one but two novels. In Aldous Huxley's *Antic Hay* the physiologist Shearwater was closely modelled after Haldane. If that were common knowledge only to Haldane's and Huxley's intimate friends, the same could not have been said of the character Mr Codling in Ronald Fraser's *The Flying Draper*. For Codling is portrayed as a corruptor of youth who, after writing *The History and Probable Future of Morality*, is chased by jealous rivals from his university chair. The resemblance to J.B.S. was unmistakable and could only have enhanced his national reputation as a daring intellect.

In Cambridge itself he naturally attracted to his home many undergraduate and academic non-conformists. Unlike the Bernal network, however, this was much more of a 'circle', with all lines radiating inwards toward Haldane at the centre. He was genuinely held in awe. One of his associates from these years would later confess that 'to me . . . he seemed to be the last man who might know all there was to be known.'[21] Such adulation was the product of Haldane's illustrious background, his great physical and scientific stature, his witty, wide-ranging essays, his 'free-thinking' attitudes about sex and, finally, his Olympian imperson-ality.* Satisfying as this heroic posture must have been to him,

---

* Both Fraser and Huxley in their novels emphasize their Haldane-figures' lack of involvement with people.

' "x^2-y^2", Shearwater was saying, "$=(x+y)(x-y)$ and the equation holds good whatever the values of x and y. It's the same with your love business, the same, whatever the value of the unknown personal quantities con-cerned. Little individual tics and peculiarities – after all, what do they matter?" . . .

'Mrs Viveash smiled agonizingly. "Here's a man who thinks personal

it did render J.B.S. a remote figure, isolated from even close friends, not to mention his many enemies who saw him as anything but an exemplar of behaviour becoming to a sober scientist.

2. Deeper Loyalties?

When the careers of Haldane, Bernal and Needham are reviewed, it is apparent how idiosyncratic and exceptional they were. But, for all their individuality, were they in any meaningful sense 'Cambridge men'? They were, at least with regard to their evaluation and understanding of the scientific enterprise. They saw the period in which they were working as one of the most promising in the history of science. For Bernal, 'it was a happy and exciting time, because practically nothing was known then of crystal structure: it was all to do, and one could, in one laboratory, see the opening up of basic knowledge of [this] enormous field'.[22] Such basic research was, according to Haldane, 'of all things most supremely worth doing for its own sake and that of its results'.[23] All three men evinced a strong aesthetic preference for pure over applied science. Needham went so far as to brush aside as 'a crude attribute of science' its power over nature.[24] He was also concerned with the effect of commercial materialism on science, but not half so much as Haldane, who warned in 1928 that

as the ideals of pure science become more and more remote from those of the general public, science will tend to degenerate more and more into medical and engineering technology, just as art may degenerate into illustration and religion into ritual when they lose their vital spark. . . The result of such a tendency would be that gradually the flow of real invention would dry up.[25]

To safeguard against these utilitarian tendencies, Bernal, Haldane and Needham pleaded – as would their ideological opponents in

---

peculiarities are trivial and unimportant," she said. "You're not even interested in people, then?" . . .

'Shearwater scratched his head. Under his formidable black moustache he smiled at last his ingenuous childish smile. "No," he said. "No, I suppose I'm not. It hadn't occurred to me, until you said it. But I suppose I'm not. No." He laughed, quite delighted, it seemed, by this discovery about himself.'

From Aldous Huxley's *Antic Hay* (New York, 1965), p. 70. See also R. Fraser, *The Flying Draper* (London, 1924), esp. p. 213.

the 1940s – for a wider recognition of the special conditions required for doing first-rate disinterested research. Of course you needed first-rate men. As Needham primly observed, 'scientific investigators are born and not made, even by the magic of a Ph.D.'[26] Such scientists next required freedom of thought, which would allow them to remain, in Haldane's lyrical view, passionately attached 'to reality as such, whether it be bright or dark, mysterious or intelligible'.[27] This was a poetic definition of that elusive but omniscient entity, the 'scientific method'. To Bernal this method circumscribed an entire way of life: 'the continuous discovery and refining of discoveries, the acceptance of organizing hypotheses as merely convenient and provisional, and the experimental critical attitude towards every dogmatic proposition or system of belief'.[28] Indeed the extension of this method to society would constitute the ultimate guarantee of scientific and social progress. 'I believe', Haldane proclaimed, 'that the future of Western civilization depends upon whether or not it can assimilate that scientific point of view.'[29] Whatever differences might have divided this trio of up-and-coming young scientists from their elders, they certainly all shared a robust confidence in the validity of their esoteric arts.

But how did consensus emerge here when it so manifestly failed to arise in other areas of their lives? The commitment to common scientific values was rooted in a set of uncommon educational experiences. Their schools, precisely because they were designed as stepping-stones to Oxford and Cambridge, were obliged to teach within and about the traditions of High Science. Even if utilitarian motivations might have originally inspired some youthful enthusiasm for research, they soon gave way to 'purer', more orthodox rationales. Bernal, Haldane and Needham were obviously also quite directly linked to Cambridge science through their membership of the Dunn and Cavendish laboratories. Nor were they any less competitive or ambitious than the people with whom they worked. Where this threesome did diverge, as in their choice of scientific specialities, it was still open to question how much of a gap divided them from their more orthodox colleagues. For in each case, Bernal, Haldane and Needham were exploring the three disciplines that would preoccupy leading biologists after the Second World War: molecular biology, genetics and developmental biology. Meanwhile these subjects were regarded as pure, hard and fashionable enough to survive in Cambridge, without encroaching on the ascendancy of particle physics and biochemistry. They were simultaneously odd enough pursuits to allow their practitioners a degree of freedom from mainstream scientific life not vouchsafed to others. Within the counter-cultures that subsequently emerged, other kinds of deviancy, not necessarily related to science, were encouraged; thereby producing the patina of protest that overlay Bernal's network and Haldane's circle. But what was striking about these sub-communities was the separation of private, political and professional preoccupations. Without any substantial overlap, it was difficult to see how even the most morally daring of their social experiments might jeopardize the progress of their scientific investigations. Where such connections were made, as in some of Haldane's essays, it was the ideology of Cambridge science that prevailed.

Yet these extraordinary individuals did have the knack of transmuting orthodox views in unforeseen ways. One such notion was how much society depended on science and its practitioners. As exceptional representatives of a Wellsian post-war generation of scientists, Bernal, Haldane and Needham naturally subscribed to this commonplace aspect of scientific folklore. But they did far more than that. They built up a picture of a world that was coming increasingly under the sway of scientific domination. Though differing in their own evaluations of whether this process was desirable, all three men were persuaded that it was irreversible. One day scientists would simply grow tired of ruling mankind indirectly through ideas and machinery and would therefore have to seize state control for themselves.

Haldane was the first of our group to celebrate the coming omniscience of scientific workers. In *Daedalus* he warned that 'science is as yet in its infancy . . .; no beliefs, no values, no institutions are safe'.[30] Whatever the moral scruples of any one scientist, 'it is his destiny to turn good into evil'.[31] In the future he will come to resemble more and more 'the lonely figure of Daedalus as he becomes more conscious of his ghastly mission and proud of it'.[32] Faced with sentiments such as these, Ronald Fraser has the Prime Minister in *The Flying Draper* predicting that 'For most people his philosophy will be like a lump of ice in the region of the heart.

There are passages in which he is completely, terribly outside human life. He observes us on our planet and reports us. The result is amusing for angels, but a little distressing to men . . . That is why Codling's book will damn him.'[33] Haldane could not have disagreed more. Indeed he forecast that the Voltaires, Benthams and Marxes of the future – the reasoners who wrecked outworn societies –would be increasingly drawn to scientific work. For, 'at present, Reason not only has a freer play in science than elsewhere, but can produce as great effects on the world through science as through politics, philosophy or literature'.[34]

In *The World, The Flesh and The Devil: An Inquiry into the Future of the Three Enemies of the Rational Soul*, J. D. Bernal did Mr Codling (and H. G. Wells) one better. Not content merely to predict the emergence of a scientific society, he attempted in 1929 to portray how it would come about and what life would be like in it. Briefly, Bernal saw the future as simply the extension of our evolving desires.[35]

The immediate future which is our own desire we seek; in achieving it we become different; becoming different we desire something new, so there is no staleness except when development itself has stopped. . . [The] dangers to the whole structure of humanity and its successors will not decrease as their wisdom increases, because, knowing more and wanting more, they will dare more, and in daring will risk their own destruction. But this daring, this experimentation, is really the essential quality of life.

The natural guardians of this scientific attitude are scientists, who are already on the brink of becoming the principal agents of social change. First through advisory bodies and later through corporations, these researchers would eventually be able to run their experiments without consulting anyone else. 'Mankind as a whole,' Bernal predicted, 'given peace, plenty and freedom, might well be content to let alone the fanatical but useful people who chose to distort their bodies or blow themselves into space'.[36] It would then be too late to break free from the scientists' hegemony: a terrifying prospect since this group's 'curiosity and its effects may be stronger than its humanity'.[37] This last fear would be manifested most directly in a transformation of the human species itself. Taking ectogenesis for granted, Bernal speculated on the fine structure of a greatly lengthened lifespan. After 60–120 years of 'larval' existence (dancing, poetry and love-making), we would move on to the 'chrysalis' stage. (So much for fine arts as the crown of civilization!) Here we would develop the mental apparatus necessary for a whole range of complex tasks. Then if any of us exhibited unusually powerful intellects, we, or rather our brains, would be literally plugged into an elaborate network of other superior beings. This world-mind or Great Being would then be in a position to manipulate or experiment upon lesser men. Finally, Bernal imagined,

consciousness itself may end or vanish in a humanity that has become completely etherealized, losing the close-knit organism, becoming masses of atoms in space communicating by radiation, and ultimately perhaps resolving itself entirely into light. That may be an end or a beginning but from here it is out of sight.[38]

'Out of sight', indeed.

One man who did shrink back from the spectacle of the scientific demiurge gone berserk was Joseph Needham. As an Anglo-Catholic with genuine mystical leanings, he was in the strange position of being a scientist who saw himself as a victim of scientific domination. Specifically, Needham identified three destructive influences that stemmed from science's commanding position in contemporary society. The first of these was widespread dehumanization through the spread of the quantitative and abstract modes of thought peculiar to modern scientists. To government bureaucrats we were numbers, not individuals; in factories we were perceived as 'hands', mere machinery rather than complex persons. There was also a widespread loss of social responsibility, which derived in part, Needham believed, from deterministic belief systems generated out of the natural sciences. Within the scientific community itself, this tendency was manifested by doctrines of ethical neutrality which rationalized researchers' indifference to how their work was used. 'No doubt,' Needham observed in 1931, 'the greatest effect which applied science has, however, is in filling the sails of . . . millenarianism, . . . the belief that there's a good time coming, actually coming here on earth, and at no distant date. This is indeed a characteristic concomitant of scientific progress.'[39] Needham himself was not nearly so certain, as some millenarian-minded scientists, that the evil that men did could be undone simply through programmes of social engineering, no matter how scientific. Instead he hoped that enough 'balanced souls' could be found to keep alive the 'sense of the holy', of human limitation and of universal mystery. Although conceding some truthfulness to 'the well known assertion that religion is the opium of the people', it was equally clear to Needham that 'we do not get very far by simply conferring this distinction on science instead'.[40]

Whatever we might feel about Haldane's and Bernal's vision and Needham's implicit reaction to them, they all evinced a set of attitudes about the nature and importance of scientific life that had 'Cambridge' stamped all over it. Such an outlook, however it was developed, implied a kind of political pose that we might not normally associate with socialists. Of course any of these Cambridge men could have practised a form of politics that was manifestly inconsistent with their behaviour as scientists: such contradictions are familiar to all of us. But in the Cambridge of the 1920s we have a context which favoured the development of a socialism made over in the image of High Science.

3. Professor Haldane's Scientific Politics

Neither the laboratories nor the colleges of Cambridge could be said to have been seed-beds of political radicalism before the Depression. There was 'very little of what today would be called left-wing thought, and still less activity . . . among either students or staff . . . prior to '31'. This was the view recently expressed by Maurice Dobb,[41] a Cambridge economics don who in the twenties belonged to the Communist Party. Dobb has also recalled how the university's unmistakably conservative ethos was manifested during the General Strike.

I happened to be lecturing at the time and can remember my audience suddenly shrinking to a front row of about four or five from . . . a nominal audience of perhaps thirty or so. These were all that had refrained from going away to answer the government's call for blacklegs to man the trains and buses.

Although one biochemist was instrumental in getting the Trades

Council to produce a strike bulletin, his action was altogether untypical of his fellow researchers.* Indeed the vast majority of Cambridge scientists could not even work up any enthusiasm for defending their own economic and political interests, let alone supporting similar struggles elsewhere. Thus the local branch of the National Union of Scientific Workers was moribund; no more than a debating society, really. When in 1927 an appeal was launched to de-unionize the N.U.S.W., it received the backing of many senior dons, including Sir Frederick Gowland Hopkins. This act of political disengagement connoted a widespread disenchantment with politics as such. Though these researchers may have had, to use C. P. Snow's phrase, 'the future in their bones',[42] the problems of present-day society were rarely on their minds. As a former member of the Cavendish once told me in confidence: until the thirties 'we didn't feel any responsibility to do anything for anyone'.

Bernal, Haldane and Needham may have thought their own attitudes were more socially responsible than those of our mythically typical Cambridge man. But their actions failed to give much reality to their beliefs, at least in this decade. Needham and Haldane were only lukewarm and inactive supporters of the Labour Party. Bernal was of course at this point a self-confessed recluse from all types of political activity. He did not even join the N.U.S.W., nor did Needham. At least J.B.S. was a member of the scientists' union. (His perfunctory participation in its affairs was nonetheless surprising in view of the assistance he had received from this organization in his fight against the Sex Viri.) In the General Strike, by contrast, it was Haldane who absented himself from the fray. Bernal refused to strike-break, even though he had been requested to serve 'the nation' in this way by his professor, Sir William Bragg, who, a few weeks before the General Strike, had broadcast over the B.B.C. an appeal from the British Science Guild for 'class unity'.[43] Amazingly enough, Joseph Needham

* B. 'Woggy' Woolf was the scientist in question. 'Woggy' was one of the two or three researchers of working-class origin to pass through the Dunn Lab in the twenties. He was also the most politically active of the biochemists at this time. In the 1930s Woolf moved to London, where he devoted more of his time to politics than research. His political assignments included a stint as lyricist for the Communist-controlled Unity Theatre. This career was abandoned after the war, however, for a genetics lectureship at Edinburgh University.

stood up to be counted – on the wrong side – by volunteering his services as an engine-driver. Only after the strike was over did Needham begin to live up to his pro-labour views, by protesting successfully against the attempted victimization of local railwaymen. Taken together, these facts did not add up to a flattering picture of Bernal, Haldane and Needham as socialists. Throughout the decade they said very little in public about their political convictions. And what they did say was rarely calculated to upset anyone, certainly not the scientific establishment. When the trio did speak out decisively, it was on behalf of the introduction of 'scientific methods' into politics. Perhaps they were more typically 'Cambridge' than they liked to admit.

That judgement is amply confirmed when one turns to the writings of J. B. S. Haldane, the best known and most vocal figure in the Cambridge counter-culture. In the 1920s Haldane wanted to be seen as a 'political' animal, but only on his own terms. On the one hand he proclaimed with some bravado that 'I have not to take many paces outside my laboratory to see the need for political and social reform. As a skilled manual worker and a trade unionist, I have a strong idea where I should find my political affinities'.[44] The problem here, however, was whether J.B.S. was prepared to leave his lab at all. For he also believed that 'the man with a gift for thought on scientific lines is of more use to his fellows in the laboratory than out of it'.[45] Haldane had no desire to become involved in what he regarded as the 'pettiness' of party politics. Nor did he feel that human biologists *at that time* had the kind of data that would allow them to advise the government on controlling human behaviour. Furthermore, J.B.S. repudiated any suggestion of moral responsibility for the uses to which his own work, however 'applied' in character, were put.[46] In other words, as a scientist, he denied that he was or ought to be politically engaged. What Haldane did concede was that he had a duty to preach to his audience about the necessity for introducing 'the scientific attitude' into politics. The nation's 'material basis is scientific, its intellectual framework is pre-scientific'. Unless, he continued, 'a fairly vigorous attempt is made in the near future to remedy this disharmony, our particular type of civilization will undergo the fate of cultures of the past'.[47] Yet who would be prepared to make such an effort? Not the ruling class, which J.B.S.

described in 1928 as 'grossly ignorant of the mental attitude which has led to scientific discoveries'.[48] No, someone else would have to push for the adoption of 'the scientific point of view'. Without it, 'human effort is so largely devoted to conflicts with fellow men, in which one, if not both of the disputants must inevitably suffer'.[49]

Not content with such an abstract presentation of his political principles, Haldane provided his readers with two concrete examples of how social problems could be approached 'scientifically'. The first of these was his defence of chemical warfare, which was first published in 1925 under the title of *Callinicus*. He began in a familiar vein by asserting that wars would not be stopped until their causes were determined 'scientifically'. In the meantime more wars were to be expected. If that were the case, then it was Haldane's wish that his country 'should be on the winning side'.[50] (So much for either scientific or socialist internationalism.) It therefore followed that Britain would have to possess larger arsenals of the best sorts of weapons. Why not poisonous gases, whose military potential had only been partly realized in the First World War? Haldane of course admitted some of the chemicals used on the battlefield could kill and maim in a very horrendous manner. But, he countered, so could explosives and a hundred other devices. Indeed to J.B.S. chemical weapons were far more humane than conventional ones. Hence he urged the government to accelerate its research and development programmes in this area. He also recommended some novel ancillary projects, such as training special units of black men from the colonies for chemical combat. For it had already been found (presumably by white scientists) that Asians and Africans suffered less than Europeans from exposure to various gases. After a slight preliminary test, Haldane suggested, 'it should be possible to obtain coloured troops who would all be resistant to mustard gas blistering in concentrations harmful to most white men'. He then quickly added, in a way that showed him still to be one of his mother's 'Children of the Empire', 'enough resistant whites are available to officer them'.[51]

Given these eminently 'rational' plans for bolstering Britain's defences, Haldane was incensed at the 'sentimental' opposition that pacifists, statesmen and even some old-fashioned soldiers seemed to be offering to them. His position was of course rather different. As 'a biochemist and therefore a person of the type who would become important if gas was returned,' he candidly admitted, 'I . . . am advocating its extension'.[52] But he likewise felt that the contrast between his 'scientific' realism and their 'sentimentalism' entailed more than a simple clash of self-interests.* In reality, 'the objection to scientific weapons is essentially an objection to the unknown'. Yet this fear of knowledge was baseless, J.B.S. contended, if we believe that 'the world is the expression of a power friendly to our aspirations',[53] or if 'we are atheists and hold that it is neutral and indifferent to human ideals'.[54] What then did he feel about the prospect of a bomb that harnessed the power of the atom? At this stage he lost the courage of his scientific convictions and simply told his readers to relax: *they* would not live to see the birth of an atomic weapon. The chance of 'constructing such an apparatus seems to me to be so remote that when some successor of mine is lecturing to a party spending a holiday on the moon, it will still be an unsolved (though not, I think, an ultimately insoluble) problem'.[55] Strange how such a fervent believer in the importance of scientific progress would soon be shown to have so under-estimated the speed of its advance.

Eugenics was the other contentious subject on which Haldane trained his scientific attitude. Of course J.B.S. was quite aware of the ideological significance of the eugenists' previous work. As he well and truly remarked in 1926 'the growing science of heredity is being used in this country to support the political opinions of the extreme right', thereby rendering 'eugenics abhorrent to many democrats'.[56] Haldane the socialist disapproved of this usage, while Haldane the geneticist scolded those writers on eugenics who on occasion were insufficiently rigorous in their understanding and selection of scientific evidence. The 'two Haldanes' also joined forces in 1928 to make the important point that 'many of the "unfit" are unfit for society as it is today . . . The attempt to prevent

---

* Haldane's acceptance of his wartime role as a biochemist would seem to make a mockery not only of his own belief in science's ethical neutrality but also of a similar defence by Needham of the social innocence of all such scientists. As late as 1931, Needham was arguing that it was not the chemist's fault 'if poison gases, explosives, etc., come into being to oppress mankind; . . . if evilly disposed persons come past and carry them off, he cannot be held responsible, and is usually much too busy to notice that anything has happened'. From Joseph Needham, *The Great Amphibium* (London, 1931), p. 24.

them from breeding really involves the appalling assumption that society as at present constituted is perfect, and that our only task is to fit man to it.'[57] But, Haldane remarked elsewhere, 'in view of the demands for intellectual and manual skill in modern civilization', it was 'an evil' that 'the unskilled workers are breeding faster than the skilled classes'.[58] The eugenists were wrong, however, to think that the best way of eradicating this 'evil' was to prevent by force the 'less able' part of the population from reproducing itself. Instead, urged J.B.S., thrust 'upon it the greatest practicable amount of liberty, education and wealth'.[59] To Haldane this would entail the abolition of hereditary wealth, as well as the provision of absolutely free and equal schooling.* Improving the standard of living of the disadvantaged was supposed to depress their birth-rate, while J.B.S.'s educational reforms were intended to equalize environment. Should these measures fail to be enacted, however, he predicted that 'we shall probably go the way of the dodo and the Kiwi'.[60] For 'civilization stands in real danger from the over-production of "undermen". But if it perishes from this cause it will be because its governing class cared more for wealth than for justice.'[61] Such eugenical views were in fact an integral part of Haldane's socialism. On more than one occasion he remarked that *until* educational inequalities were removed, 'my political views are likely to remain . . . on the Left'.[62] J.B.S. accordingly looked forward to the creation of 'a classless society', where 'far-reaching eugenic measures could be enforced by the state with little injustice. Today this would not be possible.'[63]

Whether the Labour Party, as a likely instrument for achieving socialism, was scientifically advanced enough to accept Haldane's eugenical programmes (or his defence of chemical warfare) was quite another matter. At the beginning of the twenties J.B.S. had held great hopes for the political wing of the British labour movement.

* 'That suggestion, addressed to an audience of [Fabian] socialists, may have been a sop for Cerberus. We shall not expect Mr Haldane to perform an experiment on himself to establish this thesis in a university, the life-blood of which is provided by hereditary wealth.' This was *Nature*'s sardonic if dim comment on Haldane's eugenically inspired plea for socialism. (He was certainly making it to the right audience.) See T. Lloyd Humberstone, 'Science and the Public', *Nature*, vol. 122 (1 December 1928), p. 834.

In this country the Labour Party alone among political organizations includes the fostering of research in its official programmes. Indeed as far as biological research is concerned, labour may prove a better master than capitalism, and there can be little doubt that it would be equally friendly to physical and chemical research if these came to lead immediately to shortened hours rather than to unemployment. In particular there is perhaps reason to think that that form of sentimentalism which hampers medical research in this country by legislation would be less likely to flourish in a robust and selfish Labour Party.[64]

By the end of the decade Haldane had reversed his judgement here. If the ruling class were scientifically illiterate, then so were Labour's leading lights. Consequently, he did not see how they would ever be able to understand enough about technology to make nationalized industries work. Nor did J.B.S. believe that the socialist politicians, once in power, could command the loyalties of his scientific colleagues. Things were different elsewhere. 'In Germany,' he felt, 'there are probably enough socialists . . . with scientific and technical knowledge . . . to enable German industry to work in the event of a refusal of non-socialist scientists and technicians to assist. I very much doubt whether the same is the case in England.' He therefore strongly advised his fellow members in the Labour Party, 'first of all, that a knowledge of science should be spread among socialists; and secondly, that a knowledge of socialism should be spread among scientists'.[65]

To judge from the militarism, patriotism, élitism and, not least, the scientism that informed Haldane's brand of 'anti-politics', we could be forgiven for identifying him as an 'open conspirator' operating undercover inside the labour movement. For beneath his new socialist veneer he continued to act the part of a birthright member of the scientific establishment. Remember that J.B.S. remained affiliated to the Eugenics Society. He was a contributing editor, along with H. G. Wells, to the I.C.I.-sponsored magazine *The Realist*, edited by A. G. Church. Until the early 1930s Haldane also sat as a senior scientific adviser on General Ashmore's Cabinet sub-committee on air defence.[66] Soon he would be finding his way into the Royal Society itself. Thus while his wide and varied contacts with the ruling class enabled him to recognize many of its 'scientific' defects, he was simultaneously too much the insider to break completely from its embrace. At least until the advent of a more serious social crisis, J.B.S. would therefore prove to be a most complacent and quirky critic of capitalist society. And why not, if he really believed that 'capitalism, though it may not always give the scientific worker a living wage, will always protect him, as being one of the geese which produce golden eggs for its table'?[67] That meant a lot to Haldane, who, like Sir Richard Gregory's *Nature*, tailored his politics to the requirements of his profession.

While Bernal and Needham may have dissented from some of the implications which J.B.S. teased from his political world-view,* we know that they shared with him some striking and rather controversial assumptions about how societies worked and how they changed. The most important of these was a commitment to 'scientific determinism'. Social development was seen as destined to run along tracks already laid down by past and present generations of rational scientists. Naturally the possibility always existed of localized setbacks to or temporary reversions from technological progress. Thus in 1929 Bernal was prepared to offer the following prescient disclaimer: 'A severe crisis in mechanical civilization brought about by its inherent technological weakness or, as is much more likely, by its failure to arrange secondary social adjustments is likely to be seized upon by the emotional factors hostile to all mechanism, and we may be closer to such a reversion than we suppose.'[68] By 'secondary social adjustments' he apparently meant the class structure, the state, culture, kinship, etc. But if they were 'secondary', then Bernal could only have meant that science was primary. He did; and so did Haldane and Needham. Haldane was fond of making statements like: 'I believe that the progress of science will ultimately make industrial injustice as self-destructive as it is now making international injustice.'[69] Needham pointed the arrow of causation in the same direction when he argued:

Scientifically speaking, there can be no such thing as personal responsibility, and all that can be done is to disembarrass society from its undesirable elements by killing them off. Let us note that this is the course adopted by

* In an anonymous article published in 1927 in *The Communist*, for example, Bernal did condemn the preparations for chemical warfare on the internationalist grounds that they would be used in a war that the workers of the world neither made nor wanted. See ' "X-Ray", The Great Poison-gas Plot', *The Communist*, vol. 1 (April, May and June 1927), pp. 113–20, 173–80 and 225–32.

the French Revolution and by the Russian Revolution, and let us note [further] that both these upheavals were distinctly under the influence of the scientific view of the world.[70]

In all of these statements 'science', the 'scientific attitude', 'technology' and 'scientists' were abstracted from and set over the world of which they were a part. Such an exaggerated estimate of science's power over mankind was perhaps the ultimate tribute Bernal, Haldane and Needham could have paid to Cambridge science's hold over themselves in the twenties.

Chapter Four

The Outsiders

I was expected to go to Cambridge to do research, but refused to go *on class grounds*. . . This class division still showed itself later with the left-wing scientists from Cambridge, among whom I still felt a slight outsider . . .

Hyman Levy, 1974[1]

Cambridge's influence can be assessed negatively when we turn to the careers of those who did not choose to practise their science and their socialism in that context. Lancelot Hogben's and Hyman Levy's alienation from Cambridge was already evident at the beginning of the First World War. In the twenties Hogben and Levy would distance themselves still further from the Mecca of High Science, as they developed their own somewhat novel scientific careers. These vocational idiosyncrasies to a certain extent evolved out of their exceptional commitment to different forms of socialist politics. In fact Hogben and Levy were themselves to grow apart politically after a brief period of close friendship. That breakdown in personal relations was, in turn, an indication of just how socially and ideologically fragmented the British Left had become in this decade. Everyone, even the suspect socialists from Cambridge, seemed to be 'waiting for Lefty'.

1. Professor Hogben's Political Science

Lancelot Hogben remarked in 1940, not without bitterness, that many of those who were to become communists in the thirties had 'chaffed' him before the Depression, 'because my own views on social questions were then too radical for them'.[2] He was referring here specifically to J. B. S. Haldane.

Although Hogben liked J.B.S. and has since claimed to have been 'the only one of his friends with whom he never succeeded in quarrelling',[3] their political sensibilities then diverged considerably. Hogben's opposition to the eugenics movement was unambiguous and unmarred by the kind of slurs against the working class that Haldane could still not resist. Similarly, it would never have occurred to Hogben to denigrate the intelligence either of women or of colonized people, in contrast to some of Haldane's utterances quoted earlier. Another, more abstract difference between the two men concerned their understanding of the scientific enterprise. Where Haldane showed himself to be sympathetic to idealist philosophies, Hogben was a militant materialist, who would have nothing to do with rhapsodies about the 'inexhaustible queerness' of the universe. Indeed Hogben marked himself out as much for his old-fashioned, uncompromising anti-clericalism as for his championing of the 'new-fangled' behaviourism of American psychology and Russian physiology. Yet his vigorous polemics in defence of the power and rationalism of science were not accompanied by Haldane-like hymns to the virtues of the scientific approach to social problems. Hogben not only limited the writ of science's methods but brought his profession down to earth as well, by specifying the utilitarian background to its development. Finally, as a running accompaniment to all of these divisions, there was the question of tone and style. Compared with the frivolity, lightness and charm of Haldane's essays, those of Hogben were markedly more hard-hitting, closely argued and serious.

Why should these two scientists, each of them of a socialist persuasion, have split so consistently with each other over such a wide range of political issues? Of course they derived from radically different backgrounds, which were likely to have had some effect on how their ideological views initially crystallized and later evolved. But we also might have expected that their divergent social origins would have played a reduced role, politically, the more Haldane and Hogben were exposed to an overlapping range of professional experiences. In their cases it was almost possible to speak of a 'double exposure', so much did they have in common as biologists. Each of them had a fleeting and not entirely satisfactory association with Trinity College, Cambridge. Both were biological polymaths, with strongly developed interests in the chemical processes that sustained and defined life itself. They remained 'paired' even down to the choice of mathematical population genetics as their favoured specialism. Given these shared enthusiasms, it was therefore predictable that Haldane and Hogben would collaborate in establishing, along with Julian Huxley and the Edinburgh geneticist F. A. E. Crew, a Society for Experimental Biology in 1932.[4] As leading representatives of a new generation of biologists, the S.E.B.'s founders were determined to make their discipline a more exacting, hard-edged and experimental one; compared to the more descriptive, taxonomic and historical approaches of the pre-war era. In other words, Hogben was, like Haldane, firmly in the vanguard of those who would ultimately change the direction of British biology. With his impeccable Cambridge credentials, this should have rendered Hogben a suitable candidate for conversion to the politics of the pure science élite.*

That Hogben refused to be politically coopted, despite his rapport with many up and coming biologists, was a measure of how estranging had been his earlier contacts with established authorities of all types. He had already rebelled against the repressive ways of his father, organized religion and the class-ridden mores of Cambridge. His conscientious objection to military service in the First World War had finally exposed him to the state's power to deprive him of all liberties. Initially, Hogben's response to these experiences – and to those generally endured by the working class in capitalist Britain – had been a radically socialist one. In the Bohemian world of post-war London he consequently wrote and taught on behalf of the Independent Labour Party, Sylvia Pankhurst's Workers' Federation and the Plebs League. In the context of his marriage to Enid Charles, Hogben tried hard to be a feminist. Finally, inside the scientific profession itself, he sought to introduce his own left-wing outlook by becoming a founder-member and sitting on the Executive Committee of the fledgling National Union of Scientific Workers. The upshot of all these activities was that Hogben did not intend to keep his political views to himself.

* To underline once more the predominance of eugenical ideas within the community of British biologists: Hogben was the only one of the S.E.B.'s four 'founding fathers' who did *not* advocate some form of birth control on some portion of the working class. Haldane's views have of course just been documented, while those of Huxley were discussed in the first chapter. As for Crew, he contributed a number of *Nature*'s more 'moderate' leading articles in support of eugenics.

They were a matter of public record, and, as such, inevitably invited others either to side with or to discriminate against him. In view of the 'extremity' of his ideological leanings, this was not a policy likely to assist the progress of Hogben's career. Sometimes the response to his politics was vindictively petty and wounding. While at London's Imperial College, for instance, he was periodically harassed by ex-servicemen who left white feathers on his desk, exposing what they interpreted as his cowardice during the First World War.[5] The more long-term and serious prospect was that, whatever brilliance Hogben might exhibit as a scientist, he would be tacitly debarred from at least one of British science's highest accolades, a senior position at Oxford or Cambridge. To judge from his previous actions, he had the will to endure far more exacting sacrifices than that one.

If Hogben had placed himself so firmly beyond the pale of *social* respectability, then his subsequent involvement in radical politics would seem to have been a foregone conclusion. In fact he proved to be as politically inactive in the twenties as his brethren at Cambridge. Hogben was kept busy instead establishing his reputation as an accomplished and original researcher. This endeavour not only required him to work long hours in his lab but to travel from job to job in search of better pay and working conditions as well. For unlike Bernal, Haldane and Needham, he had no private means with which to support his wife, Enid Charles, and the four children born to them in this decade. Hence Hogben and Charles were compelled to embark on an academic odyssey that would take them from Birbeck College to Imperial College in 1919, the University of Edinburgh in 1922 and, three years later, McGill University in Montreal in Canada. Then in the spring of 1926 Hogben was offered and accepted a handsomely paid full professorship in the University of Cape Town, South Africa. With barely ten years of his career behind him, he had thus managed to run through five academic assignments, three continents and several different aspects of biology.

Although these sojourns did succeed in making Hogben's name professionally, they were costly in a personal/political sense. Once out of London he lost touch with both the Plebs League and the scientists' union. Upon leaving Britain altogether, he became physically removed from the I.L.P., not to mention the events that led up to the General Strike. Still more seriously, his feminist compact with Enid Charles came under severe pressure, as much from the paucity of jobs available to women academics as from the travels of Hogben himself. They consequently had to accept for the moment that, in Hogben's words, 'few women can compete on equal terms with men, if they also bear children'.[6] Despite the burdens of being primarily responsible for raising their family, Charles was able to keep up with her own field of demography. Nevertheless neither she nor her husband was happy about the practical limitations that had been set on the development of their political beliefs and practices. Somehow they had got themselves into a position of behaving like just another respectable academic couple – the very role to which they remained, by temperament and conviction, so completely opposed. It therefore looked as if Hogben might be assimilated into his profession; certainly for as long as his research commitments prevented him from translating his radical thoughts into revolutionary deeds. With a bit of luck his exposure to the conservatizing ways of university life might even mellow him into a quite satisfactory liberal.

Hogben, however, was not about to be manoeuvred into quiescence without a fight. Rather than completely sacrifice his outside political interests to the demands of scientific life, he consciously brought his politics to bear on the kind of science he did. As a feminist who was also an experimental biologist, Hogben was drawn in the early twenties to the new field of comparative endocrinology, in order to study the hormonal bases of sex differences. As a socialist, he likewise found himself attracted to the social biology of class and racial differences. As an atheist who saw science as the antithesis of religion, he fought against all philosophers and scientists given to 'God-building' on the basis of the limitations of scientific knowledge. Hogben was, in short, engaged in a number of politically informed activities which, as far as the pure science establishment was concerned, cut much closer to the bone than any revolutionary sentiments expressed outside laboratory hours by a Bernal or a Haldane at this time.

Of all these battles, the one most crucial to Hogben's career was his fight against orthodox eugenics. As early as 1918 he had joined issue with those who decried the mental capacities of working-class people.[7] An additional impetus to oppose these anti-egalitarian

106 Before the Thirties

tendencies came in 1926 when Hogben went to South Africa. There he found a new social order arising explicitly on the twin foundation of 'adventure capitalism' and scientific racism. Even in semi-urbane Cape Town Hogben could discover no South African whites who did not subscribe wholeheartedly to the notion of 'the blacks'' racial inferiority. What infuriated him almost as much, he would assert in later life, was the intellectual strain he suffered trying to follow the arguments offered to him in support of white supremacy.

The form of sport to which I am most addicted is consequential conversation. I was deprived of it during four years' sojourn among the *chromatocracy* of South Africa by repeated attempts to communicate through the medium of dialogue like this:
Almost Any South African Graduate: If you had to live in this country as long as I have, you would know that a native can't be taught to read or write.
Myself: Have you ever visited Fort Hare Missionary College?
Almost Any S.A.G.: Don't talk to me about missionaries.
Myself: Well, I have. I have seen a class of pure blood Bantu students from the Cis-Kei working out differential equations.
Almost Any S.A.G.: What would you do if a black man raped your sister?[8]

It was one thing to put up with the most venerable and disreputable of all racist appeals coming from the lips of 'almost any S.A.G.'; quite another to hear it dolled up in the finery of modern biology. Yet that was invariably what happened whenever Hogben involved himself in academic discussions. For example, at the annual meeting of the South African Association for the Advancement of Science in August, 1927, he heard a remarkable presidential address from his fellow biological researcher, Professor H. B. Fantham. The essence of Fantham's racism was distilled and praised shortly thereafter in the leader columns of *Nature*.

Here we have the opinion of a biologist who realizes, as all biologists do, that the black skin of the Negro is the outward expression of profound differences of a more obscure kind, which mark him off from the white race as distinctly as does his non-attainment of what we call civilization, with its complex social organization, its great cities, its high art, its written languages, during all these untold centuries of his undisturbed sojourn in

Africa . . . [Hence] Racial admixture is disastrous in its results. 'When once chromosomes of Bantu origin get mingled in white families they cannot be bred out, as is so often popularly supposed, but will exhibit themselves in unfortunate ways and at unfortunate times throughout the ages.'[9]

In his opposition to such apologia for oppression, the irrepressible Hogben undoubtedly expressed himself 'in unfortunate ways and at unfortunate times' throughout this period. He has since admitted to having sympathized with 'the Communist Party (S.A.) which was the only group actively concerned with the voteless four-fifths of the total population'. Though never a party member, Hogben was prepared to speak out against the progressive encroachment of apartheid into every domain of South African life. By 1930, he claimed afterwards, 'I had indeed to get away from South Africa, because I was too articulate in my sympathy for the natives' cause.'[10]

Perhaps the most important and enduring facet of Hogben's opposition to apartheid was his attempt to discredit entirely the claims of scientific racism. He carried out this attack via a relentless examination of the arguments and evidence then commonly used by eugenists. Hogben did not reject the eugenics movement's avowed goal of contributing to the biological improvement of the human species. Nor did he wish to deny that 'extremes of intellectual accomplishment or defect are significantly determined by genetic variation'.[11] (But, Hogben was quick to add, the extreme cases had little bearing on the direction of human evolution.) What did incense him about the eugenists were their cavalier and incautious methods of analysis. Always a stickler in matters of scientific nomenclature, Hogben ridiculed the belief of some writers on eugenics that there were genes through which 'characters' such as 'sobriety' and 'improvidence' could be transmitted from one generation to another. Thus when confronted with the assertion, in Estabrook's infamous study of the Jukes family, that 'there is an hereditary factor in licentiousness', Hogben was ready to search through this monograph 'for a single indication of the way in which' Estabrook 'defines licentiousness and its allelomorphic opposite chastity'.[12] Of course he looked in vain. Hogben went on to note how this mode of explanation, like most of those employed by eugenists, made the fundamental mistake of trying to isolate heredity from environment. (The environmentalists were commonly guilty of the opposite error.) Yet, Hogben maintained, 'no statement about a genetic difference has any scientific meaning unless it includes or implies a specification of the environment in which it manifests itself in a particular manner'.[13] For such 'gene' differences could be increased or decreased, depending on environmental conditions. According to an early chronicler of the nature-nurture controversy, Hogben therefore questioned the validity of all attempts – like those of Arthur Jensen and Hans Eysenck in our own day – 'to weigh numerically the relative importance of heredity and environment'.[14] Inevitably, these exercises were not based on populations in which environmental conditions had been standardized. And by 'environment', Hogben pointed out, one was not referring simply to physical surroundings, but to pre-natal and social circumstances as well. Until such time as there were experimental controls for these non-genetic variables, the scientific credentials of racist ideologies would remain bogus. In the interim Hogben would tirelessly reiterate – into the twenties and beyond – how ignorant we were about the hereditary basis of our own behaviour: 'I do not hesitate to say that all existing and genuine scientific knowledge about the way in which the physical characteristics of human communities are related to their cultural capabilities can be written on the back of a postage stamp.'[15]

Once Hogben had put forward his own very imposing model of scientific rectitude, he felt free to lambast the advocates of eugenics for their reckless politicization of the entire subject of human genetics.

The discussion of the genetical foundations of racial and occupational classes in human society calls for discipline, for restraint and for detachment. Nothing could make the exercise of these virtues more difficult than to force the issue into the political arena in the present state of knowledge. This is precisely what the eugenist has done.[16]

(But one might ask how, in a society based on hierarchies of class, race and sex, could a science of human differences either be kept out of the political arena or, more radically, be anything other than a political subject?) More specifically, Hogben lamented how one-sidedly political the eugenists had been. He sourly observed in 1931 that 'eugenics has . . . become identified with a system of ingenious excuses for combating the amelioration of working-class conditions'.[17] Leaving aside (with great ceremony) his own pro-Labour views, Hogben excoriated the reactionary politics of the eugenists on more pragmatic and scientific grounds. First, by blocking various 'environmental' reforms, they were denying to their own science the experimental controls required to sort out more satisfactorily the inter-relationships of nature and nurture. Second, 'by . . . antagonizing the leaders of thought among the working classes, the protagonists of eugenics have done their best to . . . delay the acceptance of a national minimum of parenthood'.[18] To Hogben this was disastrous because, as Enid Charles's own demographic studies were beginning to show, Britain was already suffering from *under*-population. Yet here were the eugenists, the arch-defenders of the vitality of the British 'race', proposing massive programmes of birth control that might eventually hasten racial decline.* Finally, and this was no laughing matter to Hogben, he believed that the identification of human genetics with the extreme right might ultimately deprive the subject of the financial and statistical support it required from the state in order to survive and flourish. As a human geneticist himself, Hogben was acutely aware of the need for and the costliness of 'employing staffs of fully qualified persons working in close collaboration in . . . centres where encouragement is likely to be given to inquiries of this kind'.[19] On the other hand, Hogben did not enjoy such facilities in South Africa. Nor the more his views on human biology became known was his situation likely to improve in Cape Town.

The man who rescued Hogben from his political difficulties,

---

* Hogben often made great play of the fact that, in contrast to his own family of two sons and two daughters, most eugenists of his acquaintance were childless. 'The eugenic movement', he charged, 'has recruited its members from the childless rentiers – twentieth century bourbons who have earned nothing and begotten nothing.' (From Hogben's *Science for the Citizen* (London, 1938), p. 1074.)
Whether the eugenic concerns of Hogben and Charles inspired them to rear more than the 2.6 children then required for reproduction of their species is not absolutely certain. But my own feeling is that in a marriage such as theirs, the intellectual and ideological dimensions of birth control and child-rearing practices would have been talked through. In this case their demographic scruples would seem to have been more important than their feminist ideals in determining the direction of their sexual politics.

brought him back to England and promised him the institutional backing he required was Sir William Beveridge, the head of the London School of Economics. Throughout the twenties Beveridge had sought to wed the natural and social sciences at the L.S.E. The key to his programme were such subjects as genetics, demography and eugenics, all of which he subsumed under the heading of 'social biology'. Despite objections from the school's most senior socio-logist, L. T. Hobhouse, that biologists were rarely sociological in outlook, Beveridge realized his ambitions, with the support of other faculty members and a hefty grant from the Rockefeller Foundation. As soon as the chair in social biology had been approved by the University of London in 1929, it was offered to Hogben, clearly the most 'social' of British biologists. Hogben accepted the post on the condition that he be allowed to follow up his own, more narrowly biological research interests. In taking on this academically unique assignment, he also made explicit his expectation that Enid Charles would be permitted to join his staff and resume in earnest her work on fertility and parenthood. With those provisos out in the open, Hogben came back to London in the autumn of 1930 to tell his new colleagues at the L.S.E. how grateful he was to be among people who understood the social complexities underlying human development. Several times in his inaugural lecture he praised social scientists for inspiring 'a growing reaction against the prevalent fashion of biologists to insist exclusively on the genetic factor in social change'.[20] No one in Hogben's audience could have savoured these appeals for academic collaboration more than Beveridge himself.*

Whether establishment biologists had equal cause to rejoice in the return of the prodigal Hogben was another matter. For 1930 was the year in which he not only threw in his lot with the disreputable social scientists, but also published a major attack on the theistic and idealist philosophies of science that many senior researchers then favoured. Among those singled out for special attack in his *The*

---

* Whether Beveridge would have agreed with the specific point Hogben was making here is more dubious. For Beveridge was himself not averse to the kind of eugenic policies then being advocated by, for example, Julian Huxley. That he nevertheless chose Hogben for the L.S.E. post may therefore have reflected the shortage of reputable biologists who were then prepared to take on such an intellectually 'soft' and professionally dubious assignment.

Nature of Living Matter were the Cambridge astronomer Sir Arthur Eddington, the South African philosopher of 'holism', General J. C. Smuts, the former Cambridge mathematician Alfred North Whitehead and, not least, J. S. Haldane. Hogben associated these men in particular with contemporary assaults on the mechanistic and materialistic approaches, which he thought constituted the only sound bases for scientific advancement. Why then were they being attacked? Hogben answered: because 'mechanistic philosophy cannot offer to the privileged a supernatural sanction for the things they value most. It cannot proffer to the underprivileged the shadowy compensation of a world into which the thought of science is unable to penetrate.'[21] Yet did not mechanical materialism and secular ideologies in general flourish in the nineteenth century, within influential sections of all classes? Hogben replied: yes, but that was a period of prosperity and expansion, while 'the period in which we live is one of ferment and disintegration'. Hence the ruling class – and, by implication, its scientific apologists – have been forced to abandon its sturdy materialism along with its benevolent liberalism in an attempt to stabilize *their* social order. Hogben was consequently under no illusion that whoever had the temerity at this time to defend the mechanical/materialist point of view was likely to receive 'any laurels from his own generation'.[22]

Hogben argues against the idealists from the standpoint of what he calls 'publicism'. The cornerstone of the publicist's philosophical edifice is his sharp distinction between the private worlds of individuals and the public world of social knowledge. There is, he asserts, 'no excuse for the sophisticated person refusing to recognize where his private world ends and the domain of social knowledge or the public world begins'.[23] Social knowledge is consensual, communicable and verifiable; it is ethically neutral; it is, in other words, scientific knowledge. Although definitions of which methods, techniques and ideas are scientific can vary historically, and some fields of inquiry are more 'mature' than others, the criteria for distinguishing the public from the private and the scientific from the non-scientific are sound enough. Even in the treacherous field of eugenics, where 'social bias is apt to override scientific judgement', it is still possible for a biologist 'to make clear when he is speaking in his capacity as a private citizen'.[24] More specifically, he can draw on the well authenticated findings of experimental geneticists, nerve physiologists and behavioural psychologists. The most striking thing about these disciplines – apart from their demonstration of the environment's power to mould and reshape the behaviour of living things – is that they all derive their success from a consistent adherence to reductionist and materialist principles. This animus to discover the physico-chemical bases of our individual and social development is not limited to a handful of researchers. For it can also be found operating in an educational system that is becoming increasingly utilitarian and scientific in character. Unfortunately, the progress of public knowledge is in danger of being arrested, because it now seems to threaten the established order. Some well known elderly scientists are even trying to collapse the public world into the private one of their choice. Hence publicists such as Hogben must rally round, like their rationalist forefathers in the Victorian era, to hold back the forces of darkness and obscurantism. And science must be their bulwark. The fight that will follow, Hogben concedes, will not be an easy one.

Because science does not flatter our self-importance, because science makes stringent demands on our willingness to face uncomfortable views about the universe, . . . human nature, deeply rooted in its unsavoury past, is on the side of vitalistic theories. Social privilege is repelled by the mechanistic outlook because of its ethical impartiality. Age brings its impressive authority to reinforce both human nature and social privilege. When the spirit of intellectual adventure dies and with it the courage to face the austere neutrality of a universe which mocks the self-importance of our individual lives, when the ruthlessness of death and decay threatens to rob us of the few circumstances propitious to personal comfort, . . . it becomes all too easy to find the formula which provides a compromise for the conflicting claims of magic and science. Perhaps the time will come when our knowledge of the Nature of Life will provide an explanation of this circumstance.[25]

In its defiant stoicism this statement reminds us that Hogben was very much the pupil of Bertrand Russell, to whom *The Nature of Living Matter* is dedicated.

What made it possible for Hogben to carry on his lonely fight against the fashionable philosophical idealism of his elders? His own oblique explanation was that 'mechanistic philosophy' could only 'flourish among those who have leisure to study, when their privileges are not compromised by social unrest'.[26] In the case of someone like Hogben – a scientist without private means, who had only his brain-power to sell – there were no obvious social constraints that might obscure his perception of scientific realities. An alternative but complementary theory would be that, *for Hogben*, empirical science really was a liberating force. After all, had he not been exposed early in life to scientific interests he might never have escaped from the intellectual constrictions of evangelical religion and the physical discomforts of genteel poverty. Instead Hogben was able to find through his professional studies a mode of explanation that was simultaneously more satisfying than traditional systems of authority, yet less oppressive in scope. As he once put it, 'since we can never know everything we should like to know, every individual has a right to his own private world'.[27] Encompassing as this world did all of our ethical and political judgements, it was obvious that in matters of morality Hogben would not even trust science to be impartial in its assessment of the individual and his conscience.

Hogben's understanding of the scientific enterprise, though more detailed, incisive and compelling than that of Haldane, was nevertheless often thin and inconsistent. For instance, he was not able to pin down why some senior scientists and not others were prey to idealism; or why some sections of capital were placing greater, not fewer demands on the existing stock of public knowledge. Much more problematic were Hogben's conflicting theories concerning the development of science. Did scientific consensus rest on the foundations either of public knowledge or of class dominance? Hogben's response was a confusing 'Yes'. In theory he suggests that public knowledge was the sole arbiter of scientific inquiry. In practice, he asserted that a dominant cabal of biologists had given their blessing to racist versions of eugenics (which to Hogben contravened or neglected entirely 'reputable' public knowledge). Yet if Hogben allowed in any way that professional élites could and did control public knowledge in their own and others' (private) interests, then what became of his public/private distinction? He had only two choices. Abandon the distinction entirely and argue, as he did in his philosophical controversy, that one's class position mediated one's perception of the natural as well as the social world;

or retain his publicism and assert that all versions of biology other than his own did not conform to public knowledge and hence were unscientific. Given his faith in the emancipating power of science and his exposed position within the scientific community, Hogben opted for the tried and true empiricism of the publicist. One might say, therefore, that while he did not mind going out on a limb for his beliefs, he was unprepared to cut himself off from the communal tree altogether.

Hogben's relationship to his fellow scientists was nevertheless highly precarious. Nor did his acerbic commentaries on work he found to be substandard enhance his popularity. How would you have responded if, like Julian Huxley, you had been told that your first book of essays was notable only for its 'timid superficiality and insipid obscurantism', but that these traits were nothing 'but the defects of mental immaturity'? That was how Hogben had greeted Huxley's *Essays of a Biologist* in the pages of the *Scientific Worker*. Huxley retorted that Hogben was the unfortunate victim not only of 'a repressed complex about religion' but of 'the passing dogma of a small biological sect' as well.[28] This was a reference to behaviourism. But another of Hogben's victims, the social psychologist William McDougall, believed that mechanism, materialism, behaviourism, etc, were all firmly in the ascendancy. Otherwise, the L.S.E. would never have appointed Hogben to its new and important chair in social biology. Presumably, McDougall smirked, the school had high hopes that their young professor would 'by chemical analysis of the blood or other tissues of our legislators, . . . succeed in solving the economic and political world crisis'.[29]

A more serious and worthy protagonist for Hogben was the Cambridge biochemist Joseph Needham. Both men were familiar with and respected each other's work. Apart from their joint participation in the early days of the Society for Experimental Biology, they also shared a strong antipathy to the vitalistic theories favoured by some senior biologists. Where they did part company was on the issue of consciousness. For Hogben it was axiomatic that 'modern biological enquiry is disintegrating consciousness into an atomic nexus of reflex arcs'.[30] Uncomfortable with the notion of 'mind', he preferred instead to talk about 'conditioned behaviour'. Needham on the other hand was persuaded as early as 1923 that such a mechanistic conception 'cannot without grave logical difficulty be extended to cover the sphere of mind'.[31] That did not mean, however, that simply because 'mind' could not be pinned down to a bundle of conditioned reflexes, it became a 'meaningless', 'incommunicable' or 'unreal' subject. Rather it suggested to Needham that Hogben's philosophy, on its own, could not put us 'in contact with what is real'. What was needed to penetrate through to the 'alogical' core of the world were philosophy and religion as well as science, *plus* 'moments of insight, of mystical experience closely allied to the apprehension of the beautiful which all three of them give us'.[32] For those of a non-mystical bent, like the Communists, Needham condescendingly commended Hogben's publicism. 'In the course of time,' he predicted, 'world-communism will certainly acquire a philosophy other than the Hegelian dialectic of the Russian Marxists, and it would be possible to conceive of several worse ones than that whose germ is contained in Hogben's book.'[33] Strangely enough, Hogben would have seconded those sentiments, while strongly disavowing the Anglo-Catholicism that had inspired them. The more important point, however, is that – first with Haldane and now with Needham – not even the Cambridge counter-culture was prepared to support Hogben's onslaught on the philosophy and politics of the pure science establishment.

2. Professor Levy's Socialism

But Hyman Levy had no hesitation whatsoever in helping out the young Hogben. Levy and Hogben had been friends ever since 1919. At that time they had both been based in London and had been active in a number of common causes, including workers' education, the Labour Party and the National Union of Scientific Workers. One of their regular meeting places was the 1917 Club in Soho (where each of them, incidentally, first met J. B. S. Haldane). All of these ties were strengthened in 1920, when the two men found themselves on the staff of the Imperial College of Science and Technology. Despite Hogben's subsequent departure for Edinburgh (Levy's birthplace), their friendship did not suffer, based as it was in part on a mutual devotion to philosophizing, as well as on each other's statistical researches. These links were manifested in the publication of *The Nature of Living Matter*. Here Hogben registered his gratitude for the care and criticisms which Levy had lavished on this manuscript. When Hogben's second book – *Genetic Principles in Medicine and Social Science* – appeared, it was dedicated to Hyman Levy. For of course by this time Hogben had come back to London, renewing in the process his valued association with the eminent Scots mathematician, Professor Levy.

It would not be too long, however, before Hogben would start to recognize a growing political gulf between Levy and himself. This divergence would eventually grow into a major personal rift between them. Meanwhile they could only regret the slow dissolution of the bonds that had held them together. Their range of intellectual interests and professional dislikes was still remarkably similar. They shared a common set of friends. Yet when Levy joined the Communist Party of Great Britain around 1930, none of these ties would ultimately prove strong enough to prevent a rupture. Why this should have been the case will be explained in more detail in a later chapter. For the moment it is only necessary to say that between 1928 and 1933 a communist was expected to regard a Labourite like Hogben as 'objectively' a 'social-fascist'. Whether Levy in fact perceived his friend in this way was irrelevant to Hogben, who would soon come to see Communism as potentially a greater threat to intellectual freedom than even Christianity. Hogben's distrust of 'true believers', whether of the theological or ideological variety, knew no bounds. It would take the good-humoured Levy longer to decide that Hogben's own doctrine of publicism was itself a piece of 'bourgeois ideology'. In the interim there was a more immediate question to be tackled. Why should Levy have moved off so sharply to the left of his long-time comrade?

The short answer is that, by conscious choice, Levy was not a 'Cambridge man'; and that his relationship to Cambridge science was much more consistent and principled than Hogben's. Having refused the chance to go to Cambridge before the war, Levy then abandoned university research altogether in order to work in a lower-status Civil Service job. After 1918 his interests in aero-dynamics and numerical methods were deemed unfashionable and insignificant, compared with the 'purity' of Cambridge mathematics. To Levy this reaction was bound up with the kind of class dominance and snobbery he had learned to loathe at a much earlier age. But agitated as he was by this more recent and subtler form of class discrimination inside science, he was well and truly motivated to spend long hours, day in and day out, working as an organizer and propagandist, both for the labour movement and for the N.U.S.W. Three aspects of Levy's politics, in particular, marked him off from Cambridge's dilettantish socialists (and Hogben too, for that matter). It was practical, not intellectual work. In terms of hours and emotions expended, it was a form of practice at least as important to Levy as his research career. It brought him into touch with politicians, trade unionists and ordinary workers; not just the grandees of and apologists for his own profession. Hence Levy's political evolution was what one might have expected of many in the 1920s who were committed socialists first and intellectuals or workers second. Fed up with the timidity and betrayal of socialist principles that characterized the leadership of the T.U.C. and the Parliamentary Labour Party, Levy switched his allegiances to the more militant and tightly organized Communist Party. However comprehensible this move may have been to those on the Left, it could not help but isolate Levy still more completely as an academic renegade. The more social distance he put between himself and 'Cambridge', the easier it became for him to lead a more political, more engaged life.

Probably none of those developments would have been possible had Levy remained an employee at the National Physical Laboratory. By the beginning of 1920 he was fed up with the place. Levy was no longer finding his battles with the director, Sir Richard Glazebrook, very edifying; the two men at best cordially disliked each other. A further difficulty was that N.P.L. scientists like Levy were still being put onto very practical projects that allowed little scope for scientific breakthroughs and an expansion of their own intellectual interests. Even Glazebrook was ready to concede in 1924 that the organization of his laboratory was holding back the progress of British aerodynamics: 'we are being left behind', because of 'the daily pressure of urgent needs and the absence of a man whose sole business it is to see that the claims of pure science are not set aside'.[34] (He added that most aerodynamical advances had come from Göttingen, but neglected to mention Levy's role in bringing them into the N.P.L. itself.) There were also political as well as scientific limitations connected with Levy's job. For as a civil servant who was simultaneously an active left-wing supporter of the local Labour Party in Teddington, he foresaw a time when restrictions might have to be imposed on what he said and did (inside as well as outside the laboratory). Levy was not satisfied, finally, that he enjoyed absolute security of tenure, though as an N.U.S.W. representative of his co-workers he was trying to improve matters. By now a married man of thirty with three children, he had reached a crucial stage in his life. He could not possibly settle into a comfortable life of routine government investigations and discreet political work in the community. But his only alternative was to secure a fairly rare university lectureship, which would give him the security, leisure and freedom he required to fulfil his scientific and political ambitions.

Then in the spring of 1920 Imperial College advertised a new lectureship in mathematics. Though the college's mathematics department was headed by Professors R. W. Forsyth and A. N. Whitehead – both Cambridge-trained pure mathematicians – Levy decided to apply for the post. Even if the maths men were purists, he reasoned, the institution itself was supposed to have a distinct bias in favour of applied and technical studies. Levy therefore sent in a list of his published papers, the manuscript of his book on aerodynamics which was already in the press and proof of his academic qualifications. What he did not include in his application was the name of his employer Glazebrook as a referee. Nevertheless Levy was called for interview and was offered the appointment. Several months later, after he had begun to lecture at the college, Levy casually encountered Forsyth, who asked him in passing why Glazebrook's name had never crossed Levy's lips. Levy mumbled in some embarrassment that he didn't think Sir Richard had known much about his work.

'Well, as a matter of fact [Forsyth replied], Glazebrook was at Trinity with me. So when you applied I wrote to Glazebrook to ask about you.'

'Oh!' was all I [Levy] could say.

'Yes. Would you like to see his letter?'

'Well, if you care to show me his letter, I'd be interested to see it . . .'

So I looked at the letter, . . . [which] began with a certain complimentary remark about myself and then finished up by saying: 'Nevertheless I cannot advise you to take Levy. He is a man who consistently stands against constituted authority. He would be a most difficult man to have on your staff.'[35]

Levy then looked up at Forsyth in some surprise and asked: 'How did you come to take me, in the face of that?' By this stage Levy's professor could not suppress a broad grin: 'As I said, Glazebrook was at Trinity with me. Even then he believed himself to be constituted authority!' What a change of fortunes for Levy.

The move to Imperial College was an important and beneficial one for Levy. Yet while it solved those problems that had plagued him at the N.P.L., it also confronted him with new ones. The most important of these was that, once inside a university, Levy was much more exposed than ever before to the influence and control of Cambridge mathematics. Remember Levy's earlier rejection of Cambridge on 'class grounds' and his later experiences under the Cavendish-trained Glazebrook. To these grievances Levy now added another, more professional indictment.

On the mathematical side Cambridge was reactionary in those days, chasing the undialectical fantasy of perfect rigour in logic and proof; as it still does today with its belief in *pure* mathematics as a separate pursuit – and curiously enough all this at a time when it was very advanced on the side of experimental physics.[36]

Compared with this rarefied approach of the dominant Cambridge school, Levy's own field of aerodynamics, as well as his emphasis on numerical methods, was distinctly mundane and unfashionable. Hence the likelihood of his being recognized as a *real* mathematician – as opposed to some kind of glorified accountant with scientific pretensions – was not great.

To illustrate how strongly entrenched were these Cambridge attitudes, Levy recounted shortly before his death the saga of introducing courses on statistics and numerical methods into Imperial College's curriculum. Since neither of the Cambridge-educated professors in the maths department considered these subjects to be a part of mathematics, Levy knew he was in for a hard time. After a great cajoling they were persuaded that if Levy really wanted these thankless assignments, perhaps consent could be given. Then Levy mentioned that his teaching would be made easier if the department could purchase an arithmometer or calculating machine. When his superiors were told that one of these devices might cost £100 second-hand, they refused his request point-blank. (Surely chalk was enough!) So committed was Levy to this work that, instead of abandoning his curriculum reforms, he went out to Brentford market and hire-purchased two old calculators with his own money. One of these he stripped down in order to show students how such machinery operated; the other was eventually used 'by a succession of students who took Ph.D. degrees in this particular field'.[37]

Apart from documenting Cambridge's grip on mathematics, this story is a striking example of Levy's loyalty, dedication and ingenuity as a teacher. His lecturing style, a blend of wit, invention and clarity that had evolved and matured through his political and trade union work, delighted undergraduates long accustomed to the drone of duller minds. (Years later Levy was to become the best-liked and most trusted teacher of two of Bernal's sons.)[38] Indeed it was largely through his impressive performance as a teacher and administrator that Levy was able in 1924 to succeed Whitehead and become the college's second Professor of Mathematics. Certainly this was a salutary and consoling promotion for him, though his resentment against Cambridge's mathematical hegemony, juxtaposed against his pride in his own research, would remain for many years a source of great dissatisfaction.

Levy was now doubly class-conscious. On the one hand he had moved from the proletarian environs of Edinburgh to the professional world of London. On the other he had experienced the life of a rank and file scientist before becoming a university professor. Yet instead of turning his back on those in the slums and the laboratories beneath him, Levy kept faith with them by opposing, through political practice, the employers, the rulers and the élites that stood over them. How was he able to find the will for this gruelling and often unsuccessful struggle? Bad conscience about his own social rise? Envy of those more professionally successful than he? Neither of these unsavoury motives could be easily ascribed to Levy, who by all accounts was a remarkably equable and generous man. Even if applicable, one would doubt their durability as incentives to a lifelong involvement in radical politics. What can be maintained here is that, unlike most socialist intellectuals of his day, Levy had actually experienced at first hand the oppression which he sought to eradicate. As a rebel against the various establishments that had tried, without much success, to put him in his place, he had been driven into the labour movement at an early age. Once active in the affairs of the Labour Party and his trade union, Levy himself became a semi-professional agitator. The different forms of his political practice now began to cross-fertilize. In the National Union of Scientific Workers he pushed for closer relations with the T.U.C. and the Labour Party, which was in turn hounded by Levy to construct for itself a policy on and for science. So pervasive were Levy's efforts as a part-time politician that they began to take on a life of their own, affected by, yet in the final analysis autonomous from, his scientific career. In other words his ultimate loyalties were to the working class and not to his profession. But then Levy never saw any worth-while future for scientific men and women, apart from the achievement of socialism in Britain.

Levy's introduction to political life had come, as Marxists would say nowadays, at the 'point of production'. By the time he had arrived at Imperial College, Levy had become one of the most influential members of the National Union of Scientific Workers. Much of his authority had derived from his leadership of the N.P.L. branch, which he had helped to make into one of the largest and most active bodies within the union. Such organizational abilities were not likely to go unnoticed. Not only was Levy voted on to the N.U.S.W.'s executive, but he was made Chairman of the important Propaganda Committee as well. Besides offering a scientific news-service to the press, this committee was expected to coordinate publicity for the union's recruitment drive. Levy himself was one of the N.U.S.W.'s most active spokesmen and travelled to many parts of the country, encouraging scientific workers to set up new local branches and expand old ones.

On these missions he quite selfconsciously attempted to represent his union as the authentic voice of the rank and file scientist in government and industry. Obviously Levy felt that this type of scientific worker required a trade union, as much to increase his control over his own job as to improve salaries and working conditions. But, he emphasized, the N.U.S.W. also had broader political objectives in mind. For it was now commonly recognized that 'scientific investigation is a vital national industry that must be developed by the state'.[39] Levy went on to argue that, if Britain was now turning to its scientists 'to raise the standard of life', then they had special responsibilities to consider how their pro- duction could be 'most effectively utilized for the benefit of the community'.[40] In particular – and here Levy could not refrain from injecting his own views as a socialist – it was important for scientific workers to concern themselves as much with the distribution as with the creation of wealth; and to be able to distinguish 'between those who create wealth and those who acquire it'.[41] Otherwise, as a profession, they would find themselves drawn time and again to the side of the capitalist businessman, who naturally attempted to increase production while maintaining the existing methods of payment for labour. Yet to Levy it was apparent that 'the present stage of society, which utilizes the wage system as a means of affecting distribution, with its million unemployed, is obviously chaotic in this respect, and from the scientific point of view indefensible'.[42] What then should scientific workers do? Behind the scenes Levy's advice came through loudly and clearly: join the Labour Party and affiliate to the T.U.C.

We know of course that the N.U.S.W. ultimately spurned Levy's advice, and worse still, retreated from trade unionism altogether. But in the early twenties, it will also be recalled, Labour and the scientific establishment were enjoying the briefest of honeymoons. Levy himself undoubtedly encouraged Wells, Gregory and anyone else who would listen that this marriage between 'two movements so clearly destined to change the nature of society' would last forever. For many months Levy made a special point of drumming this message into the consciousness of Major A. G. Church, the N.U.S.W.'s General Secretary. Soon he was embellishing his 'sales talks' to Church with the promise of a parliamentary candidacy for the major, should he decide to declare himself for Labour. Throughout these colloquies, Levy had few illusions of transforming Church into a socialist. 'I put all this to Church,' he reminisced in 1968, 'and pretty well forced him to stand for the Labour Party. I never really thought he was sympathetic to the Labour Party . . . But by this time I was becoming perhaps a little less ethical about it than I should have been. I was concerned about getting the job done.'[43] 'The job' in this case was to get the N.U.S.W. represented in Parliament, expose its official spokesman to the full influence of the labour movement and demonstrate to his fellow scientists how sympathetic to their profession the socialist party really was. As it happened, Church did become an M.P. in 1924; but then went on to distinguish himself by his distinctly un-socialist actions, first in the House of Commons and eventually in his own union. At this stage, however, there is no need to rehearse the sorry history of the N.U.S.W.'s journey towards de-unionization. This must have been a heartbreaking experience for Levy, undoing as it eventually did all the organizing he had done at the National Physical Laboratory. Nor can there be much doubt about his bitterly disappointed reaction to the union's announcement in 1927 that it would henceforth be 'entirely non-political' in character.[44] That Hyman Levy could be active in a 'non-political' organization seemed a contradiction in terms.

The other side of Levy's political coin, the Labour Party, was even less of a winner for him. He began working for the party in Teddington, picking up valuable experience as a street-speaker in election campaigns. (Levy's rhetorical instincts probably owed a great deal to the many 'sermons on the Mound' that he would have heard in pre-war Edinburgh.) Through Clement Attlee and Arthur Greenwood, whom he had met at the 1917 Club, Levy was intro-duced to party affairs at the national level. In 1920 they asked him to sit on the Labour Party's Education Advisory Committee. This was one of a network of groups set up after the war by G. D. H. Cole to stimulate policy innovation. But there was no Science Advisory Committee. Early in 1924 Levy suggested that one should be established. He stressed to his colleagues on the educational policy sub-committee that, if socialism were to be achieved, the Labour Party would have to know how it intended to harness science and technology for socialist ends. After outlining a few of his own ideas, including the creation of a Ministry of Science, Levy looked round to assess the reaction.

> Attlee listened very closely to it, although I could see he was rather uncomprehending of it all, because you've got to remember that I was dealing with people who themselves had no scientific training. They were, shall I call them, the economic intellectuals of the Labour Party. I could have talked to the working-class person in the . . . party and put my points to him in relation to his experience of machinery. But I couldn't talk like that to the leadership of the Labour Party.[45]

Such a bleak reception, however indicative of the need for such a committee, was hardly much encouragement to get it going.

Yet Levy was determined to put these ideas into practice. For the next six years he kept a Science Advisory Group in existence. No records of its deliberations seem to have survived, and in later life Levy would be unable to recall with certainty the names of of those who passed in and out of it. (Most of them were probably associates from the N.U.S.W.) At least in 1939 Levy did manage to record a brief resumé of the committee's history: it is quoted here in its entirety.

This body met regularly for some six years, during which it kept Labour members informed of matters of scientific moment that were raised in the House of Commons; it pressed the MacDonald government for scientific representation on government committees of inquiry and royal commissions that involved matters of scientific moment: but without avail. In particular, it stressed the necessity of scientific representation sympathetic to the ideals of the Labour Party. In this also it was unsuccessful. The committee, relying on the most expert knowledge, produced far-reaching plans for a scheme of national electrification, for a thorough survey of the mineral resources of the country, for the development of the by-product industries of the mines, low-temperature carbonization and allied topics. The objective the committee had in mind was the creation of new industries directly under government aegis and control, from which elements of private profits had to be eliminated from the start, except in so far as they depended on subsidiary undertakings already established. Thus these new industries would be nationalized from their inception. The memoranda embodying these proposals were accepted by the executive of the Labour Party, but, as was learned afterwards, this by no means implied their sympathetic reception by the parliamentary group . . . Thereafter the committee petered out, disheartened.[46]

Once again Levy's political machinations had come to nought.* By the late twenties he had thus been robbed of both his trade union base and his toehold in the Labour Party's lower echelons.

But Levy also had other, more radical connections to the labour movement than those of the N.U.S.W. and the Science Advisory Committee. Shortly after the First World War, he had volunteered his services to that militant agency of working-class education, the Plebs League. His main job for the Plebs was to teach a course in elementary statistics at the Central Labour College.[47] As the C.L.C.

---

* 'But today science is a commonplace in the Labour Party. When Wilson makes a speech about the future policy of the Labour Party even he talks about the application of science and technology to the society. It takes a generation for that to get through into the mouths of politicians. One's got to accept that.' Hyman Levy, in an interview with the author, 10 May 1968.

began to become firmly dominated by members of the young Communist Party of Great Britain, Levy was naturally exposed to revolutionary socialist ideas, unlike anything he had ever heard expressed by Attlee, Greenwood and MacDonald. In the scientists' union he also found himself drawn to hard-working left-wingers like the Communist food technologist A. L. Bacharach. Though not yet a member himself, Levy now began to identify publicly with the C.P.G.B.'s position. Thus he supported the communist-led 'minority movement', which attempted unsuccessfully in 1924–5 to bring technicians into the N.U.S.W. Levy's friendship with scientific and other workers inside the C.P. grew apace with the debacle over the General Strike and the ensuing drift to the Right that marked the Labour Party's leadership. At the same time Labour's hierarchy was beginning to crack down on dissident individuals who belonged to the party but who were also affiliated to or at least publicly sympathized with Communism. Levy most certainly had fallen into this category by 1930. That was the year he officially became a Communist. Whether he was then 'expelled from the Labour Party for being a Communist',[48] or had already been 'expelled in the late 1920s for being too "left" and too sympathetic to Communists',[49] is not clear. What can be said is that Levy had finally lost hope in parliamentary gradualism as a viable instrument for achieving socialism in Britain. Stronger measures were required, and, at this time, only the Communists seemed prepared to take them.

Levy did not 'convert' to Communism in a blinding flash. Nor did he reject the 'moderation' of the Labour Party because of a scientist's distaste for the tactical compromises associated with daily political practice. His desire to join the C.P. was the act of a politically mature socialist who knew the Labour Party well enough to doubt the sturdiness of its socialist aspirations. If this action merited the heavy-handed opprobrium of the Labourite bureaucracy, one can imagine how Levy's evolving radicalism was viewed inside his own university. Reflecting in 1945 on his life since becoming a 'red' professor, Levy confessed that

It has not been easy to be a socialist in academic circles for the past twenty years or more, especially for one with a strong proletarian background. The professions tremble too closely on the brink of the working class, and aspire too anxiously to be regarded as the equals of their social if not intellectual superiors, to tolerate the suggestion that their position is in fact precarious. The tradition of science versus politics as against science *cum* politics, has been very strong, and those who dared to defy this tradition ten to twenty years ago did so at their professional peril. But after all individual advancement is a trivial thing when set side by side with the slums of Edinburgh and Glasgow.[50]

Perhaps to many readers that last sentence may sound embarrassingly self-congratulatory or self-righteous. Its virtue resided in its refusal to fudge the moral dilemma then inherent in the structural position of a socialist don. To succeed as an academic normally required an overriding commitment to the right sort of scholarship and to a range of professional values that transcended the specific requirements of doing 'good' work. Yet to behave in this manner was to constrain, re-shape and ultimately deny many aspects of one's socialism. This was a political/existential insight that would never have occurred in the twenties to the bright young men of Cambridge. It was glimpsed by Hogben, who then refracted it through his pioneering if narrowly based campaign to debunk scientific racism. Only Levy – the least conventionally successful member of the Visible College – went to the heart of this problem and resolved it in favour of his political principles. The difficulty with this solution was that it limited still further what Levy wanted to achieve for himself as a creative scientist. This was a real sacrifice, especially for someone who had managed to overcome poverty and demonstrate great academic potential; and it was not one that Levy would have made without the compensation of knowing that his efforts would help those still trapped in the Old Town. In other words, Levy expected the Communists to be effectively socialist in both theory and practice.

A more positive interrelationship between Levy's political and professional acitivities was his increasingly dialectical view of science. Through his work for the scientists' union and the Labour Party, he already had direct experience of the many political dimensions of British scientific life. As a distinctly 'impure' mathematician, Levy had also discovered that the range of socially acceptable research problems in his community was subject to tacit limitations, which also carried with them subtle connotations of class control. Finally, his years at the National Physical Laboratory had persuaded him that the 'purity' of Göttingen's mathematicians and the destructive power of aerial bombardment were locked together in a powerful unity. All of these observations were now starting to coalesce in Levy's mind, as he inched his way towards the view that social needs might enter into the very construction of scientific theories. One writer who did not share this notion was H. G. Wells, who had met Levy through the National Union of Scientific Workers. 'What worried Wells', Levy would later observe, 'was that I embedded science in society . . . To Wells science was something which impacted on society . . . He didn't like the idea that science wasn't the essence of clear thinking.'[51] Nor did Bernal, Haldane, Needham and even Hogben, all of whom were as apt to isolate science from its social context as a leader writer in *Nature* trying to cap an argument for more research funds from the state. To account for this difference between Levy and the rest is to ask, among other things, which form of practice, political or professional, mattered most to them in the 1920s?

3. 'Waiting for Levy'

It has taken us four chapters to make three apparently simple observations. There were natural scientists in Britain who were socialists prior to the 1930s. At a time when their profession was coming increasingly under the sway of capital, they found it difficult to think and act consistently as radicals. The more reflexive they were about such difficulties, the more effective they became in the practice of their socialism.

Perhaps the most fascinating aspect of their collective biography so far has been their interaction with the scientific profession. We have observed that the dominant personalities and institutions of British science were not 'above' politics. On the contrary: they were structurally and ideologically committed to strengthening British capitalism at home and abroad. Such support was manifested on at least four different levels: a) overt propaganda on behalf of science-based monopolies and 'free enterprise' generally; b) advice to the state on how to enhance the productive and military powers of the nation; c) 'scientific' philosophies and theories directly supportive of class domination and bourgeois ideology; and d) the maintenance of élite control within the scientific community itself. All of these dimensions, juxtaposed upon the very narrow social base from which 'pure' scientists were recruited, thus conspired to set very real limits on the development of socialist attitudes, both inside and outside the ranks of science. Not many young researchers had the political experience, emotional strength and professional assurance necessary to recognize the consequences that this heavy burden might have for their socialism. They and their ideals suffered accordingly.

Hopefully the weight of these social forces making for conformity has been leavened to some extent through our exposure to such exemplary deviants as Hogben and Levy. In Chapters Two and Four we saw Hogben and Levy bearing witness to their beliefs in very unfavourable circumstances. Each thereby paid a heavy price: in that sense their actions could be called heroic. But although such heroism may have had its own rewards, it could find no issue at a time when the labour movement was conspicuously weak and divided. In Hogben's case the lengths to which he was driven just to keep his own counsel *and* earn his living as a biologist were so great that he had no energy left for organized politics. That made Levy's tireless, unrewarded and ultimately misplaced devotion to the Labour Party and the National Union of Scientific Workers all the more remarkable.

The tone of Part One would have been lighter and more 'optimistic' had it been recounted in the light of what we know was going to happen in the thirties. Greater stress would then have been placed on two submerged features of our narrative. One of these is that the science establishment's fairly unequivocal support for British capitalism rested, in part, on the assumption that state and industry would never go back on the 'scientific' lessons of the First World War. When in the early 1930s research funds became temporarily scarce, scientists began to lose their jobs and Hitler started dismissing professors from German universities, the flaws in *Nature*'s political assumptions became apparent, thereby giving socialist scientists the opening they needed for a comeback in their own scientific community. The other alteration in emphasis would have been a revaluation of the Cambridge men's political evolution. More might then have been made of Bernal's anonymous articles in 1927 for *The Communist*,[52] Haldane's trip to the Soviet Union in 1928[53] and Needham's growing interest in socialist theory after the General Strike.[54] Each of these episodes could easily have been used to date a new beginning or significant breakthrough in their progress towards becoming activitists for the socialist cause.

Yet as of January 1931 neither of these reappraisals would have seemed justified. The lack of change in all of their outlooks could be deduced from their myopic views about the Soviet Union. To Sir Richard Gregory and his associates 'the Russian large-scale experiment in scientific education' was nothing compared to the 'world-portent' of the election of an engineer, Herbert Hoover, to the American presidency.[55] J. B. S. Haldane evaluated the Soviet system more highly than that. But he was not certain whether the Bolsheviks would merit his esteem by evolving into a scientific state. 'The test of the devotion of the Union of Socialist Soviet Republics to science will', Haldane thought, 'come when the accumulation of the results of human genetics, demonstrating what I believe to be the fact of innate human inequality, becomes important.'[56] By that time, however, Bernal believed that the Soviet proletariat would probably already be under the thumb of a powerful scientific élite. That was the scenario he forecast for those workers in his *The World, The Flesh and the Devil*.

In a Soviet state the scientific institutions would in fact gradually become the government and a further stage of the Marxian hierarchy of domination would be reached. Scientists in such a stage would tend very naturally to identify themselves emotionally rather with the progress of science itself than with a class, a nation or a humanity outside science, while the rest of the population would, by the diffusion of education in which the highest values lay in a scientific rather than in a moral or a political direction, be much less likely to oppose effectively the development of science.[57]

The U.S.S.R.'s new rulers would of course require a philosophical world-view far more scientific in character than the outworn Hegelianism of Marxian dialectics. That was Joseph Needham's view as late as July 1931, when he was still commending Hogben's publicism to Soviet statesmen and philosophers. Besides documenting their uniformly high ignorance (Haldane aside) of what was actually happening in the Soviet Union (see Chapter Six), all of these commentators – from Gregory to Needham – were demonstrating that science was the lynchpin and arbiter of their politics, whether of the Right or of the Left. And that had been true now for well over a decade whenever scientists had concluded that the needs of their profession were more compelling than those of the people.

5

This was at best a bizarre position for socialists like Bernal, Haldane and Needham to have upheld. For it arrogantly implied that there was nothing fundamentally amiss about their own situation. In present-day parlance they saw themselves not merely as 'liberated' but also as prototypes of the new scientifically oriented men that would emerge in the coming struggle to build socialism. Such an élitist sensibility was normally the hallmark of talented bourgeois radicals who had passed through the exclusive rites of passage of their class straight into one of the many privileged niches reserved for them. Once installed there – in this case, the Cambridge community of High Science – they found themselves far removed from 'the people' whom they wished to succour. Even Joseph Needham, who despised various forms of scientific domination and tried to mingle with 'the masses', could not escape the condescension bound up with his role as a self-appointed trustee for the liberation of others. In his essay on Cambridge life (1932) he tried to make amends, with the following mixed results.

It is a truth, indeed, that those who disdain to mix with the people miss a very great deal. Their idea of paradise is that of the man who woke up in a dream in an empty place and remarked, 'This certainly must be Heaven. There isn't a soul in sight.' Paradise Creek in summertime would certainly not please them. Returning one hot summer evening after some particularly pleasant exchanges at the Town Sheds [the public bathing place], I got out my commonplace-book and turned to a page on which I had written a number of passages come upon at various times celebrating the easiness of intercourse with people in general which the kind of sincere people I admire usually show. It would be too portentous to call it a due sense of humility, but the intuitive recognition on the part of complex and learned people that simple and unlearned people are of the same essence as themselves is, to my mind, the root of the charm which the truly great possess.[58]

An extraordinary confession: especially because, in its historical context, it was meant to be a model of liberality. Yet in his well-meaning attempt to communicate with the 'locals', Needham was adopting the attitude of a colonial anthropologist dispatched to study the 'natives' in some remote part of East Africa. Needham's field-work, however, was situated in the wilds of East Anglia, where Bernal, Haldane and other aristocratic sympathizers with the labour movement usually maintained their distance from workers as individuals. These were not the best of conditions for encouraging a belief in socialism as the *self*-emancipation of the working class. Whether our Cambridge men would take that view as seriously in the thirties as Levy had in the twenties was, at best, an open question.

Part Two

The Thirties

Chapter Five

Increased Visibility

I tried to keep to my own field, but politics would keep breaking in.

J. Needham, 1941[1]

In the 1930s the Cambridge men – Bernal, Haldane and Needham – did adopt a new attitude to politics. They became far more politically active. They tried much harder to relate their thoughts and actions to wider, more collective efforts to bring about socialism. Still more remarkably, they began to apply their socialist convictions to their own circumstances as scientists. Such was their unconscious homage to the strategies evolved a decade earlier by Hyman Levy, who now welcomed, perhaps a trifle nervously, his new-found allies from Cambridge. While that spectacle may at first have amused Lancelot Hogben, it in no way appealed to him. In fact by the end of the thirties he would emerge as a socialist critic of the Communist-dominated Popular Front; a George Orwell for the scientific Left. What we therefore want to discover in this chapter is how, why and to what extent these men transformed themselves ideologically.

Between 1931 and 1933 they started to widen the scope of their political activities. Even the formerly apathetic Joseph Needham began to write pamphlets, give speeches and serve on numerous committees. That was the tribute which he and his friends paid to the gravity of the social crises through which they were living. As socialists, they were alarmed at the fate meted out to workers: whether in Britain, where one man in five was unemployed; or in Germany, where the Nazis were about to destroy Europe's strongest labour movement. As socially conscious scientific workers, they strongly objected to the many ways in which their science was being placed at the service of militarists, racists and fascists. To our subjects these attacks upon the working class and the scientific community were among the more ominous signs that European capitalism was in a dying but dangerous state. As the title of one of this period's most influential books declared, *The Coming Struggle for Power*[2] was nigh. If that were so, then our erstwhile radicals might not have another chance to uphold their political beliefs. They acted accordingly.

Their response, multiplied many times over, was both a cause and an effect of a revived left-wing movement, set apart from parliamentary politics and largely organized by the Communist Party of Great Britain. The 'moderate' leadership of the Labour Party and Trades Union Congress was partly (and proudly) responsible for diverting this new socialist militancy into unorthodox channels. By their steadfast refusal to put forward more radical policies they helped to convert thousands of manual and mental workers into 'extremists'. On the other hand, it would take the Communists several years before they could fully reap the harvest of this discontent. For as of 1931 'the party's' pathetically small, almost exclusively proletarian membership was still cut off from the rest of the labour movement, thanks in no small measure to the self-isolating 'left turn' it had taken three years earlier. Thereafter the C.P. began to moderate its sectarian attitudes, not only about the class position of its adherents – radicalized students, teachers, academics, artists and professionals were now actively recruited – but about its tactics as well. By the mid-thirties it was committed to a 'United Front', made up of workers and their allies, and dedicated to the immediate defeat of fascism and the ultimate triumph of socialism. When the Second World War commenced, the British Left was effectively led by the Communists and numbered at least 60,000 supporters.[3] With its new networks of factory militants and Marxist intellectuals, here then was a Left which no one who pretended to be a socialist could ignore any longer. One way or another they had to relate their politics to it. Bernal and Co. were no exception to this rule.

The more they put their socialist beliefs to work, the more relevant did these become to their science. Like other intellectuals attached to the United Front, our subjects were expected to proselytize their uncommitted colleagues in the labs. Another way of connecting up their scientific and political practices was to discover how research was conducted in the world's first socialist state, the U.S.S.R. This supremely practical demonstration of the relationship between science and socialism, along with their introduction to the basic texts of Soviet Marxism, helped Bernal and the others to identify the social bases of their own intellectual work. Those insights were in turn used to persuade more researchers to throw in their lot with the scientific Left. So successful were these early initiatives of left-wing scientists that the entire Communist-dominated Left, already under the sway of science-based Russian theories, subsequently took on a more scientific cast. And if, as Bernal argued, science were communism, was it also not possible that communism could itself become a science? Never had Frederick Engels' famous notion of 'scientific socialism' been treated so literally.

Yet without that degree of apparent compatibility between their politics and their profession, it is possible that these men, as socialists, might not have evolved so far or achieved so much. For though they believed that their science could not survive under capitalism, there were in fact a variety of conflicts between their own situation as High Scientists and their advocacy of socialism. Some of these were 'merely personal'. For example: all of them, save Levy, were professionally ambitious. How much time could they spare for political duties? In a tight situation, what would they choose to do – perform the crucial experiment or attend the critical meeting? If they failed to get the balance right, then they risked their standing with the elders of science, not least those who regarded left-wingers as congenitally unsound. Even more liberally minded members of the establishment were apt to question the enthusiasm of a Bernal or a Haldane for the life of their 'unfree' Soviet counterparts. To the left of our scientific radicals came the hesitant criticism that their political and professional practices were élitist and, as such, did not square very well with their socialist beliefs. For the moment, however, the main thing to remember about all of these conflicts is that, in the thirties, they were successfully fudged, forgotten or resolved. Only in the Cold War would Bernal, Haldane, Levy and others have to spend much time proving that science and Communism could be reconciled.

Such was the 'ecological' background to the unique niche which our subjects came to occupy in British cultural and political history.

To the public at large they would appear as scientific apologists for the coming socialist transformation of Britain. To their fellow scientists, they would become spokesmen for the emergent culture of science. But they were unable to assume either of those roles until they had seen more clearly the connections between their science and their socialism. In that respect, we are in the unusual position of knowing precisely when and where their political vision dramatically improved. It was at the Science Musuem, South Kensington, on Saturday morning, 4 July 1931.

1. A Russian Roadshow

Scientists sometimes make the headlines; historians of science never do, and for good reason. Having little interest in the world, the world takes no notice of them. This tacit conspiracy allows them to share their erudition with each other, in peace. As an additional guarantee that their gatherings will not be deemed newsworthy, agendas listing topics, speakers and commentators are drawn up and published far in advance of the meetings themselves. The subsequent discussions prove to be as uneventful as those earnest and orderly men can make them. For where there are no 'events', there can be no news.

The second International Congress of the History of Science and Technology, scheduled for London in the summer of 1931, ought to have been a model of such anonymity. Not only was the history of science in its professional infancy, but 'the world' was looming abnormally large at this date as well. Weaving in and out of the pages of Britain's national press were sensational stories about the international economic crisis and the impending collapse of Mac-Donald's second Labour government. Placed against those momentous developments, 'The Sciences as an Integral Part of General Historical Study' or the 'Historical and Contemporary Interrelationships of the Physical and Biological Sciences' were bound to come across as fairly peripheral topics. Yet these were among the high points of the congress's prearranged programme – along with a special luncheon for delegates at Cambridge's Trinity College. A stimulating pot-pourri for the participants, perhaps; but not very exciting to a Fleet Street editor.

Therefore, imagine how bewildering it must have been to open a morning newspaper on Tuesday, 30 June 1931, and discover that 'the Russian government is taking an important part in the International Congress of the History of Science and Technology'.[4] That was how readers of the *Manchester Guardian* were informed of the impromptu arrival of a large Soviet delegation, led by no less a figure than Nicholai Bukharin, one of Lenin's closet associates after the Bolshevik revolution. No one could have been more surprised than the congress's organizers, among them Lancelot Hogben and Joseph Needham. For months they had been assuming that only one Russian – a Professor Zavadovsky – would be participating. Now they were confronted with a small battalion of politicians, administrators, scientists, historians and philosophers, all of them armed with lengthy and detailed addresses that they wanted to deliver to the congress (and to the world).

What was still more extraordinary was that as late as 22 June not even the Russians themselves had known they would be coming to London. Though there had been some special conferences on the role of science in the new Five Year Plan, no one had as yet prepared any special material for delivery in the West. Then on 23 June Stalin officially brought to a close eighteen months of political warfare between the Soviet state and its intelligentsia.[5] 'Bourgeois specialists' who performed their jobs well were henceforth to enjoy greater intellectual autonomy. This unforeseen dispensation was accompanied by a new propaganda drive designed to make Westerners more familiar with the Soviet Union's industrial and scientific progress. As it happened, the congress in London looked to be a convenient forum for launching this campaign with unprecedented speed. Bukharin, who was simultaneously the head of the Academy of Science's section on the history of science and the Director of Industrial Research for the Supreme Economic Council, was the obvious choice to select and lead the delegation. He picked, among others, the U.S.S.R.'s leading physicist (A. F. Joffe), its best-known biologist (N. I. Vavilov) and an obscure historian and physicist named Boris Hessen. After three days of frenzied activity, they threw their belongings together, dashed to the Moscow airport and took off for England. Unfortunately, one hour later, they had to return to Moscow. In the confusion and haste surrounding their departure, Bukharin had managed to pack everything, except the speech he was supposed to read out to the congress.[6]

When they flew into London – a newsworthy event in itself, given the rarity of transcontinental flights – their first mission was to contact the congress's President, Professor Charles Singer of University College, London. Their meeting with Singer took place just two days before the congress was to begin. What had to be decided was how much time the Soviets would be allowed to speak. Naturally they were under considerable pressure to make their presence felt, in the meetings and in the press. Singer, on the other hand, had neither the rooms nor the days to offer them. He did suggest that an additional half-day meeting could be scheduled for the following Saturday. While Bukharin accepted this arrangement, he pressed the congress's committee to cancel the one-day junket to Cambridge, so that the Soviet papers could be read out in full. But Singer would not deny to the assembled historians and scientists of twenty-four countries their special treat. At this predictably tense point in the proceedings, Lancelot Hogben intervened. He asked Bukharin: would it be possible for your associates to get their addresses translated, printed and published as a book by the end of the week? It was an audacious suggestion, to say the least, and Bukharin liked it. He decided to launch the project there and then with, he hoped, Hogben's assistance.

The Russians accordingly threw themselves into what the *Guardian* came to describe as 'The Five Days' Plan'. The Soviet embassy was turned into a publishing house. Authors worked over the shoulders of translators supplied by the Society for Cultural Relations with the U.S.S.R. As soon as a provisional manuscript had been completed, it was whisked off to compositors, who were working round-the-clock shifts. Back came the galleys, and then the arguments began. 'What does this sentence mean?' 'You can't say it that way in English!' 'But I thought Engels was perfectly clear on that point . . .' Yet somehow they managed to move on to page proofs and the final printing. When the delegates filed into the Science Museum's lecture hall on the morning of 4 July, they were able to pick up copies of all the Soviet papers. Three days later a bound edition of the essays appeared under the title *Science at the Cross Roads*. By the following Saturday it had already been reviewed by J. D. Bernal in, of all places, *The Spectator*.* Whether this was a

* Bernal found his way into the columns of this normally conservative weekly because its reviews were then managed by one Celia Simpson. Both

record in the history of British publishing, it was certainly to become a landmark in the history of British science.

Meanwhile the Soviets were putting in a daily appearance at the congress's formal sessions. Not content to remain off-stage until Saturday, they injected themselves into the proceedings whenever humanly possible. When, for example, on 30 June the historian G. N. Clark and the physiologist A. V. Hill suggested that historical studies should be broadened to include the record of intellectual advances, no less than 'five members of the Soviet delegation' asked the Chairman if 'they might be allowed to contribute a Marxian view to the symposium'.[7] The upshot of their collective commentary was that the recommendations of Clark and Hill would only result in new forms of hero worship; Newton and Darwin over Marlborough and Lincoln. What was required instead, they insisted, was to replace these individualistic or 'bourgeois' philosophies of history with the Marxist approach. For Marx and Engels had, in the Soviets' view, correctly emphasized the ways in which social and economic forces moulded (and repressed) Great Men. Whatever the merits of this intervention, it went on and on. Indeed they would have embellished their theme still further had the presiding officer not had at his disposal a rather formidable 'silencer'. 'Instead of a discreet red light, they had this enormous ship's bell,' Needham has recalled, 'and I have vivid recollections of Charles Singer trying to shut the Russians up.'[8] He succeeded, but not for long.

Undeterred by this indignity, B. M. Zavadovsky and A. F. Joffe turned up two days later to support Hogben's and Needham's attack on 'vitalism' and idealism in biology. After Hogben had wondered aloud whether Western fears of social decay had led to a declining enthusiasm for scientific materialism, Zavadovsky felt able to assert that 'these tendencies characterize the general disillusionment of bourgeois society in the possibilities of material culture'.[9] The Soviet biologist added that, for the dialectical materialist, the

---

of them were intimate friends of John Strachey, whom Simpson would later marry. In 1932 the *Spectator* dismissed her for being too left-wing in her sympathies. (See Hugh Thomas, *John Strachey* (London, 1973), p. 113.) As if to add journalistic insult to ideological injury, the *New Statesman* 'scooped' the *Spectator* on the same Saturday when it published a short article by Bukharin himself on 'Science and Politics in the Soviet Union'.

dilemma posed by this particular session – could 'life' be explained in purely physical terms – was a false one. To admit that the biological level was qualitatively distinct from the physical merely implied the need for novel experimental tools and a subtler version of the materialist viewpoint. The overall framework, he contended, had already been laid out 'in the classical works of . . . Marx and Engels, and, in our own times, in the profound works of Lenin'.[10]

All this trumpeting of Marxism was merely a foretaste of the 'dialectically' heavyweight discussion that would take place on Saturday. The addresses by Hessen and Bukharin on that day deserve special consideration here. In reviewing them we should remember that they were delivered before a collection of academics who knew little about the Soviet Union and even less about Marxist philosophy. Most of them were certain to be sceptical about any overly positive claims about the U.S.S.R.'s scientific achievements. Yet this would be the burden of Bukharin's paper. They were also unlikely to view science as anything other than a body of ideas fathered by a succession of scientific geniuses. Thus if they were told that Isaac Newton's great work, the *Principia*, was in any sense 'rooted' in the social and economic life of seventeenth-century England, we might have expected them either to giggle or to get very angry. Yet that was the proposition that Hessen was about to put to them.

In one sense the *Principia* was merely a peg on which Hessen was able to hang a highly compressed history of the physical sciences. His most startling proposition was that capitalist entrepreneurs had been ultimately responsible for the scientific revolution of the seventeenth century. On the one hand, they had promoted a tremendous expansion of world trade. As the pace of economic activity increased, so had the need for solving a new range of technical problems connected with gunnery, sailing, navigation and mechanics. To Hessen it was perfectly obvious that these topics not only constituted the 'earthy core' of the *Principia*, but had fundamentally 'determined the theories of physical research' in the period as well.[11] By this statement, he did not mean to imply that Newton's tools of analysis had been directly related to economic factors. Here his listeners were enjoined to take into account the superstructure of philosophical theories and religious beliefs which had guided Newton along certain lines of thought. Hessen next dissected the *Principia* into its conflicting philosophical components, in order to suggest that Newton's great work was the scientific equivalent of the social and political compromises of the late 1600s. And why had these cultural pacts been such a prominent feature of the Newtonian era? Because the English bourgeoisie had neither vanquished nor been defeated by the old feudal aristocracy. Instead power was shared between two classes, two world-views. That split was also reflected in Newton's writings. Indeed Hessen went so far as to assert that the more enduring portions of the *Principia* were technologically rather than ideologically inspired. The political moral which he derived from all this was that science could not advance in a society which restricted technical progress: 'Science develops out of production, and those social forms which become fetters upon productive forces likewise become fetters upon science.'[12] At the close of his speech, Hessen confidently drew a parallel between the Puritan and Bolshevik revolutions by remarking that, 'as in all epochs, in reconstructing social relationships we are reconstructing science'.[13]

That was a lot to take in, even in summary form. But consider the unsuspecting delegates, who were then asked to assimilate as well Bukharin's 'Theory and Practice from the Standpoint of Dialectical Materialism'. At least Hessen had referred, in however unfamiliar a way, to the familiarities of British history. Now the audience was going to be force-marched through the uncharted wilds of contemporary Russia by a guide who spoke only 'Marxism', not English. Would the journey be worth it?

Bukharin began his address by asserting that science had three major social functions. They are: to increase our knowledge of the external world; to invent and perfect technical processes; and to overcome those forces opposed to human advancement. To perform any of these tasks satisfactorily scientific theorists must be closely linked to those who, in one way or another, apply science; including engineers, technicians and other production workers. But, Bukharin argued, such a union can never be fully achieved in a capitalist social order, where mental workers are placed over and divided off from manual workers. Indeed the scientists themselves are split between those whose research has a quick technological pay-off and those whose investigations do not. Because the latter often work in isolation from an industrial setting, they are encouraged to think of their science as 'pure' and practised 'for its own sake'. To Bukharin this notion of purity is myopic and dangerous. Whatever professional scientists might subjectively feel about their work, it is objectively 'determined by aims which are practical in the long run – and this . . . can and must be considered from the standpoint . . . of social development'.[14] Furthermore, as long as scientific theorists remain divorced from agricultural and industrial workers, there is always the possibility that their theories will go awry and the economy will stagnate. This is one reason why capitalist nations have been unable to achieve a satisfactory system of production. By contrast, averred Bukharin, the Soviet Union has already taken the first steps toward the fusion of mental and manual labour. He emphasized, in particular, the possibilities of planning not just the economy but science itself.

[One] can feel with one's hands, as it were, how the requirements of the rapid and extensive growth of the U.S.S.R. imperiously dictate the solution of a number of technical problems, how the solution of these problems, in its turn, dictates the posing of the greatest theoretical problems . . . And all the poverty of the idea that the 'utility' of science means its degradation, the narrowing of its scope, etc., becomes crystal clear and apparent. Great practice requires great theory . . . But this means that thereby we are arriving not only at a synthesis of science, but at a social synthesis of science and practice . . . Science is reaching the summit of its social self-recognition.[15]

After this passionate outburst, Bukharin went on to outline how scientists and workers have already been united in the building up of a new socialist culture. Thus 'it is not only a new economic system which has been born' in the U.S.S.R. 'A new science', concluded Bukharin, 'has been born' as well.[16]

Any questions? Silence. Then coughs, shufflings of feet and a miasma of mutterings. But no laughter, no anger and no questions. Sitting in the audience next to Hyman Levy was a twenty-year-old Cambridge mathematics student named David Guest.[17] Guest had just returned from a spell at Göttingen, the same university where Levy had studied as a post-graduate. What had drawn Guest and Levy together, however, was politics rather than science. For both men were members of the Communist Party, which had only three weeks earlier approved the establishment of a university 'cell' at Cambridge. Now, as the silence droned on in the Science Museum's lecture hall, Guest leaned over to Levy and whispered 'Should I speak?' Levy replied matter of factly: 'Yes, of course, if you've got something to say.' Hesitantly, Guest uncoiled himself from his folding chair and cleared his throat. After a quick glance at his elders, this mere undergraduate began to congratulate the Soviet speakers on their performance. He also managed to support their general analysis of Western science, with references to various contradictions in pure mathematics. Upon finishing his commentary, Guest sat down to the same non-reaction that had greeted the Soviets.

Eventually two historians of science did voice some opposition. Yet the prevailing mood was essentially passive: simply let this session end as quickly and quietly as possible. Part of the problem of course had been the utterly alien quality of the Soviets' language and philosophy. Even 'in quarters anxious to understand the new Russia', reported the *Guardian*'s science correspondent, J. G. Crowther, there was a feeling that 'the Soviet would advance its cause more quickly and receive more sympathetic understanding if it would explain its ideas in the idiom of other languages, instead of merely translating expositions cast in the new Russian turn of thought'.[18] Certainly Bukharin and Hessen did not advance their cause with Dorothy Waley Singer, a noted Renaissance scholar and wife of the congress's presiding officer. Later she would write to Needham about her reactions to the Saturday meeting: 'I listened hard and with open mind, and the impression gained was that they adopted toward Marx exactly the medieval attitude towards Aristotle – that nothing could be right unless it could be traced to his words'. 'How', she queried, 'can that really help human development?'[19] It was left to J. D. Bernal to surmise the feelings of those less sympathetic to the Bolsheviks. He thought that the appeal to Marxism, far from impressing the Western academics, probably 'disposed them not to listen to the arguments which followed'. Indeed the probable consensus was that 'anything so ungentlemanly and doctrinaire had best be politely ignored'.[20]

The performance of the Soviet delegation was not entirely overlooked, however. In its summary of the congress's proceedings, *Nature* spoke of Marxism as a 'communistic explanation of scientific development, in which the integrative work of the masses is exalted at the expense of the glorification of genius'. Its reporter further maintained that 'the attitude of the Soviet delegates can scarcely explain any history, however stimulating their message and their endeavours to put it into practice'.[21] Three weeks later, in a review of *Science at the Cross Roads* that had been commissioned by *Nature*, the historian F. S. Marvin was rather more generous.[22] He agreed that knowledge was, in part, a social product. But he doubted whether such an insight could account for all aspects of the history of science. Though overtly sympathetic to the Bolshevik régime, he also expressed anxiety over the effect which dialectical material- ism might have on the direction of Soviet research. No such tenta- tiveness of judgement was evinced in the *Times Literary Supplement*, whose anonymous reviewer unhesitatingly derided and dismissed *Cross Roads*:

these papers were meant as contributions to the history of science, and judged as such they are so thoroughly doctrinaire as at times to be laughable ... A long analysis of Newton's position ... is intended to show that 'its physical content arose out of the tasks of the epoch, which were raised for accomplishment by the class entering into power'. The writers have no conception of devotion to science simply for the sake of science. Consequently science throughout means technology to them.[23]

Apart from these less than enthusiastic notices, the publication of *Science at the Cross Roads* appeared to be something of a non-event.

Yet judged by their lasting impact on left-wing scientists, the Soviets really had performed a five-day wonder. The 'most impor- tant meeting of ideas that has occurred since the Revolution' – that was Bernal's immediate reaction to the congress.[24] For the Soviet delegation had succeeded in altering not only his own scientific and political ideas but those of his colleagues as well. Zavadovsky's paper, for instance, had greatly impressed Needham, because its conclusions – so similar to his own – had apparently been derived independently with the aid of Marxist philosophy.[25] Hessen's contribution made an even deeper and wider impression. As Hogben has since reflected, it 'reinforced my interest' in Marx's historical outlook 'as an intellectual tool for expository use'.[26] Hyman Levy now found most works on the history of science inadequate, because they did not 'give an account at the same time of men's social and economic background'.[27] A far more surprising convert was Joseph Needham. For at the beginning of 1931 Needham had published an historical account of the development of embryology, his own special field. What was striking about this work was its 'internalist' conception of the history of science as nothing more than a record of the intellectual advances made by Great Men. Yet only three years later Needham would disavow this approach. Indeed he had now become confident that 'further historical research will enable us to do for the great embryologists what has been so well done by Hessen for Isaac Newton'.[28] Speaking for his comrades as well as himself, Bernal was thus able to look back on the congress as 'the starting point of a new evaluation of the history of science'.[29]

While the scientists were duly grateful for these historical and philosophical insights, they were even more strongly drawn to the Soviets' political message. This was especially true of the two Communists, Bernal and Levy. As Levy would reflect in 1939:

the standpoint consistently adopted by these delegates crystallized out in remarkable fashion what had been simmering in the minds of many for some time past. What became clear was not only the social conditioning of science and the vital need for planning, . . . but the impossibility of carrying this through within the framework of a chaotic capitalism.[30]

That perspective was further elaborated during the intense discussions which took place between the Soviet delegates and the British left-wingers. Both sides got tremendously excited about this interchange. Great friendships were struck up. Bukharin, Hessen and the others even spent an evening at Hogben's home. But of course the Russians soon had to take leave of their new British comrades. To the accompaniment of many bear-hugging farewells, the delegates flew back to Moscow, back to the business of constructing a new socialist order. What they did leave behind them was a dilemma, which Bernal nicely captured at the time. 'Is it better', he asked the Spectator's readers, 'to be intellectually free but socially ineffective, or to become a component part of a system where knowledge and action are joined for one common social purpose?'[31] Neither the Spectator nor Bernal was in any doubt (or agreement) over the answer to that challenge.

Indeed Bernal found the events surrounding the congress so stirring that he was inspired to set off for the Soviet Union. Within a matter of weeks he arrived in Leningrad with a small party of 'leftish' individuals who were interested in science. They included the *Guardian*'s Crowther, the historian of science John Pilley and a young Cambridge biochemist Bill Pirie. In contrast to the sumptuous Russian junket that Crowther had already arranged for a large number of senior British scientists, Bernal's party roughed it. However, their hard travelling did allow them to penetrate quite a bit further into the new U.S.S.R. All of them were deeply impressed with the political, scientific and economic activities that they encountered there. Even twenty-five years after their occurrence, the memory of these events could still overwhelm Bernal.

> I went round the Soviet Union in those rather rough, primitive and casual days when one saw very much of the difficulties as well as of [the] achievements. I saw the construction camps for the Dnieper dam, and at the same time saw something of the hard times that were produced in the period of early collectivization – a consequence of the concentration of all efforts for the building of heavy industry, very remote from immediate enjoyments . . . And yet there was no mistaking the sense of purpose and achievement in the Soviet Union in those days of trial. It was grim but great. Our hardships in England were less; theirs were deliberate and undergone in an assurance of building a better future. Their hardships were compensated by a reasonable hope.[32]

The strangely exalted realism of this passage tallies fairly well with Pirie's recollection of the extraordinary intensity which Bernal managed to sustain through the trip. Pirie was especially struck by an incident in Kiev, where Bernal decided to conduct his own private tour. Upon rejoining his companions many hours later, Bernal was asked what he had been up to. He replied that he had been meditating in Kiev Cathedral on the meaning of socialism. In Pirie's retrospective and somewhat cynical view, all this communion with the struggles of the Russian people smacked just a bit too much of religion. But then he added, as if to soften his blow, 'is "faith" not an occupational hazard for a theoretical physicist?'[33] Perhaps scepticism is the characteristic vice of biochemists.

Crowther's later reminiscences of the scientists whom he accompanied to the Soviet Union in 1931 are more detached, though equally acerbic. He recorded his amazement over 'the uniformity of outlook of Cambridge scientists, in spite of wide variations in personality and political beliefs. John Pilley, who was an Oxford man, also commented on it.'[34] To those who recall our earlier speculations about 'Cambridge Man', this is a rather tantalizing remark. Unfortunately, Crowther did not bother to add anything here about the content of that outlook. What he did spell out were his very serious reservations about the politics of all these scientific workers, Bernal and Pirie included. It was his belief that they were then, at best, 'politically underdeveloped'.

It must be remembered that several of them, since famous, were then young scientists establishing their scientific reputations. They were working very hard at science, and their activities outside it were part-time and additional, and often appeared to me juvenile. These scientists only became mature during the Second World War, when they first had experience of serious responsibilities outside science.[35]

Those are hard words and, as we shall soon see, they came very easily to a man who prided himself on his hard-boiled 'realism'. In my own view Crowther's judgement is terribly unjust when juxtaposed against the movement of left-wing scientists in the late thirties. But it does ring truer for men who, as of 1931, were newly active on the Left.

Nevertheless they were becoming not only more involved in socialist politics, but also more aware of what socialism was about and how it related to their science. Much of the credit for the rapidity of their political evolution must of course be given to the Soviet delegation, and more particularly Bukharin and Hessen. The irony and tragedy of this exchange is that, while their ideas would now serve as the cultural foundations for a scientific Left in Britain, they would subsequently be ignored in the U.S.S.R. itself. Yet in the early 1930s such a scenario was indeed difficult to imagine. The Soviets were, against all odds, building a socialist society. It was now time for Bernal and the others to participate in the rebuilding of a socialist movement in their own country.

2. Personal, Professional or Political?

Despite their new-found taste for political engagement, they did not achieve much prominence as the scientific Left's leading spokesmen until the late thirties. Since there was no movement of radicalized scientists as of 1931, this delay was hardly unexpected. Indeed it might have taken more than a decade to have launched such an

enterprise, had not the fascists made so many striking gains on the
Continent. Even with that measure of assistance Bernal and his
cohorts had an immense task ahead of them; assimilating Soviet
Marxism, propagating their version of scientific socialism and
organizing their fellow scientific workers. What made those
endeavours all the more daunting was the historical novelty of a
sizable number (1 per cent, perhaps) of bourgeois intellectuals who
apparently were prepared to support the aims of a revolutionary
movement. Neither the Communist Party of Great Britain nor the
doyens of High Science were prepared for this upcoming shift to
the Left. Hence it was difficult for these young scientists to judge
precisely what form their politics would take, let alone the effect
it might have on their careers. That made it all the more important
to negotiate as quickly as possible the ground rules that would
govern their political commitment. For they could not make
significant and lasting inroads into their own profession until they
had devised a formula that effectively meshed the demands of their
science and their socialism.

Unfortunately, no ready-made solution to these problems was
forthcoming from Britain's only viable revolutionary party, the
C.P.G.B. In fact for the first decade of its existence the party had
quite consciously refused to organize intellectuals on the grounds
that they were 'objectively' allies of, if they did not actually belong
to, the ruling class. Natural scientists were explicitly shunned.
Useful though their researches would be to the proletariat after the
revolution, they were for the moment only made available to the
bosses and the generals. That was the argument Cambridge economist Maurice Dobb put to readers of the party journal *Labour
Monthly* in December of 1925,[36] and it was to be repeated three
years later in one of Bernal's anonymous contributions to *The
Communist*.[37] By that stage the C.P., like other 'sections' of the
Soviet-dominated Communist International, was following a policy
of 'class versus class'. The logic of this line was that the rank and
file of the labour movement had to be turned away from its social
democratic leadership, in preparation for the impending 'general
crisis' of world capitalism. Yet if the outstanding representatives of
the T.U.C. and the Labour Party were now to be regarded as
agents of 'social-fascism' where did that leave bourgeois scientists?
At the best of times they had been dismissed as capitalist lackeys.

The new tactics would appear to have placed them irredeemably beyond the pale of Communist respectability.

As it happened, the sectarian excesses of the 'class versus class' phase encouraged the C.P.G.B. to reconsider its earlier opposition to the active recruitment of intellectuals. For contrary to the party's official pronouncements, the rising unemployment and lower wages of the Depression era were dampening rather than provoking class conflict at the 'point' of industrial production. Nor were the supposedly 'social-fascist' policies of Labour's leaders driving British workers into the arms of the Communists. Instead the labour movement remained what it had been since the time of the General Strike: weak, divided and demoralized; thanks in some small measure to the C.P.'s own tactics. On the other hand, the world slump did seem to inspire an incipient radicalism inside the universities, whose undergraduates were beginning to manifest a social conscience and whose graduates were already suffering from some under-employment. Once again the logic of 'class versus class' was being confounded. Hence, as early as 1931, the Communists felt obliged to start violating the spirit, though not the letter, of the Comintern line. One instance of covert 'deviation' was their support for new, more broadly based 'front' organizations such as Wal Hannington's National Unemployed Workers' Movement. Another was their unprecedented attempt to recruit mental as well as manual workers into the party. Yet it was not until 1938 – three years after the Comintern had switched from the tactics of 'class versus class' to those of the 'united front' – that the C.P.G.B. could publicly admit to itself 'the importance of "work amongst the middle class and professional sections"'.[38] Old inhibitions died hard.

The party, however, could not be too careful in its relations with would-be bourgeois allies, scientists included. It had to guard itself not only against exaggerated notions of the intelligentsia's capacity for self-radicalization but against the political adventurism of recently converted intellectuals as well. That at any rate was the firm opinion of the *Guardian*'s science correspondent, J. G. Crowther, who was himself a *de facto* party member. As we might have expected, his advice to Communists and scientific workers alike was singularly hard-headed. Though Crowther of course believed that only communism could satisfy the true interests of scientific workers, he was equally well persuaded that many if not most of them would never come round to his view. In 1941, long after the C.P.G.B. had committed itself to working with scientists and other intellectual 'workers', he recognized that

The relatively attractive conditions of research work dispose many scientists towards conservatism and indifference. They are apt to ignore external circumstances, because discovery cannot be made without intense concentration. They become detached from external affairs and may lose the faculty of thinking about them. The greater the detachment, the greater the difficulty in returning to ordinary matters, and this increasing difficulty widens the detachment still more. [Indeed] the material conditions of scientists contain elements that dispose them to fascism . . . The immediate economic and class interests of scientists tend to make them fall in with authority.[39]

Crowther's understanding of the scientific community's under-lying conservatism ought to have favourably disposed him to those researchers who had nevertheless decided to 'come out' as socialists. In fact he was almost more upset by the activist minority than the apathetic majority. For Crowther detected a desire on the part of the newly radicalized 'to drop the tantalizing ardours of hampered research and enjoy some hot and straight agitation against social abuses in general and scientific abuses in particular'.[40] Whatever the short-term satisfactions of dropping out might be, it was a course of action which in Crowther's view was politically unsound. If, as he explained to members of the Association of Scientific Workers in October 1936, it was important to oppose right-wing views in science and turn the profession in a progressive direction, then socialist drop-outs hurt their own cause. They denied to other scientists the benefit of their counsel, example and support. They were no longer able to use their scientific credentials as a means of getting non-scientists to listen to them. Most importantly, their withdrawal from the professional community could be used by the establishment to show that the true socialist had a low opinion of science. Indeed the consequences of their 'radicalism' were so uniformly reactionary that Crowther was compelled to cast doubt on the sincerity of their motives. Most of them were either making a political exit as 'a disguise for evading professional failure', or they had proved themselves to be 'mentally unstable'. Either way, 'after a few years of bohemian agitation' they usually tried 'to find a rich wife and join a Rotary Club'.[41] So much for these political adventurists.

Apart from developing one's ability to spot neurotic, incompetent 'crypto-Rotarians', what was to be done, if one was a scientist of socialist persuasion? Stay in science, snapped Crowther, in order to carry out the following political assignments:

1. The exposure of errors in science which are quoted in support of reactionary politics, and the exposure of the scientific errors in the works of reactionary scientists.

2. The organization of exposure in a cooperative manner . . .

3. Solid and scholarly demonstrations of the relations between science and social affairs, so that scientists may be convinced of the need for taking an active and progressive interest in politics *for the sake of science*.

4. The extension of demonstrations of the frustration of science by a bad social system, and how frustration would be increased in still worse social systems . . .

5. The persuasion of scientists . . . to support progressive parties on the ordinary political grounds of economic interests and prospects, and social justice.

6. The involvement of all scientists on all rational grounds in support of the United Front of progressive parties against social and intellectual reaction, and war.[42]

In performing these tasks Crowther also made it clear that left-wing scientific workers could mightily enhance their political effectiveness by achieving greater professional recognition. That meant, among other things, attaining Fellowships in the Royal Society. For, 'in a scientific age, the official scientific societies contain a good deal of progressive spirit, even if it is mixed with much reaction. Scientists should therefore take these societies seriously, and qualify themselves for the appropriate organization to which they should belong.'[43] Those recommendations merely echoed the C.P.'s maxim that, however important it was to mobilize scientific workers and popularize scientific socialism, the first duty of a Communist scientist was to be a 'good', i.e. a conscientious and successful scientist. A more practical demonstration of the compatibility of science and socialism was hard to imagine.

Whether these ground rules would satisfy the professional scruples of High Science's elders remained to be seen. As we noted back in Chapter One, the tacit convention of *their* scientific community certainly did not include support for, among other things, organized exposés of the work of politically reactionary scientists. What they did positively sanction was self-absorption in one's work and self-isolation from the world. Even in the thirties, according to Hogben, the popularization of one's own science was still considered to be slightly risqué.

A presbyterian divine once said that a man who plays golf neglects his business, neglects his wife and neglects his God. Many of the older statesmen of science hold that if a younger one writes a book which can be read painlessly, he neglects his students, neglects his laboratory and neglects his golf.[44]

Yet the science establishment was said to be fairly liberal and tolerant. It did not *really* mind whether (successful) eccentric researchers sought unusual functional equivalents for golf – so long as they did not participate in left-wing agitation. Such was the position adopted by Professor A. V. Hill in his Huxley Memorial Lecture of 1933. As a well connected member of the intellectual aristocracy (J. M. Keynes was his brother-in-law), a Nobel Prizewinner in physiology and a powerful figure within the Royal Society's inner circle, Hill did not bother to mince his weighty words. He reminded his younger colleagues that the Royal Society's Charter specifically enjoined its Fellows not to 'meddle with politics'. 'Such', Hill continued, 'is the normal condition of tolerance and immunity for scientific pursuits in a civilized state'. Moreover, science 'should remain aloof and detached, not from any sense of superiority, not from any indifference to the common welfare, but as a condition of complete intellectual honesty'.[45] Hill buttressed this argument with an allusion to the experience of those academics whom Hitler had already hounded out of Germany.

At the moment in England we are free. We rejoice in our freedom. We cannot imagine it otherwise, in spite of all our young communists and fascists. A year ago Germany was free . . . Neither Russia nor Italy today can claim – their rulers indeed would probably deny – that honesty and intelligence are safeguards for unpopular opinion. Who knows when the next epidemic of mass insanity may appear?[46]

Many years later Hogben would wryly observe that Hill was, in effect, urging 'young scientific workers' to 'take their views from the *Daily Telegraph* and entrust the destiny of Britain to Stanley Baldwin'.[47] His encouragement took the form of a twin condemnation: communism was 'irrational' and activities to that end were 'anti-scientific'. For the benefit of his scientific juniors, *Nature* published and endorsed the substance of Hill's message. Even toward the end of the thirties when the establishment briefly relaxed its 'anti-political' biases (see Chapter Seven), it was widely understood that at least one form of politics could not be practised: under no circumstances could the British public be told 'the truth' about its own scientific community. Bernal at least had the courage to acknowledge the existence of this rule.

Unfortunately it is not possible in any published book to speak freely and precisely about the way science is run. The law of libel, reasons of state and still more the unwritten code of the scientific fraternity itself forbid particular examples being held up alike for praise or blame. Charges must be general and to that degree unconvincing, and lacking in substantiation.[48]

The extraordinary thing about this statement was that it appeared in Bernal's *The Social Function of Science*, which, by comparison with the general run of books then available about British scientific life, was monumentally indiscreet. It was yet another measure of the limits which 'the profession' could still set on the political activities of its members.

Here then was the complex dilemma which confronted every radicalized scientific worker in the 1930s. They were not asked to choose between their science and their politics. Indeed the Communist Party was particularly anxious that socialist militants remained in their labs and were seen to be 'good' scientists. But that policy, for all its political cunning and overt deference to the norms of High Science, could never fully overcome the lingering hostilities of the science establishment. The elders continued to believe that the pursuit of one's politics as an avocation could not but do injury to the practice of one's vocation, namely science. Nor, as members of the dominant class, were they ever likely to be *that* tolerant of those researchers who sought to abolish the class system. So it was not entirely clear whether it was possible for any researcher to be regarded by his political and professional peers alike as both a 'good' scientist and a 'good' socialist. This dilemma was sharper at the beginning of the decade – when the C.P.G.B. largely ignored

intellectuals and leading High Scientists were unreservedly anti-
political – than at the end – when a left-wing intelligentsia had been
formed and young scientists were permitted to be 'socially
conscious'. It was also felt most keenly, needless to say, by those
who had already embarked on a scientific career but had yet to
establish their reputation. Nevertheless, it was always a reality for
all politically active researchers, whatever their seniority or their
particular brand of socialism.

Certainly this was the case with our five subjects. For despite
their varying ages, temperaments, ambitions and political views,
they were equally devoted to the causes of science and socialism.
Thus unlike the twenties political engagement was to become for
each of them almost an existential necessity. That at any rate was
how Bernal retrospectively understood the many initiatives which
he was about to undertake on behalf of his socialism:

if it had not been for that activity and the real contact it brought me with
the people, I, as an intellectual, would have found existence intolerable. To
watch impotently . . . the destruction of all the advances that humanity
seemed to have made as a consequence of the scientific and industrial
revolution . . ., would have been to make meaningless the whole work we
were doing as scientists to add to human culture.[49]

And had their work been rendered 'meaningless', then so too
would their lives. For we cannot doubt that at the core of their
personal/social identity was their love of the scientific enterprise.
The origins of their attachment have already been displayed. Here
we need only add that, to judge from their reactions to the publication in 1934 of C. P. Snow's first serious novel *The Search*, this
devotion did not abate in the thirties. The main story line in the
book is that after a promising start to his career Arthur Miles, an
X-ray crystallographer, decides to abandon science altogether, in
order to become a politically minded writer and critic. The problem for many High Scientists who read *The Search* was that they
could not understand how anyone who had experienced the joys of
scientific discovery could ever abandon such a life. Lord Rutherford
made this criticism to Snow,[50] as did J. B. S. Haldane.[51] At least
Dorothy and Joseph Needham, in their review of the novel for
Nature, suggested that one reason for the implausibility of Miles's
decision was that his political aspirations were so indeterminate.

We are given to understand that the psychological and political education of mankind came to seem more important to him than the search for detailed scientific truth. But the outlines of this need greater clarity. Had he turned to propagate a robuster political faith, this would not have been so necessary as it is when his aims seem so mild and moderate, so Lowes-Dickensonian, so L.N.U. [League of Nations Union].[52]

There was, however, at least one figure in Snow's work who showed no signs of wanting to desert his scientific career: 'Constantine', the brilliant, polymathic and highly successful crystallographer. In fact he represents, as we noted in Chapter Three, a somewhat mythical portrait of the young J. D. Bernal – just at the moment when Bernal's socialism was beginning to 'break in' more insistently on his science. Having come full circle, it ought to be clear how concerned they all were to honour both their professional and their political commitments.

How then did they choose to harmonize these loyalties? Obviously that decision depended in part on the more idiosyncratic aspects of each man's life. Had he not yet attained, for example, his Fellowship in the Royal Society, he might not wish to become as politically active or prominent as someone who had already got his 'F.R.S.'. If someone worked in an isolated laboratory with relatively unsympathetic colleagues, his politics might necessarily have to take on an individualistic cast; especially in a city where the organized Left was quite weak. Should one of them find himself estranged from the Communist Party – and, by extension, the Popular Front – his very identity as a socialist would be called into question. Obviously the precise impact of these different circumstances would depend upon the dynamics of individual life histories, not to mention those of a society and world that were eventually to be plunged into total warfare. Nevertheless out of this welter of variations there would emerge at least two common strategies. All of them would work punishingly long hours, inside their labs and outside in the world, thereby earning themselves the high esteem of scientists and socialists alike. Still more important, they were united in their belief that the fortunes of science could not be advanced without the achievement of socialism, and vice versa. Thus to play upon the C.P. maxim quoted earlier, they came to believe that the second duty of a good scientist was to become a good socialist. That would represent their ultimate resolution of the so-called conflict between their politics and their profession. However, beneath this significant degree of unanimity, Bernal and the others still had to resolve for themselves how they would relate *their* science to *their* socialism, and how each in turn could best be worked into the other dimensions of their lives.

3. Red Professors

None of our subjects encountered greater difficulties en route to that resolution than J. B. S. Haldane. For J.B.S. had assumed his birthright place in the ranks of the science establishment before he felt obliged to reassess his rather liberal political stance. The problem here was that, as in his infamous divorce case, Haldane's zeal for scientific rigour was to combine with his aristocratic code of personal integrity, so as to produce a passion for consistency in his own behaviour. Hence the early 1930s were relatively tranquil years for Haldane, because his social outlook then appeared to be all of a piece with his membership of the Royal Society, his professorship at University College, London, and his public reputation as a stimulating, not *too* serious observer of contemporary life. Like the 'enlightened' High Scientist he was, Haldane accordingly described himself to a former student 'as a "lukewarm" supporter of the Labour Party and referred to a friend's membership of the Communist Party as "unexpected"'. He also criticized in this period 'the no doubt naïve political activity of his junior colleagues' and, Bill Pirie continues, 'had little connection with the "anti-war" movements in which we were active'.[53] When J.B.S. turned forty in 1932, it therefore looked as if he had become and would likely remain a 'progressive' spirit – but well within the terms and limits laid down by the conservative managers of High Science. In Haldane's world the dilemmas we mentioned earlier simply did not exist.

His tranquillity proved to be short-lived, however. By 1938 he had declared himself a Marxist and a supporter (though not a member) of the Communist Party of Great Britain. This apparent departure from the predestined trajectory of his life was for Haldane as psychologically painful as it was politically necessary. Here is how it came about. Soon after the Nazis had assumed power in Germany, he was quickly persuaded that they had to be contained and ultimately defeated. Otherwise the security of Britain and the well-being of international science would be permanently placed at risk. While that was not in itself a radical perspective – it could be found in Hill's Huxley Lecture – it became so for one who had increasingly grave doubts both about the willingness of the ruling class and the ability of the Labour Party to resist the menace of fascism.[54] Haldane's disenchantment with orthodox politics reached its apogee during the Spanish Civil War, not least because, in his view, the policies of the Labour opposition as well as those of the Tory government favoured Franco's fascists. At the same time 'Spain' brought him more directly in touch with the struggles of the revolutionary Left. First his stepson, Ronald Haldane, decided to fight with the anti-Franco forces. Shortly after Ronald's death in combat, his mother, Charlotte Haldane, decided to join the C.P.G.B. By this time J.B.S. had himself come forward as an adviser on civil defence to the Spanish authorities. When Haldane returned from these 'journeys to the frontier', he naturally took an active part in the Communist-led campaign on behalf of the Republican cause. 'As a scientist whose business it is to discover and publish truth', he declared to one rally, 'I am proud to do what I can to . . . see that [Foreign Secretary Anthony] Eden does not keep the truth from the people of Britain'.[55] Unfortunately, the leadership of the Labour Party did not want to know 'the truth', as Haldane saw it, about Spain, about the need to protect the British people from aerial attack (see Chapter Seven) and, of course, about the importance of science to socialists. But the Communists did. Their accord was symbolized and sealed when the first of J.B.S.'s weekly science columns appeared in the C.P.'s own newspaper, the *Daily Worker*. Now here was a truly 'unexpected' affiliation.

Indeed Haldane had undergone a political transformation. He did not eventually support the Communists merely because, to quote his biographer, they represented 'in an imperfect world . . . the least unsatisfactory option'.[56] They were that for Haldane; but they were also the only significant Marxist revolutionary party in Britain. And J.B.S., by the late thirties, had decided that Marxism was 'true',[57] and that the prospects of achieving socialism in Britain, without recourse to violent revolution, were growing slimmer every year.[58] In other words Haldane came to see and affirm communism as the antithesis rather than the apothesis of bourgeois liberalism. Hence we must resist the temptation to perceive him as a liberal who, in the perverse circumstances of a 'low, dishonest decade', could only uphold his values through an alliance with the C.P.G.B. That interpretation comes too easily to mind, not only because it has been used so often and fits so well the history of certain (formerly) left-wing poets like Stephen Spender;[59] but also because it is rather difficult to capture on paper just how the 'alternation'[60] in J.B.S.'s political vision led him to reinterpret the events that were, allegedly, responsible for driving him into the arms of the Communists. Unfortunately, it was not quite that simple. For the social reality of Haldane the revolutionary was, in crucial respects, very different from that of Haldane the liberal.

The central motif in the 'new' Haldane's political outlook was that the ruling class – his class – had to be divested of its control over the means of mental and material production. Socialists therefore had to develop, within the labour movement, institutions that were dedicated to the obstruction – and eventual destruction – of the smooth administration of the capitalist state. Obviously both axioms were derived from the writings of Marx, Engels and Lenin. As early as 1933 Haldane had begun to study their works in earnest.[61] What they had to say increasingly helped him to make sense of what was happening to his world, and vice versa. In fact J.B.S. was uncharacteristically overwhelmed and humbled by the complexities and insights of 'dialectical materialism'. Only after he had mastered to his own satisfaction the Marxist 'world-view' did Haldane allow himself, in 1942, to be put forward as a full member of the Communist Party. By that time he had already become a veteran of revolutionary politics, and not just in public. True to his canons of personal integrity, J.B.S. felt obliged to wage the class war with himself and his family. Sometimes the results could be very alarming to, among others, his sister Naomi Mitchison:

I suppose he wanted to join the Communist Party, partly as a kind of affirmation that he was through with his comfortable pre-war life; that he was casting off his bourgeois origins. Often he did this rather violently, as the time when my father died [in 1936]. There was a cremation in London. The ashes were to be taken up to Cloan [the Haldanes' ancestral home in

Scotland] to be scattered. We were going up by the night train, and my
Aunt and I – it had been a pretty gruelling time – got sleepers. And he not
only wouldn't have a sleeper, but he insisted on having the ashes with him
in a third-class compartment in the rack; just to show what sort of person
he was now.[62]

By stage-managing this break with his aristocractic past, Haldane
was, quite consciously, increasing his reliance upon a new range of,
shall we say, less than aristocratic associates. That, however, was
only the initial step in what was bound to be a long and complicated effort to change himself. When asked in 1940 what he required
from life, J.B.S. replied with a transparent honesty that indicated
how far his self-transformation had proceeded, as well as the
distance he still had to cover.

I require friendship. Particularly I require the friendship of my colleagues
and comrades in scientific and political work. I want the society of equals
who will criticize me, and whom I can criticize. I cannot be friends with a
person whose orders I have to obey without criticism before or after, or
with one who has to obey my orders in a similar way. And I find friendship
with people much richer or poorer than myself very difficult.[63]

These sentiments were not unusual for someone of Haldane's background. What was peculiar was the admission that they were, in
any sense, problematic. Perhaps it was J.B.S.'s new-found sensitivity
to his own condition that made it possible for Hyman Levy to
befriend him for the first time.[64] In view of their very different
histories, not to mention Levy's congenital uneasiness with
Cambridge men, this was a striking testimonial to the deep
changes which had made it possible for Haldane to become a
Communist.

But Lancelot Hogben, retrospectively, offered a rather different
explanation for J.B.S.'s altered behaviour: 'Coming from a Calvin-
istic tribal background, Haldane had swallowed hook, line and
sinker dialectical materialism, which I regarded at all times as
obscurantist rubbish.'[65] While Hogben's religious determinism
cannot, I believe, account for Haldane's situation in the thirties, it
works rather well when applied to his own. For unlike J.B.S.,
Hogben did not undergo any personal/political transformation in
this period. He remained instead the perennial non-conformist,

6

the troublesome gadfly of all 'establishments', the nit-picking nemesis of any 'true believer'.

Prior to the formation of a communist-led left-wing intelligentsia, his had been, by any reasonable definition, a radical stance. From a point of near-heroic isolation, Hogben had kept faith with his own socialism and had discomfited a number of reactionary (and quite powerful) scientists. Along the way, however, he had also cultivated some of the psychological and philosophical defences we might have expected of someone who occupied such an exposed position. One of these was a tetchy disposition, which prevented Hogben from becoming too closely involved with any individual or institution. This pattern allowed him to keep his own counsel, though the price he paid for this independence – the periodic loss of close friends and his detachment from the labour movement – was obviously a heavy one. Another form of self-protection was his ferocious defence of science's ethical neutrality. Once again, in the context of the 1920s, Hogben's defence of 'public knowledge' had served a progressive end, because it validated his one-man stand against the dominance of politically motivated eugenic ideas within the scientific domain of British biology. That it likewise served to buttress his profession in the future against any outside influence from the Left was then a purely academic point. Hogben was, in short, the complete individualist, who pursued quasi-revolutionary ends with purely liberal means.

That combination worked well enough until the time of the Popular Front. Thereafter the fragile life-style, through which Hogben had stitched together his personality and his philosophy, his profession and his politics began to unravel. For the first time he had enemies to the left as well as to the right of him. The scientific community had become politically animated in a manner that both pleased and repelled him. Socialist intellectuals were now sufficiently numerous to justify organized, collective protests, in which their individual personalities were often submerged. Furthermore, Hogben did not yet feel that he had secured adequate recognition for his experimental work. All of these developments were bound to inhibit his wholehearted participation in the political movements of the 1930s. But his experiences at the London School of Economics, coupled with his early disaffection from Soviet communism nearly moved him to abandon politics altogether.

His sojourn at the L.S.E. proved to be especially traumatic.* By many academic criteria Hogben's Department of Social Biology ought to have been counted a great success. Apart from his own work on population genetics and sex hormones, Hogben sponsored the demographic studies of Enid Charles and supervised the earliest researches of a number of promising students, including David Glass, J. L. Gray and Pearl Moshinsky. Together they produced in 1938 under Hogben's editorship the volume *Political Arithmetic*. Among their investigations was a tightly argued account of how up to 60 per cent of Britain's most gifted children were excluded from higher education. Although this work appeared both to confirm Hogben's previous criticisms of the eugenists and to transform demography into one of the leading social sciences, it was only published after the L.S.E. authorities had dismantled Hogben's department. Hogben had already left the school, as had Beveridge, his principal backer.

He had many reasons to be disenchanted. Hogben still felt professionally insecure. If his fellow scientists judged his own research to be competent and worth-while biology, they did not always extend that accolade to social biology as a whole. That judgement was likely to be reinforced in the case of eugenically minded biologists, whose old arguments about the genetic inferiority of the working class were now being pulled apart by Hogben's students. Hogben of course might have stood firm had he received unwavering support from other social scientists, not least at the L.S.E. But they were frankly envious and resentful at the relative ease with which he was able to fund his work and that of his students. Hogben, in turn, was openly contemptuous of the 'aimless' theorizing of his colleagues, whether they were right-wing economists like Lionel Robbins and Frederick von Hayek, or left-wing followers of the political theorist Harold Laski. He charged these 'secular Platonists' with conspiring

to protect the study of human society from what is called empiricism (of approved topics) and muckraking (when the subject is a forbidden one) . . . Today active opposition to realistic research is mainly directed against

* The full details of this episode are discussed in José Harris's forthcoming biography of Lord Beveridge. I am grateful to Ms Harris for allowing me to see part of her draft manuscript, from which the comments of Beatrice Webb, quoted below, have been extracted.

attempts to study how man can enlist the new powers which science has placed at his disposal for the satisfaction of common social needs and the prolongation of human life.[66]

Then for good measure he chivvied his enemies with the 'unscientific' nature of their ideologies and research methods. Perhaps there was some guile in these attacks. As Beatrice Webb commented of Hogben at the time: 'Partly because of his anti-Marxism and anti-politics, he has got on the right side of Beveridge.' He therefore 'gets all the money and freedom he wants for [the department] and Enid's investigations'. But Hogben was quite genuinely estranged from the rest of the L.S.E.'s academic staff. He not only tended to stay away from the Senior Common Room but got away from London every weekend as well. Thus when the Rockefeller Foundation announced in 1936 that it would be unable to continue its massive subsidy for social biology, Hogben lost no time in applying for a vacant Chair of Physiology at the University of Aberdeen. Having secured this professorship, he was overcome with relief – and bitterness. 'That will end an inglorious and rather humiliating chapter of my life,' he admitted in a letter to Beatrice Webb. 'Just now I am on top of the world again. The biological opportunities are stupendous. But if what is called social science is what is done at the L.S.E., thank heaven I am still a biologist.'

Aberdeen was not exactly a centre for revolutionary ferment. Yet to Hogben that had almost become a point in its favour. Though he still saw himself as a Marxist and a socialist, he could not bring himself to support the organized Left of the thirties. We know some of the 'deep background' that helped to account for this response. What we have not considered are his specific objections to the form and content of the Popular Front. The main difference between Hogben and more orthodox left-wingers in the thirties was his rejection of the philosophical outlook, economic direction and repressive policies of the Soviet state. Even at the 1931 congress, he had been anxious to dissociate Marx's conception of historical development through class conflict, which he accepted, from the Russians' mania for dialectical 'laws', which he immediately dismissed as 'mere logic'.[67] The influence of the U.S.S.R.'s Marxism was, however, not half so baneful as its (understandable) obsession with industrialization. For just as Hogben had been about to campaign against the horrors of an 'over-developed' Britain (see Chapter

Six), his fellow socialists became fascinated with the new production targets of the Five Year Plan, thereby reviving what Hogben later termed 'the discredited ideology of early industrial capitalism'.[68] What finally disillusioned him about the Communist Party 'as such' was 'the execution of Bukharin and others in the purges of 1936–38'.[69] He abhorred the C.P.G.B.'s 'cover-up' of the Moscow trials and suspected that life would be no different should the party ever come to power in England. On the other hand Hogben could summon up no enthusiasm for any form of collaboration with the Labour Party. Ideologically speaking, he was adrift and the political tide had already turned against him.

Later Hogben would manage to recover his bearings and renew his opposition, as a socialist, to the orthodox Left. But in the thirties he did momentarily lose his way. His main political role, as we shall soon see, was to popularize a new approach to the history and presentation of science. Yet even that apparently uncontentious enterprise was difficult for Hogben to launch, so uncertain had he become about his normally assured (and fearless) moral judgements. In this case he hesitated over the publication under his own name of *Mathematics for the Million*. Written while Hogben was recuperating from a long bout of illness and destined to become an international best-seller, the book prominently featured a Marxist emphasis on the social background to scientific discovery. At first he decided that this work might damage his scientific reputation, at precisely the moment when he hoped to be considered for admission to the Royal Society. Hence Hogben pressed his still close friend, Hyman Levy, to place his name on the title page instead of Hogben's.* While Levy admired the text and understood its author's diffidence in showing it to the world, he declined the request. His grounds for doing so were that, however much on the periphery of pure mathematics, he could not assume the authorship of a work whose mathematics were entirely 'pre-Newtonian' in character, and still call himself a professional mathematician. Eventually Hogben gave the go-ahead to his publisher, Allen & Unwin, who brought out *Mathematics for the Million*, by . . . Lancelot Hogben. That was in

* Levy first related this incident to me on 10 April 1968, but he made me promise not to make any mention of it to Hogben. Three months later Hogben spontaneously told me the same story, which he forbade me to take back to Levy.

1936, one year after Hogben's election to a Fellowship in the Royal Society. As with his health, his friends and his politics, the thirties had the effect on Hogben of stretching him to the furthest reaches of his rugged individualism. The retreat to Aberdeen came none too soon.

When we turn to the political course taken by Bernal, Levy and Needham, we find no trace of the internal upheavals which Haldane and Hogben were experiencing. As we might have expected, Levy's situation in the 1930s was the easiest to understand. For he was already 'there', well before the Popular Front had commenced. Levy was professionally secure within the limits which he (and others) had placed on his scientific ambitions. He had become a Communist, on terms of mutual respect, at a time when the party was not overly keen on intellectuals. Still more remarkably, in his attempts to unionize scientific workers and popularize scientific socialism, Levy was once again well in advance of the strategies favoured not only by the C.P.G.B. but by his Cambridge allies as well. (His brief broadcasting career is discussed below.) Here we need only add that, if there was any change in Levy's politics, it was in the direction of an even more intimate relationship with the party's internal development. In particular he would devote himself to making improvements in the Communists' educational programmes for its own members, while more conventionally successful intellectuals – Bernal and Haldane, for example – were put on public display.

Indeed Bernal was, somewhat paradoxically, to prove his loyalty to the Communist Party by leaving it as early as 1933.[70] In 'losing' his party card, he was of course free to operate in public as an 'independent' intellectual of Marxist persuasion. Yet like John Strachey Bernal would remain very closely in touch with the party's leadership. His resemblance to Strachey increased when by the late thirties he had emerged as the most widely respected theoretician of the scientific Left. The irony of Bernal's political evolution was that the anonymity and apathy which had previously characterized his Communist leanings would now be officially preserved and put to good use. Hence his most explicitly 'Communist' writings continued to be produced anonymously, at least before the Second World War.[71] Although this ploy had the effect of abetting Bernal's career, its main purpose was to protect his 'uncommitted' status within the scientific community. His own research work was already widely respected: at the age of thirty-six he was elected to a professorship of physics at Birkbeck College, not to mention a Fellowship in the Royal Society. Meanwhile he had become a model Popular Front intellectual, involving himself at one count in more than sixty committees devoted to peace, anti-fascism, civil liberties, Spanish aid, friendship with the U.S.S.R., etc., *ad infinitum*.[72] (On one occasion, when Bernal literally had to be in three places at the same time, Hyman Levy was reputedly driven to inquire: 'Where is that sink of ubiquity?!')[73] Why the pace of Bernal's politics increased so dramatically was not very mysterious. Having undergone his 'conversion' to Marxism in the twenties, he still lacked the means and motives for putting his ideology to work. These missing ingredients finally turned up in the early thirties, not least in the form of a Soviet delegation to an international gathering of historians of science. Thereafter Bernal threw himself into the business of creating what had not previously existed in Britain: namely organizational channels that helped to translate intellectual discontents into socialist grievances. For that job it was useful to be widely known, but not as a 'card-carrying' communist.

Bernal's progress was recapitulated in a rather more muted fashion by Joseph Needham. It was not simply a question of Needham's retiring manner – Bernal was himself a shy man. Nor did they diverge that radically in their political outlooks. Both men were attracted to dialectical materialism, counted themselves as supporters of the Soviet Union and jointly participated in a variety of Popular Front activities. They did, however, differ as to party affiliation. For Needham the Labour Party still represented the most likely agency for bringing about a social revolution in Britain. Naturally he was aware of its many faults, including the conservatism of the party's current leadership. That is why he was one of the most active supporters in Cambridge of the Socialist League, a left-wing ginger group of Labour supporters that tried unsuccessfully in the thirties to turn the national party in a more radical direction.[74] Despite this failure, Needham could not bring himself to admit that his only option was to turn to the Communists. His reticence to do so indicated a number of tacit reservations about their policies. Perhaps the one doubt that came closest to the surface of his public utterances was that the Bolsheviks were possibly too obsessed with social order – and scientific rationality. This objection, which will be elaborated in the next chapter, was perhaps not so surprising, coming as it did from an Anglo-Catholic who still believed in the virtues of a 'balanced' soul. Indeed Needham went out of his way to link together his religious faith and his political principles. For the benefit of his fellow socialists he helped to produce one of the period's most famous documents, *Christianity and the Social Revolution*.[75] But he also spent five years with a small circle of his co-religionists, including the anthropologist Bronislaw Malinowski and the poet T. S. Eliot, who laid the foundations for the Modern Churchman's Conference, which was held in 1937.[76] These efforts helped Needham to prevent his life from being collapsed into a single 'mould of understanding'; in this case political action informed by a Marxist world-view. He was therefore more than prepared to allow Bernal to become, in Needham's words, 'the St Paul of the "science and society movement" of the thirties'.[77]

One final regulator of Needham's political activity was his aspiration to be admitted to the Royal Society. Since the publication of *Chemical Embryology*, his scientific career had gone slightly awry. It was not that his work on 'organizing relations' in embryological development – a collaborative project with Dorothy Needham and C. H. Waddington – was unpromising. No, the problem for this gifted team was finding funds for their expensive and esoteric research. By the mid-thirties they, like Hogben's social biology department, had lost their support grant from the Rockefeller Foundation. While Needham now suffered directly from the world-wide decline of American capitalism, the effect of his victimization was to make him slightly more cautious in his public efforts to weaken that system. For he still did not have his F.R.S. However, Needham by no means ceased to place himself 'on the line' for his political beliefs. Indeed at the beginning of 1936 he wrote to *Nature*,[78] attacking the racist views of Professor E. W. MacBride, an extreme eugenist and a member of the Royal Society's selection committee for Needham's field. When Hogben read Needham's letter, he recognized exactly what his fellow-biologist was risking. 'How brave you are,' read Hogben's message of congratulations and commiseration.[79] But Needham was now prepared to be more selective about the political enterprise to which

he lent his name. A case in point was his decision to publish anonymously a short book he had written on the English Civil War.
'The reason for this', Needham would later confess,

was that I was by this time . . . hoping to get into the Royal Society; and,
as I felt that I was already quite unpopular enough in the *bien pensant* circles,
I thought I never should get in it if I started publishing books about the
Marxist interpretation of the Civil War, etc., however disguised, as a young
scientist should not do. Therefore I wrote it under an assumed name, but I
gave an introduction to it under my real name.[80]

This volume appeared in 1939, bearing on its soft orange cover the
title of *The Levellers and the English Revolution*, the pseudonym of
'Henry Holorenshaw' and the imprint of the Left Book Club.*
Fortunately for Needham, his days of concocting these useful
'fictions' were numbered. In 1941 – less than a year after MacBride's
death – he got his Fellowship and could now be regarded by one
and all as a fully paid up, 'card-carrying' member of the High
Science party.

Though it is fascinating to contemplate the very different ways
in which Bernal, Haldane, Hogben, Levy and Needham worked
their science and their socialism into their lives, we must not lose
sight of their common political role in the thirties. Quite briefly, it
was to serve as socialist spokesmen for the emergent culture of
science. Of course there were variations in how they interpreted
this brief. Some of them concentrated on bringing their message
to scientists rather than non-scientists, party workers instead of
'fellow-travellers' and informal seminars as opposed to large rallies.
But in all contexts they used their prestige and rhetoric to drive

---

* In order to give 'Holorenshaw' a more substantial identity, Needham
managed to persuade the *Cambridge Review* to send his *alter ego* some books to
review on the English Civil War. This was not good enough for a young
Oxford historian named Christopher Hill. 'Who is this guy?' he asked his
friend Roy Pascal. Hill wanted to know more about the author of *The
Levellers and the English Revolution*, for he had a very high opinion of Holorenshaw's work. (C. Hill, letter to R. Pascal, n.d. (c. November, 1938).)

Thirty-five years later 'Holorenshaw' resurfaced, 'as one who knows
[Needham] better than most people', to write an essay on Needham's life. See
'Henry Holorenshaw', 'The Making of an Honorary Taoist', in M. Teich and
R. Young (eds.), *Changing Perspectives in the History of Science* (London, 1974),
pp. 1–20.

home the point that the advancement of science and socialism mutually presupposed one another. As intellectual advocates they could not have been more effective. All of them undeniably had a way with words. They were also well known and controversial enough to fill a lecture hall, found a journal, broadcast over the B.B.C., publish a letter in *The Times* or *Nature* and get their books speedily into print. In other words, they belonged to that restricted part of the population who were expected to exercise political and cultural leadership. As such, they were destined to become some of the brightest 'stars' in the left-wing firmament.

The man who led the way here, yet again, was Hyman Levy. One reason why Levy became a pioneering spokesman for the scientific Left was that, through his involvement with workers' education in the 1920s, he had encountered an extraordinarily energetic biology tutor named Mary Adams. She admired Levy's ability to communicate complex scientific ideas in simple, every-day language. As it happened, Adams was also a producer of wireless talks for the British Broadcasting Corporation. In that capacity she therefore asked him in the autumn of 1930 whether he would like to help plan and execute a series of radio programmes on 'Science in a Changing World'. Naturally he was delighted at the prospect of proselytizing a far larger audience than he had ever reached before. His talks, finally broadcast in the autumn of 1931,[81] were apparently judged to be a great success, for he quickly received offers to do two more batches of programmes. One of these featured a number of interviews between Levy and 'experts from a variety of different fields', including a skilled manual worker. The purpose of these programmes was, in Levy's words, to fashion an 'approach to an activist as opposed to a contemplative philosophical outlook, consistent with scientific possibilities',[82] Through this 'Web of Thought and Action' – the collective title for these dialogues – Levy was introducing his audience to a Marxist perspective on how people come to know the world. Why the knowledge gained in this manner was used in particular ways was the subject of a further set of broadcasts on 'Scientific Research and Social Needs', in which Levy collaborated with Julian Huxley. Though Levy would find it more difficult in later years to use B.B.C. facilities, he had already created a style of popularization, a vocabulary of politics and an image of science which presaged and made easier the subsequent efforts of his left-wing colleagues to communicate to the public at large.

But on at least two counts, Levy was still dissatisfied with these efforts. First, he believed that the impact he made on the wireless would be wasted unless there was a corresponding literature where his listeners could reflect more easily on his ideas. This, too, was an important activity because, as Levy recollected to me in 1968,

Science was [then] a strange thing to people. It was part of their everyday life, but they didn't know it was science and to . . . talk about it in terms that were understandable to them was a very difficult thing, because we had to get rid of all the special scientific terms and speak in simple language, in order to get the ideas across . . .[83]

Levy finally got the Rationalist Press Association's publishers, C. A. Watts, to print under Levy's general editorship not only the broadcasts but other books on the social aspects of science as well. The series was dubbed 'The Library of Science and Culture', and this was its credo.

The outstanding feature of the present age is the extent to which the life of man is affected by the remarkable growth of science. Not only has the development of scientific processes had a profound and disturbing effect on social conditions, but the extension of scientific knowledge and the increasing application of the scientific method in all directions have transformed our mental outlook and evoked new conceptions in history, ethics, philosophy, religion and every phase of culture.

The library of Science and Culture is designed to present to the general reader a picture of the world, both of action and of thought, as science is shaping it. It will reveal how mankind had sought in science the means of satisfying its varied needs, and how, in turn, science is stimulating fresh aspirations, inspiring loftier deeds of progress and awakening hopes of increasing mastery over the destiny of the race.[84]

The bracketing of 'Science and Culture' was itself significant at this time. 'You've got to remember', Levy would later emphasize, that the series was produced 'towards the end of the period when culture was necessarily classical. You weren't a cultured person unless you could read Latin and Greek . . . Mathematics . . . wasn't culture in any sense at all. But now we were . . . passing from one concept of culture to a new outgrowth of culture, a new development of cultural understanding'.[85]

Levy recognized, however, that the popularization of this emergent culture of science had to be carried on in more explicitly political contexts and made an organic component of the labour movement's ideology. That meant seizing every opportunity to hector the Left in the thirties, much as he had harassed the Labour Party in the twenties. For example, as a Communist intellectual, Levy was able to become one of the Left Book Club's most sought-after speakers. Thus when his *A Philosophy of a Modern Man* became an L.B.C. book of the month in 1938, 'Levy was sent on a lecture tour round the [club's] groups to explain his book.' 'He was', in the view of the club's Secretary, John Lewis, 'a brilliant speaker and a considerable wit. He aroused great interest everywhere and people turned to the book with high expectations – which were by no means always satisfied. The book was as tough and recondite as the lectures were racy and delightful.'[86] In his mixture of highly serious writings and down-to-earth lecturing, as well as in his earlier struggles to unionize scientists and work within a political party, Levy deserves to be remembered as the scientific Left's prototypical activist.

The others followed, singly and then collectively; and Levy's contribution began to become eclipsed. The Library of Science and Culture was only a limited success compared with Hogben's 'Primers for an Age of Plenty'. After the mammoth sales of his *Mathematics for the Million*, Hogben wrote the still more widely acclaimed (and sold) *Science for the Citizen* of 1938. The sub-titles of these books offered a clue as to why they were more popular than Levy's. For they were 'Self-Educators Based on the Social Background of Scientific Discovery'. In other words Hogben set out to teach his readers some of the techniques and facts of the science whose social history he was narrating. The 647 pages of *Mathematics* aimed to remove 'the inferiority complex of some of the million or so who have given up hope of learning through the usual channels';[87] while the 1,078 pages of *Science* provided the kind of information Hogben thought would be necessary to equip men and women for full citizenship in a scientific age. The utilitarianism of this approach infuriated pure mathematicians like G. H. Hardy.[88] But it delighted, if not millions, then at least thousands of non-scientists and made Hogben a small fortune.

Behind the format of his primers there was a strong conviction that workers' education had to be rescued from the professional researchers who were taking it over. Indeed Hogben believed that watered-down versions of academic science were very far removed from his projections of a people's science. As he told a W.E.A. annual conference in the thirties:

The adult education movement has no need for biology courses of the kind which exist in the universities. What it needs are courses on malnutrition, public health policy and the revolution of agricultural techniques made possible by present biological discoveries . . . It has no need for elegant expositions of useless literature. It should further the study of languages as a means to peaceful communication between nations. It has no need for university economics, university sociology or university political science. It should be its business to organize courses on the changing structure of industrial management, the recruitment of social personnel, the distribution of income, leisure and educational opportunities, the powers of local government, the new problems of population growth, the social influence of finance capital.[89]

What made Hogben's arguments especially persuasive was the popularity of his books, compared with the declining percentage of workers enrolled in W.E.A. classes, only about 6 per cent of which were devoted to science.[90] In any event, the practical orientation of his writings proved to be more attractive to the reading public than the 'loftier' aspirations embedded in Levy's.

Meanwhile, Bernal, Haldane and Needham were taking up other aspects of the communications breakthrough pioneered by Levy. It was Bernal's achievement to develop further many of the insights which had first been adumbrated in Levy's earlier broadcasts. When his book *The Social Function of Science* appeared in 1939, Bernal was widely acknowledged as the scientific Left's most penetrating theoretician. Unlike Levy, his favoured audience was a more restricted one, whether it was a Communist summer school or an informal discussion with like-minded scientific workers. Such small-scale gatherings were also favoured by Joseph Needham. Haldane, on the other hand, preferred a grander political role; the larger the lecture hall, the better. He had of course the flamboyant manner, the prestigious family name and his own considerable scientific reputation, all of which could guarantee him a relatively large following. But the essential ingredient that made J.B.S. such a great public success was his ability to talk clearly, directly and wittily on any subject. As a stylist he had no peers among the popularizers of science. His science column for the *Daily Worker* in the thirties and forties is still a pleasure to read. Later he would pass on this advice to anyone who intended to write a popular scientific essay

When you have done your article, give it to a friend, if possible a fairly ignorant one. Or put it away for six months and see if you still understand it yourself. You will probably find that some of the sentences which seemed simple when you wrote them now appear very involved. Here are some hints on combing them out. (Remember, by the way, that I am only giving my personal opinions. Professor Hogben writes sentences longer than some of my paragraphs and his books sell very well, as they ought to.) Can you get in a full stop instead of a comma or a semicolon? If so, get it in. It gives your reader a chance to draw his breath. Can you use an active verb instead of a passive verb or verbal noun? If so, use it. Etc. . . .[91]

Haldane adhered to these precepts in his public lectures as well as in his writings. They allowed him to cover an immense range of problems in a very short space of time, often with breathtaking results. By demonstrating his mastery of words in a variety of circumstances, J.B.S. undoubtedly became in the thirties the most widely known member of the Visible College.

Needless to say, the total literary output of these left-wing scientists was prodigious. Besides their hundreds of experimental papers, they produced at least thirty books on 'social' topics between 1931 and 1945. How many speeches and broadcasts they gave is unclear, but Haldane alone was reputed to have kept to a schedule of about a hundred public lectures a year.[92] When they were dissatisfied with the opportunities that already existed for spreading their political message, they simply created new ones. Apart from Hogben's 'primers' and Levy's Library of Science and Culture, they collectively supported the establishment of new periodicals. Thus Hogben, and later Needham, would serve as science editors for the magazine *Fact*, founded in 1937 by Leonard Barnes and Raymond Postgate. The American 'Marxian quarterly', *Science and Society*, numbered among its seven original foreign editors the names of Bernal, Hogben, Levy and Needham. This editorial bias towards scientists was also manifested back in Britain when the *Modern Quarterly*, a heavy-weight intellectual journal controlled by the Communist Party, was founded in 1938. Of the fifteen people who sat on this magazine's Editorial Council, eight were scientists; and they included Bernal, Haldane, Levy and Needham.

So: as advocates and popularizers of scientific socialism, they had no equals on the Left. These men accordingly became its chief spokesmen and leading ideologues on all questions connected with science, through their extraordinary production of published and unpublished material. (Indeed to employ the Soviet jargon of this era, they were veritable 'Heroes of Mental Labour'.) No opportunity or audience would be missed in their double-barrelled efforts to enlighten the world about the scientific dimensions of socialism and the social relations of science. To non-scientists in the Communist Party, the Popular Front and the public at large, they would hammer away at the liberating role that science had played in the early days of capitalism and could play again, once it had broken free from its capitalist shackles. These points would be brought home even more forcibly to their fellow scientists, who were told that there was no certain remedy for their profession's present frustrations, no reasonable hope of personal, scientific or social progress, unless they aligned themselves with the progressive forces of the Popular Front. The extraordinary thing about these appeals (Hogben's dissent aside) was that, unlike in the 1920s, there were now groups of socialists and scientific workers who were ready to heed them. This was partly a tribute to how much the political climate had changed. But it was also a reflection on the efforts of our five central characters that they had got themselves accepted as serious political figures on the Left and as highly esteemed colleagues inside their own professional community. For the two forms of legitimation reinforced one another, simultaneously enhancing the intellectual authority and political effectiveness of these left-wing scientific workers. They were *real* scientists and *authentic* socialists. With these credentials they became uniquely qualified to define and articulate a socialism that was truly scientific.

Chapter Six

Theory

In its endeavour, science is communism.   J. D. Bernal, 1939[1]

Apart from their own research, the main intellectual task of our subjects in the thirties was to meld their political and professional commitments into a coherent outlook, that simultaneously drew scientific workers to the Left and contributed to the development of a Marxist cultural tradition in Britain. No one defined this job with greater accuracy, or carried it out with more skill, than J. D. Bernal. Thus in 1964, twenty-five years after the publication of his *The Social Function of Science*, he could modestly observe that 'we are no longer concerned, *as I was then*, merely to vindicate the growth and use of science in modern civilization'.[2] However, the substance of Bernal's vindication – his detailed presentation of science both as a social institution and as a model socialist enterprise – also represented a novel extension of Marxism. Indeed Bernal went so far as to assert that science, in all its manifestations, was the chief agent of change in society. Though many latter-day left-wingers would dismiss that proposition as untrue and 'un-Marxist', it was not widely disputed within the pre-war Popular Front. Nor, given the historical context, can we imagine how a defence of science by socialists could have resulted in anything other than a fairly literal approach to the question of scientific socialism.

There were many compelling reasons why science came to be perceived as a powerful force that could not be contained within the social framework of a capitalist society. Well before the onset of the crisis-ridden 1930s, socialists as well as scientists had affirmed that, in an important sense, the laws, methods and facts of science transcended all national and social limitations. The difference between the two groups was that, according to the Left, this socially neutral scientific knowledge could never be fully or humanely used under capitalism. John Strachey, undoubtedly the most widely read radical of the inter-war period, ably summed up this tradition when he reminded his followers in 1933 that

For the last half century and more socialists have said with varying degrees of clarity, one thing. They have said that the continued and ever accelerating growth of technical and scientific knowledge . . . did not in itself, as the liberals supposed, ensure a steadily rising standard of life and civilization for the mass of humanity. They said that, on the contrary, . . . it would cause poverty and chaos instead of peace and plenty. They therefore alleged that, since to check technical and scientific progress was both impracticable and profoundly at variance with the permanent interests of the race, it was becoming urgently necessary to abolish the system of the private ownership of the means of production.[3]

In a time of scientific retrogression the urgency of Strachey's argument could not be ignored. The world slump was destroying the industrial fruits of progressive science. In Britain it became more difficult for scientific workers to devote their lives to research. Across the Channel the Nazis appeared to be launching a frontal attack against scientific rationality itself. Meanwhile, as the socialists' old prediction of a growing incompatibility between science and capitalism was being confirmed, no effort was spared in demonstrating that there would be no such conflict in a socialist society. On the one hand, the Left did point with pride to the material and ideological support which scientists in the U.S.S.R. enjoyed. Sidney and Beatrice Webb, in particular, rejoiced in their discovery that, unlike 'the groups of landed proprietors, lawyers, merchants, bureaucrats, soldiers and journalists in command of most other states, the administrators in the Moscow Kremlin genuinely believe in their professed faith; and their professed faith is in science.'[4] But British socialists could also boast of their own efforts to make the Popular Front into, among other things, a platform for the defence of scientific progress. A young communist, writing in 1939 indicated how much importance was then attached to this strategy:

the new approach . . . implied a patient effort to discover those issues which are capable of stirring all honest intellectuals whatever their philosophical, religious or political outlook, into action. These issues proved to be the affirmation that science exists for the furtherance and not for the destruction of human welfare, that man was not made for the machine, but the machine for man; the claim that art and science are worth preserving from fascist savagery and the holocaust of war; the realization that, in a world writhing in agony along the blood-trail of facist aggression, all who have the cause of humanity at heart must unite to preserve our heritage.[5]

Here was an apt, if overwrought restatement of the thesis that the pursuit of science not only stood above the class war but was actually opposed, in the long run, to the preservation of any class-based society as well.

This theme – that it was the advancement of science, not the actions of the working class, which was bringing about the downfall of capitalism (and vice versa) – became a significant one in any country where the Communist Party was allowed to operate in the thirties.[6] Nevertheless, no left-wing movement ever became quite so obsessional about the scientific road to socialism as the one in Britain. That difference in degree was mainly due to the very grave defeat which the British Labour movement had so recently suffered in the General Strike. By comparison with the French proletariat's political *élan* and the dramatic organizational gains of trade unionists in the United States,[7] workers in the U.K. were neither economically nor politically militant. Hence the class struggle was more often than not a submerged feature of the thirties' crisis of British capitalism. What was demonstrably playing havoc with the existing social order was its inability to stage an economic recovery through an effective utilization of the power and instruments of science. While the French and American bourgeoisies were faced with similar problems, they were at least historically allied to a dominant culture that esteemed scientific and technological pursuits.[8] Such was not the case with the British ruling class, which remained wedded to cultural forms that were aristocratic in origin and often hostile to anything that smacked of industrialism, science included.[9] So despite the scientific devotion of monopoly capitalists such as Lord Melchett of Imperial Chemical Industries, Ltd, science still retained a somewhat disreputable aura. It could accordingly be used much more easily by British left-wingers than by their counterparts in France and the U.S.A. as their own distinctive cultural symbol. Yet not even the C.P.G.B. could fully realize what a powerful weapon it now possessed until *The Social Function of Science* had appeared. Indeed Bernal's greatest political achievement was to show his comrades how the socialist transformation of Britain had become a scientific necessity and virtually an historical inevitability.

In view of the range, depth and importance of his writings, we shall therefore devote the major portion of this chapter to Bernal's social thought. As an introduction to 'Bernalism', we can consider the different ways in which Soviet Marxism – the most important intellectual tendency within the Popular Front – influenced the scientific Left's leading ideologues. After examining Bernal's views of science, capitalism and socialism, we may then consider the reservations which Hogben and Needham had about these ideas. Finally, we shall need to remind ourselves of some developments in the U.S.S.R. that, even in the thirties, were already running counter to Bernal's expectations.

1. The Science of Marxism

The widespread dissemination of Soviet Marxism greatly enhanced the British Left's already high estimation of science's progressive role in history. For 'the scientific attitude' was itself deeply rooted in the world outlook of the Communist Party of the Soviet Union. The C.P.S.U.'s doctrine was called dialectical materialism, and it consisted of an interpretation of natural as well as human history. What linked these two phenomena together was that, supposedly, both moved in accordance with the same dialectical laws. The party was of course the custodian of those laws and the guarantor of their 'correct' application to social practice. Actually the communist leadership appeared in this respect to operate more like a scientific than a political élite. Nor was this surprising, in view of its close involvement not only with the planning of science in the U.S.S.R. but with the integration of scientific knowledge into its own world-view as well. An important consequence of the Bolsheviks' ideas and circumstances was that, with some notable exceptions, they, too, revered modern science as a revolutionary force under capitalism, and as an essential ally in their bid to build 'socialism in one country'.

Naturally there were, in theory, other versions of Marxism besides the Soviet model. But they were not readily available to British Marxists in the 1930s. The writings of continental Marxists who criticized the Bolshevik party for its over-valuation of science

– its 'scientism' – were either unpublished or untranslated,[10] as were
the most explicitly 'humanist' works of the young Marx.[11] At least
Leon Trotsky's critique of Stalin's régime could be explored. Yet
its influence was as minimal as the small number of Trotskyists in
Britain at this time might have indicated.[12] This meant that the
Left's sole remaining ideological resources were the local adaptations
of Marxism which had been made by earlier generations of socialists
here. Yet the revolutionary followers of William Morris and the
pre-1914 syndicalists had long since given way to the authority and
discipline of the Communist Party of Great Britain.[13] Consequently
the C.P.G.B. was able to select the texts and interpretations which
together would constitute the 'authorized' version of Marxism.
Besides such standard volumes as *Capital, The Communist Manifesto*
and *State and Revolution*, the party distributed in 1937 *A Handbook
of Marxism* and other guides to the new orthodoxy. Among the
books that were especially recommended to those who wished to
unravel the mysteries of dialectical materialism were Lenin's
Materialism and Empirio-Criticism and Engels' *Anti-Dühring*. Later
they were supplemented by Stalin's own pronouncements and the
first English translation of Engels' *The Dialectics of Nature*, not to
mention Hyman Levy's *A Philosophy for a Modern Man*. Such was
the literature which introduced British socialists to a new world-
view and led them to equate Marxism with Soviet-style *diamat*.

The concept of science occupies a pivotal position in orthodox
textbooks of dialectical materialism from this period, because
persons and even social classes do not. To the Soviet dialectician
this assertion represents a monstrous parody. Therefore his interest
in this (false) idea is to explain how it arose. Our interest in his
explanation is that it may help us to understand how his philosophy
works.

1. My *idea* runs counter to Soviet Marxism.
2. That idea belongs to an *ideological 'superstructure'* that helps to preserve
the power of the ruling class.
3. That ideological superstructure, in turn, reflects the needs of the
economic base, which comprises the class system and the production system.
4. The economic base, however, is socially *unstable* (hence the need for the
superstructure), because changes in the *production system* are undermining
the class system.
5. The production system is changing, because *new technologies* have

brought about changes in the division of labour, the efficiency of firms, etc.

6. The new technologies have arisen through the application of *science*.

7. Though science is closely wedded to production, its advancement has come through its willingness to follow and discover the laws of *nature*.

8. But what is nature, if not a series of complex aggregations of *matter in motion*?

9. The achievement of Marxism-Leninism has been to unravel the *general laws of motion* which underlie all natural, social and human phenomena.

10. These laws are '*dialectical*' in character, and they include: 'the law of the transformation of quantity into quality; the law of the interpenetration of opposites, and the law of the negation of the negation'.

11. Hence any attacks on dialectical materialism are an affront to scientific rationality and the laws of nature, as well as of the Soviet Union. As such they are 'irrational' and presumed therefore, to be 'ideologically inspired'.

Many Soviet proponents of dialectical materialism were then quite fond of this type of reasoning (despite Engels' warnings about such 'reductionism' and 'mechanical materialism'). Ideas often became mere 'reflections' of class interests. Technological changes were seen to 'determine' the course of social development. Perhaps most seriously of all, the 'general laws of motion' tended to replace the self-emancipation of the working class as the prime mover behind the eventual – and 'inevitable' – triumph of socialism. In this philosophical universe the closer one got to 'nature' and production, the more one's ideas would evolve in a 'scientific' and 'Marxist' direction. Even the metaphors betrayed how deeply implicated the dialectical materialists were in their defence of the (ideologically neutral?) natural sciences.

As we might have expected, Soviet Marxism's emphasis on scientific necessity made good sense in the Soviet Union. On the one hand, it bolstered the Bolsheviks' future-directed faith that the forces of natural as well as human history really were on their side. On the other, it focused attention upon the scientific and industrial prerequisites which this underdeveloped country had to fulfil, if its revolution were going to survive in an openly hostile world. As Stalin declared only six months before Bukharin's delegation flew off to London: 'In ten years at most we must cover the distance which separates us from the advanced countries of capitalism'. How could this awesome task be accomplished? Stalin answered: 'The Bolsheviks must master technology. It is time for the

Bolsheviks themselves to become specialists,' for 'during the period of reconstruction *technique decides everything*'.[14] By 'technique' he meant pre-eminently the science and technology of Western capitalism.

But the Soviet dictator was interested in scientific knowledge as a means of advancing the party's ideological hegemony as well as the U.S.S.R.'s economic development. This attempted integration of the natural sciences with the 'science' of Marxism had the effect of bestowing upon the C.P.S.U.'s Central Committee the power to define the scientific limits of natural and social reality. In the pursuit of that objective it was, as one British Communist put it in 1930, about 'as dogmatic as . . . a group of biologists charged with overhauling the educational system of a Fundamentalist Middle West' community in the United States.[15] This was the political background to the Soviets' tremendous interest in the philosophy and practices of theoretical science. Hence 'it was no accident' that an American historian would one day discover that dialectical materialism, as a 'systematic interpretation of nature', was 'the most original creation of Soviet Marxism' in this period.[16] Nevertheless, this chorus of praise for science did not prevent the régime from closely overseeing the activities of its scientific workers, most of whom were still 'bourgeois specialists'. As long as Soviet researchers were led by these potentially untrustworthy elements, Stalin would refuse to declare *officially* that their research had become an ideologically neutral 'force of production'. Yet in practice that was how their work was normally treated. And that was as it should have been; because no world-view could have been more heavily underpinned by the theories, methods, findings and applications of science than dialectical materialism.

While the C.P.S.U. had no difficulty in exporting *diamat* to its British comrades, it could hardly expect them to recreate the social context which supported this formidable philosophical system. Shorn of its Soviet trappings, we must admit that dialectical materialism did display the kind of objectivity, austerity and 'lawfulness' that we normally associate with a piece of 'hard' science. Yet deprived of its specific social function – the ideological prop of Stalin's absolutist rule – this world outlook quickly broke down into its many component parts. The most important of these was historical materialism, which consisted in the main of Marx's account of the social processes that had given rise to (and would lead to the decline of) international capitalism. As for the science of the general laws of motion, or the dialectics of nature, or Marxist biology, they were initially seen to be peripheral, possibly bogus aspects of Soviet philosophy. Certainly that was Hyman Levy's immediate reaction. In 1933 he remarked that 'the almost medieval language in which . . . references to the laws [of dialectics] are phrased is itself repellent to the scientific man. He finds it difficult to believe that generalities of this nature can really mean much in practice', especially when compared with 'the carefully detailed phraseology of his own scientific findings'.[17] Such a response infuriated party philosophers like Clemens Dutt, who lamented in the same year that 'the bulk of scientific workers in England, even among those who are inclined to support Marxism as a scientific reading of social developments [historical materialism], are profoundly unacquainted with dialectical materialism'. What alarmed Dutt here was that, in his view and that of his Soviet mentors, historical materialism had no 'scientific basis' without the dialectical system, which dealt with both the 'content and form of the laws relating to physical nature, history and thinking'.[18]

By the end of the thirties our subjects had partially mended their 'undialectical' ways. Haldane was now able to show how easily the recent findings of physics, chemistry and biology could be expressed in the new Soviet idiom.[19] Needham had in the meantime been drawn to the dialectics of nature, which, like his own philosophy of 'organizational levels', was predicated on the existence of evolutionary forces that were inexorably bringing about world socialism.[20] Levy made a remarkable *volte face* by becoming the scientific Left's most assiduous popularizer of the dialectical method of thinking, both in science[21] and in 'everyday life'.[22] Yet, as we might have expected, it was Bernal who first affirmed his allegiance to Soviet Marxism, with the striking assertion in 1934 that 'dialectical materialism is the most powerful factor in the thought and action of the present day. Even its most bitter enemies are forced to recognize its analysis and ape its methods.'[23] Whether Bernal's nostrum applied to other opponents of Soviet thought, it certainly did not inhibit Lancelot Hogben's unrepentant hostility to dialectical materialism. In his book of 'dangerous thoughts' Hogben amplified his earlier dismissal of all this 'obscurantist rubbish'.

The inner necessity of the dialectic, which supposedly guarantees the overthrow of the employing class, rests on the identification of history with the reasoning process; as a corollary of the belief that ultimate reality is mental. In other words, the dialectic is a purely idealistic device which has no special relevance to any creed which is essentially behaviouristic; as are the views which Marx sets forth in his notes on Feuerbach. Hence dialectical materialism is a confusion of terms.[24]

Clemens Dutt retorted that Hogben's materialism was naïve and 'vulgar'.[25] Otherwise Dutt ought to have been well pleased with the progress made by his scientific confederates.

At the same time we must admit that the leading ideologues of the scientific Left had in no way made their science and politics dependent upon their belief in dialectical materialism. The bulk of their Marxist studies were still concerned with the historical and, more particularly, the contemporary aspects of the 'social relations' of science. It was also apparent that, aside from occasional ventures on the part of Bernal, Haldane and Needham into theoretical biology,[26] their excursions into dialectics remained external to their mainline scientific researches. They were reluctant to go further, partly because, as mature scientists, their investigations were already enmeshed in a web of fully tested methods, techniques and assumptions. Hence even Bernal was prepared to concede that

the essential task of any comprehensive understanding of the universe is not to build up an abstract system of connections and deductions in which experience will fit; but to use experience in its already most highly organized state of scientific knowledge, where it exists, to suggest its own form of interconnections and developments. The game must come before the rules and not the rules before the game.[27]

However much Bernal's rules/game distinction begged the very questions which dialectical materialism had been supposed to answer, it testified to the weight of the scientific 'givens' in his life. Indeed he and his associates believed not only in the relative autonomy of science but also in the possibility that dialectical materialism could be, in Bernal's words, '*derived* from . . . [natural] science'.[27] Joseph Needham agreed, when he described Marxism as the 'quintessence of the scientific method itself'.[28] Whether it was 'kosher' in a Marxist sense to make dialectics dependent upon science, it was logically consistent with the exalted political and ideological roles which Soviet Marxists had assigned to scientific knowledge. Was orthodoxy thereby being transformed (dialectically) into a 'scientistic' heresy?

That was not the way it appeared to Bernal, for one, in the 1930s. He prided himself on his understanding of and allegiance to orthodox Marxism; and he was absolutely convinced that the Soviet world-view had both confirmed and illuminated his belief in science as the most powerful and progressive force in human history. On the basis of his scientific and socialist convictions Bernal was accordingly able to construct an intellectual framework that was as arresting as it was influential.

2. 'Bernalism'

The central purpose behind all of Bernal's writings is to show that only in socialist society can science take its rightful place as the chief servant of human liberation. To bolster this argument Bernal regularly relies upon his considerable ability to speculate concretely and persuasively about the future. Once he has sketched out how good things could be, his next move is to show how the structural limitations of capitalism as a social system prevent it from using science effectively and humanely. Obviously Bernal would like to see those constraints removed, but the great question is 'How?' Here his imagination fails him. Yet he is quite certain that the transformation he seeks will take place. His faith apparently derives from the irreversible historical tendencies which he has detected in the course of his many examinations of the social relations of science. Of these forces, the most important by far is science itself: the prototype of all human action, not least the organizational forms of a socialist world order. Hence if we are to understand Bernal's socialism we must first come to terms with what he takes to be science.

His definition of science is exceedingly broad, ultimately asocial and highly reified. For a start Bernal uses the term to connote and relate a series of connected, albeit distinct activities. The usage is implicitly followed in *The Social Function of Science*, to the great annoyance of some reviewers. But in his later work, *Science in History*, Bernal openly avows and justifies this practice. There he remarks that science is, variously, an institution, a method, a cumulative tradition of knowledge, 'a major factor in the maintenance and development of production' and 'one of the most powerful influences moulding beliefs and attitudes to the universe and man'.[29] With that range of practices in mind, it is inescapably the case that science has social relations, and that these will vary over time and between different modes of production. In a capitalist society, for example, it is the dominant class which, in the final analysis, decides the direction, pace, amount and applications of basic research.[30] Moreover, Bernal continues, capitalism's rulers can also use their control of the educational system to pre-select the kind of people they wish to see operating inside the scientific community.[31] He finally concedes that the philosophical and political *interpretations* usually placed on scientific theories are simply elaborate forms of bourgeois ideology.[32] In all these senses we can speak of 'capitalist science'.

But Bernal also recognized that, for many workers in twentieth-century Britain, science as such must now appear to be indistinguishable from capitalism. At no time was his recognition of this view sharper than after the first explosion of a 'nuclear device' in 1945.

The identification of science with the governing and exploiting classes has from the earliest times of class division . . . engendered a deep suspicion of science . . . in the minds of the peasants and, to a lesser degree, of the working classes . . . In the Middle Ages science existed only on sufferance, and, even after its rebirth, the same popular reaction was to be seen in the machine wreckers of the Industrial Revolution. Today we can still see it in the reactions to the latest triumph of science, the atomic bomb. The combined effects of the contempt and ignorance of the learned, and of the suspicion and resentment of the lower orders, has been through the whole course of civilization a major hindrance to the free advance of science. [But science] has replaced an unwilling and grudging cooperation for the free and active exchange of practical and theoretical knowledge that can, as experience in socialist countries is now beginning to show, greatly increase the rate of technical and scientific advance.[33]

Here Bernal is both asserting and denying the 'class character' of science. On the one hand, he seems to be saying that the machine wreckers and their successors were correct in their perceptions of scientific technologies as capitalist tools of social domination. On the other hand, such opposition has had the effect of hindering the 'free advance of science', a process whose essentially classless and non-oppressive nature can only be revealed in a socialist setting. So Bernal apparently does believe that science, here defined as 'the free and active exchange of practical and theoretical knowledge', both transcends particular societies and is neutral with respect to social values. Science can thus be a class or classless activity, depending on whether it is practised under capitalism or socialism.*

The way is now clear for the treatment (reification) of science as a quasi-human entity endowed with extraordinary capacities. Thus: 'Science, conscious of its purpose, can in the long run become a major force in social change. Because of the powers which it holds in reserve, it can ultimately dominate the other [economic and political] forces.'[34] On first reading those sentences make no sense. Something called science can no more be 'conscious of its purpose' than a cabbage. Only human beings possess that attribute. But the substitution of scientists for science would imply the possibility that they can (and very well may) seize power from the ruling class (or the proletariat, for that matter). The absurdity of such a notion, save in science fiction, is quite apparent to Bernal (see below), though his earlier *The World, the Flesh and the Devil* had suffered from such scientific megalomania. Are we therefore simply confronted with a stylistic lapse, or a convenient figure of speech? Unfortunately we are not; or rather Bernal's language expresses quite well his belief that there is a being – and not merely a tradition – called science, and it is the prime mover of human history. Here then is a fuller version of his main thesis.

We have spoken of science in its application both to the satisfaction of human needs and to the processes of productive industry . . . So far science comes in . . . only as a means of satisfying desires *in which science itself takes no part*. Science appears as *a slave to social forces foreign to itself*; it appears as an external and uncomprehended force, useful but dangerous, holding a

* In *The Social Function of Science* (London, 1939, p. 409), Bernal admits that 'capitalism was essential to the early development of science, giving it for the first time a practical value'. However, this admission of modern science's historical specificity is not seen to have any bearing on the use of that knowledge in a socialist society. Indeed Bernal and other Marxists in this period believe that scientific theories are ideologically neutral precisely to the extent that their 'practical value' can be demonstrated in production.

position in society like that of a captive workman at the court of some savage monarch. To a large extent this does represent the position of science in modern capitalist society; but if this were all, we should have little to hope for either from science or from society. Fortunately science has a third and more important function. It is the chief agent of change in society; at first, unconsciously as technical change, paving the way to economic and social changes; and latterly, as a more conscious and direct motive for social change itself.[35]

This credo becomes more intelligible if we recall how Bernal defines science. While he insinuates it deeply into the cultural and productive systems of humankind, he simultaneously removes science from any particular historical context. He thereby preserves its detachment from the specific and diverse forms which our understandings of nature have taken over the centuries. The power of this vision lies in its presentation of an almost redemptive force that is slowly but surely leading men and women from one social order into another. However, its strength is also its weakness. For the logic of Bernal's system impels him to attribute to science – say, the atomic bomb – what others would assign to the actions of specific social groups (scientists included). In other words, at the heart of his dialectical materialism we find a purely idealistic conception of science.* That is why Bernal's Marxism, like that of his Soviet counterparts, is always in danger of becoming 'History with the people; i.e. social classes left out'.

If we accept Bernal's comprehensive, almost cosmic definition of science, then we must also follow his ideological lead. As he rightly observes, 'any widespread appreciation of the results of science, of the possibilities that it offers to humanity, or of its

---

* This divided aspect of Bernal's social thought, and that of the scientific Left in general, has tripped up numerous commentators. Thus on page 57 of his *Science and the Social Order* (New York, 1962 ed.), Bernard Barber first sums up the work of Bernal and his cohorts this way: 'The burden of the Marxian view on these matters is that science is a wholly dependent part of society, moulded fundamentally by the economic factor; . . . [with] no reciprocal influence between science and the other components of society.' But 235 pages later Barber concludes his examination of the British 'scientific humanists', principally Bernal, by saying: 'they tended to absolutize science as a value in itself, or at least they ignored its interdependence with many other needs and values of a society'. Barber's confusion is understandable: Bernal at times seemed to hold both of those positions.

methods of criticism, cannot fail to have large social and political implications'.[36] Indeed an important measure of social progress is the degree to which scientific workers are 'free' to pursue their investigations. But for Bernal scientific freedom does not merely mean 'the absence of prohibitions on this or that research or theory'.

The full freedom of science [he maintains] goes much further. It is useless to permit a research if at the same time the funds to carry on that research are unprocurable . . . But even if means are provided . . ., science is yet not fully free. The complete circle of scientific activity is only closed when that discovery is fully incorporated, both as an idea and as a practicable application, in contemporary society.[37]

Bernal concludes that the 'freedom of science needs to be considered in its modern aspect as freedom to act and not merely to think'.[38] In an ideal state scientific change would encounter little or no social friction. Yet to reach that state of perfection, society itself would have to be remodelled along scientific lines. That in fact is the visionary 'punch-line' to be found on the final page of *The Social Function of Science*:

in the practice of science we have the prototype for all human common action . . . In its endeavour, science is communism. In science men have learned consciously to subordinate themselves to a common purpose without losing the individuality of their achievements. [Only] in this willing collaboration can each man find his goal . . . Facts cannot be forced to our desires, and freedom comes by admitting this necessity and not by pretending to ignore it.[39]*

By this stage we should realize that Bernal's analysis of the social

* This is the central and most widely quoted passage in all of Bernal's writings. Hogben uses it to cap his own ideological credo. (See *Lancelot Hogben's Dangerous Thoughts* (London, 1939), p. 24). The biologist C. H. Waddington also cites it as 'a very fine statement of the aims and method of science, whether or not one agrees that in acting this way scientists are behaving like communists'. (From Waddington's *The Scientific Attitude* (Harmondsworth, 1941), p. 77.) In fact, the notion that science is a form of communism is not so partisan as it might sound. Robert Merton, the American functionalist sociologist, employs it as well in his *Social Theory and Social Structure*, 3rd ed. (New York, 1968), pp. 610–12. Whether this is a useful concept for understanding how scientists actually function has been questioned recently, in S. B. Barnes and R. G. A. Dolby, 'The Scientific Ethos: A Deviant Viewpoint', *European Journal of Sociology*, vol. 11 (1970), pp. 3–25.

relations of science represents nothing less than an attempt to fashion a 'new philosophical and historical outlook', which he hopes 'will serve to integrate human society as effectively as but more intelligently and flexibly than did the religions of past ages'.[40] Some commentators have dubbed this creed 'scientific humanism'; I should prefer to call it 'Bernalism'. Whatever its designation, it is the scientific world-view that allows Bernal and his cohorts to mount a comprehensive attack upon the capitalist institutions of their day.

Bernal's indictment of capitalism rests upon the following paradox. Many would agree that, especially in a time of widespread unemployment and privation, our 'primary social aim' must be the establishment of 'a working productive organization consciously directed to the satisfaction of human needs'.[41] If this endeavour ever materializes, then it will be thanks in no small measure to the collective efforts of natural scientists. For it already 'lies within the immediate capacity of physical science to solve completely the material problems of human existence'. Yet, Bernal observes,

this often repeated statement carries no conviction or satisfaction. Most people feel by actual experience that physical science will not be applied in this way, and, even if it were, the result would not be a real improvement of human welfare. The best application of science is conceived of as producing such a fatuous and stultifying paradise as Huxley's *Brave New World*; at worst, a super-efficient machine for mutual destruction with men living underground and only coming up in gas masks.[42]

So many distrust and fear science, even though it alone can deliver them from the material circumstances which most directly deform their lives. To Bernal this disturbing 'contradiction' arises out of the inability of the ruling class to apply scientific knowledge fully, effectively and humanely. Rather than admit that inefficiency and inhumanity are inescapable components of a profit-oriented production system, the bourgeoisie encourages the belief that it is science which is responsible for these evils. Obviously this pose not only shields the capitalists from their would-be critics but, in a social crisis, endangers the scientific enterprise as well. On behalf of his profession and his politics, Bernal must therefore persuade 'the people', scientists included, who their real oppressors are.

In the context of British capitalism in the 1930s, it is easy to see how the efforts of all scientific workers are both wasted and restricted. Science, according to Bernal, has already been transformed into 'an industry supported by large industrial monopolies and by the state'.[43] Yet the cult of science's 'purity' flourishes as never before. What helps to nourish this illusion is that, in Britain at least, industrialized science is undercapitalized and poorly managed. Only a tenth of a per cent of the Gross National Product is devoted to scientific research and development.[44] (In the 1960s this country's 'R. & D.' bill was anything from twenty to thirty times that figure.)[45] But not only is the amount of money available for scientific investigations 'ludicrously small, but also the greater proportion of what is spent is wasted on account of internal inefficiency and lack of coordination'.[46] Hence funds are poorly distributed. In industry small firms do not have the capital, while monopolistic enterprises, in Bernal's view, lack the incentive, to extend the writ of science in production.[47] At the universities financial support for long-term investigation is wildly sporadic and biased in favour of the physical over the biological sciences.[48] All of these distortions point to a common pattern of mismanagement. Perhaps this is to be expected of civil servants and industrialists who are commonly unversed in scientific matters. Their ignorance, combined with their mania for shrouding all types of researches in secrecy, effectively stymie all attempts to coordinate and apply science more effectively.[49] Bernal is, if anything, even more critical of senior academics, who are the self-appointed managers of High Science. Indeed so removed is this 'gerontocracy' from the frontiers both of pure and applied work, that it constitutes 'the greatest factor in holding up the advance of science'.[50] Whether that is the case or not, we cannot deny that today the morale of all scientific workers, whatever their institutional location, is as low as their pay and their status. However, the key to the solution of all these problems is currently in the hands of the ruling class. Science will only be supported when those who control production wish to expand it. They cannot do so at the moment because, if they did, still more millions of people would be thrown out of work.[51] Consequently, science is now relatively starved, unapplied – and 'pure'.

Yet this enforced retreat of academic scientists into the 'cleaner' atmosphere of abstract theory may not prove to be an adequate refuge for long.[52] For example, a bourgeoisie that lost the ability both to use science and to rule in the old way might encourage the public to revolt against scientific rationality itself. That is how Bernal accounts for the rise of fascism in Germany.[53] Whatever the cause, it is quite self-evident that, once in power, the Nazis have quite consciously set out to attack international science, in the name of their half-baked, mystical and irrational ideology. They have concocted the disciplines of 'Nordic biology' and 'Aryan physics', in order to justify their racist outrages against the German Jewish community, including of course a number of distinguished scientists led by Albert Einstein. Meanwhile the quantity and quality of pure research practised under the Nazi regime has declined. What scientific investigations are tolerated seem to be bent toward predominantly military ends. That of course is an ominous sign, which would suggest that other European scientific communities are no longer immune from Hitler's attack upon science. Already in Britain Oswald Mosley's fascists are using eugenic and other pseudo-scientific arguments to whip up anti-semitic feelings. Though not strong at the moment, British fascism is poised to advance should the economic crisis worsen. The more immediate threat to science and democracy here, however, still emanates from Germany. For the Nazis' militarism and nationalism, unchecked by any rational or humane considerations, are bound to lead them into war. That is why, in September 1938, Bernal is convinced that 'science itself, for the first time since the Renaissance, seems in danger'.[54]

Indeed simply the menace of fascism is at this moment transforming British science, in the form of its increasing militarization. Between 1933 and 1937 expenditure on defence research rose by 50 per cent.[55] A year later Bernal is able to estimate that, conservatively, 'between one-third and one-half of the money spent on scientific research in Britain is spent directly or indirectly on war research . . . And this in peace time'.[56] While this support helps to fatten up the body scientific, it nonetheless serves to weaken Bernal's profession. Once again science becomes identified with the destructive tendencies of capitalism. The secrecy of military research leads not only to a further breakdown in science's internationalism (and its efficiency) but to a decided curtailment of many scientists' civil liberties. To make matters worse, it is not

4. J.B. Bernal *(back row, centre)* in Cambridge around 1935, with members of the Cavendish's Crystallographic Sub–Laboratory. Dr W.A. Wooster stands at the far right of the back row

5. Dorothy and Joseph Needham in 1927 at a workbench in the Dunn Biochemistry Institute, Cambridge

6 and 7. Getting their message across to the public: Hyman Levy *(above)* broadcasting a science programme for the BBC in the early thirties; J.B.S. Haldane *(below)* attempting to stir up a 'United Front' meeting in Trafalgar Square in January 1937

8. An experiment that backfired. In 1938 the Cambridge Scientists' Anti-war Group attempted to confirm a report from Spain that an incendiary bomb could set alight a multi-storey building by burning through several floors in succession.

The experiment was entrusted to Maurice Wilkins, then an undergraduate protégé of J.D. Bernal and W.A. Wooster. Wilkins set up his apparatus in Wooster's garden. But, as the photographs show, Wilkins' wooden planks were more than a match for his 'bomb'.

Despite his failure here, Wilkins decided to continue his scientific career, which subsequently led to his Nobel Prize-winning collaboration with Crick and Watson on the structure of DNA

9. Needham in China. As Director of the Sino-British Science Co-operation Office, Joseph Needham inspects the scientific facilities of Ch'engtu, Szechuan in 1943

10. Author and publisher. Sir Stanley Unwin *(left)* with his best-selling author, Lancelot Hogben in 1944

11,12. The Soviet connection. A Russian teenager appears to have Hyman Levy *(above, head on hand)* stumped in a chess game played at a 'Pioneer Camp' near Moscow in the early 1950s. *Below*, Nikita Khruschev greets J.D. Bernal *(right)*, then chairman of the World Peace Congress, Peking 1959.

13. A smiling Hogben leaves
Birmingham Crown Court in
1952 after being acquitted of
a charge of driving 'while
under the influence'

14. Hyman Levy in 1972 at
the age of 83 as ready as ever
to make his point

15. J.B.S. Haldane in Indian dress on the streets of Monaco in 1961

16. Joseph and Dorothy Needham, sixty years in Cambridge and fifty years of married life

even clear whether Britain's armed services will ever be deployed in Bernal's oblique phrase, on behalf of 'the principles of democracy and civilization',[57] by which he means in defence of Britain and the U.S.S.R. against the fascist powers. The one positive feature of science's assimilation into the war machine is that, 'more than anything else', it 'has made scientists look beyond the field of their own inquiries . . . to the social uses to which their discoveries are put'.[58] The limitations of the retreat into pure science have at last been discovered. Perhaps researchers will now begin to appreciate that the frustration of their science is, as Bernal claims, an inescapable feature of the capitalist mode of production.

That argument is enormously strengthened when one considers the very different fate of science under socialism. For 'the cornerstone of the [Soviet] Marxist state', Bernal assures us, 'is the utilization of human knowledge, science and technique, directly for human welfare'.[59] Let us rely here, as Bernal himself does in *The Social Function of Science*,[60] on the observations of Martin Ruhemann, a physicist who had actually worked at a Russian research institute in the 1930s.[61] Ruhemann notes that both ideology and necessity have led the Communist Party of the Soviet Union to push the scientific method into all spheres of social life.

> The most fundamental concept in the Soviet world outlook is that the arrangements which people make among themselves for producing the necessities of life . . . depend on the extent to which the inhabitants have made nature serve their needs. To a people with such a 'philosophy', scientific research – that is, the process of mastering nature's laws – must acquire particular significance, since *its results are considered to determine the whole structure of society*. That the specific needs of the Soviet people, and their position in relation to the rest of the world, literally forced this outlook upon them, can only enhance its effect, and explain the constant attention paid to scientific research by the Soviet authorities . . .[62]

Besides confirming our earlier judgements about the 'scientism' inherent in Soviet *diamat*, Ruhemann is able to demonstrate how and to what extent the scientific attitude has entered into the lives of the Russian people. His favourite example of a people's science is 'Stakhanovism'. Named after a coal miner in the Donetz Basin, the Stakhanovites are celebrated in the U.S.S.R. for their efforts to boost production. Most of their improvement came through their own rediscovery of piece-rate methods of work,

7

which had the effect of putting them into competition with each other for a larger wage-packet and of breaking down a complex job into a series of simple, monotonous tasks. Such techniques are also well known to workers in a capitalist society. The difference is that here piece-rates and other forms of speed-up have to be imposed in the form of 'scientific management', whereas in Russia they can be introduced as the invention of, literally, scientific workers. Of the many conclusions that might be drawn from this contrast, these are the ones selected by Ruhemann.

It is nowhere contended that these 'Stakhanovites' are particularly clever, and probably their results might have been attained by any normally intelligent person giving his mind to the question. The point is that the kind of reasoning applied by Stakhanov and his followers is in no way different from the reasoning of a scientist confronted by a problem in his own sphere. To be a Stakhanovite requires not so much cleverness or even an undue stock of intelligence; what it does require is just the scientific outlook of which we have been speaking. The fact that many thousands of persons are beginning to share this outlook is a momentous fact in Soviet history: not only does it bear out Marxist theory and justify the government policy, but it enables things to be done from below which could never have been done from above.[63]

In this context the repeated stress on 'intelligence' is rather jarring, as is the implicit suggestion that the regimentation of working life is a *direct* consequence of applying the scientific method to problems of production. Yet Ruhemann unflinchingly makes that connection. So, too, does Bernal: Russian 'workers are encouraged in every way to assist actively in the application of science to industry . . . In the Soviet Union the great Stakhanov movement is an impressive proof of the possibility of workers themselves taking a leading part in transforming the processes of industry.'[64] The essential background to this development is a state that stresses the supreme role of science in all spheres of social life.

Such whole-hearted commitment is bound to be reflected in the lives of Soviet scientists. Because their work is identified with the liberation rather than the oppression of the people, the morale of professional researchers is correspondingly much higher. They are esteemed figures in Soviet popular culture and important advisors to the state planning authorities. Given the low level of scientific achievement in pre-revolutionary Russia, it is not surprising that the quality and quantity of research there does not yet exceed that done in Britain. But the Soviets have already established the pre-condition for a *scientific* revolution that will exceed in size and comprehensiveness all previous leaps forward in the history of science. For a start the U.S.S.R. spends proportionately ten times as much as the U.K. on all aspects of research and development.[65] Moreover this expenditure is not dissipated in the form of periodic restrictions on funds, gross mismanagement and poor coordination between different sectors of the scientific-industrial complex. For the common ownership of the means of production in the Soviet Union allows the state to engage in long-range economic planning. In these conditions it is also possible, in close consultation with the scientific community, to plan the advancement of science itself. However, the *conscious* integration of scientific workers into the vaunted Five Year Plans means that Soviet scientists can enjoy greater 'freedom' than their counterparts in the West. Not only is there widespread recognition of the need for unfettered basic research, but scientific investigators can be confident that their ideas will be fully incorporated into production and culture as well. Compared to that picture, the consolations of pure science strike Bernal as 'mean', in both senses of the term.

At last we can appreciate the breadth and power of Bernal's critique of capitalist society. Clearly he has offered many good reasons why 'the present economic system and the advance of science cannot for much longer go on together. Either science will be stifled and the system itself go down in war and barbarism, or the system will have to be changed to let science get on with its job.'[66] Though both of these contingencies are possible, Bernal believes that, on balance, the hour of the socialist transformation first predicted by Marx is fast approaching.[67] Nevertheless he cautions the Left against any overly optimistic reading of history. Capitalism, which had originally 'made science possible', is in a dying but dangerous state. It would be wrong to think that the ruling class will be overthrown simply because 'science [now] makes capitalism superfluous'.[68] In other words, science can only bring the people to the brink of a revolution; it is they who must finally initiate it. As Bernal almost grudgingly concedes, 'the events of the future do not come to [men] as blind fate, but partly, ever so little, as the result of their own efforts'.[69]

How the transition to socialism is to be made is nowhere clearly
stated in any of Bernal's writings. He is confident that this change
will be achieved through the guidance of the Communist Party,
whose 'revolutionary leaders . . . represent most completely and
consciously the social forces actuating the great mass of their
followers'.[70] Why should the party be allowed to exercise this
degree of hegemony over the revolutionary movement? Bernal
replies: because its leadership has been and will continue to be drawn
from the ranks of 'those who can see the wider possibilities, through
the discipline of science, natural and dialectical, philosophy [etc.,
and who] can therefore analyse, plan and act for humanity as a
whole'.[71] This formulation, while it prefigures the role Bernal will
allot to the intelligentsia of a socialist society, still does not tell us
how the revolution will be carried out. All he will concede is that
'changing societies are full of violence and apparent cruelty: the
cruelty that unhesitatingly sweeps aside all the sentiments of people
who for one reason or another cannot adapt themselves to the rate
of change'.[72] Since Bernal is already persuaded that, in the absence
of a proletarian revolution, such cruelty (and worse) is likely to
visit the working class in the form of fascism, he has no hesitation
in opting for the socialist alternative. For in a general crisis of
capitalism there is ultimately no middle way between fascist and
socialist dictatorships; between a production system that serves a
tiny minority and one that works on behalf of all the people.

The superficiality of the similarities between fascism and socialism
immediately becomes apparent when we examine Bernal's vision
of the social relations of science in a post-revolutionary society.*

* We must be careful here about our characterization of Bernal's projection
of an ideal science. In *The Social Function of Science* he simply notes (p. 241) that
'to allow science to grow freely for the benefit of humanity presupposes a
change in society itself. For our immediate purpose it is not necessary to
stipulate in detail what that change should be. It will be sufficient to assume
that it would be a society that actively desired that science should be developed
and used for human welfare, and that it would be prepared to provide the
means for that development and for the most effective utilization of its results.'
Whether it would be possible for a capitalist society to move in this direction
depends partly on problems of definition and partly on one's estimates of the
viability of capitalism as an economic system. Because in the thirties it is just
plausible to imagine that the world economy might break down completely,
Bernal is exonerated from specifying which part, if any, of his scientific
reorganization of society could be achieved in a more prosperous phase of

The first priority of any socialist regime must be to establish an optimal biological and social environment for all its citizens. Everyone will therefore have the right and duty to work for their own and the common good. Since 'the part that people play in the productive mechanism will for a long time determine the quality of their social relations',[73] the moral authority of the new order will necessarily be founded on cooperative values.

The central demand of the new morality [Bernal makes clear] is that we should work our best with our fellows for a common purpose. This implies many demands both on the individual and on society that were never made before. It demands goodwill and cooperation; it demands intelligence and initiative; it demands unlimited responsibility for every action. These are not separate demands but linked closely with each other. The new society is not a society of instinctive robots like those of bees and ants: it is one of conscious and diverse human beings. It is not one ruled by a 'Fuhrer Prinzip', in which each man is only responsible for carrying out the demands imposed on him by his superior. It is up to everyone to find his place and to do his best in it, not for himself but for the society of his fellows.[74]

This means that men and women are free to take up any position that suits their fully developed talents and fulfils a socially useful purpose. The fraternity gained from the realization of an efficient system of production thus becomes, in the eyes of society, the source of equality between all of its members; true liberty flows from the recognition of social and natural necessity. At this juncture we perceive that 'from each according to his abilities, to each according to his needs' is a maxim affirmed by Bernal not as an ideal but as 'the only way in which a productive mechanism will ever work satisfactorily'.[75] Out of that experience, or so Bernal believes, will come an enlargement of individual responsibility, as well as an enhancement of social solidarity. A new religion – built on collective pride and scientific knowledge – might even be possible; one which fostered a 'deep sense of community and human brotherhood'.[76]

Already the importance of science in Bernal's severely practical utopia is quite striking. Furthermore, as a result of recent developments in the social relations of science, Bernal can now envisage how scientific knowledge can be more effectively placed at the

---

capitalism. Capitalism is already in decline. Therefore, the implied argument runs, Bernal's scientific renaissance can only take place in a socialist society.

service of society. For in a Marxist state these investigations can be planned. Science's main social function will be to supply 'answers on the basis of controlled experiment and statistical results' to 'all problems of production, agriculture, health and strategy'.[77] In the context of a society so committed to the promotion of productive efficiency, the role of 'basic research' in providing the knowledge for new technologies will obviously be an important one. Indeed Bernal looks forward to the creation of a 'science of science' which can enhance the creativity of the theoreticians.

What is needed is a more thorough analysis of those characters in scientific work that make for initiative in discovery and theory, and for critical thoroughness in the establishment of facts. It has already been found in practice that it is possible to retain these characters, combined with extensive organization, as long as the scientists are given responsibility and allowed to arrange their own work . . .'[78]

Bernal's awareness that 'the fate of science depends upon the preservation of liberty'[79] is so great that he feels obliged to grant scientific workers an unusual measure of autonomy within the limits of the Five Year Plan. As in the Soviet Union, it will be basic researchers who are made responsible for overseeing a vast network of technical institutes, industrial laboratories and agricultural field stations. In consultation with the state, they will determine what fundamental investigations ought to be undertaken. How much such research will cost is a matter that will be left to the discretion of the academicians (!) themselves.[80] One final guarantee of scientific independence is that an individual scientist should be allowed some time to pursue his/her own 'private' investigation, even if that effort is not directly essential to the immediate goals of his/her lab.[81] Once those conditions have been satisfied, science will most certainly take on the reified supra-social status that Bernal has always ascribed to it.

Science so organized can now assume its rightful place in a socialist society as the chief source of technological and cultural transformation. Under the guidance of a master plan, scientists will direct their attention, on the one hand, to: anomalies in basic theories; previously neglected areas of research; and new fields where rapid progress is likely. On the other, they will be sensitive to those discoveries in physics, chemistry and biology which can be exploited for human benefit. In 1939 Bernal mentions such possibilities as full automation, cybernetics, nuclear energy, plastics and (eventually) qualitative population control. Prospects for the more distant future should include disposable clothing, the gradual replacement of traditional food sources by plankton, algae and similarly ubiquitous substances on land and sea, and, quite certainly, 'the totally enclosed, spacious (and) air-conditioned town'.[82] But all such progress will be either futile or unlikely unless the cultural context offered by society is itself transformed along scientific lines. The outlook and knowledge of science – the ultimate ground of our freedom through their definition of natural and social necessity – must suffuse our educational and political institutions.[83] Of critical importance is a revaluation of school curricula such that scientific subjects will not only encompass historical, literary and visual dimensions but become integral to the understanding of the arts as well.[84] Finally, the dialectically conceived social sciences *and* the conduct of socialist politics will both have to be placed on a sound experimental basis. Then and only then will the full implications of the scientific world-view be realized:

> Science implies a unified and coordinated and, above all, conscious control of the whole of social life; it abolishes or provides the possibility of abolishing the dependence of man on the material world. Henceforth society is subject to the limitations it imposes on itself. There is no reason to doubt that this possibility will be grasped. The mere knowledge of its existence is enough to drive man on until he has achieved it. The socialized, integrated scientific world organization is coming.[85]

Yet, Bernal emphasizes, his utopia will not be 'a happy ecstatic state but [solely] the basis for further struggles and further conquests'.[86] Under anti-scientific capitalism we are confronted with the destructive contradictions of a class society. The adventure and promise of scientific socialism will gradually evolve out of the discovery of what it means to be 'truly human'.[87] Such is the hope at the heart of 'Bernalism'.

3. Hogben's Dissent, Needham's Aside and Stalin's Surprise

Bernal's social thought may be assessed from many different angles. With the advantage of forty years' hindsight, it is easy to detect several underlying weaknesses, not least in his assessment of the short-term durability of British capitalism. Yet after reading Chapter Seven it will be difficult to deny the persuasiveness of Bernal's arguments in the thirties itself. For they helped not only to push a number of scientists to the left but to prod the Left into becoming more scientific as well. In this section, however, we want to find out whether any of Bernal's associates dissented from the main lines of his philosophy. The brief answer is that, with two exceptions, they did not. Hogben and Needham, the two non-Communists, did have some reservations about, respectively, Bernal's industrialism and his scientism. But even their disagreements were made within the boundaries of a Bernalist universe. Nor was this surprising, given that Bernalism was ultimately very much a personal synthesis of a much wider, more collective endeavour. What they all had more difficulty in reconciling with their world-view – at this time – were some unexpectedly 'unscientific' developments in the U.S.S.R.

Let us begin with Hogben's less traditional and more problematic rationale for the overthrow of contemporary capitalism. Hogben concurs in the general criticisms that Bernal has made of capitalist Britain. In particular he is convinced that 'only collectivism by its encouragement of technology can now afford science with the means for its further development'.[88] Where Hogben departs from Bernal and the others is in his analysis of what was then thought to be a widespread fear of technical change. To the Bernalist such anxiety is epiphenomenal and will assuredly disappear once the means of production are communally owned and operated, as they are in the Soviet Union. Hogben on the other hand cannot dismiss so easily this reaction to the evils of a capitalist-inspired nexus between science and other productive forces. Is it conceivable that at least some of the problems which most concern the scientific Left are not specific to capitalism, but inherent in all forms of society that rely predominantly upon industrial technologies?

The 'reason from reason' so characteristic of the age has its origins, he believes, deep in human history: 'From earliest antiquity the backward state of biology [has] made towns the centre of any scientific culture . . . Hence . . . hypertrophied urban squalor . . . has been tacitly accepted by most people as the price we pay for what is gratuitously styled a high standard of life.'[89] Because of the early maturation of the physical sciences and their related technologies, the first scientific-industrial revolution had to result in a system of mass production which pollutes everything it touches. The increasing availability of goods became the hallmark of such a society and led to an invidious fetishism of commodities. In order to produce and secure these products, the populace has since been herded together in urban environments that are both physically and socially undesirable.

Hogben's horror of the city is virtually unbounded.* Its overall congestion and typically cramped living quarters are iniquitous in themselves and destructive of privacy. But when these aspects are combined with inducements to the employment of women in a time of declining population, they become dangerously 'incompatible with fertility'.[90] (In the thirties some demographers, notably Enid Charles, believed that Britons were then witnessing the 'twilight of parenthood' in their own country.)[91] Another source of allurement, not just away from the home but away from any sort of meaningful activity, are the overwhelmingly passive pleasures of city life. 'The cinema', Hogben argues, 'is mainly used to compensate the unbearable tedium of life in a model flat. Crowds assemble to watch games which are only played by experts or gentlemen. Having abandoned the family pew and the choir practice, we turn on the radio and listen to the crooner.'[92] His indictment of capitalism is that it is too committed to the exacerbation of all those problems to countenance the unglamorous alternative of a less diversified, smaller scale, de-urbanized but self-sufficient economy – made possible, so he asserts, by modern bio-technology.[93]

What maddens Hogben about contemporary socialists, especially orthodox Marxists, is that they concentrate upon transforming the *administrative* machinery' rather than the 'creative policy of industry'.[94] The Labour Party offers little hope here: 'its

* Hogben's own life-style reflected this antipathy. In *Science for the Citizen* (London, 1938, p. 10), he describes his own retreat from London in the early thirties: 'Life in South Africa had completely unfitted my children for continuous incarceration in the sooty squalid depression of the English metropolis . . . I therefore bought a cottage in Devon for a family of four who had grown up barefoot and daylight-conscious . . . On Friday nights we [Hogben and his wife Enid Charles] took an express to rejoin the fast fattening four in surroundings which should be the birthright of every British boy or girl.'

spokesmen have made it clear that they would concentrate on the nationalization of well established industries. They have even sought to soothe the middle classes by promising that initiative in creating new industries would be left to private efforts.'[95] As for the supporters of the Popular Front, they have become obsessed with Soviet Russia's programme of industrialization, thereby reviving what he terms 'the discredited ideology of early industrial capitalism'.[96] At this point Hogben cannot avoid criticizing Bernal, who was possibly the British Left's most eloquent advocate of socialist industrialism. 'The utopia of Professor Bernal', he caustically observes,

is a beehive city with a single glass roof, plus an artificial climate. As far as I can see, biologists would have no function except to inspect the plumbing and the factories where any food not synthetically manufactured would be produced by water culture. The rest of the population would live without the inconveniences of propinquity to any form of living matter, except other human beings . . .[97]

Hogben concludes: 'It may be a chemist's paradise, but it has no attraction for me.'[98]

In order to counteract the influence of all these industrializers, Hogben must therefore revert to the earlier socialist visions of Robert Owen and William Morris, and then revamp them in the light of modern 'bio-technology'. He first reminds us that

Men like Owen and Morris were far less taken in by the glamour of capitalism than we are. They were not content to criticize it because it distributed its products unjustly, or because it was incapable of producing as large a quantity of goods as a planned economy could deliver. They also, and more especially, attacked it because it was not producing the kind of goods which are good for people to want and to strive for, and they were not hypnotized by the liberal delusion that things people have been educated to demand by capitalist advertisement are necessarily the things they *need* most.[99]

What these pioneers of British socialism inevitably lacked, however, was any 'clear recognition that science could [one day] create the prospect of a new heaven for uncongested traffic and a new earth for spacious living.'[100] But in Hogben's 'bio-aesthetic' utopia, science would achieve, as it does in Bernal's fantasies, cultural as well as productive pre-eminence. The first step to be taken – through the gradual process of 'piecemeal planning by peaceful persuasion'[101] – is the socialization of all 'technical resources which private enterprise has failed to exploit in the interests of social welfare'.[102] With the aid of an appointed parliamentary chamber of experts,[103] an inventory of human needs – determined by 'the science of human nature' – can then be compared with an appraisal of available resources. Afterwards it will at last be possible to draw up a thermodynamical balance sheet for the entire society.[104] The provision of basic necessities would be followed up with a long-term plan 'to restore the serenity of small community life'[105] through the exploitation of hydro-electric power, light metals, fertilizers and a host of applications stemming from recent work in biochemistry and genetics.[106] Furthermore, Hogben proclaims, 'mobile power, aviation and electrical communications make it possible to distribute population at a high level of productive capacity without the disabilities of cultural isolation'.[107] Yet underlying all of his hopes for social progress is 'an educational reformation which will make the world outlook of modern science an open Bible'.[108] If the scientific enterprise is inextricably linked to the recovery of England's green and pleasant land, then it becomes the primary ingredient of intelligent citizenship. Such is the only set of proposals known to Hogben that might unite 'different sections of the productive population in a common endeavour to prevent the frustration of science by social parasitism'.[109] Distinctive as this vision may be, however, does it not bear a strong structural resemblance to the socialism advocated by Bernal?

Where Hogben is critical of left-wingers who overvalue industrialism, Joseph Needham is distressed to find that many Marxists are intoxicated by what he describes as 'scientific opium'. The two components of this rather heady drug are said to be ruthlessness in the face of deviation and imperfection, and blindness to the 'numinous' aspects of human experience. Accepting the potential need for pre-revolutionary violence, Needham anxiously wonders whether the pattern of cruelty against those who, in Bernal's words, 'cannot adapt themselves to the rate of change' will be continued and extended in a post-revolutionary society, particularly one 'based on science'. 'The ruthlessness with which a biologist throws out an anomalous embryo useless for his immediate purpose . . .

may', Needham fears, 'too easily be applied to human misfits and deviationists in the socialist world order.'[110]* A more ineluctable quality of scientific socialism may be its denial of the tragic side of life through an overly blithe definition of the Necessity which stands over mankind. Here we should allow Needham to speak at length.

Shall we substitute for the opium of religion an opium of science? It has always been the tacit conviction of the social reformer and the person occupied with the practical application of scientific knowledge that by man's own efforts, not merely minor evils, but the major evils of existence may be overcome. This is expressed in that great sentence of Marx: 'Philosophers have talked about the universe long enough; the time has come to change it.' But the problem of evil is not capable of so simple a resolution. So long as time continues, so long as change and decay are around us and in us, so long will sorrow and tragedy be with us. [Hence] there is little to be gained by trying to replace [these considerations] by a eupeptic opium, derived from too bright an estimate of the possibilities of scientific knowledge. Driven out, it will return in the end with redoubled force.[111]

Thus Needham hopes that, as an antidote to scientism, it will be possible to preserve the ritual and liturgical forms of traditional religion and, partly through them, the sense of 'the Holy'.[112] His goal is clearly a *regnum dei* populated by human beings balanced between scientific pride and religious humility.[113] Such qualities can be ascribed to Bernal personally by Needham,[114] who nevertheless retains some ill-suppressed doubts about their viability under a 'scientifically' socialist regime. At the same time he believes that, in the main, 'communism provides the moral theology appropriate for our time'.[115] Needham also affirms that the defeat of capitalism is just a matter of time.[116] Finally, his long-standing belief that 'the natural sciences [can] only come to their most perfect fruition in a socialist society'[117] leaves us in no doubt that he, too, is a Bernalist.

---

* Bernal, however, would later disagree: 'Science is not something limited to electrons, chemicals and machines; it ranges over the whole field of living creatures, and it is now coming more and more to deal with human beings in their social and economic relations. Thousands of scientists, in production and in operational research, have had concrete experience in dealing with them during the [Second World] war. The scientist is thus the man least likely to underrate the importance of the individual and the need for the democratic working of society.' (From Bernal's *The Freedom of Necessity* (London, 1949), pp. 87–8.)

The leading spokesmen for the scientific Left therefore evinced considerable unanimity in their views on the social relations of science; and this was all to the good. For in the late thirties they began to receive some disturbing reports of a major attack on the science of genetics in, of all places, the Soviet Union. Apart from any other consideration, this news was an embarrassment to anyone who, like Haldane and Hogben, had unfavourably contrasted the poor opportunities which British geneticists had to teaching and research[118] with the tremendous support which their counterparts in the U.S.S.R. were receiving.[119] Yet they could hardly deny the Soviet controversy's existence. Here then is how it came across to Bernal and the others, based on the published and unpublished information they had managed to obtain by 1940.[120]

There is an anti-genetics trend in the U.S.S.R. The Soviets' disgust with biological racism, notably in Nazi Germany, has already led them to close down their institute of human genetics, and to arrest some of the leading specialists in that field. Plant geneticists have also been attacked for their failure to apply their work successfully to the problems of agricultural practice. So for the moment the Soviet authorities seem to be relying upon the approach of T. D. Lysenko, an agronomist of peasant origin, following his earlier triumph in increasing grain yields. His secret weapon is what he calls 'vernalization', a set of techniques designed to expose seeds to unusual environmental conditions prior to sowing. The nub of the problem is that, not content with overseeing the development of agricultural practice, Lysenko has attempted to enforce his unorthodox theory of heredity on all Soviet biologists. He disagrees with the view expressed by most geneticists that, apart from random mutations, no change in environment can alter the hereditary potential of an organism. However, according to Lysenko, his experiments reveal that such 'genotypical' transformations do take place. (The belief in 'the inheritance of acquired characteristics' is commonly associated with the name of Lamarck, a nineteenth-century biologist.) He therefore has not hesitated to attack geneticists both for their undialectical perspective on the 'nature-nurture' question and for the bourgeois distortions associated with their discipline. Naturally orthodox genetical theorists have resisted the notion that their work – like that of other scientists – is not ideologically neutral. They have also suggested that Lysenko's experimental results either have been ill-founded or could be explained without resort to outmoded scientific doctrines like Lamarckism. Nevertheless, the gene theory's proponents still suffer from a double handicap. Not only can their science not promise immediate benefits for Soviet farmers, but it seems to contradict the egalitarian sentiments of Marxism's founding fathers as well. Hence Lysenko has been able to gain the upper hand, despite his manifest ignorance of the widely verified theories and practices on which classical genetics is based. Fortunately this dispute has not been finally resolved. As of 1939 it looks as if Lysenko's branch of biology will be subjected to thorough tests in the fields, as well as in the laboratories. Meanwhile geneticists are able to continue their own investigations, handicapped though they are by their lack of contact with Western science.

Even this incomplete assessment of the early stages of Lysenkoism deeply troubled British left-wing scientists. First, it contradicted their notions of how the Soviets were – and ought to have been – dealing with scientific matters. They found it inconceivable that the Bolsheviks might have gone back on their earlier pledges to respect the findings of world science and make them the foundation of their socialism. Yet that was what appeared to be happening in the case of genetics. For here, apparently, was a clear indication that the reins of scientific authority were being handed over to those who cared more for Marxist orthodoxies than scientific facts. Certainly that was the interpretation that anti-communist scientists were applying to this episode. As early as 1937, a leading article in *Nature* was citing it as a prime example of 'the atmosphere in which scientific investigators in totalitarian countries have to live and work'.[121] The possibility that more attacks would be made on this vulnerable front was the second major concern of the scientific Left. The third and perhaps most significant problem was that some of Britain's leading radical researchers were among the world's foremost advocates of classical genetics. J. B. S. Haldane certainly fell into that category, as did Lancelot Hogben. Inside the Theoretical Biology Club, Bernal and Needham were regularly exposed to the view of their trusted colleague C. H. Waddington that 'the broadening and deepening of our understanding of the behaviour of genetic factors is probably the most obvious advance in biology in the last twenty-five years. It has been shown that genes, whose interactions seem finally to control all the properties of the living organism which contains them, are arranged in a linear order on the chromosomes in the cell-nucleus.'[122] While Needham accepted Waddington's observation with some reservations,[123] Bernal was completely won over. By 1937 'Sage' was regularly engaged in experiments and discussions designed to elucidate the molecular structures underlying the basic hereditary units.[124] In other words, all of these men were fundamentally committed to the very theories that had been called into disrepute inside the U.S.S.R. Such were the professional and political pressures that weighed heavily on their consciences.

In the face of all these complexities, they managed to evolve a simple but effective strategy. Its main premise was that the Soviet genetics controversy was a genuine scientific dispute, and nothing more than that. Bernal summed up the debate in this way: 'geneticists were criticized for attributing all inherited characters to specific unitary factors in the chromosomes, and neglecting cyto-plastic [sic] and environmental factors, whose importance was probably exaggerated by their critics.'[125] Within this narrowed perspective the spokesmen for the scientific Left were able to take sides against Lysenko without calling his scientific credentials into question. Thus Haldane suggested that some of Lysenko's admirable results may have been due, not to environmentally induced changes in hereditary material, but to virus infections common to the types of plants the Soviet breeder had used.[126] Even so, concluded the authors of a *Modern Quarterly* article, 'there has so far been nothing in Lysenko's experiments which classical genetic theory cannot explain'.[127]

Apart from their criticisms of the scientific foundations oi Lysenko's views, left-wing researchers were quite confident, in public, that the genetics controversy would be resolved in accordance with the rules that had previously governed the Soviet scientific community. One of these, Needham maintained in 1937, was a due regard for the limitations of Marxist philosophy.

Dialectical materialism is so sharp an instrument that, although there can be no question about its value as a general system, the detailed application of it must always be a delicate and difficult matter in which dogmatism must at all costs be avoided. Specific interpretations, if made with undue confidence, may be dangerous. For example, most biologists believe . . . that during the recent discussion on genetics in the U.S.S.R. classical gene theory has suffered some criticism which was not well based.[128]

Needham also believed that the Lysenko episode illustrated, as he put it five years later, 'the benefit which would be derived could the scientific workers of the Soviet Union in the future come into much closer contact with those of other countries'.[129] He was nonetheless certain that 'further discussions and experiments which are still going on, and for which . . . the U.S.S.R. offers more material support than any other human community, will assuredly in due course put matters straight'.[130] J. B. S. Haldane shared those sentiments. Indeed he was so bold as to predict that, whatever its specific limitations, Lysenkoism would ultimately advance and not merely confirm biological theory and practice.

The controversy among Soviet geneticists has been largely one between the academic scientist, represented by Vavilov and interested primarily in the collection of facts, and the man who wants results, represented by Lysenko. It has been conducted not with venom, but in a friendly spirit. Lysenko said [in the October discussions of 1939]: 'The important thing is not to dispute; let us work in a friendly manner on a plan elaborated scientifically. Let us take up definite problems, receive assignments from the People's Commissariat of Agriculture of the U.S.S.R. and fulfil them scientifically.' Soviet genetics, as a whole, is a successful attempt at synthesis of these two contrasted points of view.[131]

The virtue of this rationale, first advanced in 1941, was that it not only normalized the Lysenko debate, but also reclaimed it as a positive feature of scientific life in a socialist society.

Nevertheless, even Haldane's perspective could not adequately explain some of the most important developments in Soviet biology at this time; including the demise of his own subject, human genetics. For many reasons this was a worrisome episode. As an example of 'ideologically-inspired' state interference in the affairs of science, it evoked an exact and uncomfortable parallel between Stalin's treatment of scientists and Hitler's. The difference – now the complications begin to mount – was that the Nazis invoked genetic determinism to justify the doctrine of Aryan superiority, while the Bolsheviks opposed all forms of scientific racism, with the aid of Lysenko's Lamarckian credo. (Indeed the abolition of intelligence testing in the Soviet Union in 1936 coincided with the closure of the human genetics institute.)[132] Back in Britain, on the other hand, Haldane was busily combating the Lamarckianism of anti-communist eugenists like E. W. MacBride. As J.B.S. noted: 'Reactionary biologists . . . naturally use the theory of the transmission of acquired habits for political ends. It is silly, they say, to expect the children of manual workers to take up book-learning, or those long-oppressed races to govern themselves.' Fortunately, he added, 'laboratory experiments agree with social experience in proving that this theory is false'.[133] Yet alongside this polemic we must set Haldane's opinions that the mean intelligence quotient of the British population was declining – and that this was due to the relative over-production of working class children.[134] In short, his views ran counter to the egalitarian as well as the environmentalist emphases of Lysenkoist biology. Hence J.B.S. was in a cleft stick. He was a good enough Marxist to recognize that the biologist 'is himself a member of a particular class and profession within it. The first prerequisite for a relative objectivity is to realize that these facts make an absolute objectivity impossible.'[135] That made him plead all the more insistently that 'biology should not be harnessed to the car of any political party'.[136] Yet Haldane was late twice over, because in the context of human genetics neither the fascist nor the communist regimes were prepared to honour his carefully phrased distinctions between science and ideology. If such actions continued to strike him as irrational when perpetrated by Hitler, they were at the very least unintelligible when undertaken by Stalin.

While Lysenkoism in some ways dumbfounded Haldane and the others in the 1930s, it in no way caused them to revise either their views on the social relations of science or their commitments to socialism and the U.S.S.R.* They felt with good reason that this

* Inevitably in a book on left-wing intellectuals in the 1930s, the question must be raised: how did these men react to the great terror unleashed by Stalin in the late thirties? The answer is that, in public, they said nothing one way or another. Privately, the news of this massive repression was a bitter blow to the hopes that they had nurtured in themselves and others about the U.S.S.R. That they did not broadcast their reaction to the world at large has been taken by David Caute (*The Fellow-Travellers* (London, 1973), *passim*) and other writers to constitute moral calumny of a high order.

Rather than revive the old ends-means debate here, we should note that, as accredited left-wingers, they all somewhat naïvely hoped that their past episode was untypical of Russian science as a whole. In any case Lysenko's 'agro-biology' only momentarily coexisted with ortho- dox genetics. So long as Soviet scientific workers settled their differences here as they had done in other subjects, they and their well-wishers had little to fear. If anything, the genetics controversy only confirmed the Bernalist view that science was and ought to be relatively autonomous from the social systems which nurtured it. Why then have we dwelled so long on Lysenko? Apart from the evident turmoil which he helped to create within the pre-war scientific Left, Lysenko's importance is purely futuristic. His is the only shadow to darken the brightly optimistic outlook of our subjects. But only when he assumed control of Soviet biology in 1948 would they understand his true significance as the misbegotten disciple of a new 'socialist' science.

In the meantime Bernal, Haldane, Levy, Needham and, in his own way, Hogben contented themselves with the advocacy of what they called scientific socialism. Their long-term goal was: a planned economy; producing an abundance of socially useful goods and services; that are equitably distributed to all sections of the

---

loyalty to the Soviet Union could be used to secure the release of at least some of the lesser political prisoners. An example of this strategy – which proved in this instance to be more effective than public protests – was the campaign to free Frederick Houtermanns, a German emigré physicist at Kharkov, who was imprisoned toward the end of 1937. Among those who sought his release was J. D. Bernal. Along with P. M. S. Blackett, Bernal went directly to the Soviet Ambassador in London, Ivan Maisky. At the time, Maisky told them, there was nothing he could do. However, Houtermanns was eventually released, only to turn up in the early fifties as a supporter of the anti-communist Congress for Cultural Freedom. (I am grateful to Ms. Margaret Gardiner for this information about Bernal.)

As a footnote to this episode, it is instructive to consider Maisky's reminis- cences of this period: 'Socialists and reformists of all kinds quickly seized on the news of arrests and repression in the U.S.S.R., and popularized it in the factories, saying: "Look what Communism leads to." I well remember how English Communists whom I used to see in those years would ask me with bitterness, almost with despair, the same question as [H. G.] Wells: "What is happening in your country? We cannot believe that so many old and honoured party members, tested in battle, have suddenly become traitors." And they told how the events in the U.S.S.R. were alienating the workers from the Soviet land and undermining Communist influence among the proletariat.' (From I. Maisky, Bernard Shaw i drugie (Moscow, 1967), p. 183; as quoted in R. Medvedev, Let History Judge (London, 1972), pp. 254–5.)

population; who feel themselves practically and morally bound to one another in this great collective endeavour. Underlying all of these dimensions is an unswerving commitment to science: as a model for the organization of all social activities; as a set of methods for determining human needs; as a complex of technologies for generating and circulating a new abundance of products; and as an ideology that binds men and women to one another through its dominion over their definitions of natural and social necessity. As society changes, so of course will the scientific enterprise. It will grow larger. Its organization will become more industrialized. It will play an increasingly dominant role in the spheres of education and culture. In the strict sense of the term, however, this will not be a 'technocracy'. For scientists as such will not themselves directly rule the country. Rather society shall be governed, on the one hand, by 'meritocratic' principles and scientific notions of expertise and, on the other, by the ethos of its scientific world-view and the findings of its scientific community. Only in these circumstances – and not those of contemporary capitalism – will science reach the summit of its social (self-) recognition. This aspiration, first enunciated by Bukharin at the 1931 Congress, lies at the core of the scientific Left's social philosophy, whose greatest exponent was most certainly J. D. Bernal.

Chapter Seven

Practice

When I meet men of science on their own ground, I find them 'scientific socialists'. They argue, most violently, how the results of their own work could be applied for the benefit of mankind, if only it was not for that few, who may be the government . . ., or the industrialists who either refuse to accept progress or accept it only to exploit it. Yet outside their own departments they are the most arrant diehards. They are, in fact, socialists in their laboratories and Tories in the Athenaeum.

Ritchie Calder, 1934[1]

As Bernal sat at his desk writing *The Social Function of Science*, he must at times have found it difficult to imagine how anyone could be anything other than a socialist. Yet his many-sided involvement in the affairs of the British scientific community was sufficient to keep his powerful imagination in check. For he was painfully aware that, laid end to end, the labs in the country constituted a great bog of political apathy and unconsciousness. To dispel the apolitical mists that enveloped their fellow scientific workers, Bernal and his cohorts therefore had to do more than propagandize the capitalist causes of science's current frustrations. They were also obliged to organize the maximum number of researchers, either on a trade-union basis, or as a distinctive grouping within the Popular Front. This strategy proved to be successful, first at Cambridge and later in other scientific centres. In fact, at least one historian has since claimed that by the late thirties a radicalized ' "social relations of science movement" . . . *seemed* almost to dominate the British scientific world'.[2] The initiative shown by left-wing scientists was, however, only one of the factors that led to such a happy outcome. Of equal importance were the activities of the science establishment's liberal wing, which, under the duress of an approaching war, found itself able to back the young radicals' more limited aims. While the durability of this coalition was questionable, its formation was rightly viewed by friend and foe alike as a victory for the scientific Left. It was also, for the Communist Party of Great Britain, a strong inducement to attach itself still more strenuously to the cause of science.

1. Who Wants to Know?

Younger scientists may have been, in the words of Noreen Branson and Margot Heinemann, 'at once the most fundamentally hopeful and the most frustrated of intellectual workers' in the 1930s.[3] But the number who would ever articulate their grievances in political terms, as socialists, was small indeed. This gap between the power of the stimulus and the poverty of the response surprised neither the C.P.G.B. nor the leading spokesmen of the scientific Left-to-be; nor, by this stage, should it shock us. All of us were or are aware that it would require very special circumstances to create a significant left-wing 'fraction' within the conservatized community of British science. However, to identify through political practice just what these conditions were proved to be a far more difficult task than the creation of political tracts. Thanks yet again to the intervention of Bernal, we can, at least in retrospect, discover how a particular set of appeals, made to a specific audience at a crucial moment, could engender the semblance of a social movement. Whether or not the power, influence and numbers of radicalized researchers were more apparent than real, relative to their previous strength – and in relation to other groups of intellectuals – they had to be treated as a social force in their own right. Anyone who has ever tried his or her hand at political organizing will recognize the significance of that achievement. For those who have not, the socio-logical 'whodunit' which follows should help to sharpen their appreciation of the odds against those who sought to translate private frustrations into public grievances.

All of our subjects realized that, by social origin, occupational status and vocational tradition, scientific workers tended to be both politically inactive and ideologically conservative. As Bernal complained in 1933: 'The coefficient of political consciousness of scientists is low, because . . . they are a particularly sheltered section of the middle class' who have been 'psychologically selected for an absorbing interest in special problems'.[4] Moreover, in the economically depressed circumstances of the thirties, an overriding concern with job security was to be expected when the typical scientific worker was 'as much a salaried official as the average civil servant or business executive'.[5] Such conditions in Bernal's view were likely to promote greater rather than less political conformity, especially on the part of those employed in government and industry.[6] Even within the universities there were constraints, some more subtle than others, that operated against the investigator with 'dangerous thoughts'. Had not each of our central characters, Haldane aside, encountered these countervailing forces as an inner as well as an outer reality? Yet if such prohibitions could be applied to men about to receive professorships and F.R.S.s, then how much more binding they must have seemed to their more junior or less eminent colleagues. Indeed the potentially radical constituency afforded by academics could be pared down further still. We could, for a start, eliminate most of the professorate: they were too old, too tied to the science establishment and too much a part of the state élite. Chemists and engineers might also be safely ignored, because of the intimate connections between their disciplines and the immediate productive requirements of the ruling class. Finally, where the Left was in general very weak – notably at the provincial universities – it was highly unlikely that science students would be in the vanguard to put that weakness right. All in all, the scientific community offered very slim pickings for any would-be political organizer from the Left.

Who then has made our short-list of candidates for recruitment to the cause of socialism? So far the scientist most likely to become a left-winger would be: young; neither too senior nor too junior; a practitioner of a fairly esoteric subject; at a major scientific centre; in a university; where the Left was fairly strong. That leaves us with Cambridge, London and Oxford as possible locations. Oxford can be provisionally eliminated, as a result of the then depressed position of science vis-à-vis the all-powerful, arts-dominated colleges there. Within the University of London as a whole, scientific morale was much higher, and the city itself was of course an important locus for left-wing agitation. But the fragmentation of academic, political and neighbourhood activities defeated for a very long time all attempts to build up a radical sub-culture for scientific workers. That leaves us with Cambridge – the bastion of High Science itself. From our previous discussions of this place, we might now want to conclude that a scientific Left simply was not 'on'. Yet it did happen, and its point of origin was Cambridge.

The scientific Left arose at Cambridge for three reasons. A determined nucleus of radicalized researchers, already in residence and led by Bernal, made it their business to see this endeavour through. They in turn received support from the best organized and most serious-minded of Britain's university-based left-wing movements. Ironically, however, none of this work would have been to much avail had not the Cambridge scientific community been structured in the way it was.

How the pursuit of High Science could, in the context of the 1930s, both abet and shape the growth of radicalism is, needless to say, an involved but interesting story. But before we become immersed in the telling of it, let us remind ourselves that nowhere in Britain were so many researchers concentrated into such a confined space. Indeed if we break down the University of London into its component parts, we find that Cambridge boasted more than twice as many pure scientists as any other academic institution in the country.[7] Since a commitment to some form of socialist politics was bound to be very much a minority affair, the significance of Cambridge's size should be apparent. With its basic research corps of approximately 500 faculty, senior research workers and post-graduate students,[8] it would only take, say, 5 per cent of them to form a viable, left-wing sub-culture. Once organized, they would of course benefit from their access to a geographically compact environment, in which political conspiracies could be as easily pursued as collaborative research projects. Yet prior to the early thirties the prospect of such an organization ever materializing seemed remote. Cambridge scientists were simply too absorbed in the business of being Cambridge scientists.

As it happened, the excellence of the Cambridge scientific community was now to inspire at least some of its members to move to the Left and become politically active. This change emerged out of a social 'contradiction' which these men and women were helping to exacerbate. On the one hand they, especially the particle physicists, were participating in what was even by Cambridge standards an exceptionally fruitful period of

scientific advance. To be quite specific: '1932 was the most spectacu-
lar year in the history of science.'[9] So says C. P. Snow, who was
then a Christ's College don and a practising physical chemist. His
evidence? Cockcroft and Walton had split the atom, James Chad-
wick had discovered the neutron, P. M. S. Blackett the positron;
and all of them were based in the same Cavendish Laboratory.
'Living in Cambridge,' Snow continues, 'one could not help picking
up the human as well as the intellectual excitement in the air.' It
was 'an intellectual climate different in kind from anything else in
England at the time'.[10] Here is how Snow sums up its impact on the
social outlook of these fortunate young men and women.

The scientists were themselves part of the deepest revolution in human
affairs since the discovery of agriculture. They could accept what was
happening, while other intellectuals shrank away. They not only accepted
it, they rejoiced in it. It was difficult to find a scientist who did not believe
that the scientific-technical-industrial revolution, accelerating under his
eyes, was not doing incomparably more good than harm.[11]

However full of insight Snow's remarks might be, he errs in one
very crucial respect: a good part of the 'scientific-technical-industrial
revolution' was not accelerating. On the contrary, the world
economy was stagnating. Unemployment and malnutrition were
rife in Britain. Japan had already invaded Manchuria, and Hitler
was preparing to take power in Germany. The upshot of these
developments, when juxtaposed against the intellectual progress
being made at Cambridge, ought to have been clear and striking.
For if ever scientists were to become aware of the great gulf that
existed between the immense promise of their theories and the
grim realities of a world filled with impoverished workers and
embittered nations, then surely this was the moment.

In Cambridge those problems were brought to the fore by a
strong left-wing movement, first organized and then led by the
Communist Party.[12] The Communists enjoyed this dominance
mainly because their commitment to proletarian politics attracted
the support of the more able and committed young socialists. That
at any rate is the view now taken by a distinguished historian and
former Communist, Roy Pascal.

It was a principle whenever a Communist group was formed that it
should undertake work in the working class, distributing party literature,

carrying on party propaganda of various kinds, helping in industrial struggles and so on. [Thus] the first thing that the group in Cambridge thought of was what could be done . . . We proceeded to create tasks . . . and to carry them out, working among railway workers, the bus workers and taking every opportunity to help. And in fact some quite considerable things were done [such as]: organizing the bus men into a union branch, which hadn't existed before; helping tenants with their problems; and all this sort of thing. This was looked on as natural and right, and . . . I think it must be said that people tended to join the Communist Party and leave the Labour Party because of this sort of requirement. You felt something was being done, that you weren't just sitting up in a study and thinking about the political situation.[13]

A powerful stimulus to this kind of activity was the periodic appearance in Cambridge of the Hunger Marchers, bands of unemployed workers who had been mobilized largely by the Communist Party. The importance of these demonstrations, according to Maurice Dobb, was that they confronted gilded youths and privileged academics 'with a disciplined group of workers such as they had never probably met before. This gave them . . . a [novel] picture of the working class acting in an organized way and taking the lead'.[14] The C.P. encouraged this perspective not only through its local projects but also by its placement of undergraduates in summertime camps run by the University Labour Federation for the benefit of the unemployed.[15] On the basis of these commitments the party was able to attract a succession of able students leaders, including David Guest, John Cornford, James Klugmann and Maurice Cornforth. Together with various dons like Bernal, Dobb, Pascal and the biochemist 'Woggy' Woolf, they constituted themselves as the most important single force inside the Cambridge Left.

Within the university itself, the Communists also took charge of a number of campaigns that attempted to unite left-wing and later even liberal sentiments. Many issues were taken up, the most important of which proved to be resistance to war and opposition to fascism. In 1932 the C.P. helped to establish an umbrella organization, the Cambridge Anti-war Council, that was supposed to coordinate activities in this area. However, not until November 1933 did the council decide to stage a large meeting in the Guildhall (chaired by Needham and addressed by the German novelist Ernst Toller);[16] at the same time it mounted a major Anti-war Exhibition in St Andrew's Hall. But by common consent it was the Armistice Day march organized by the Student Anti-war Council that marked the beginning of Cambridge's left-wing renaissance. For while attempting to lay a wreath at the town's War Memorial – 'To the Victims of a War They Did Not Make, from Those Who are Determined to Prevent All Similar Crimes of Imperialism' – the demonstrators were attacked by a group of right-wing students. Many of the marchers were of course not socialists at all. Indeed some of them, like Eric Burhop, then an Australian research student in physics, were Christian pacifists.

I remember marching in the Armistice Day procession, the first time I'd ever marched, with a little badge in my lapel which said 'Christ Claims You for Peace'. During the procession, which was quite a large one . . . the fascists attacked [us] and seized the banner. I stopped an egg and a tomato and spoiled one of my suits. Well, of course, I was furious about this. Then I saw the evening newspaper, the *Evening Standard* of that day. I opened it and saw there was a leading article which read 'Hooligans at Cambridge'. And so I thought: 'Oh! This is very good! The newspapers are attacking the hooligans and putting them in their place.' But when I read the article, I found that we were the hooligans, and not the fascists who had attacked us. I think this was the first thing that brought home the realities of the political situation . . . in Great Britain.[17]*

Partly thanks to the injustice of those charges, anti-war groups began to proliferate in Cambridge. In 1934 the Anti-war Council

* The *Evening Standard* of 13 November 1933 in fact stated that 'The behaviour of the Oxford and Cambridge undergraduates who made violent pacifist demonstrations, which in one case ended in a free fight round their respective War Memorials on Armistice Day, is a disgrace to every member of both universities . . . Since the university authorities seem unable to control these young hooligans' excesses, I suggest that their fellow undergraduates procure some tar. The pacifists already have the feathers.'

The 'hooligans' were probably a group of Tory 'hearties'. This is a message that one of them sent to a Mr R. N. Mitchell of Peterhouse College. 'Tell your friends: "Tories of the World, Unite." All well affected persons should make an effort to be present at Parkers' Piece at 11.15 a.m. on Saturday when a pacifico-communist demonstration proposes to lay an insulting wreath on the War Memorial. From: Peterhouse Branch, Cambridge University Conservative Association.' Unfortunately for the Tories, this missive was opened by the wrong Mr Mitchell, who happened to be a left-winger himself. He passed it on to Joseph Needham who, in turn, drew it to the attention of the university authorities.

was able to stage a still larger exhibition, this time on 'Fascism and War'. But the stronger the anti-war movement became, the more problematic was its conjunction of pacifism and anti-fascism. For the Left at least, these difficulties were removed two years later with the outbreak of the Spanish Civil War. 'Spain' was quickly adopted as the rallying cry for the Cambridge Left. While a handful of students enlisted in and died fighting for the International Brigade, most stayed in the university, taking on a variety of agitational and fund-raising activities. The anti-fascist cause continued to dominate the university political scene thereafter. Indeed so persuasive were the arguments of its proponents that, shortly after the signing of the Munich Agreement, the undergraduate Socialist Club was able to attract more than 1,000 members.[18] The Cambridge Left had grown unprecedentedly strong.

Thus the university provided the scientific and political preconditions for the emergence of a distinctive grouping of left-wing scientists. It also contained within its ranks established researchers who were already politically active. In addition to the Communists Bernal and Woolf, one encountered Labour supporters on the far Left like Dorothy and Joseph Needham, or Bill and 'Tony' Pirie. (Like the Needhams, the Piries were *both* products of the Dunn Lab, members of the Socialist League in the 1930s and, later, Fellows of the Royal Society.) All that was now required to set the whole thing in motion was an organizational framework, a provocative issue and a form of action that could politically engage the specific skills and interests of scientific workers. That was in fact to be the prime function of the Cambridge Scientists' Anti-war Group. How the C.S.A.W.G. helped to launch the scientific Left is consequently of some interest to us.

But, first, let us scrutinize the Anti-war Group's supporters, in order to determine exactly who at Cambridge finally decided to 'come out' as left-wingers. Although no membership list survives, a letter of protest against the militarization of research was widely circulated by the group, signed by seventy-nine faculty, research workers and post-graduate students, and published in the *Cambridge Review* on 1 June 1934. A statistical analysis of its signatories' scientific backgrounds is appended below (pp. 339–42). Here we need only concern ourselves with its main results.

1. Overall support for the letter was low. Despite its mildly liberal and pacifist tone, less than 12 per cent of Cambridge's pure scientists signed it. It is therefore entirely possible that the total number of left-wing activists in the research community at this time was less than 5 per cent.

2. Post-graduate students were more than twice as likely to sign the letter as faculty members. But post-doctoral research workers without teaching positions made an even stronger showing than post-graduates. No professors and only one reader in pure science (Needham) put his name down.

3. More than half the pure scientists who signed the letter were drawn from only two labs: the Dunn Biochemical Institute and the Cambridge Laboratory. Yet these biochemists, particle physicists and X-ray crystallographers constituted less than a fifth of all pure scientists working in Cambridge.

4. Possibly the most interesting and certainly the most unexpected result was that women post-graduates and faculty members engaged in basic research were four times more likely than their male counterparts to sign the letter. (Incidentally, of the 423 Cambridge researchers in this category, only thirty-one of them were female. Twelve of these women supported the Anti-war Group here.)

Otherwise the profile that emerges here is very much what we expected it would be. Left-wing politics were not fashionable among Cambridge scientists. Those who were politically to the left of centre were young in age, junior in status, 'pure' at heart and, quite often, female by sex.

Only two of these findings require further comment here. The strong showing made by the 'second sex' is important and cannot be explained away with a passing reference to women's traditional pacifism. For at least nine of the twelve women signatories were also active in left-wing organizations apart from the anti-war movement. Dorothy Needham and Tony Pirie, for example, worked hard in the malnutrition campaigns and stood as Labour candidates for the City Council. Nora Wooster, an X-ray crystallographer, was not only the first Co-secretary of the Cambridge Scientists' Anti-war Group, but the original convenor of Cambridge's Left Book Club Group as well.[19] Reinet Fremlin was a Cavendish research student who became in 1938 the National Organizing Secretary for the Association of Scientific Workers.

Other women who joined Left groups either then or later included another X-ray crystallographer, Dorothy Crowfoot (Hodgkin), the zoologist S. M. Manton and the biochemists Barbara Holmes, Shirley Hughes and Marjory Stephenson. At least one of their male associates, the late C. H. Waddington, was able to appreciate the importance of their political contribution:

they were undoubtedly a very important part of the whole social group, [and] not only in making contact between people . . . Some of them were very politically active, and in some cases more politically active than the menfolk. At that time, I think it would be said, to take one instance, that my wife [the architect Justin Blanco White] was much more inclined to politics than I was. And there were people like Mrs Fremlin, Mrs Wooster and Mrs Pirie who were all at least as involved and, in many cases, more involved than their husbands with politics . . . So they were very important . . . to the whole social group, which was not just a set of isolated men, but a really coherent group of friends of both sexes.[20]

Why women scientists were often drawn to the Left is not an easy question. Though they belonged to the first post-suffragette genera-tion, they received little encouragement, either from the Popular Front or from wider social forces, to develop an explicitly feminist perspective. On the other hand since their sex accounted for less than 10 per cent of all Cambridge natural scientists, they were by definition a gifted *and* suppressed minority. Their self-awareness was probably heightened both by their concentration mainly in biological disciplines, and by a high degree of intermarriage with male co-workers in their respective labs. As biologists some of them may have come into radical politics via the malnutrition issue. As women with their predominantly liberal and genteel backgrounds, the pacifist orientation of the Left in the early thirties may also have been a decisive factor. But whatever the causes, these women proved to be more sensitive to the social crises of their time than male scientists. Nevertheless it was the men who publicly dominated the scientific Left, especially as its leading theoreticians. Hence, neither for the first nor the last time, the political contribu-tions of such women would be almost completely 'hidden from history'.

Such a fate has not, however, been reserved for the (male) Cam-bridge biochemists and physicists of that era. Many general argu-ments have already been put forward to explain why practitioners of these sorts of subjects might have been inclined to radical politics. So let us confine ourselves here to two remarks about the qualities specific to the inmates of the Dunn and Cavendish labs. First, they were not all *that* politically active. Eric Burhop has since estimated that, of his co-workers in physics, no more than 25 per cent – 'if as high as that' – could be said to have held left-wing views.[21] Bill Pirie would not even go that far with regard to his fellow bio-chemists. 'After all,' he told me, 'more than half the staff were fairly ardent Conservatives . . . [Malcolm] Dixon had no political interests. Eric Holmes didn't do anything political. Tim Hughes was a Conservative, and so on. Don't overrate our position. There was a lot of opposition inside.'[22] If the radical tide was not exactly overwhelming, it was at least tolerated by the labs' directors, Lord Rutherford and Sir Frederick Gowland Hopkins. Though politically conservative, Rutherford was himself disturbed by the signs of industrial stagnation in Britain and fascist repression in Germany. Indeed these trends ultimately inspired him to volunteer his services both to the Department of Scientific and Industrial Research and to the Academic Assistance Council (which will be discussed later on in this chapter). He could therefore at least sympathize with those of his 'boys' who also wanted to do something about those problems. As long as their 'communism' did not get in the way of their experiments, Rutherford could lump their politics. Gowland Hopkins, by contrast, was not merely tolerant of his left-wing protégés, but a staunch supporter of the Labour Party in his own right. Famed for his early work on nutrition, he also publicly backed the exhibitions mounted by the Cambridge Anti-war Council in 1933 and 1934. (Apparently he did not, however, feel it prudent to sign the *Cambridge Review* letter.) Knowing what we now do of the low support that the Left received from Cambridge's two most radical laboratories, we must also recognize how critical were the stances adopted by Rutherford and Hopkins. For what would have become of the scientific Left had the Cavendish been headed by a reactionary physicist like Oxford's F. A. Lindemann; or the Dunn been led by the biochemical equivalent of A. V. Hill or E. W. MacBride?

In short, not even the most ideal of scientific environments could be said to have been favourable to the organizational schemes of left-wing researchers. History may have been on their side, in theory. But in practice they would have to make their own history, in circumstances that were hardly of their own choosing. It is against this ungrateful background that we must consider the origins and achievements of the Cambridge Scientists' Anti-war Group.

2. The Cambridge Scientists' Anti-war Group

Nineteen-thirty-two witnessed not only the *annus mirabilis* of nuclear physicists but the first signs of political awakening on the part of Cambridge scientists as well. For in that year an attempted rejuvenation of the local branch of the Association of Scientific Workers was accompanied by the formation of a Cambridge Scientists' Anti-war Group.[23] The date is politically significant. It coincides in fact with the first serious efforts by the Communists to launch a major anti-war campaign inside the university. The C.S.A.W.G. would appear to have been an integral part of that exercise, especially since the group's earliest surviving members have all credited J. D. Bernal with its inspiration. Bernal, as we shall see, also played a leading role in reviving the A.Sc.W. The historical importance of the two organizations is that, between them, they would serve as the organizational foundations of an influential and distinctive grouping within the Popular Front. Indeed in a sense, they *were* the scientific Left.

But, at least until the academic year 1935–6, both bodies were anxious to maintain a low ideological profile. This was true even of the more explicitly 'political' Anti-war Group. The group at first mainly concerned itself, recalls its first Chairman, W. A. Wooster, 'with educating its own members. It felt that the causes of international tension really wanted to be studied carefully before trying to take any particular action.'[24] The process of political education turned out to be a frustrating and arduous one. As late as June 1936, the group – now with about eighty members[25] – was unable to achieve a consensus on *any* ideologically sensitive issue.[26] Nor was this surprising. Though originally formed by a left-wing coterie, its programmatic blend of pacifism and anti-fascism was self-consciously 'liberal' and somewhat self-contradictory. Neither quality helped the group in the establishment of a clear perspective, around which a definite set of political practices could be organized.

All the Left scientists could hope for was that at least some of their liberal and Christian pacifist associates might be cajoled into becoming 'radicals'. In the meantime, the C.S.A.W.G. naturally supported the activities of the Cambridge Anti-war Council, to which it was affiliated. These included a demonstration in near-by Duxford during the Royal Air Force's 'Air Display' of 1935. That action so provoked the patriotism of spectators and police alike that the constabulary was moved to confiscate the protestors' specially prepared newspaper, the 'Air Display Special'. Later Wooster would successfully sue the Chief Constable for this action.[27] Otherwise the group supplied speakers to other anti-war organizations, wrote letters to, among other places, Nature[28] and, above all, kept on talking. Compared with the remaining 90 per cent of the Cambridge scientific community, such activities were almost revolutionary in character. Yet Bernal and his comrades were well aware that the scientific Left was still in the making.

One academic year later it had been made, in Cambridge if not elsewhere. The immediate cause of this extraordinary political transformation was Spain. How the Spanish Civil War was used to energize the Left in this country is not a story we need to re-tell here.[29] What does demand emphasis is that the armed defence of Republican Spain against the forces of General Franco at last allowed left-wingers here to 'de-pacify' their anti-fascism. The new and more consistent line was: if one were interested in peace, then one had to curb the aggressive tendencies of the fascist powers. Hence, without coming out explicitly in favour of rearmament, the peace movement was used to propagandize the virtues of an alliance between France, Great Britain and the Soviet Union, whose governments could then act together to deny the fascists any further territorial gains. One form of military preparation that the emerging Popular Front did support, however, was civil defence. Indeed it was in this arena that the C.S.A.W.G., which really ought to have been renamed the 'Cambridge Scientists' Anti-fascist Group', was to be politically 'blooded' for the first time in its short existence. Partly through that experience and partly as a result of the more overtly socialist content of their new activities, at least some of its members felt obliged to move leftwards. That shift was in turn sufficient to allow the group to arrive at a firmer, more radical stance.

Just how radical can be seen from its joint sponsorship, with the local branch of the Socialist League, of the leaflet 'Why are They Fighting in Spain?'

Certain newspaper millionaires with fascist sympathies [they claimed] are actively supporting the Spanish fascists in the British press. In many papers the fascist rebels are described as 'patriots', while the supporters of the [Republican] government (which contained no Communists) are denounced as 'Reds'. When the freedom of the press in England is so abused by newspaper millionaires, it is time for those who have some regard for the truth to do something about it . . .

In Quiet England it is difficult to imagine the Spanish working-man standing up to the fascist tanks and aeroplanes with insufficient ammunition, or just with shot-guns and sticks. But the Spanish loyalists are fighting for your freedom not only for their own, for if fascism wins in Spain *France and England will not be safe*. See that all your friends clearly understand the nature of the Spanish struggle, and

SUPPORT THE SPANISH PEOPLE![30]

This document was released sometime in 1937. Like all Popular Front literature, it suffered – sometimes consciously – from certain characteristic defects; not least in its 'liberal' emphasis on the coming struggle between English 'freedom' and fascist tyranny. (Britain was of course a liberal democracy, but, like Germany, this society was still based on the 'freedom' of workers to sell their labour-power to those who controlled the means of production.) However, so long as the Communist Party instilled in its own membership an awareness of the long-term need to bring about socialism at home, then the short-term fight against fascism *could* become a tremendous aid to political enlightenment. At any rate, it would be difficult to deny that from a socialist standpoint the C.S.A.W.G. had made a remarkable advance over its previous policy – which, roughly speaking, had been that war was a Bad Thing. Indeed it now deserved to be known as the vanguard of the scientific Left.

The group first achieved prominence when in the mid-thirties it made a dramatic intervention into the nation-wide debate about the adequacy of Britain's civil defences. Fears of aerial bombardment with poisonous gases sparked off the controversy, after Prime Minister Stanley Baldwin made his infamous, incautious and, as it turned out, incorrect observation that 'the bomber will always get

8

through'. In order to allay such anxieties, the Home Office's Air Raid Precautions (A.R.P.) Department started issuing handbooks in 1935 for those homeowners and shopkeepers who wished to 'gas-proof' their premises and make them structurally stronger. The dual emphasis of these early publications was that, on the one hand, 'A.R.P.' was ultimately the responsibility of individual citizens and not their government; and, on the other, that if the detailed instructions of the Home Office were carefully followed, people would be well protected from the worst effects of atmospheric poisoning, heat, blast and splinters. Privately, however, it is clear from the files of the A.R.P. Department (now housed in the Public Records Office) that a number of its officials were far from satisfied about the adequacy of their procedures.[31] Despite this awareness, the department would prove unable for several years to persuade either the Cabinet or the fighting services to make available the funds and facilities necessary for substantial improvement in the A.R.P. system. In particular, there was strong resistance to the notion of constructing public air raid shelters, both because of their cost and because, it was said, they would negate the 'self-help' aspects of earlier A.R.P. policy. Hence the government was obliged to argue that, within limits, the British people could protect themselves from enemy air attacks.

In the earlier phase of the great A.R.P. debate, attention was focused primarily upon the destructive potential of chemical warfare and the adequacy of the Home Office's measures to defend the civilian population against it. Though many believed that high explosives would ultimately prove more dangerous, it was the memory of gas attacks during the First World War that still captured the public's imagination. Among the A.R.P. Department's strongest defenders were several chemists and military officials who had previously handled poisonous gases. These included Major General C. H. Foulkes,[32] J. Davidson Pratt – in a lecture chaired by the former Chairman of Imperial Chemical Industries, Lord Melchett[33] – and Professor James Kendall, F.R.S., of Edinburgh University. While believing that 'the average man mistrusts nothing more deeply than scientific brains or scientific intelligences',[34] Kendall apparently still thought it worth-while to use his scientific authority to persuade the 'average' reader that, 'in a home-made gas-proof room, the civilian is perfectly safe against the most severe gas attack'.[35] Thus the disarming (or re-arming) title of his book: *Breathe Freely! The Truth about Poison Gas*. As for the public's fears about the development of a new generation of superweapons, they were assured that 'no authority on explosives anticipates that the world will see, in the near future, a new super-explosive, many times more powerful than T.N.T. . . . Control of atomic energy may ultimately put a new angle on these problems, but that is a dream of the very far distant future.'[36] Indeed to Kendall it was those whom he called the 'alarmists' about chemical warfare who were the real danger, not the fascists, with whom he proposed, in 1938, a peaceful settlement.[37] Such a novel form of A.R.P. obviously had some appeal for Neville Chamberlain as well.

The Home Office also had its critics, ranging from organizations like the Union for Democratic Control and the Socialist Medical Association to pacifists such as Bertrand Russell and Aldous Huxley. The U.D.C. described the government's earliest A.R.P. plans as a 'very cruel deception'.[38] Not only did they presuppose a standard of dwelling which only the wealthy could afford, but they were only proof against the gases known at the time of the 'Great War' as well. Surely, asserted the U.D.C., new and more persistent gases have since been secretly developed. Thus the only value of these measures must be to develop a war psychology among the masses. The S.M.A.'s Science Committee reiterated these arguments in 1936, in its pamphlet *Gas Attacks – Is There Any Protection?* There was for some, it concluded, but not for, say, the 280,000 London families living in one- or two-roomed flats.[39] However, unlike the pacifist U.D.C., which stated that the only defence against air attack was the prevention of war itself, the S.M.A. castigated the Home Office for failing to advocate the single most adequate form of protection, namely heavy bomb-proof shelters. Assuming for the moment that these critics were correct and the A.R.P. programme was not reformed, what then would be the consequences in wartime? Bertrand Russell in his *Which Way to Peace?* painted a grim enough picture,[40] which Aldous Huxley was then able to embellish in the *Encyclopaedia of Pacifism*. 'A bombardment with a mixture of thermite, high explosives and vesicants', Huxley asserted, 'would kill large numbers outright, would lead to the cutting off of food and water supplies, would smash the system of sanitation and would result in general panic. The chief function of the army would be, not to fight an enemy, but to try to keep order among the panic-stricken population at home.'[41] Even without resorting to fantasies about an atomic bomb, the pacifists were able to pile one horror upon another, thereby hoping either to make war unthinkable or to render Britain more secure.

Unfortunately, in the view of 'Ten Cambridge Scientists', 'such easily controverted statements' too often allowed the government to hold up the entire peace movement to ridicule.[42] This was one reason why the Cambridge Scientists' Anti-war Group decided in November 1936 to test the efficacy of the Home Office's gas-proofing procedures for itself. In taking on such a practical task, the group was also politically engaging its members as scientific workers. Its 'labs' were located either in a basement room on King's Parade or in the sitting-room of Peter and Nora Wooster. Such after-hours experimentation, measuring the rate of 'half-time' gas leakage out of a room, often proved to be a time-consuming and discomfiting experience. But it had its pleasures as well. Nora Wooster recalls one of the tests with particular amusement.

We used to evaporate large quantities of solid carbon dioxide into the air until we got something like 10 per cent of the atmosphere CO_2. And at that time it had a quite profound effect on your breathing. You used to pant very hard at every breath, and it was really quite exhausting. This went on for a period of two or three hours. On one occasion, a couple of friends of ours went into the drawing-room and sealed themselves up. After they'd been in there a time, we heard peals of laughter. And this went on until about two o'clock in the morning. Naturally we were very intrigued to find out that this was due to their discovery of a copy of *Little Black Sambo*, which they hadn't come across before. So they read *Little Black Sambo* and proceeded to laugh, and then they read it out again, and then they laughed again. Perhaps this was really the effect of large quantities of CO_2 on one's sense of humour, I don't know.[43]

At least they had the pleasure of getting 'high' from their work, in contrast to the luckless research student John Fremlin. Fremlin got so caught up in this work that he very much neglected his own investigations at the Cavendish. One of his political experiments involved the liberation of tear gas in his college rooms. Having cleared the gas from his lodgings, or so he believed, Fremlin tried to go to sleep. He failed to do so. Even though his

windows were wide open, the gas was still there. Luckily he had a
respirator-mask which he put on before retiring yet again. Fremlin
continues the saga:

I slept in that respirator all night and woke up in the morning feeling a
bit odd, turned over and got about half a pint of cold water down my neck,
which had condensed in this thing while I was asleep. Then my bedder, who
was a Mrs Cronin, came in weeping copiously. She was very concerned
about what was happening to me. But she very nobly went down the stairs,
wiping her eyes, and prevented one of the college porters coming up,
because this might lead to trouble . . . As it happened, the gas still had two
or three days to evaporate.[44]

(One side-effect of Fremlin's misfortune, however, was to arouse
his doubts about the effectiveness of the respirator mask: but that
is another story.) Fortunately for the Anti-war Group, its main
gas-proofing experiments never managed to cause as much havoc
as Fremlin's.

In February 1937 the results of the group's first set of investigations were published by Victor Gollancz under the title of *The
Protection of the Public from Aerial Attack*. Since this book provided
the first substantive challenge to the official A.R.P. programme,
its conclusions were bound to become noteworthy. The most
important points made by the Cambridge scientists were these:

assuming that the air outside contains enough mustard gas to kill a man in an
hour, it would be possible on an average to remain alive for about three
hours in the gas-proof room; in other words the 'gas-proof' room is not
gas-tight. Completely gas-tight rooms can only be constructed, at great
expense, by experts.

Emphasis has [also] been laid on the fact that, first, one million of the
population do not possess a room which can be set aside for gas-proofing
and that, secondly, seven millions more would have to live under conditions
which are officially defined as overcrowded if one of their rooms were set
aside as a gas-proof room.[45]

In short, the group found that the Home Office's provisions were
technically unsound and would discriminate against the urban
working-class. This challenge, to quote from the 'official' history
of civil defence during the Second World War, caused the government 'some concern'.[46] The C.S.A.W.G. was twice invited to
speak to M.P.s in the House of Commons. They in turn put
questions to the Home Secretary. The press began a campaign that

was gingerly critical of official A.R.P. policies. But it was not until 16 November 1937 that Geoffrey Lloyd, the junior minister for civil defence, officially responded to these charges. On the following day the *Guardian* reported that his principal tactic had been to attack the 'politically motivated' character of the Cambridge group.

Criticism of the efficiency of the gas-proofing recommendations of the Home Office had come before a body called the Cambridge Scientists' Anti-war Group (Ministerial laughter) [!]. He wished to make it clear that this group was quite distinct from the general body of Cambridge scientists, and their using a name which was liable to be taken as investing them with a certain authority was gravely resented by the senior members of the faculty. This group, to say the least, has a political tinge. (Ministerial cheers.)

Lloyd went on to report that experiments conducted on the Salisbury Plain by the Chemical Warfare Research Services on 'a gamekeeper's cottage in a good state of repair' – 'not even a modern town house', Professor Kendall would later harumph[47] – easily controverted the Cambridge group's results. Outside of Parliament, the Left scientists received uneven support from their professional peers. The Association of Scientific Workers strongly endorsed their work,[48] as did J. B. S. Haldane. Nevertheless J.B.S. did find the government's new evidence impressive and believed furthermore that the C.S.A.W.G. had overestimated the persistence of lethal concentrations of gas in the atmosphere.[49] *Nature*, however, published a damning review of the book by General Foulkes, a former commander of the British Army's chemical warfare section. Foulkes accused the Cambridge scientists of perverting 'scientific theories . . . for political ends' and attempting 'to create panic'.[50] As far as he was concerned, the Home Office's recommendations 'are generally sound and reasonable, and it is important that public confidence in these measures shall not be shaken unnecessarily'.[51] To judge from all these comments the line between science and politics was getting thinner all the time.

Despite the strictures of the government and its supporters, the Anti-war Group held its ground and indeed tried to widen the debate still further. 'We have no desire to create panic,' it replied to Foulkes, 'but those who persuade the people of Great Britain to believe that they are safe when they are not are inviting panic and worse than panic in the case of war.'[52] While the group did not dispute the Salisbury Plain experiments, it noted that vital details, such as whether the cottage had been subjected to explosives as well as gas, had not been disclosed.* In any event, the radical researchers were unrepentant about their own experimental procedures, which had shown, among other things, the need to fill up cracks in skirting- and floorboards; an important detail omitted from and eventually added to the Home Office's handbooks. Yet the most stunning omission of all was the A.R.P. officials' refusal to address themselves to the issue of public shelters and the probability that high explosives, not poisonous gases, were likely to pose the greatest dangers to a civilian population. For all these reasons the group remained adamant in its opinion that the Home Office's programme was 'a tragic deception of the people of this country'.[53]

The second stage of the A.R.P. campaign then moved on in 1938 from the controversy about gas-proof rooms to the efficacy of government-issued gas masks and the necessity for a large-scale, state-financed scheme of civilian shelters. The first issue was taken up by Fremlin, by this time an employee of Standard Telephone and Cables in London. For this investigation he succeeded in enlisting the support not only of his former Cambridge colleagues, such as the biochemist R. L. M. Synge, but of the *Daily Express* as well. The *Express* agreed to purchase gas-masks and gases, and to give the story prominent coverage, if, as Fremlin claimed, the masks proved to be ineffective against arsenical smokes. They did. Thus on 17 August 1938 the *Express*'s readers found splashed across the front page: 'GAS MASKS: AN INVESTIGATION – Government's civilian designs fail in *Daily Express* tests – INEFFECTIVE AGAINST CHEMICAL SMOKES.' Spread across three columns was a picture of Synge, who 'is here seen awaiting first aid' after the fumes had got through his mask. This was one of a number of actions that would lead the government to devise a more effective filter for its 2s. 6d. mask.[54]

Of far greater importance, however, was the shelter issue. In

* Indeed the Cambridge group had good reason to be sceptical. For while working in the Public Record Office on the A.R.P. Department's archives, I came across two revealing photographs (D8101/02 in H.O. 45/17632) of the Salisbury Plain work. These photos demonstrated three things. First, the 'gamekeeper's cottage' was in fact a modern structure built of sturdy bricks. Second, it was located in an open field where the gas would be easily blown away. Third, from photograph D8102 it is clear that the gas was fired at the one wall of the house which had no windows.

September 1938 the Left Book Club launched a massive campaign based solely on this aspect of the A.R.P. debate. The L.B.C. initiative featured the combined talents of Bernal, Haldane and John Strachey, who between them addressed mass meetings in over forty cities. At the same time Haldane's long-awaited study of *A.R.P.* was published. Drawing on his experiences in both the First World War and the Spanish Civil War, J.B.S. was able to put forward an authoritative, independent and fresh critique of the Home Office's programme. He quickly discounted the menace of gas, adding that the effect of the A.R.P. Department's proposals was to confine people to their homes and thus leave them tragically exposed to the full effects of high explosives. Therefore, in his view, 'the entire air raid precautions schemes so far adopted are rather worse than useless'.[55] Haldane called instead for a two-part emergency reconstruction of the nation's civil defence system, including such measures as the appointment of a minister in this area, the replacement of ex-servicemen by civil engineers in the A.R.P. Department, the digging of trenches in open places, the use of tube stations appropriately modified as underground shelters and, in the long run, the initiation of still more ambitious projects. But J.B.S. was doubtful about how far the government would go in admitting its previous errors. He was therefore 'convinced that nothing short of a great national movement on non-party lines will force the government to protect the people from the real and terrible dangers which await them'.[56] In these circumstances Haldane very much valued how seriously the shelter question was treated by the C.P.G.B. Shortly thereafter he decided to become a Communist.

For once, history proved to be on the side of the scientific Left. Just as the L.B.C. began its A.R.P. campaign, Britain became gripped in a war scare that lasted until the Munich settlement. Even after Chamberlain's pact with Hitler it was evident that many people had lost confidence in the Home Office's rationale for side-stepping the issue of public shelters. Within the government itself, doubts were also being raised, up to and including the Cabinet itself. As Sir Samuel Hoare, then at the Admiralty, confidentially conceded to the Chancellor of the Exchequer, Sir John Simon:

We are dangerously backward in protection against the consequences of high explosives, especially in the vulnerable areas represented by important industrial cities with crowded populations . . . It is clear that the country is anxious for large developments in the shelter policy, and the government must adopt measures which will secure vigorous and quick progress with all practicable schemes for providing such protection.[57]

Later an official historian would recount how the 'public demand that the government should take steps, regardless of cost, to provide some form of universal protection' finally compelled the Home Secretary to admit that 'a more comprehensive policy was needed'.[58] In less than a year the A.R.P. budget rose to £42,000,000, an increase of nearly 500 per cent. A distinguished civil servant, Sir John Anderson, was appointed to oversee this vastly expanded programme. Shortly after his assignment to the Home Office, Anderson attended an All Souls' garden party in Oxford. There he was introduced to a wiry, red-haired physicist who proceeded to tear apart the existing arrangements for civil defence. Anderson's antagonist was of course Bernal, who was now based in London. Afterwards the new A.R.P. major-domo insisted on having as one of his principal advisors in the Home Office this refugee from the Cambridge Scientists' Anti-war Group.[59] Such an action was a credit both to Anderson's judgement and to the success of the scientific Left's intervention in the great A.R.P. debate.

Apart from its specific contributions to the reformation of Britain's civil defences, the Cambridge Scientists' Anti-war Group helped in two ways to educate its members politically. First, as J. F. Danielli pointed out in the *Scientific Worker*, their experience had demonstrated 'the absolute necessity of independent criticism of government statements on technical questions, whenever there is the least suspicion that policy, as well as accuracy, is influencing the mind of the government'.[60] This visible politicization of science, their own as well as the state's, greatly enhanced the left-wingers' plea that scientists had to take a stand and commit their own professional skills to the struggle of their choice. Science did have social relations, which scientific workers could ignore only at the peril of themselves and their society. The scientific Left's second political gain was that, by moving from discussion to action, it involved its members with a greater diversity of individuals and institutions than they would have ever encountered by remaining in and around King's Parade. For example, shortly after the

Anti-war Group's book was published, John Fremlin found himself dispatched as a speaker to, among other places, the Epsom Trades Council, the Royal Free Hospital, the Hornsey Labour Party, a meeting of the National Association of Labour Teachers in Hackney, the Walthamstow Peace Council, the Halifax chapter of the Peace Pledge Union, a women's guild in south London, the Paddington Communist Party branch, the Streatham Left Book Club and, last but not least, the Harrow Green Contact Club – 'an adventure in comradeship for men of goodwill'![61] Apart from those wider contacts with the British labour movement, the Left scientists linked up in 1936 with their French counterparts to establish a Science Commission within the International Peace Campaign.[62] This kind of international cooperation between 'progressive' researchers would later result in the foundation of a World Federation of Scientific Workers. In the short run, however, the net effect of all these endeavours was to drive many of the Anti-war Group's members into taking up a more explicitly left-wing position. That was how the scientific Left grew up in Cambridge. Given what Cambridge represented to the rest of British science, it was now unlikely that the momentum of its 'young turks' could be contained within the boundaries of a rather sleepy East Anglian market town.

3. A Popular Front for Scientists

The influence of the scientific Left quickly radiated outwards from Cambridge after 1935. London now became more important for radicalized scientists, not only as a well-organized sub-culture in its own right but, almost inevitably, as the administrative hub of what was increasingly a national movement. A clear indication that left-wing researchers had 'arrived' within their own profession was the sympathetic attention they were starting to receive from some of the more liberally minded members of the science establishment. One reason for these unprecedented overtures was that, by design and persuasion, the radicals and liberals had moved closer to one another on several key issues. The approach of a major European war also helped to push the two sides together, in spite of their remaining ideological differences. But we should also recognize, as did the more astute elders of High Science, that unless they took a greater interest in the social relations of their community, they would lose ground to the left-wingers who did. In fact that was why they had already lost control of the Association of Scientific Workers. For the establishment had not adequately reckoned with the tactics of the Cambridge Left, led as ever by the irrepressible Bernal.

Had the radicals not been so active, on the other hand, the Association of Scientific Workers might have collapsed altogether. By 1932 the A.Sc.W. had become a floundering organization with a declining membership. Three years later, following the resignation of the 153-strong branch at the National Physical Laboratory which Levy had originally organized, it was left with only 600 senior members.[63] But it was also in 1935 that the Association revised its general policies and appointed a new Honorary General Secretary, W. A. Wooster. These changes were to save the organization. To understand why they were made we must go back to 1932 when Wooster's predecessor, Professor B. H. Holman, came to Cambridge to recruit new members. Much to Holman's own surprise, his efforts were handsomely rewarded, largely because they coincided with the same political ferment that had led to the founding of the Cambridge Scientists' Anti-war Group. Within the space of eighteen months, Bernal and Wooster, along with Bill Pirie, made their way onto the local steering committee. The presence of strong contingents from the Dunn and Cavendish labs thereafter helped to boost the Cambridge branch's reputation as the most lively group within the A.Sc.W.[64] Then in 1934 Bernal was elected to the association's national Executive Committee. In a tremendous burst of energy, the 'Sage' subsequently prepared the draft of a new policy statement and persuaded Wooster to succeed Holman. By December 1935 this statement of aims, officially put forward by the Cambridge branch, was adopted; and so was Wooster.[65] During the next three years more representatives from the Cambridge Left gained seats on the Executive. Eventually they were strong enough to force the resignation of the association's ineffectual Organizing Secretary, Dexter Smith. He was replaced on 1 January 1938 by Reinet Fremlin: a former Cavendish research student, Cambridge Scientists' Anti-war Group activist, recently Honorary Secretary of the Cambridge A.Sc.W. branch and wife of John Fremlin. By common consent if was Mrs Fremlin's dynamic conception of her role as an organizer that was critical to the association's revival.[66] By 1939 the A.Sc.W. had 1,319 members, a figure that would double only two years later as it moved back into the area of industrial organizing. The scientific workers' organization was at last thriving under a radical leadership that unquestionably had its roots in the Cambridge Left.

What these newly organized scientific workers were after was recently highlighted by Reinet Fremlin.

There was a liveliness of effort to make the association represent the growth of feeling among scientists that something needed to be done. We stood for a greater use of what science could give in improving industry, medicine, agriculture – science for the benefit of mankind. We saw that this involved raising the status of scientists themselves. Science needed more government support. It needed better laboratory conditions. We wanted better pay and promotion responsibilities. These all came into our aims, but, in general, we wanted to educate the general public in what science could do if given the opportunity. And we wanted to educate scientists themselves to demand these opportunities to do it. That's my feeling as to what we were aiming at, at that time.[67]

It was this aggressive optimism about science, combined with the association's new determination to fight against scientific frustrations and for scientists' material interests, that gave it such vitality. It proposed through the Parliamentary and Scientific Committee a comprehensive reorganization of British academic, industrial, medical and agricultural science.[68] (We should not be surprised to learn either that this scheme was prepared by Bernal, or that it was turned down by the government, principally because it gave scientists too much autonomy from Parliament.)[69] The association also gave its wholehearted support to a number of Popular Front causes, including the defence of academic freedom, the resettlement of German refugees and the various malnutrition campaigns. But its propaganda extended to broader themes as well. Thus in the spring of 1937 the A.Sc.W. sponsored a series of public lectures on historical and contemporary aspects of the social relations of science. About 200 people attended them on average, and the series was credited with having led a number of people to join the organization.[70] More prominent among the causes for increased membership, however, were the association's decisions not only to admit research students as associate members but to organize industrial laboratory staffs, including technicians, as well. This was a foretaste of the direction which the A.Sc.W. would take in the following decade.

But it was also a tremendous vindication of the perspective adopted many years earlier by Hyman Levy, who had for too long, in the words of one admirer, 'been buried and almost suffocated beneath the association's cloak of academic respectability'.[71] Levy was no longer a loner. He was now an integral part of a movement that was making its presence felt both inside and outside the community of science.

As the scientific Left grew more prominent, its locus began to shift to London, where some of its leading personalities – Bernal, Haldane and Levy, for example – had taken up professorships. The London branches of the A.Sc.W. had already played an important role in the left-wing takeover of their organization's National Executive. In addition to their trade-union activities, the city's radical researchers had also begun to overcome their isolation from one another by forming in 1937 a Scientists' Group within the Left Book Club. Organized from the East End by Harold Rose and strongly supported by Hyman Levy, this organization was the first and most active of its kind.[72] It put together a travelling exhibition on 'the Frustration of Science', arranged its own lecture series on science and society (attended by an average of two hundred paying customers) and, perhaps most impressively of all, set out to educate itself, both about Marxism and world affairs. The group's activities were widely publized through the L.B.C.'s *Left News* and probably served as a model for the Scientists' Groups subsequently formed in Birmingham, Bristol, Cambridge, Derby, Leeds and Leicester.[73] (It was even rumoured that some *industrial* scientists, who were members of the Left Book Club up in the north-east of England had also come together.)[74] Another manifestation of a radical trend within Britain's laboratories was the establishment in 1937 of a Scientists' Peace Association in Manchester.[75] How many such institutions were launched, how long they lasted and how effective they were, are questions for which there will probably never be answers. For the structure of British political life and the prestige of High Science both conspire to drag us back time and again to Cambridge and London. Nevertheless that was where left-wing researchers were able to make the most substantial impact.

No one was more aware of and disturbed by the gains of the scientific Left than the editor of *Nature*, Sir Richard Gregory, and his associates.[76] Representing as they did an important body of 'middle opinion'[77] inside the science establishment, it is not surprising that, for the better part of the thirties, their own publication's leading articles were overtly hostile to the radicalism of the Bernalists. Hence *Nature* could always be relied upon to criticize severely such left-wing initiatives as the Cambridge Scientists' Anti-war Group's experiments,[78] the association of Scientific Workers' proposals for reorganizing research[79] and even Bernal's *Social Function of Science*.[80] It also took every opportunity to score the Soviet Union for its restrictions on the intellectual autonomy of its scientific community.[81] In fact, apart from its praise of the U.S.S.R.'s polar expedition of 1937,[82] the journal never once uttered a favourable comment about Soviet science in any of its leading articles, from the revolution of 1917 to the outbreak of the Second World War. On the basis of this record, the emergence of a scientific 'popular front' that united the Left with some of its staunchest critics appeared to be most improbable.

However, beneath the surface of *Nature*'s composed anti-communism, there was actually a good deal of ideological turmoil.[83] Contrary to the earlier expectations of Gregory and the scientific establishment, British capitalism was proving unable to evolve with ease an economic and political environment conducive to the development of a scientific renaissance. Not only were scientists under-employed but their advice to the government was quite plainly ignored as well. While the Depression was breaking down scientific morale at home, the rise of fascism was playing havoc with the vaunted internationalism of science. The Nazis constituted a special problem for *Nature*. Not only were they guilty of persecuting the German scientific community, but – and this was a real embarrassment – their eugenic policies were not all that different from those which the journal was still backing. A further blow to its hopes for the development of science as a progressive force came in the form of new schemes for the militarization of the British research community. The net effect of all these tribulations was to demonstrate to Gregory and his associates that society, not science, had the final say in the direction of scientific as well as social change. To the extent that they saw the emergence of

historical forces inimical to their self-interests, *Nature* and the establishment were accordingly obliged to revise their political outlook
and rally their fellow scientists to it. Otherwise they might lose
that initiative to those infernal young Marxists.

These ideological uncertainties presented the scientific Left with
opportunities both to compete for the leadership of their peers and
to pull some of their elders in a more liberal direction. Although
science's senior statesmen remained committed to capitalism, albeit
of a more planned and scientific variety,* they were ripe for conversion or co-option on a number of lesser fronts. These included
their assimilation into organizations devoted to the relief of German
refugees, the defence of civil liberties, the fight against malnutrition,
the attack on biological racism and the prevention of war. The
younger radicals were also keen to prevent the more progressive
members of the establishment from completely abandoning the
Association of Scientific Workers, which therefore retained them
in various honorific positions. What ultimately made these unprecedented alliances more plausible, however, was the growing evidence
of the scientific Left's professional respectability. By the late thirties
no one in his right mind could deny its adherents' devotion to the
advancement – and defence – of scientific virtues. Their leaders
included some of the most brilliant researchers of the inter-war
period. Their political allies in the wider Popular Front were
becoming ever more scientific in their orientations. And then one
began to pore over the left-wingers' writings on the social relations
of science, all of which were dedicated to the widest possible extension of scientific knowledge. If the message about the relative
'soundness' of these men and women had still not been received,
then, finally, this was no fault of their faithful publicists: Ritchie
Calder of the *Daily Herald*; J. G. Crowther of the *Manchester
Guardian*; and C. P. Snow, in his capacity as editor of *Discovery*

* The impulse to a planned capitalism was an important ideological strain
in the politics of the 1930s. It was most prominent in 'The Next Five Years'
group, which included radical Tories like Harold Macmillan and Liberals such
as A. D. Lindsay. Among the signatories of its manifesto were a number of
personalities associated with the scientific community: Samuel Alexander, Sir
Richard Gregory, Lady Daniel Hall, Julian Huxley, Sir Oliver Lodge, C. S.
Myers, Lord Rutherford and H. G. Wells. (See *The Next Five Years; An
Essay in Political Agreement* (London, 1935), pp. v–x.) Incidentally, it was
Macmillan's family publishing house that produced this volume and *Nature*.

magazine.[84] Here indeed was a combination of forces that ought to have won the sympathy of all but the most conservatively minded figures.

Rather than give a detailed account of how these processes developed and interacted throughout the thirties, let us instead concentrate on how they affected just one individual, Julian Huxley, and a single institution, the British Association for the Advancement of Science. Huxley, we may recall from Chapter One, was a prototypical scientist of 'middle opinion' in the 1920s. Among other things, he was a 'moderate' eugenist, the President of the Association of Scientific Workers during its most apolitical phase and the proponent of a rather Victorian form of scientific humanism. But like many of his ilk, Huxley was alarmed by the scientific retrogression he saw around him. His immediate response was to jump on the 'planning' band-wagon, both as a foundation member of the Society for Political and Economic Planning (P.E.P.) and as an associate of the Next Five Years Group. So far he seemed to be an unexceptional figure who had happily steeped himself in the wisdom of *Nature*.

At the same time, however, Huxley was prepared to accept the tutelage of his left-wing friends when it came to three crucial issues: the U.S.S.R., eugenics and the social relations of science. It was Crowther who first introduced Huxley to the achievements of Soviet science, in the summer of 1931. Huxley's initial impression of socialism, as *A Scientist among the Soviets*, could not have been more favourable. Of course the Russian economy was 'planned throughout'.[85] But, much more importantly,

Science is an essential part of the Russian plan. Marxist philosophy is largely based upon natural science . . . Not only does it assert that the method of science is the only method in the long run for bringing phenomena under our control, not only does it assert that this is applicable to social as well as to biological and physical phenomena, but it asserts that the scientific attitude must form part of the Communists' general outlook.[86]

Through 'the elevation of science and scientific method to its proper place in affairs', Huxley concluded, 'the new Russia . . . is in advance of other countries'.[87] Nevertheless, his experiences in the Soviet Union neither persuaded him to become a socialist nor moved *Nature* to soften its anti-communism. What they did allow was the growth of a somewhat more generous estimate of the Soviet Union's scientific achievements.*

Huxley's views on eugenics underwent a similar transformation, in part because Lancelot Hogben did not hesitate to inform his friend that, in propagating them, he was acting like a neo-Nazi.[88] Thus, in contrast to his complaint in 1931 that the 'stupid' and the 'shiftless' were inheriting the earth, Huxley emerged in 1936 to address the Eugenics Society on the need to take an environmentalist perspective. After quoting Hogben – who was anathema to most eugenists[89] – on the need for equalizing educational opportunity before measuring levels of intelligence, Huxley finished his Galton Lecture by asserting that 'we shall only progress in our attempt to disentangle the effects of nature from those of nurture in so far as we follow the footsteps of the geneticist and equalize environment . . . We must therefore concentrate on producing a single equalized environment'.[90] Three years later Huxley would join Haldane, Hogben and Needham in defining as a suitable productive environment one that was organized 'primarily for the benefit of consumers and workers'.[91] Once that had been done, biologists could more readily determine the genetic background to good health, high intelligence and 'those temperamental qualities which favour fellow-feeling and social behaviour, rather than those . . . which [make] for personal "success", as success is usually understood at present'.[92] Though he still sought biological explanations for social behaviour, Huxley had at least abandoned his previously reactionary approach to these questions.

* Gregory may have been unusually reluctant to concede any of the Soviet 'experiment's' good points, but his friend H. G. Wells was not. Indeed Wells felt that the direction of Soviet history actually confirmed his own belief in the power of scientific necessity. In some respects, his judgement here was acute. Thus: 'Contact with reality . . . has obliged communist socialism to become progressive and scientific in method, in complete defiance of its founder and of its early evangelical spirit. Lenin conjured government by mass-democracy out of sight . . . by his reorganization of the Communist Party so as to make it a directive élite, and by his organization of the soviets in successive tiers.' The U.S.S.R., Wells concludes, 'is now no longer a communism . . . It is a novel, experimental state capitalism, growing more scientific in its methods every year. It is the suppositious child of necessity in the household of theory'; which all sounds fine, except for one thing. What, Mr Wells, did you mean by 'reality'? From H. G. Wells, *Experiment in Autobiography*, vol. 1 (London, 1969), pp. 265–6.

Having become something of a progressive liberal in his attitudes towards the Soviet Union and social biology, Huxley was now ripe for conversion to a 'Marxist' perspective on the workings of the scientific community. The year is 1933. His 'tutor' this time is Hyman Levy. The scene is set in a B.B.C. studio, where Levy and Huxley are about to launch a series of broadcasts on 'Scientific Research and Social Needs'. Action. Levy begins by asking his biologist companion how he would define science. Huxley replies: 'Well, I generally like to think of science as a body of knowledge . . . This knowledge can generally be applied to controlling nature, but most scientists, I think, would say that there definitely is something that can be called *pure science*, which has a momentum of its own and goes on growing irrespective of its applications.'[93] To which Levy responds: 'Well, Huxley, I think that to state things in this way is to lay a false emphasis on pure science.'[94] 'It does not seem to me', Levy continues,

that science becomes 'pure' because there are individual scientific workers whose personal motive in carrying through investigations is that they desire simply to extend the boundaries of knowledge. The existence of such a motive does not necessarily enable them to lift themselves outside their historic social epoch, but it may mean that they will concentrate their attention on problems more remote from direct application. Science, however, does not cease at discovery. It is also concerned with application, and the applications are to the systems of society in being . . . Moreover, since scientists, like other workers, have to earn their living . . . to a large extent the demands of those who provide the money will, very broadly, determine the spread of scientific interest in the field of applied science . . . I know of no scientist who is so free that he can study absolutely anything he likes, or who is not restricted in some way by limitations such as the cost of equipment.[95]

After this interchange Huxley conducted a tour of different research establishments. By the final broadcast he was persuaded that 'the form and direction which it [science] takes are largely determined by the social and economic needs of the place and period'.[96] Huxley concluded that the chief moral of the series was that

science is not the disembodied sort of activity that some people would make out, engaged on the abstract task of pursuing universal truth, but a social function intimately linked up with human history and human destiny. And the sooner scientists as a body realize this and organize their activities on that basis, the better both for science and for society.[97]

From this brief survey of Huxley's 'pilgrim's progress' we can readily understand why subsequent commentators have lumped him together with his radical associates. But Huxley always differentiated between his political outlook and, as he once wrote, that of 'extreme left-wing socialists like Levy and Needham'.[98] When the political climate changed in the late forties, he would amply substantiate this claim.

In the interim, however, Huxley did appear to drift on to the periphery of the Popular Front; and so did *Nature*. Leaving aside its continuing antipathy to the Soviet Union, the journal did reverse itself on a number of issues, not least eugenics. After January 1936 Gregory ceased to commission any leading articles from eugenists, whether moderates or extremists. Instead his journal came out squarely in favour of the sentiments put forward in Huxley's Galton Lecture.[99] Temporarily at least, the Eugenics Society began to suffer a loss of scientific respectability.* Even before its conversion to environmentalism, *Nature* had been won over to the 'social relations' perspective that Huxley had imbibed from Levy. Thus shortly after their joint broadcasts, the journal's most prolific leader writer, Rainald Brightman, could proclaim:

> The conception of science as a social function intimately linked up with human history and human destiny, moulding and being moulded by social forces, should summon forth from scientific workers something of the energy required to translate into policy and action the knowledge acquired by their work. Such energy will find its expression . . . in . . . the faith that human reason, by using wisely the scientific method, can give us the control of our destiny.[100]

To the extent that this approach was originally identified with those who regarded themselves as Marxists, we might therefore wish to

---

* The eugenists nonetheless clung to their belief that 'the principles of eugenics, being based on science, should appeal to all political parties'. They therefore continued to aim 'at improving the race by 1) permitting the fertility of superior, healthy and useful stocks, and 2) restricting . . . the multiplication of those . . . stocks with bad heredity'. (From the inside cover of a Eugenics Society pamphlet issued in the early forties and prefaced by Julian Huxley.) But, given the unemployment of 'able' workers through no fault of their own, 'it was a bad time', the Eugenics Society's Secretary would later concede, 'for eugenists to assess their values in terms of class.' From C. P. Blacker, *Eugenics: Galton and After* (London, 1952), p. 141.

agree with Neal Wood that 'the Marxist conception of the function of science and the role of the scientist in society gained wide currency, dominating the British world of science within a decade'.[101]

But Wood's formulation, with its implication that the scientific Left occupied a commanding position within the scientific community, is misleading in at least three ways. First, *Nature* represented in the 1930s, at most, only a progressive minority within the science establishment. For example, according to A. V. Hill, the Royal Society officially refused to take part in the social relations of science debate, on the grounds that the society 'didn't want to get mixed up with what might turn into politics'.[102] Second, when it came to liberal causes, senior scientists of middle opinion were often level with, if not in advance of, the scientific Left. Thus within a matter of weeks after the first expulsions of Jewish scholars from Germany, researchers like Hill and Lord Rutherford were able to set up an Academic Assistance Council (later renamed the Society for the Protection of Science and Learning).[103] Furthermore, of all the initiatives taken in the fight against malnutrition, none made a more decisive impact than the publication in 1936 of Sir John Boyd Orr's *Food, Health and Income*.[104] Finally and most surprisingly, it was Gregory, along with Lancelot Hogben, who featured most prominently in the establishment of the Trader Union Congress's Science Advisory Committee in 1939.[105] Though this organization eventually co-opted Bernal and Blackett, it effectively pre-empted any similar initiative on the part of the Association of Scientific Workers, much to its own chagrin.[106]* Third, we must not forget that *Nature* continued to abhor Soviet communism quite as much as it did German fascism. Hence its equation of the threats posed by Hitler and Stalin to the internationalism and freedom of science led the journal to support the exclusion of both Germany and the U.S.S.R. from the councils of world science. *Nature*'s rationale for this decision was that 'in these countries at present scientific workers are bound much more closely to their respective government than is the case elsewhere'.[107]

* The T.U.C.'s alliance with the scientists never got off the ground, however. Ten weeks after its formation, the Second World War began and the organization simply packed up. In any event, by the war's end, the Association of Scientific Workers had become affiliated to the T.U.C.

In short, the perception that science had social relations was not, in itself, a radicalizing influence. Such a perspective could have been used to show up communist as well as fascist regimes. Nevertheless, in its time, it had progressive, even socialist overtones. Perhaps that is why, in 1939, Hyman Levy was so pleased to observe that, after trying 'to find a compromise way out of the obvious dilemmas that faced the scientists', *Nature* was finally obliged to lend its support to 'the growing demand for a study of the social relations of science'.[108]

This then was the background to the alliance which liberal and radical scientific workers were finally able to forge in the late thirties. Its institutional locus arose out of the foundation of a Division for the Social and International Relations of Science, within the venerable British Association (or British 'Ass', as it is known to its friends and detractors alike).[109] One of the advantages of this format was that no corporate decisions would be taken by the new organization on matters of social policy. Instead the 'purpose of the division', as explained at the time by the Assistant Editor of *Nature*, 'would be to further the objective study of the social relations of science. The problems with which it would deal' were, principally, 'the effects of the advances in science on the well-being of the community, and, reciprocally, the effects of social conditions upon advances in science'.[110] The role of the new division was *discussion*; it was carefully designed *not* to become the kind of forum already realized by the radicals in the Association of Scientific Workers, whose members could collectively speak out on controversial questions. On the contrary: in the very act of drawing together, liberals and left-wingers signified how far apart they really were. Nevertheless, in a special supplement which appeared in *Nature* in the spring of 1938, all sides agreed that the formation of such a body was a Good Thing.[111] Among its radical supporters were Bernal, Haldane, Hogben, Levy, Needham and the entire A.Sc.W.[112]

The division was formally christened four months later at the British Association's annual meeting – held fittingly enough on this occasion at Cambridge. It was, by all accounts, an extraordinary gathering. As Crowther drily observed in the *Guardian*, 'the remarkable unanimity in support of the new division astonished many members. Persons with contrary political opinions were equally strongly in favour of it.'[113] At one level the whole affair seemed to connote a major victory for the Left, which certainly was able to make a great show of strength on its own (well-rolled) Cambridge 'turf'. Special discussions were organized by the Cambridge Scientists' Anti-war Group, the International Peace Campaign, the Left Book Club's Scientists' Group and the Association of Scientific Workers. (No prizes will be awarded for the correct guess as to who was the principal speaker at every one of these events.)[114] If one blinked in the direction of the liberals, however, one could also note how firmly in control they were of the new organization. Gregory was not only the incoming President of the whole association, but Chairman of the General Committee which managed the social relations division as well. While four left-wingers (Bernal, Blackett, Hogben and Levy) had found their way on to the Divisional Committee, their influence was utterly swamped by the presence of no less than thirty-four other members of rather more moderate persuasion. Radicalism was therefore still very much a minority affair, especially when placed in the context of this final observation of Crowther concerning the Cambridge meeting: 'It provided a splendid illustration for the general public of the quality and vigour of British academic science. But the atmosphere was still that of the educated and ruling upper classes; full evening dress and dinner jackets were worn by nearly everybody at the chief social functions. It was still the science of the British Empire.'[115] Whether the new division advanced beyond this definition of the 'social functions' of British scientists remained to be seen.

Despite the division's shortcomings, the scientific Left was keen to praise it. A particularly fulsome evaluation of its potential was made by J. D. Bernal, who wrote as follows in the *Reynolds News* of 28 August 1938:

The Cambridge meeting of the British Association may well prove a turning point in the history of science, for it announced a discovery of an importance altogether different from any of the great discoveries that have been announced there in the past. This discovery was not in science, but about science. It was that scientists for the first time have become conscious of the need to concern themselves with the social consequences and possibilities of science . . .

Up till now the scientist has been isolated. Now, coming together in his own association, he can, for the first time, effectively demand that science should be properly used, and lend force to a popular demand that these evils should be no more, that science is made for all men and not for the profit of a few.[116]

Crowther was of a similar opinion, arguing that 'by its courageous action' the B.A. had not only 'saved' itself but also 'strengthened the hope for a better world through . . . the solution of social problems by the application of scientific method'.[117] Levy, on the other hand, described the division – somewhat tongue in cheek, perhaps – as likely to 'have gladdened the heart of Condorcet'.[118] Yet even if he genuinely believed that this century-old association had only just caught up with the 'advanced' thinkers of 150 years ago, this perception did not prevent him from participating in its affairs and lecturing on its behalf.[119] Nor did its less than radical orientation preclude the A.Sc.W.'s cooperation with the B.A.'s efforts to study more closely the industrial employment of scientific manpower.[120] Bernal, as we might have expected, was active in the division, preparing with Julian Huxley a lengthy memorandum on the need for the 'Further Coordination of Scientific Research in Great Britain'. Impressive though these initiatives were, their impact on the British Ass. was minimal. For one year after the division had been inaugurated, the Second World War began.

Indeed it is only against the backdrop of a rapidly developing war psychology that we can fully appreciate the alliance between liberal establishment figures and younger left-wingers. For whatever degree of consensus they had reached on specific issues, the two camps remained seriously divided, not least over the fate of scientific workers in the Soviet Union. Having agreed that science had social relations, they still held very different views about what social relations it ought to have. But in a time of national emergency such divisions carried much less weight than the evident need to collaborate with one another in the face of a common enemy. Certainly this was the ethos which the Communist Party had been projecting through the Popular Front. It was also the attitude which the government had adopted, both in its consent to the appointment of a prominent left-winger, P. M. S. Blackett, to the secret committee that would oversee the development of radar,[121] and in its co-option of Bernal as an adviser on civil defence. Given those precedents, it was most unlikely that socially conscious researchers would not join hands for limited purposes at an extraordinary moment in British history. One symbol of the pressures which those circumstances exerted was that *Nature*'s first and most detailed proposal for the wartime mobilization of scientific workers was anonymously written by J. D. Bernal – the only leading article he ever wrote for the journal.[122] Another sign of change was the B.A.'s division, founded in the shadow of Munich and organized when the hope of 'peace in our time' was fast fading.

But we should also recognize that, had the scientific Left failed, either organizationally or intellectually, to coalesce as effectively as it did in the 1930s, the science establishment would never have been confronted with the necessity for an alliance in the first place. To that extent we must credit left-wing researchers with a substantial political achievement. Against very severe odds, they had been able to generate, out of their own limited resources and those of the Popular Front, a sense of radical movement within an exceptionally staid scientific community. Obviously the scientific Left had its problems, very severe ones, not least with regard to the numbers of those who were prepared to commit themselves fully to political struggle. As C. H. Waddington has cautioned:

> Remember it was a very tiny movement, . . . primarily of people who were not the slightest bit professional either in administration or in politics. Some got themselves tied up with . . . Marxist communism, in a strictly interpreted manner. As for others it was relatively peripheral to their interests . . . It wasn't the major concern of their lives really until they got absolutely involved in the war effort and it was a question of survival as it were.[123]

Given those limitations, the great visibility which the scientist-activists did achieve for their endeavours was all the more remarkable. Ultimately we kept coming back, did we not, to the same names: the Fremlins, the Woosters, the Piries and the Needhams; Levy, Haldane and, without doubt the most dynamic member of this tiny coterie, J. D. Bernal. Having created something of a progressive momentum inside their own peer group, however, they were now faced with the task of sustaining and accelerating it, in a decade that would prove to be both scientifically and politically very different from the times which had engendered them. One of the most important of these changes would be an intensified involvement on the part of the Communist Party of Great Britain in the affairs of science.

4. Making the Left Safe for Science

The scientists were of course not the only section of the British intelligentsia which the Communist Party attempted to organize in the 1930s. Indeed in the earlier part of the decade it was the left-ward drift of younger writers and poets, as well as of university undergraduates, that captured the imagination of the public and the party alike. Though these groups were initially more vocal and better organized than the radicalized scientific workers, the primary reason for their greater prominence was the more central position they occupied within Britain's dominant culture. Poetry and literature still constituted the lifeblood of high cultural life. Oxbridge retained its monopoly position both as a finishing school for the ruling class and as a way station for those who were destined for entry into the state élite. So strategically placed were these two sectors that the slightest hint of a subversive tendency was bound to be detected. Hence when a coterie of young poets published a semi-political manifesto, or the Oxford Union vowed not to support King and Country in a future war, or Cambridge students staged a pacifist demonstration on Armistice Day, the press and college authorities (over-) reacted accordingly. So did the Communists, who had recognized as early as 1931 that the ancient universities might prove to be a novel and important arena for agitation. Through the creation of special forums and publications such as *Left Review*, the C.P. also sought to encourage the political development of certain members of the literati, who welcomed new opportunities for writing, speaking and dramatizing what was on their mind. These were the years of Auden, Spender and Day-Lewis, of MacNeice and Isherwood and of Ralph Fox and Edward Upward. (Note how, with the exception of the socialist novelists Fox and Upward, they have remained household names to this day, in contrast to the relative eclipse suffered by their scientific counterparts.) Given the attention they received from the commanding heights of British culture, not to mention the C.P.G.B., it is not surprising that their initiatives at first made a greater impact than did those of radical scientists.

The party was also not entirely clear at first what it should make of the scientific obsessions of left-wing researchers. Above all the Communists were not certain in the thirties whether Bernalism was a Marxist heresy, or a sound extension of orthodox Marxism. As late as 1939, the *Labour Monthly* reviewer of *The Social Function of Science* could still criticize Bernal's tendency 'to idealize science as a revolutionary factor in itself and of itself'.[124]* That remark probably represented the view of many Communist intellectuals who were not themselves scientists. It most certainly conveyed the alarm felt by Benjamin Farrington, a party member and classicist, who had returned to Britain in the mid-thirties after a spell of teaching in South Africa. Here is what he encountered.

Well, my impression when I got to London and began to meet people was that at least half the Marxists whom I met were scientists. But I had the impression also that their Marxism was of a peculiar brand. They seemed to be under the impression that Marxism had originated from scientific sources, I mean the physical sciences, and not to be so much aware of the social and philosophical background. And I was alerted to this owing to the fact that we in Cape Town . . . the Marxists whom I had come across . . . were very alert to Trotskyism, very keen on Leninism and just ready to be alarmed at the way Stalin was developing, you see. And this picture of communism was in my mind.

But in England, chiefly also among scientists, I found a complete optimism about Marxism and science. It seemed to them and I heard the actual words from them, that Marxism was the theory which gave science its opportunity . . . And it seemed as if science and Marxism had absolutely been married to one another – they were the same kind of thing. And this used to worry me and disappoint me, because I hadn't looked at Marxism in that light.[125]

Though Farrington probably gives too much credit to the scientists

* Later in *Science in History* (London, 1954, p. 739), Bernal would implicitly accept the force of this criticism. Thus during a discussion of Marx's social thought, he observes: 'The victory of the class which can bring about productive relations more in harmony with the contemporary productive forces leads to a higher stage in society, and also to a rapid further improvement in the means of production. That improvement, which has been immensely accelerated by science in the last two centuries, has been a factor in creating social instability, but cannot in itself be a cause of social change, which must always have a human motive force.' This is a reasonable and consistently Marxist standpoint, which Bernal unfortunately never quite managed to feed back into his work on the social relations of science.

for creating the Left's obsession with science, he was aggrieved at the ways in which they specifically magnified the role of scientific and technical advances as the key factor in social change. Bernal, he felt, was particularly guilty of this error.

> Perhaps the most impressive champion of Marxism was J. D. Bernal . . . a most attractive man in every way. But I remember the first time that I heard him giving a public lecture, saying to myself: 'Well, Bernal is obviously under the impression that Marxism is a product of the physical sciences'. . . And then when *The Modern Quarterly* was founded, Bernal contributed an article on the social function of science, in which he said: 'The discovery of civilization was a local event. It had acquired nearly all its essential features by the sixth millenium BC, but only at its centre somewhere between Mesopotamia and India. We cannot trace in the succeeding thousands of years, right up to the Renaissance and the beginning of our own times, any substantial changes in the quality of civilization.' As I say, this kind of mentality, you can understand, made me gasp. I mean my life was spent trying to persuade people that they should learn Greek; and then that they should learn Latin and read Virgil and Tacitus and Cicero; and then that they should understand the astonishing change which had taken place when religion derived from the third great centre of antiquity, the Jewish religion, conquered the pagan world and became the religion of Europe, without which you can't understand the history of Europe. And to find the whole thing dismissed as – 'we cannot find right up to . . . the beginning of our own times any substantial changes in the quality of civilization'; I mean most of the world that interested me was ruled out by those judgements.[126]

The interest of Farrington's testimony here is that it comes from a Communist who worked closely with and greatly respected Bernal, Haldane and Levy, in particular. Moreover, as a noted historian of ancient science and sympathetic biographer of Francis Bacon,[127] he cannot be charged with the traditional biases of an arts man who ignores or denigrates scientific knowledge and its practitioners. What Farrington did find objectionable was the 'scientism' of Bernal and his associates, their over-evaluation and reification of their science as *the* revolutionary force behind the collapse of capitalism and the rise of socialism. In that respect, he undoubtedly spoke for other Marxists who were less than scientific.

Nevertheless, as a result of the scientific Left's organizational gains, the influence of a 'scientized' Soviet Marxism, the Popular Front's defence of science and civilization, and the containment of class conflict in an unscientific Britain, scientific workers were beginning to establish their own cultural pre-eminence within the Left. This shift in emphasis was symbolized in 1938 by the simultaneous demise of *Left Review* and the birth of *The Modern Quarterly*. In contrast to the literati who controlled the review, the quarterly's Editorial Council was dominated by natural scientists, including five Fellows of the Royal Society. Moreover, of the seven articles which were featured in its first issue, three were written by Levy, Bernal and Needham, while a fourth, contributed by Farrington, was devoted to the science of classical Greece. But in case the drift to a more scientific Marxism was not self-evident, the new journal's 'Statement of Aims' admirably clarified this tendency.

We live in an age of great intellectual activity, of great achievement in the social and material sciences. Investigators are probing more and more deeply into the nature of matter and developing more perfected methods of controlling our environment. All the technical conditions for vast advances in knowledge and in social progress seem to be present.

But it is becoming increasingly apparent that in modern society these achievements are not being utilized to the full; we are accustomed to the company of war and poverty, and to the perversion of scientific discovery to ignoble and injurious ends . . .

One aspect of this crisis is an increasing scepticism as to the validity of scientific thought and a growing disregard for human values . . . Already in the fascist countries this tendency has reached its most extreme expression as a national cult cynically enforced by an authoritarian state.

We believe that it is urgently necessary to combat such tendencies. We hold that the great advances in science and learning are not only contributions to our knowledge of truth, but should be put to the service of society as a whole. We wish, therefore, to contribute to a system of thought which will correspond to the real world which science analyses and in which we live. In this connection we recognize the arts and sciences as an integral part of the social progress of mankind.[128]

This was the credo that heralded the approaching ascendancy of Bernalism within the Communist Party.

In this loud and clear affirmation of 'the validity of scientific thought', Bernal, the scientific Left, the C.P. and the Popular Front were committing themselves to a particular political strategy. Its most obvious objective was to bring many more scientists into the socialist movement. Its most convincing tactic was to contrast the frustration of science under capitalism with the scientific achieve-ments of the Soviet Union. The force of this argument would derive in part from the authority of the distinguished researchers who put it forward. When the different elements of the new approach were combined, they were intended to convey the message that science, modernity and communism were much the same thing. However, by associating the scientific enterprise with their politics, the Communists were also obliged to tailor their policies to science. Banal and tautological as that may sound, it is an important point. For the Left had now denied itself the option of treating science as, fundamentally, an artefact of capitalism – as opposed to a model of socialism.

What then were the political consequences of upholding the ideological neutrality of scientific knowledge? Theoretically, it was no longer 'on' to assert, as did Clemens Dutt in 1933, that 'it is not merely fields like eugenics and race theory which are permeated by class prejudices. In a wider sense the character of scientific theory in a particular society reflects the existing social relations'.[129] What Dutt had joined together – science and ideology – had now to be teased apart *and* turned into opposites: truth versus distortion. The practical corollaries of that belief were that Communist scientists in a capitalist society should have no qualms about their professional work. Not only were their methods and findings valuable in them-selves but the more successful they were in their careers the more effective would they be in their political work. Hence the first duty of a Communist researcher was to be a good researcher. That was the line that was to be pushed forward in the forties; and with good reason, in view of its successful application in the 1930s.

But suppose for a moment that the science/ideology distinction was not so absolute. Imagine further that British capitalism recovered its economic stride and scientifically reformed itself. Then consider the possibility that, in attempting to clear away the barriers between intellectual and manual workers, the U.S.S.R. discovered that it had to break with both the theories and the practices of bourgeois science; otherwise the aims of socialism could not be achieved. If all of these fantasies – and that is how they would have been regarded in the late thirties – ever materialized, in what direction would Communist scientists in Britain have had to start changing their personal, professional and political lives?

To the best of my knowledge only one man in this period took those sorts of propositions seriously and tried to work out what bearing they might have on the conduct of bourgeois socialists. His name was Christopher Caudwell: an engineer-turned-freelance writer, a Communist based in the East End of London and one of a select number of young intellectuals who died in the Spanish Civil War. In his *Illusion and Reality*, first published in 1937, Caudwell maintains that people like himself have 'three possible roles in relation to the proletariat – opposition, alliance or assimilation'.[130] His usage of 'alliance' and 'assimilation' is ambiguous. At times it seems to denote nothing more than a distinction between those who are and are not members of the Communist Party. But these terms also have wider connotations for Caudwell. Thus to be assimilated fully into the working class – to become a real communist – entails, on the part of bourgeois revolutionaries, the fulfilment of two obligations above and beyond party membership. One of these is the development of a shared existence, materially as well as politically, with the proletariat. (Caudwell lived for two years with dockers in a Poplar lodging house before he went off to Spain.) The other is the acceptance of proletarian leadership in one's own special field. On neither count does he feel that left-wing intellectuals are trying to change the character of their lives and their consciousness.

To Caudwell this split between their proletarian ideology and their bourgeois life-style is fraught with personal and political dangers. (Though his discussion concentrates upon the situation of art and its practitioners, he makes it clear that his analysis can be equally well applied to science and scientists. Thus in subsequent quotations I shall be substituting 'science' for 'art'.) Here is how he characterizes their dilemmas.

They announce themselves as prepared to merge with the proletariat, to accept its theory and its organization in every field of concrete living except that of science. Now this reservation – unimportant to an ordinary man – is absolutely disastrous for a scientist, precisely because his most important function is to be a scientist. It leads to a gradual separation between his living and his science – his living as a proletarian diverging increasingly from his science as a bourgeois. All his proletarian aspirations gather at one pole, all his bourgeois science at the other. Of course this separation cannot take place without a mutual distortion. His proletarian living bursts into his science in the form of crude and grotesque scraps of Marxist phraseology and the mechanical application of the living proletarian theory . . . His bourgeois science bursts into his proletarian living in the form of extraordinary, and quite unnecessary, outbursts of bourgeois 'independence' and indiscipline, or quite apparent bourgeois distortions of the party's revolutionary theory. It leads to an unconscious dishonesty in his science – as of a man exploiting the revolution for his own ends . . . This is only dishonest because it is unconscious – if open, it would be a fair working alliance, an acknowledged treaty like that which politically unites the different parties of the People's Front.[131]

What disturbs Caudwell about the reservations of Left intellectuals with regard to *their* 'freedom' in a future socialist society is that, if '*all* these different petty-bourgeois claims were granted, they would, when lumped together, negate any proletarian society at all, and simply equal the retention of the present system against which they revolt'.[132] Naturally this criticism does not 'affect the individuals who make the demand, for they have carefully segregated their particular fields of interest from the field of life as a whole, and the scientist is, for example, quite content to see the artist proletarianized'.[133] 'It is for this very reason', Caudwell concludes, that 'the more the petty bourgeois becomes revolutionary, the less he can operate in his own organizations with other bourgeois revolutionaries, and the more he becomes an individual under the hegemony of the proletariat'.[134]

Caudwell's perspective, however acute and challenging, simply could not be applied immediately to the circumstances of the British intelligentsia. It was hard enough, as we have seen, to get scientific workers to act positively as liberals, let alone revolutionaries. Nevertheless his observations did have the value of reminding socialist intellectuals that they were unlikely to transform society unless they changed themselves before as well as after the revolution. Hence at some point the Popular Front mentality that 'we are all scientists now' must give way to a more painful, demanding and liberating form of politics. Otherwise Communist scientists shall be forever tempted to place their science before their socialism or, even worse, collapse the latter into the former. To reverse that tendency Caudwell asks his fellow intellectuals to begin merging with the proletariat.

The contrast between his 'utopian' strategy and the 'realistic' one adopted by the C.P.G.B. is evident when we turn to the political evolution of J. B. S. Haldane. Haldane, we may recall, was highly sensitive to the gulf that his aristocratic past had created between him and his proletarian allies. He was, still more remarkably, willing to break with many aspects of his bourgeois world. At the same time he knew, as did the C.P., that 'who-he-was' could be exploited in the service of the Popular Front. And they were right, of course. Whether it was the Albert Hall or Trafalgar Square, J.B.S. could pack them in. One indication of his drawing power was that a lecture he gave in 1937 on 'A Dialectical Approach to Biology' – not exactly everyone's idea of fun – attracted an audience in London of more than 180 people.[135] Another testimonial to Haldane's charisma has come from Lord Ashby, who in 1936 was just embarking on his academic career at the University of Bristol.

I do remember there being a group [of us] who were so interested in the Spanish War that we asked J. B. S. Haldane down to Bristol, and we couldn't get a hall big enough for him to talk in. There was an enormous sympathy and interest in . . . what Haldane was then standing for, which was really that scientists as an élite – and that's how scientists used to think of themselves in those days – should stand up for their political principles. Haldane gave a talk on the Spanish war. I remember he arrived with a beret and sheaves of notes, having come from Spain . . . He got a most enthusiastic reception, and I was one of the people who stayed up all night, because we had to put him on the first train in the morning to get back to London.[136]

That scene was to be re-enacted hundreds of times in the coming decade. Each time Haldane would find himself at the centre of these rituals, through which his aristocratic status was restored to him.

Haldane regretted his entrapment in this vicious circle, but he accepted the political conventions that put him there in the first place. Indeed only a few years later he would consent to the release of an extraordinary hagiographical account of his life. This was part of the C.P.'s strategy to turn J.B.S. into a hero of the people.

HE SPEAKS TO MILLIONS

This is the story of Professor John Burdon Sanderson Haldane, Fellow of the Royal Society, member of the French Société de Biologie, honorary member of the Academy of Science of the U.S.S.R. and member of the Executive Committee of the Communist Party.

It is the story of an outstanding British scientist whose life has been dedicated to the investigation of problems that will help ordinary men and women to live and work under healthier and safer conditions . . .

Above all it is the story of a professor whose teachings have been taken to millions of people through popular books, magazines and newspapers, especially through the columns of the *Daily Worker* . . .

All his work is related to the fight for human progress and the seeking of truth for the benefit of the people, but he will deny that everything he does is of immediate practical value . . .

Meantime, he believes in giving ordinary people an understanding of scientific matters, and equipping them with a scientific way of thinking. The popularity and fame of his *Daily Worker* articles proves how right he is in this view.[137]

'Haldane . . . Royal Society . . . U.S.S.R. . . . . Communist Party . . . outstanding British scientist . . . dedicated to . . . ordinary men and women . . . whose teachings have been taken to millions of people . . . his work . . . the fight for human progress . . . seeking of truth for the benefit of the people . . . giving ordinary people . . . a scientific way of thinking.' Here we see J.B.S. turned into an object of reverence; a man *for*, but, inevitably, not *of* the people; an Olympian figure whose 'teachings' could inspire 'ordinary men and women'. It would be an absurdity to countenance the 'assimilation' of such a person into the proletariat.

Yet placed against the uncertain rewards (and certain perils) of Caudwell's politics, J.B.S.'s choice – and, by extension, that of his comrades – was, in the context of the thirties and the ideology of Bernalism, a sensible and 'correct' one. Indeed, compared to his outlook on the eve of the 1931 History of Science Congress, Haldane could now present himself to the world as a mature and committed socialist. So could Bernal, Levy, Needham and, though many would have disputed it at the time, Hogben. Behind them was a decade in which they had created from scratch an impressive literature on the social relations of science and a still more remarkable Popular Front for their fellow scientific workers. On the basis of those achievements they would now press forward not only to new gains but to new problems as well.

9

Part Three

Since the Thirties

Chapter Eight

Two Cultures, Two Camps

Why is it that so many party members adopt the fashionable habit of using the word 'scientific' to mean 'true' and the word 'emotional' to mean 'false'?
A Communist schoolteacher/poet in
Edward Upward's *The Rotten Element*[1]

The test of the devotion of the Union of Socialist Soviet Republics to science will come when the accumulation of the results of human genetics, demonstrating what I believe to be the fact of innate human inequality, becomes important.　　　　　　　J. B. S. Haldane, 1928[2]

On 1 September 1939, the oldest of our central characters (Levy) had just turned fifty; the youngest (Bernal) was approaching his thirty-eighth birthday. Already those men, along with Haldane, Hogben and Needham, had become the British Left's most outstanding spokesmen on scientific affairs. During the next three decades they would not only consolidate and extend that position, but add to their scholarly honours as well. They were also able to witness within their own society a series of scientific transformations that they had advocated (and predicted) in the thirties. Consequently, as they approached the end of their lives, these socialist statesmen of science had numerous academic and political reasons for feeling contented with their respective lots. Above all, they had not abandoned their pre-war commitment to socialism.

Yet, from the angle of the political hopes and successes they had nurtured in the thirties, their story now assumes a darker aspect. For we are about to enter a period of right-wing backlash within the labour movement and the scientific community. The post-war impact of organized anti-communism on left-wing scientists was especially severe, because of the strategic position they had come to occupy among progressive intellectuals. Indeed, while the literary Left had already gone into decline, the scientific Left was still, as of 1945, in its ascendancy. Buoyed up by the triumphant application of their notions of 'planned' science in wartime, riding high on a wave of widespread demand for the reform and modernization of British society and avidly courted by the Communist Party, it was inevitable that figures like Bernal and Haldane would be placed among Britain's leading left-wing theoreticians. As such, they were ideal and important targets for intellectual Cold Warriors bent on discrediting communism, the Soviet regime, leftist 'subversives' and, above all, the scientific ethos of Marxist ideologies. Although these attacks failed to alter, in any fundamental way, the ideological standpoint of their victims, they did encourage a new generation of scientific workers not to meddle in (radical) politics.

Despite those personal and political setbacks, the thirties' generation of radicalized scientists did manage to regroup themselves in the early 1950s: some to organize around the issues of peace, malnutrition and the Third World; others to extend their theoretical and historical perspectives on the social functions of science. In two instances at least – the Campaign for Nuclear Disarmament and the Labour Party's later call for a 'white-hot' technological revolution – their organizational and intellectual initiatives had significant political repercussions. But it was not until the foundation in 1969 of the British Society for Social Responsibility in Science that the old scientific Left could be certain that there would be a new generation of socialists to carry on its work into the future.

1. Scientific Warfare

The scientific Left, with some notable exceptions, whole-heartedly supported the national war effort from the very onset of the Second World War. Indeed, the greatest fear of many radicalized scientific workers was that their skills would not be effectively utilized by the fighting services. After all, asserted the Association of Scientific Workers in October 1939: 'It is a war in which science will play an important part, and it is necessary that our scientific resources should be used in such a way that they can be of the greatest effect in supporting the whole defence machinery of the country'.[3] These sentiments were to be amplified many times over during the first year of the war, not least in the leader columns of *Nature* (by Julian Huxley)[4] and the *Manchester Guardian* (by J. G. Crowther).[5]

But the most famous and influential broadside on this subject was a Penguin Special entitled *Science in War*. The book was an anonymous product of the 'Tots and Quots', a London-based dining club regularly convened by an urbane Oxford biologist named Solly Zuckerman.[6] Among its regular members in the period 1939–40 were Bernal, Crowther and Huxley, as well as the physicist P. M. S. Blackett, the biologist C. D. Darlington, the economist Roy Harrod, and C. H. Waddington, another biologist. By the summer of 1940 this liberal–Left coterie was eager to publicize its collective anxieties about the state's under-utilization of scientific workers. To that end, Zuckerman invited Allen Lane, the founding father of Penguin Books, to come along to the Tots and Quots. Lane was, in turn, so impressed by the quality and urgency of the discussion that he commissioned a book on the spot – provided that the club could produce the manuscript in less than a month. It did, and in August 1940 *Science in War* charged on its bold orange and white covers that 'The full use of our scientific resources is essential if we are to win the war. Today they are being half-used.' The attack continued on page one.

It should be appreciated that until now, the world of science has had little say about the use to which scientific advances are put. Had it been otherwise, and had scientific methods played their part in home and international affairs, war might have been avoided . . .

(For) science is the most orderly expression of normal ways of acting and thinking: there is therefore a great need today for quick scientific thought. Only scientific method can deal effectively with the new problems which turn up daily, and the issue of the war depends largely on how quickly and how effectively science is used.

In other words, science 'should be used not only to improvise immediate new methods of offence and defence, but also for surveying the whole field of war needs and war methods'.[7] These sentiments revealed at a very early stage not only the scientific Popular Front's depth of commitment to the war effort but also what scientific lessons Bernal and others would draw from their experiences, once hostilities had ceased. In the meantime *Science in War* was well received, widely read and reprinted less than three months after its first appearance.*

The only one of our central characters who did not throw himself immediately into the campaign for making warfare more scientific was Hyman Levy. Levy believed that, as a member of the Communist Party, he was obliged to support the party's 'phoney war' policy. Briefly, the upshot of this line was that, as a result of the Nazi-Soviet non-aggression pact, the conflict between Germany and Britain had to be viewed as an imperialist war, which served the interests neither of the British, German nor Soviet working classes. Now, caught between its pre-war and quite genuine hopes of an anti-fascist alliance and its current near-defeatist theoretical position, the party struggled to produce a coherent strategy. This took the form of a call for a 'people's convention' that would generate support for the replacement of the Chamberlain government with one committed to a 'people's peace'.[8] Until Hitler's invasion of the U.S.S.R., Levy vigorously spoke and wrote on behalf of the convention movement,[9] and by these initiatives earned in equal measure the opprobrium of many non-Communists[10] and the respect of the party's leadership. Like many party members, he was therefore considerably relieved when the Soviets were compelled to join forces with the Allies.

J. B. S. Haldane shared in this relief. For, prior to June 1941, his position had been even more complicated (and apparently contradictory) than Levy's. In fact, while publicly defending the concept of a 'phoney war' in the columns of the *Daily Worker* – which the government closed down in January 1941 – he simultaneously conducted a number of investigations for the military and contributed one of the chapters in the Tots and Quots' Penguin Special.[11] His biographer has attributed this behaviour to 'a form of geological fault which separated Haldane's actions on to two

---

* The anonymity of *Science in War*'s authors allowed them, somewhat unscrupulously, to review their own book. Crowther and Huxley did so in the *Manchester Guardian* and *Nature* respectively, while Zuckerman was given space in *Nature*'s leader columns to commend the volume that he had been so instrumental in producing. See 'Men of Science and the War', *Nature*, vol. 146 (27 July 1940), pp. 107–8.

distinct planes'.[12] It could be argued that J.B.S.'s opposition to the war as it was being prosecuted was in fact consistent with the aim of most of his early wartime researches (see below), designed as they were to save the lives of civilians and service people previously placed at risk by various forms of governmental neglect. Whatever rationale really guided J.B.S. through this politically confusing period, its rationality was undoubtedly enhanced once the war had become an unambiguously anti-fascist, pro-Soviet and, not least, an increasingly scientific conflict.

The specific contributions of the scientific Left's adherents to the war effort would make an interesting book in their own right. Hogben and Levy virtually reversed the positions they had occupied during the First World War. As a result of his political activities between 1939 and 1941, Levy was simply reserved as a lecturer at Imperial College. (Among his wartime students were two of Bernal's sons.) Hogben, by contrast, exchanged his old status as a conscientious objector for that of a colonel attached to the War Office. There, under the nominal supervision of his old friend, Brigadier Frank Crew, he comprehensively reorganized the British Army's section on medical statistics.[13] J. B. S. Haldane, however, remained true to his past record of daring self-experimentations.[14] His most important investigations were designed to improve the respiratory systems and escape procedures used in submarine warfare. As always, J.B.S. insisted on carrying out the most dangerous parts of the research either on his own or in collaboration with his most trusted associates. Apart from his official work as an adviser to the Royal Navy, he continued to function as the nation's leading unofficial expert on, and critic of, the civil defence system.

As for Bernal and Needham, neither of whom had seen action in the 1914–18 war, their wartime records were rather more exotic. After serving on the Biology War Committee and making what was, in effect, a propaganda tour of American universities, Needham was asked by the government to represent the Royal Society on a brief visit to 'Free China'.* Once there, he was able to persuade

* Needham's interest in Chinese affairs and culture was already well known. Apart from his activities on behalf of the Free China Campaign in 1939–40, he had already embarked on an intensive study of Chinese language and history. On the origins of his interest in this then highly esoteric subject, see the account of Needham's *alter ego*, Henry Holorenshaw, 'The Making of an

the British Ambassador to keep him on, not only as his embassy's Scientific Counsellor, but also as the head of a Sino-British Science Cooperation Office as well.[15] It was through the latter organization, in particular, that Needham was able to establish close contact with the Chinese people and their scientific traditions – an experience that was to alter profoundly the subsequent course of his life. Bernal, too, found himself transported around the world several times and, even more importantly, into the higher reaches of the British war machine. His pre-war interest in civil defence was extended to include his collaboration with Zuckerman on the physics of air raids. He was then moved from the Home Office to Bomber Command and ended up as Lord Mountbatten's scientific adviser in Combined Operations. His working brief ultimately encompassed nearly all significant aspects of strategic planning. Indeed, when J. G. Crowther came to write one of the War Cabinet's official histories, *Science at War*, he discovered that the 'weight of opinion was for Bernal' as the British scientist who 'had done the most to win the Second World War'. Furthermore, 'the persons who spoke most highly of (Bernal's) military scientific work were those who were most sharply opposed to his political views'.[16] One striking confirmation of Crowther's observation was the American government's award of its Medal of Freedom (with palms) to Bernal in 1945.[17]

In short, the scientific Left's leading ideologues had what came to be called a 'good war', and it was made even better when placed in the context of their pre-war utterances, actions and hopes. Then they had projected in their more utopian writings a Britain transformed through the combined efforts of a politically awakened scientific community and a scientifically enlightened labour movement. Now that improbable vision was beginning to materialize, thanks to the prosecution of a long and arduous 'people's war'. For the social dynamics of total warfare had not only shifted large sections of public opinion to the Left but compelled politicians, industrialists and generals to make some amends for their old, unplanned and unscientific ways as well.[18] More specifically, by the General Election of 1945 four scientists in five were prepared to vote for the Labour Party,[19] whose leaders were themselves becoming slightly more science-minded. The Communists had grown still more vociferous in their support of scientific socialism, while the Association of Scientific Workers and British Association for the Advancement of Science had both emerged as thriving havens for 'socially responsible' scientists, engineers and technicians. These were some of the many indications of a new convergence of commitments to science, planning and, above all, 'the people'. It all sounded enough like Bernalism to make our subjects believe that history, here and now, really was on their side.

Of course they did what they could to help history on its appointed way. As individuals who had in the thirties warned of the Nazi threat to international science, recommended the state's adoption of a scientific approach to social problems and spoken out on behalf of the needs and aspirations of scientific and other workers, Bernal and the others were inevitably involved in wartime debates about the forthcoming reconstruction of their society. They continued to regard the A.Sc.W. and the British Association as the main forums for the discussion of their ideas. But they also spoke and wrote a great deal for Communist-controlled organizations like the Anglo-Soviet Friendship Society and the University Labour Federation. Exposure to a wider audience was made possible through sporadic B.B.C. broadcasts. (One particularly interesting series entitled 'Science, Capitalism and Fascism' was produced in 1942 for the Indian Service by Eric Blair (George Orwell) and featured Bernal, Needham, Crowther and Benjamin Farrington.)[20] Last came their ever growing volume of published work: two collections of Needham's political and philosophical essays;[21] cheap, reprinted editions of Haldane's earlier works;[22] two new books by Levy;[23] and, not least, J.B.S.'s column for the *Daily Worker* whose circulation increased to over 100,000 once it was allowed to resume publication.[24] In none of these spoken and written contributions was an attempt being made either to extend the theoretical discussion of the past or to depart from the political strategies evolved during the Popular Front period. Rather they were crafted with a view to consolidating gains that left-wing scientists had already made in scientific and labour circles.

The intellectual restraint and political caution exercised by the scientific Left were handsomely rewarded, especially within the confines of the Association of Scientific Workers and the Communist Party of Great Britain. For the A.Sc.W. in particular, this was a remarkable period. On the one hand, it continued to operate as a progressively minded professional interest group, sponsoring among other things a series of conferences on the social benefits of planned science. On the other, the Association in 1941 decided to register as a trade union which in turn became affiliated one year later to the T.U.C. By mid-1943 the A.Sc.W. had attracted over 11,000 members – 10,000 more than had been on its books in 1939. Such a phenomenal rate of growth was almost entirely due to the A.Sc.W.'s determination to recruit in earnest industrial scientists and technicians. At first the interests and outlooks of the pre-war and wartime memberships were difficult to reconcile. The association's political initiatives had only a limited appeal to those based in industry, while its new status as a trade union troubled many academic 'brothers' who, in the words of one A.Sc.W. pamphlet, 'ascribe to trade unionism a character which belongs to past history and not to the present, a background of direct action, strikes, lockouts and violent demonstrations'.[25] Shortly after the war's end this split looked well on its way to being healed. For, despite its overwhelmingly industrial constituency, the organization was more firmly committed than ever to functioning as a critic of state science policies. The difference between the old and new A.Sc.W.'s was that this role was now being undertaken within and on behalf of the labour movement. That was the underlying message of *Science and the Nation*, the association's Pelican Original of 1947. No development could have pleased more the incoming President of what had become an 18,000 strong trade union. His name was J. D. Bernal.

This rapid assimilation into the labour movement of large numbers of scientific workers led by left-wing academics was one reason why the C.P. paid increasing attention to the claims of science in the 1940s. Even before the war, the party had begun to allow natural and social scientists to share some of the cultural limelight with their more erratic arts-based comrades. That tendency was reinforced in a world war where scientific 'boffins' were being transformed into back-room heroes. The Communists proceeded to capitalize on these developments in three ways. First, they brought to the fore of their own political agenda Bernal's old complaints about the frustration of science under capitalism. As Palme Dutt declared to the C.P.'s annual congress in 1943:

> The Communist Party stands with modern science. In contrast to the niggardly treatment of science at the hands of the old state and the monopolists, we stand for the fullest support . . . and facilities for scientific research, and the fullest utilization of the great discoveries of science in the interests of the nation. It is the scientists and the workers in alliance who will build the new Britain.[26]

The direct appeal to scientific workers as, at the very least, co-equals in the coming struggle for socialism was a second facet of the party's efforts to make itself over in the image of science. In this endeavour it had the full support of Haldane – now a member of the party's Executive Committee – who explained in a pamphlet of 1945 *Why Professional Workers Should be Communists*.

> The answer is that if you are good at your job, you would (in a socialist society) have more power and more responsibility than you have now. The leading commissars in the Soviet Union who direct great socialized industries, compared to which I.C.I. or any of the British railways are small fry, are business executives mostly trained as engineers. The leading scientists, writers and artists are very important people.

Some might say these promises were easy to make, coming as they did from a political party unlikely to assume control of the state. Just how earnest the C.P. had become about the scientific aspects of its socialism was therefore best judged in the light of the serious and extended discussions which it launched between 1945 and 1946 on the history, philosophy, social relations and politics of science. For the first time economists, historians and philosophers inside the party were seriously debating a range of scientific issues that had first been raised by Bernal, Haldane, Hogben, Levy and Needham. Echoes from these debates reverberated through the pages of *Modern Quarterly*. But the main forum here was the Engels Society, an organization set up in 1946 to deepen and publicize the party's interest in the past, present and future situation of scientific workers.

The political good fortune of the scientific Left was not limited to gains made on its own 'turf'. Things were also looking up inside the British Association for the Advancement of Science. Because of various wartime exigencies, the association was obliged to operate through the largely London-based committee which ran its Division for the Social and International Relations of Science. Given its brief (and its effective membership, which included Bernal, Hogben and Levy), the Divisional Committee was bound to place the parent organization quite firmly on the social terrain favoured by the Left.

Just how advantageous a position this was for progressive scientists became apparent in September 1941, at the B.A.'s Conference on Science and the World Order. One of the most remarkable aspects of this three-day gathering of ambassadors, governments-in-exile and Cabinet ministers, not to mention a cast of thousands, was that the Divisional Committee had only decided to sponsor it on July 17.[27] The committee was then responding partly to the suggestion of a joint meeting with the A.Sc.W. and partly, perhaps, to Hitler's recent invasion of the Soviet Union. Whatever its precise origins, the conference was quickly built up into a major propaganda exercise on behalf of both the Allied war effort and, as it transpired, the proponents of scientific planning and planned science. Its deliberations were recorded by the B.B.C., filmed by Pathe News, printed in full in the association's new magazine[28] and abridged as a Penguin Special.[29] Bernal, Haldane, Hogben, Levy and Needham were among the featured speakers,* as was the Soviet Ambassador, Ivan Maisky. Although, as expected, the conference endorsed the nostrums of intellectual freedom contained in a Charter of Scientific Fellowship, its political significance lay

* Our central characters did not fare equally well at these sessions. While Bernal proved to be a star performer and was given the job of summing up the entire conference, Hogben was unexpectedly and bizarrely humiliated during the presentation of his address. His tormentor was the session's Chairman, H. G. Wells, who, still suffering from a request to cut his own speech short the day before, was now out for blood. Seated behind Hogben and obscured by the rostrum, Wells counted the minutes, then the seconds. When Hogben's time ran out, Wells, without warning, grasped Hogben by the seat of his trousers and began to pull the slightly built biologist downwards. Before Hogben knew what was happening, he found himself sinking majestically into the ground in front of a thousand amazed spectators. He did not take the trouble to resurrect either his person or his oration. The next speaker, J. G. Crowther, took no chances and cut his remarks to the bone. See Crowther's *Fifty Years with Science* (London, 1970), pp. 232–3.

elsewhere. 'An interesting fact', noted in the journal *Chemistry and Industry*, 'is that of the sixty or more speakers at the B.A. conference, the great majority expressed, or implied, the conviction that scientific planning could be wholly successful only under a non-profit system, which would automatically remove probable sources of opposition to the schemes science would propose.'[30] That did not mean, however, that the venerable British Association was about to become a para-socialist institution. But at least its Divisional Committee was now prepared to attempt an injection of the scientific ethos into social and economic planning. To that end it set up a number of new sub-committees, organized several smaller scale conferences and established contact with a number of planning bodies. One small step for the scientific Left; a giant leap for the B.A., at least compared to its rather sleepy existence of a decade before.

However, when wartime changes in the image and outlook of the association are compared with those of other, still more august institutions, its transformation seems less remarkable. For the war enforced upon many sections of the British ruling class a new awareness of the potential benefits of a scientifically re-tooled society. This perspective probably came most easily to senior military commanders, who now often relied upon the operations research performed by their own scientific advisers.[31] But it was also being adopted by increasing numbers of industrialists, social scientists, civil servants and politicians. Evidence for this trend can be found in a series of reports emanating from the Federation of British Industry,[32] the Parliamentary and Scientific Committee,[33] and Nuffield College,[34] all of which emphasized the need to expand quickly and greatly the resources available for scientific research and development both in the public and private sectors. In this period of buoyant optimism about science, not even the officers of the Royal Society could resist the urge to meddle, albeit most delicately, in various affairs of state.[35] Admittedly, the consensus that was emerging about the need to render British capitalism more scientific was not sufficiently powerful to result in major changes in the organization of civil 'R & D' during the war. Yet year by year this tendency was growing stronger, whether measured by the number of semi-official recommendations emanating from 'the great, the good and the powerful', or by the ever rising budgets of

the Department of Scientific and Industrial Research.[36] Perhaps the
most impressive sign that science had arrived as a serious political
issue was the growth of the Parliamentary and Scientific Committee
from a rather pathetic body of fourteen M.P.s in 1938 to a much
more formidable group of 146 parliamentarians in 1946.[37]

Why, then, were so many influential people and organizations
now prepared to think harder about and spend more on scientific
means to the achievement of particular social ends? Most would
say 'the war', meaning that science was seen to deliver the goods,
whether in the form of new hardware like radar and, above all,
the atomic bomb, or in the guise of novel techniques devised by
scientists, notably operations research. But that still leaves us with
the question as to why science and scientists – as opposed to technology and engineers, or factories and workers – were perceived to
be so uniquely critical to the war effort. There were many reasons
for the popularity of this explanation. One of them was the existence
of the very campaigns, which we have already described, to propagate the ideology of scientism and link it to aspirations for social
change. A closely related cause was the equation that the British
people were encouraged to make between science, democracy and
the Allies on the one hand and anti-science, tyranny and the Axis
powers on the other. Once Britain and its partners had subdued
Nazi Germany, in particular, the force of that logic was widely,
if not deeply, appreciated. Nowhere was it spelled out more fully
than in *Science at War*, the official history (published in 1947) of
Britain's scientific achievements in wartime.

> This is the major conception – the reduction of war to a rational process.
> It is the contrary of that held by Hitler, who had a romantic view of war.
> He believed that wars are to won by great strokes of inspiration . . . System-
> atic scientific work on known weapons paid larger and quicker dividends. It
> beat Hitler . . . [For example,] Hitler and his generals failed to produce any
> operational research comparable to the British development. If they had,
> they would probably have won the submarine campaign and the war. But
> it was impossible for them to collaborate on a basis of equality with the
> rational, equalitarian scientists . . . (etc.).[38]

The prevalence of this reasoning, so remarkably similar to the
attitude adopted by Bernal and his comrades before the war, did
in fact owe something to their thoughts and actions. For their

perspective was not only transmitted through their writings and personal contacts with the scientific and military establishments but also embodied in the public stance of their key reference groups, not least the A.Sc.W., the British Association and the Communist Party. Heavily mediated though the scientific Left's influence may have been, it was acknowledged from at least one unexpected quarter as early as December 1940. In welcoming J. B. S. Haldane and the physicist P. M. S. Blackett onto the Royal Society's council, Sir William Bragg, P.R.S., remarked that

those who like himself could compare the present with the past, are happily and proudly convinced that the young men of today [Haldane was then forty-eight] are maintaining in full force the tradition they have received. But they are doing something more and something new. It is a chapter of novel importance, because, as they extend the record of the facts of nature they find themselves compelled at the same time to consider a new problem – the relation of those facts to society and to the government of nations.[39]

What these 'young men' had in fact done was to invest their vocation with a social significance which did not make itself felt until a war had been won partly through and on behalf of their science.*

Certainly that was how they tended to interpret their own war-time experiences. But in doing so Bernal and the others tried to separate the scientific achievements of the war from the capitalist context, albeit heavily 'socialized', in which they had been made. As Bernal would later observe, 'all that I had thought and written about the possibilities of the ordered utilization of science, I now saw enacted in practice, and I saw that where I had erred was not in overestimating but in underestimating the constructive power of

* During the war the Royal Society showed itself to be open to at least one key aspect of the scientific Left's political programme, namely the planning of science. In October 1943, Blackett and another physicist asked the society's secretaries to initiate a survey of university departments concerning the measures that would be necessary to ensure the post-war progress of fundamental research. Their proposal was accepted and, two years later, a report *On the Needs of Research in Fundamental Science after the War* was privately circulated to all F.R.S.s. Though this document did not entirely satisfy Blackett, it did indicate a willingness on the part of some elders of science to consider what in pre-war days might have been regarded as a dangerously radical proposal. (From B. Lovell, 'Patrick Maynard Stuart Blackett', *Biographical Memoirs of the Fellows of the Royal Society*, vol. 21 (1975), pp. 101-2.)

science'.[40] At the same time he fully realized 'how crazy a system was which found its only efficient and complete utilization of science in the service of destruction'.[41] Bernal was nevertheless decidedly coy in 1945 as to whether 'the successful transition from a pre-scientific and planless economy to a fully planned one' could be made through parliamentary channels 'with the minimum loss of efficiency and liberty'.[42] What he did most earnestly believe was that science – its methods, theories, discoveries, techniques and above all, its practitioners – was indispensable to the success, humanity and openness of any state plan. In particular, he stressed

how much science itself can do in removing the arbitrary and despotic elements which many persons of genuine liberal feeling imagine to be inherent in all planning . . . [For] the more scientific the analysis of the situation, the more possible it is to find a solution which will really answer the need and at the same time be the most acceptable one as demonstrably reasonable. Science, by accepting corporate opinion and reason as its criterion, is itself a democracy: one always open to conviction but not accepting any dictum until it has been convinced. In so far as science infuses government, it enhances all the democratic elements in it.[43]

Such a linkage of science, democracy, planning and social reform, though comparatively new in the thirties, was fast becoming a commonplace of liberal-Left thinking at the war's end.[44] Perhaps that ought to have been a sign to Bernal and his more advanced comrades to turn their minds to the more detailed implications of practising science not only in a socialist context but in a socialist manner as well.

However, the election in 1945 for the first time in British history of a Labour government backed by a substantial parliamentary majority, and mandated to enact far-reaching social and economic changes, was an event sufficiently momentous to preoccupy left-wing scientists with reforms in the here and now. Somewhat surprisingly, it was an open question whether Prime Minister Attlee's administration would respond to the aspirations of its many scientific supporters with the same enthusiasm it was expected to show towards those of its traditional working-class constituency. At first, the new government moved rather cautiously on the scientific front, despite the multi-levelled and overlapping campaigns for the re-organization and expansion of British science. Indeed, its most decisive act during the period 1945–6 was to appoint a Committee

on Scientific Manpower headed by Sir Alan Barlow of the
Treasury. Though the Parliamentary and Scientific Committee
welcomed this effort 'to consider policies governing the use and
development of scientific manpower and resources in the next ten
years',[45] it represented a minimal and highly orthodox response to
a set of ideas whose time had already come. More importantly,
the Parliamentary Labour Party was still openly bereft of a coherent
science policy.

There were nevertheless some encouraging signs that the P.L.P.
and other mainstream institutions of the labour movement were
beginning to assimilate the new scientific wisdom of the age. In
the forefront here was, rather incongruously, Herbert Morrison
who, as Lord President of the Privy Council, was responsible for
overseeing the state's civilian research and development programmes. At a conference organized in February 1946 by the
Association of Scientific Workers, Morrison went so far as to
declare that 'upon there being a scientific approach to human
problems depends the future of man'.[46] As if to demonstrate that
this was no mere rhetorical flourish struck off for the benefit of
assembled scientists, he went on to exhort them to put their work
in a social, indeed a political perspective.

Much of the hard work of scientists has been wasted because they have
been content to lose interest in its final development and distribution. Great
benefits have been misused because the scientists have been satisfied to be
specialists and have failed to give their work a social context . . . For that,
society is also to blame. There has been far too little imagination and understanding by governments, industries and other powerful influences of the
value of the scientific method.[47]

After making this very Bernal-like observation, Morrison went on
to pledge renewed commitment to planned science and scientific
planning in peacetime.

In Britain today we are attempting to reorganize our affairs and to do so
in a planned, tidy and scientific way. We are trying to make the best uses of
our full resources of men and materials, to bring about an orderly and
certain recovery of trade and living standards with the minimum of waste
and as soon as we can. To do this, to make this plan and carry it through,
we must recruit our scientists. We are taking a progressive step in coordinating the work of all kinds of scientists – the economists, the medical men, the

dieticians, as well as the physicists and the chemists – and harnessing their thought and effort to the machinery of the government.[48]

Morrison was followed on the platform by a T.U.C. representative who wanted members of the Association of Scientific Workers 'to feel that we in the labour movement generally and in the Trades Union Congress wish to see you as part of the great democratic movement which alone can bring about the salvation and the progress of the world'.[49] To that end the T.U.C.'s General Council re-established its long dormant Scientific Advisory Committee and filled it this time with scientists drawn exclusively from, not the British Association, but the A.Sc.W. It was yet another hopeful sign for everyone on the scientific Left that the long awaited marriage between science and British socialism might at last be consummated.

When set against so many unanticipated trends that favoured their pre-war stance, it was unlikely that Bernal, Haldane, Hogben, Levy and Needham would seriously alter their personal, professional or political arrangements in the post-war period. It is true that in 1945 Charlotte Haldane divorced J.B.S., who in turn promptly married his tough-minded and outspoken research assistant, Helen Spurway.[50] Perhaps a more remarkable change of circumstances was Needham's decision to abandon (at least temporarily) scientific research altogether and become the first Director of UNESCO's Department of Natural Sciences. (Indeed, he played an important part in implanting the S in an organization whose brief had been originally restricted to educational and 'cultural' affairs.)[51] Accompanying that decision was a subsidiary one taken in 1946 to 'spend a year writing a book on the history of science and technology in China'.[52] (Thirty years and many volumes later he is still trying to finish off that 'little book'.)[53] The only political departure that approximated the personal and professional changes undergone by Haldane and Needham was Bernal's short-lived period of 'intense respectability' in the eyes of the establishment.[54] In addition to his election in 1946 to the council of the British Association, he was appointed Chairman of the Ministry of Works' Scientific Advisory Committee. Almost by way of compensation for his entry into the corridors of power, Bernal played a leading role in the establishment on 21 July 1946 of the World Federation

of Scientific Workers.[55] The W.F.S.W. quickly gained an international reputation as a progressive 'front' organization dedicated
to world peace, dominated by British and French Communists or
fellow travellers and funded (partly) by the Soviet Union. Bernal
not only wrote its charter but also served as one of the federation's
first Vice-Presidents. Otherwise there was little variation in the
lives of the scientific Left's leading ideologues. Hogben, as was his
wont, had picked a quarrel with the Aberdeen authorities in 1941
and moved on to Birmingham University, which created a special
Chair of Medical Statistics for him in 1947. Hyman Levy, by contrast, began his third decade of service to Imperial College by
becoming simultaneously the head of its mathematics department
and Dean of the Royal College of Science. In short, they had all
in their own ways carved out suitable contexts in which to work
on the social and scientific problems that had come to define their
lives.

The coincidence of their personal, professional and political
maturity with the radical reformism of 1945–6 therefore constituted a highly auspicious beginning to the post-war era. Labour
was securely in power. The membership of the Communist Party
of Great Britian had reached an all-time high, as had that of the
Association of Scientific Workers and the Parliamentary and
Scientific Committee. A new and widely shared consensus about
the importance of science in national life seemed to be emerging,
while larger numbers of scientific workers were apparently becoming politicized. As the Left grew more scientific and scientists
took to radical ideas more easily, the prospect of a truly and fully
scientific Left was at last able to be seriously entertained by those
who could rightly lay claim to being its founding fathers – Bernal,
Haldane, Hogben, Levy and Needham.

2. Cold Warfare

Yet by 1950 the British Left, scientific or otherwise, was in disarray
– when it had not been absolutely routed. Such a precipitate decline
was ultimately the result of a series of confrontations between the
'two camps' – the 'Free World' led by the United States and the
Communist Bloc dominated by the U.S.S.R. In this 'Cold War'
the Labour government, out of ideological inclination as well as

economic necessity, fell in behind the Americans. The anti-Soviet initiatives orchestrated by the U.S.A. abroad were quickly paralleled by anti-Communist drives inside the British labour movement. At the same time a cultural Cold War was being mounted in the West against intellectual supporters of the East and on behalf of 'liberal' values. Inevitably, in the heat of these momentous controversies, distinctions between socialism and communism or militancy and subversion were dangerously blurred. It also became progressively more difficult to mount a *critical* defence of one's chosen camp; not to choose caused one even more problems. Domestically the practical outcome of these global developments was not merely to foreclose a second round of radical reforms but to put the Parliamentary Labour Party firmly behind the economic and cultural rejuvenation of the British ruling class.[56] Whether or not one finally attributes the concomitant decline of the Left to the machinations of American imperialism, one cannot understand how it all happened without reference to the government's manipulation of the labour movement, the Communists' tactical responses to the Cold War[57] and the intellectual Cold Warriors' efforts to discredit Marxism and its donnish adherents.[58] Together they stifled the war-born resurgence of radicalism among workers and professionals alike.

In these circumstances the scientific Left was bound to be attacked from many sides and with great energy. For not only had it engaged the support of many academic scientists but it had also encouraged the Communist Party, in particular, to stress the Left's monopoly of the causes of science, modernity and industrial progress. Leading Communist scientists like Bernal and Haldane were naturally singled out in the ensuing onslaught. Bernal was gradually stripped of his various jobs as a state scientific adviser. In 1949 he was not re-elected to the British Association's council, whose members had taken umbrage at a pro-Soviet speech he had earlier delivered in Moscow. Meanwhile tremendous pressure was being applied to J.B.S., both from Communists and anti-communists, to simplify his position on T. D. Lysenko's post-war leadership of Soviet biology. By 1950 Haldane – along with numerous other party scientists – had been driven into a highly cramped corner over this issue. He subsequently resigned from the party (though not officially because of the Lysenko affair). Apart from the humiliation meted out to particular individuals, the scientific Left suffered other, more institutionalized reverses. The Association of Scientific Workers lost thousands of members in the late forties and early fifties.[59] Partly as a result of its continuing attachment to the World Federation of Scientific Workers and other pro-Communist organizations proscribed by the T.U.C., the association also gave up the little influence it had briefly gained inside the labour movement.[60] Indeed the Labour government was to turn its back quite quickly on the A.Sc.W.'s approach to science policy-making.[61] Despite some new programmes (including the National Research Development Corporation and the Atomic Energy Authority) and a lot more money for research and development generally, Attlee and his ministers abandoned the rhetoric of scientific planning, failed to enlarge the specialist role of scientific civil servants and, not least, oversaw the effective militarization of large areas of British science.[62] These were only some of the many indications that left-wing scientists were unable to sustain either their hopes or their numbers in this period.

To a limited extent the scientific Left was the victim of its own theories and tactics, which had not radically changed since their first appearance in the early thirties. Then Bernal and the others had agreed that science, as an international and progressive force, was endangered. It could no longer either prosper or be humanely applied under capitalism. Therefore the scientific endeavour would either be destroyed by a fascist response to the world crisis or be saved and renewed through a socialist revolution. Now in the early post-war period, those premises began to look very shaky, if not highly irrelevant. The major fascist powers had been defeated and scientific workers in Germany, Italy and Japan would once again be able to govern their own internal affairs. In Britain itself that measure of freedom was guaranteed to (senior) academic scientists who were also about to enjoy, along with their industrial counterparts, an expansion of funds for pure and applied research. Such portents of prosperity (and some political influence) suggested that the British capitalist system, with the assistance of social democracy, had become more than capable of supporting and advancing science and its associated technologies. If that were so, then much of the material and ideological basis of Bernalism's appeal to his fellow researchers was about to be removed. The only new issue of any importance was not whether but how science was to be used, and to what ends. Those of course were value-laden and potentially divisive questions in a period when, for example, the militarization of British science could be characterized as a new form of barbarism and/or a development essential to the defence of the 'free world'. A number of scientists, once politically active, publicly ignored that dilemma because of a desire either to preserve their links with the military, or to prolong the flow of state resources into their laboratories, or to uphold the authority of a reform-minded Labour government. Others were persuaded that the Soviet threat to the West was real and important, not least because of Stalin's repeated attacks on his own scientific community. Whatever might be said about such motives and arguments they constituted a new political reality that seriously contradicted the received Bernalist wisdom of the thirties.

To reverse these trends left-wing scientists were obliged to re-evaluate their own politics and produce a coherent and per-suasive counter-reality. Yet they had neither the 'mental space' nor the inclination to do so. Here we should recall that the strength of their political tactics in the thirties had resided in a defence of scientific practices to which they had been as committed as their less radical peers. Nor had their wartime experience led them to revise in any way their pre-existing conceptions of science and its social relations. Unfortunately for Bernal and his allies the logic of their rather conventional views began to run counter to their political aspirations as the Cold War grew colder. Even if they had now wanted to countenance a socialist science radically different from the old bourgeois model, they were unlikely to find the time to piece all that together and put it to work. For the reverses suffered by the scientific Left simply came too hard on the heels of its greatest victories to allow for that kind of innovation. Indeed far from being able to sit back and plan where the radical cause should next be advanced, Bernal, Haldane and the others were about to be put perpetually on the defensive by an articulate and increasingly well-organized band of anti-communist intellectuals.

The 'band' consisted of two sections. First, we have the defenders of High Science, who sought to protect their laboratories from the encroachments of would-be scientific planners. Second, there were the advocates of High Culture, who likewise feared 'outside' interference in the management of their artistic preserves. Members of both groups generally set themselves against a variety of attempts to: debunk some of the social mythologies surrounding the practice of science and art; inject some new, often progressive social content into these cultural pursuits; and open them out both to more practitioners and to a wider audience. Because such proposals tended to emanate from the Left, they were also closely associated with an antipathy toward bourgeois values and an enthusiasm for the kind of scientific materialism that appeared to permeate Soviet cultural life. The apostles of an élitist culture pursued |for its/their own sake were therefore driven to speak out on behalf of the moral and material framework of a bourgeois society that supported their endeavours. Not surprisingly, this fight was to be led from the Right, where the defence of Christianity and capitalism was most assured, and by the literati, whose cultural dominance was still secure. Together with some volubly anti-communist scientists they accordingly set out to take the middle ground – the moderates and the liberals – away from the Popular or People's Front, by showing how illiberal were the barbaric practices of Stalin and the scientific theories of his British supporters, not least the Bernalists.

The cultural Cold War, in so far as it was waged in an organized fashion against the scientific Left, dated back to the formation in the spring of 1941 of a Society for Freedom in Science. The S.F.S. were very much the creation of a pair of Oxford biologists, John R. Baker and A. G. Tansley, and a Manchester chemist, Michael Polanyi. In retrospect they criticized themselves for not realizing sooner how 'the power of influencing public opinion was tending to pass from the hands of those who believed in pure science and freedom in science into the hands of those who did not'.[63] Their awareness of that danger had greatly increased just before the Second World War with the publication of Bernal's *Social Function of Science* and the launching of the British Association's new division. Just how dangerous a turn this was for the B.A. to have taken was confirmed at the Science and World Order Conference. To one of the society's scandalized supporters this meeting seemed to take on,

as it progressed, more and more the nature of a camp meeting for the Marxian religion, with pious celebration of the scientific achievements of

Soviet Russia, as a state in which . . . political theory and action were supposed to be based upon natural science. That was the direction in which I was conscious of an immediate danger of science becoming 'entangled in politics through the over-eagerness of its advocates and champions to invoke the sanction of science . . . in the support of any special political doctrine . . .'[64]

Thereafter it became easy for the S.F.S. to identify as its main function the formation of

a solid body of opinion ready to present the case for freedom if the threat to suppress scientific liberties should develop dangerously in the period of reconstruction after the war. Those who lay all the stress on the applications of science and consider that research should be centrally planned are not only highly organized and extremely active, but also influential in certain political circles. Only a state of preparedness can make it certain that the case for freedom in science will get a proper hearing if and when such a crisis arises.[65]

To that end the society recruited academic scientists who explicitly pledged themselves to the 'free' pursuit of pure science. According to its own records, the bulk of these members were initially drawn from universities (Leeds, Manchester and Oxford) when the scientific Left was weak and scientific life was relatively small-scale. That membership drive was supplemented with the publication of letters, articles and books, designed to counteract Bernalist propaganda.

The society's two main protagonists in the ensuing battle of ideas were undoubtedly Baker and Polanyi. While they displayed a number of striking philosophical, political and temperamental differences, both men agreed that Bernal and other left-wingers had endangered the cause of High Science. The central problem with the scientific Left, according to Baker and Polanyi, was that it had wilfully confused science – a valid body of theories that could only be successfully modified in accordance with its own rules and needs – with technology – the practical mastery of nature for particular social ends. Given that basic confusion, the Bernalists had been unable to comprehend why pure scientists either required complete freedom to choose their own research topics and publish their results, or failed to contribute directly to the solution of technical problems. Furthermore, because they had seriously underestimated the intellectual and creative powers involved in doing first-rate scientific work, progressive writers on science had been able to talk blithely about the potential of team research, planned of course in advance for human, i.e. material, welfare. In short, Baker asserted, 'Bernalism is the doctrine of those who profess that the only proper objects of scientific research are to feed people and protect them from the elements, that research workers should be organized in gangs and told what to discover, and that the pursuit of knowledge for its own sake has the same value as the solution of crossword puzzles'.[66] This approach had already been applied in the Soviet Union and, contrary to the opinion of the Bernalists, had not only failed in its own terms but had produced great human suffering as well. Even in 1939 it was perfectly obvious to Polanyi that 'scientific thought is . . . nowhere oppressed so comprehensively as in the U.S.S.R.'[67] Yet it was the Soviet model of planned science that the scientific Left was pushing in Britain. That alarmed Polanyi, who would subsequently write a number of eloquent articles on the mutual dependency of scientific progress and liberal democracy on each other.[68] Such faith in democratic processes did not, however, commend itself to Baker. As a conservative, even reactionary eugenist, he sought to reinforce High Science as a buttress against the egalitarian claims of the masses. Indeed, in his *Science and the Planned State* of 1945, he went so far as to argue that 'the false attachment of special virtues and talent to people who by definition do not possess them has become so widespread as to constitute a serious threat to civilization. People are beginning to cease honouring great men and to honour instead the masses of humanity or the publicists who reiterate their praise.'[69] But what was so wrong with praise of the common man or woman? Baker replied:

the common man has not an urgent desire for liberty or action, and is prepared to use the vote granted to him by liberal-minded people to destroy not only his own liberty, but that of uncommon people as well. It is impossible to imagine that the common man understands the condition under which great work in science, philosophy or music can be done: he is prepared and actively encouraged to think the only thing that matters is his own mutual welfare.[70]

Though Polanyi and Baker were not directly in conflict here, their distinct approaches nicely illustrate the political range represented within the Society for Freedom in Science's membership.

Until the late forties it was difficult to judge the society's effect either on the scientific Left or on liberal academic researchers. To Bernal and his associates the 'freedom in science' controversy was rather unreal. For none of them had ever disputed the need for scientists to manage their own affairs. (This point was so unexceptional to Needham that he felt able – much to Baker's surprise – to join the S.F.S. in 1942.)[71] However, unlike Baker and Polanyi, they believed that as the scale and expense of research work increased, free science could only be preserved and advanced if it had the optimum mix of human and physical resources at its disposal. In short, planning for science was seen to be a necessary condition for freedom in science. That had been shown, the Bernalists asserted, not only in the war but in the Soviet Union as well. Neither contention immediately evoked much opposition from liberal or even conservative members of the scientific establishment. Their administrative responsibilities during and after the war had slowly sensitized them to a new form of science politics. Where they diverged from political outsiders like Baker and Polanyi was in their recognition that various freedoms in science could no longer be

expected to retain all their earlier validity, under the new conditions for the support and encouragement of research, which had grown up since the beginning of the present century . . . And [continued Sir Henry Dale, F.R.S., in a speech to the Society for Freedom in Science in 1951] under such conditions, however much we may desire that government advisory councils, charitable foundations or a benevolent industry should be ready to show their faith in individual scientists, by simply endowing them to do whatever researches they fancy, this cannot be expected as a regular policy.[72]

Acceptance of some limitation on the free pursuit of pure science by those enmeshed in state affairs was matched by their short-term willingness not to air their own, usually hostile views of Soviet scientific life. Such restraint was politically necessary so long as the U.S.S.R. was a military ally. Even after the war, hope was expressed officially and semi-officially that Soviet scientific workers would continued to enjoy the civil liberties necessary for the practice of their vocation.[73] Hence the ideologues of the scientific Right were at first unable to generate either a great debate with their left-wing counterparts or the public endorsement by the science establishment of their anti-communist views. On the other hand, it did not appear that the freedom of High Scientists was to be discernibly diminished in post-war Britain. For the S.F.S.'s supporters this all added up to a great victory. 'Very little is heard nowadays', the society's *Bulletin* reported in July 1947, 'about the movement against freedom in science, which . . . reached the peak of its development at the meeting of the British Association in September 1941'.[74] By contrast, some of Bernal's friends concluded that it was 'the movement' for freedom in science which 'died soon after the war, when it was realized that no one was going to brow-beat British scientists into doing things against their will and for which they were not trained'.[75] Round one of the clash between the two movements could accordingly be judged a draw.*

That was not, however, the only challenge to its political, moral and intellectual authority which the scientific Left received between 1945 and 1947. Indeed, a better publicized and more immediately effective attack against Bernal, in particular, had already been launched by an ideologically heterogeneous grouping of literary intellectuals. Prominent among these writers were E. M. Forster, Arthur Koestler and George Orwell. Anti-communist to a man, they regarded the rise of the scientific Left not only as a threat to the artist's strategic role in British culture but as the sign of an increasing sympathy for totalitarian means and ends as well. For were not these scientists prepared to sacrifice the moral integrity and free development of the individual, so long as they might be allowed to speed up material progress under the aegis of an

---

* In fact neither side could claim to be completely happy with the projected direction of British scientific affairs in this period. If strategic planning for the advancement of science was becoming commonplace, so was the militarization of many areas of research. And while High Scientists in a few universities were able to investigate what they wanted (within a set of pre-determined norms), their interests were already being subtly modified by an élite group of scientist-administrators, many of whom continued long after the war to maintain close links with the military. The mixed blessing of 'free science' planned for human destruction and administered from the top were such that the battle between Left and Right would have to be fought out on different terrain. Hence in the post-war period the underlying political differences between pro- and anti-communist scientists were allowed to come more sharply to the fore, as their debate shifted to the plight of scientific workers in the U.S.S.R.

all-embracing scientific state? Their uncritical defence of the U.S.S.R. seemed to indicate that much to those writers who, by the war's end, had come to realize how difficult it would be to justify their own culture and values without explicitly rejecting the Left's package of support for science, materialism and Soviet socialism. The most efficient way to confront that doctrine was to go for one of its principal authors, J. D. Bernal.

At the beginning of 1946 Bernal presented his arts-based adversaries with a convenient summary of his views entitled 'Belief and Action'. Appearing as it did in the first number of a revamped *Modern Quarterly*, this article could have been and was interpreted not merely as Bernal's credo but that of many other Left intellectuals, too. What he had to say here was by now very familiar to his associates and ourselves. 'We are at the beginning of a new era,' he claimed, 'in which the people, at last firmly in power, can plan and act.'[76] Bernal believed that it would now be possible, even without a socialist revolution, 'to ensure that all human beings have a chance of full development'.[77] Such an advance could only be achieved if 'the people' were allowed to construct a well-organized productive and distributive system. To guide them in this mammoth undertaking they would have to strike a new moral balance between the claims of the individual and those of society. Here was how Bernal approached this touchstone of moral philosophy.

> Too great an insistence on individuality means an anarchy in which the material conditions necessary for the realization of full human possibilities cannot be achieved. Too little insistence on it means a tyranny in which the individual is limited to a particular function and in which, by demeaning man, the purpose of the organization itself is frustrated: The maintenance of the balance between these extremes is the greatest of responsibilities. It is too great to be borne by individuals; it is the responsibility of the people.[78]

In this context Bernal advised the people to rely on the 'theories and the practice of Marx, of Lenin and of Stalin'[79] in which 'the achievements of liberal philosophy have themselves been incorporated'.[80] Indeed he believed that the wartime experiences of most Britons had already begun to transform them into (*de facto*) dialectical materialists. Hence his optimism: 'This time there is no mistaking the people's purpose. Everywhere in Europe and, most important of all, in Britain, elections have shown that the great majority are determined to control the forces which science and technology have provided and to use them for the common good and not for private profit, for peace and not for war.'[81]

The most coherent critique of Bernal's theses appeared as an unsigned leading article, written by George Orwell, in the journal *Polemic*. For nearly a decade Orwell had been simmering with indignation against what he took to be the dangerous pretensions of scientific socialists like Bernal. His antipathy to left-wing researchers was, in part, the result of a more general prejudice against scientists, whom he regarded as 'much more subject to totalitarian habits of thought than writers'.[82] That tendency was manifested to Orwell's satisfaction when he reviewed the defences of Hitler and Stalin that had been offered over the years by German and British scientists respectively.[83] He attributed such behaviour to a 'power-hungry' mentality that supposedly pervaded the salaried middle class – the very group that provided the Communist Party with most of its intellectuals.[84] But in the case of scientific workers Orwell believed that the specific attraction of totalitarian regimes, whether of the Left or the Right, was their apparent devotion to the advanced technologies and outlook associated with scientific materialism. He himself was not so enamoured of material progress. Indeed Orwell tended to favour a leaner version of socialism, based very much on certain ethical first principles like justice, liberty and common decency.[85] Given that orientation he could scarcely avoid commenting at some stage on the work of Britain's foremost Bernalist.

His occasion for doing so was an attack made in the *Modern Quarterly* against *Polemic*, which was charged with making 'persistent attempts to confuse moral issues, to break down the distinction between right and wrong'.[86] Orwell countered with the assertion that it was Bernal's 'Belief and Action' which played havoc with the established ethical balance between individual and societal needs. To Bernal 'any action which serves the cause of progress is virtuous'.[87] Therefore, deduced Orwell, 'right action [for the Bernalist] does not lie in obeying your conscience, or a traditional moral code: right action lies in pushing history in the direction . . . of the classless society which all decent people desire'.[88] All this, in Orwell's view, opened the way to a relativistic morality in which power and virtue were confused to the disadvantage of liberal values and personal freedoms. The disastrous human consequences of that perspective had already been displayed in the Soviet Union. Yet Bernal continued to endorse 'the practice of Stalin', and, why not, Orwell challenged, when he had already proved himself to be a theoretical master of Stalinist ethics. 'We think we have said enough', concluded the *Polemic* leader, 'to show that our real crime, in the eyes of the *Modern Quarterly*, lies in *defending* a conception of right and wrong, and of intellectual decency, which has been responsible for all true progress for centuries past, and without which the very continuance of civilized life is by no means certain'.[87]

Arthur Koestler offered a similar analysis of Bernal's article, but to a rather different audience. Instead of addressing a few thousand readers of *Polemic*, Koestler broadcast his broadside to an audience of five million. For this was the first of eleven 'lay sermons' on 'The Challenge of Our Time' put out by the B.B.C. on Sunday evenings during the spring of 1946. From soundings taken among its various cultural advisers the corporation had been able to define this challenge as 'the lack of synthesis in modern thinking and in particular the wide gulf between the scientific and the humanistic approach to life'.[88] The elaboration of these problems was to be tackled by a team of arts men assembled by the Canon of St Paul's and a panel of scientists invited by J. D. Bernal. In addition to Koestler they selected three researchers (J. B. S. Haldane, Michael Polanyi and C. H. Waddington), two historians (E. L. Woodward and Benjamin Farrington), two philosophers (Lord Lindsay and A. D. Ritchie) and the novelist E. M. Forster. Between them they not only gave substance to C. P. Snow's subsequent lament about the 'two cultures' but demonstrated the political and ideological bases for that cleavage as well. The non-scientists (Farrington aside) were lining up with the Right against the Soviet Union and in favour of individualistic ideals. With the exception of Polanyi, the scientists obligingly leaned to the Left, supported the Communists and stressed the need to engage the people in a great co-operative venture to improve the material foundations of their society. It was of course the initial clash between Bernal and Koestler that helped to bring about this remarkable convergence of polarities.

The arts men feared that the scientists, in their zeal to render life more comfortable through technical gadgetry and top-down planning, were endangering personal freedoms, if not the 'human spirit' itself. Among the writers there was some consensus as to why this was so. Forster argued that the rising social and political fortunes of scientists during the war had separated them 'from ordinary men and women' and made them 'unfit to enter into their feelings'.[89] That experience had encouraged researchers to believe, quite wrongly in Polanyi's view, that 'the decisive problems of our world can be solved by applying the methods of science'. Yet 'our troubles today are political and not technical.' 'After all,' Polanyi added, 'if all we wanted was scientific planning we could have had that through Hitler.'[90] But Hitler put science at the service of totalitarianism. So, too, had Stalin, whose suppression of civil liberties did not, or so it appeared to Koestler, really bother Bernal and other pro-Communist scientists. For example, Koestler continued, Bernal's article did contain

some reservations to the effect that there should be no question of 'blind and obedient carrying out of orders', which, he says, leads to the Fuehrer prinzip. He doesn't seem to have noticed that blind obedience plus the Fuehrer prinzip are nowhere more in evidence today than in the party to which Professor Bernal's sympathies belong.[91]

In other words to Koestler and his comrades the challenge of their time was to defend human freedom and individual enterprise from their fashionable detractors. But that project could only succeed if free men and women could strongly oppose the corroding and allied influences of scientism, materialism and communism. As Lord Lindsay noted, each of us had to reject the idea that 'an indefinite multiplication of riches will of itself make us either good or happy'.[92] Though the arts coterie was somewhat vague as to where 'real' goodness and happiness might be found, they were agreed that 'the people' should take their moral cues from literary rather than scientific intellectuals. Indeed Forster was not even prepared to accept scientific workers on anything like equal cultural terms. Thus:

I am writing like an intellectual, but the intellectual to my mind is more in touch with humanity than is the confident scientist, who patronizes the past, over-simplifies the present and envisages a future when his leadership will be accepted . . . We want him to plan for our bodies. We do not want

10

him to plan for our minds, and we cannot accept, so far, his assurance that he will not do this.[93]

At least Forster had some hope that the 'confident scientist' was not yet beyond redemption: 'it is high time he came out of his ivory laboratory'.[94] Koestler, by contrast, was unshakeable in his belief that 'much confusion could be avoided if some scientists would stick to their electrons and realize that human beings do not fit into mathematical equations'.[95] It was to say the least a happy coincidence that the political idealism of the literary spokesman dovetailed so well with their cultural self-interests.

Bernal, Haldane, Levy and their friends welcomed this abuse (and publicity) of their ideas to such an extent that they helped to organize a further series of London-based public lectures in 1946 called 'The Communist Answer to the Challenge of Our Time'. Their confidence here resided in a belief that the war-born impetus to transform Britain into a more just and efficient society had not yet run its course. By emphasizing the scientific and socialist dimensions of this new political consensus they now hoped to reinforce it intellectually and at the same time show how far removed the apostles of High Culture were from the feelings and aspirations of 'ordinary men and women'. In other words, the scientific Left was only too eager to race ahead to the corner into which the anti-communist writers wanted to drive them.

The principal aim of Bernal and his comrades was to show that scientists and socialists were not only the friends of liberty and freedom but the two groups most likely to defend and extend these desired aspects of modern civilization as well. They therefore set out to destroy the literary men's contention that scientific planning was incompatible with the needs of individuals to develop freely and keep their own moral consciences. Bernal laughed at the falsity of this dilemma during his B.B.C. broadcast.

> There are some people who would like you to believe that once you start trying to run the world in a sensible and conscious way, something terrible will happen to human values, that men will be considered only as machines, that human society will be reduced to that of the white – why not red? – ants. This is sheer nonsense. In fact, it is the other way round... The position of the individual in the new world will be far more important and interesting than it ever was in the old, and the way individuals will work together will be something far more democratic than anything we have known.[96]

Later in the series Haldane would reject the anti-communists' implied belief that, in the absence of state interventions into social and economic life, individuals were free to think and act in whatever way their 'spirit' demanded. 'The plain fact', J.B.S. contended,

is that we are all suffering from spiritual planning which has been so efficient that most of us have not even noticed it, and described any protest against it as 'subversive propaganda'. Professor Polanyi, who opposes scientific planning in the name of freedom, has suggested that we should compile a complete code of moral behaviour. I only wonder he didn't suggest a world conference on Mount Sinai to draw up a code. How easily one is led into spiritual planning if one rejects economic planning.[97]

Bernal would later interpret this 'campaign against science in favour of mystical religion, against planning and against the belief that the people can run the show by themselves' as part of the ruling class's desire to damp down the populist trend of recent years. 'All this', he told a London audience in the autumn of 1946, 'saps self-reliance and must inevitably lead to economic decay and disaster.'[98]

The antidote to such poisonous despair was for the people to reaffirm their desire and ability to take control of their own lives – at whatever cost to the tender sensibilities of a few aesthetes. That was Bernal's advice to the millions who listened to his broadcast.

We cannot leave this challenge to be taken up by soured intellectuals with their eyes fixed on the past. It must be taken up by those who have the hope, the knowledge, the ability and the drive to define the problems of our time and to solve them. We will throw off our anxieties and quell our fears not through any metaphysical searching of heart but by getting down to the urgent practical job of securing the conditions for a good life for all the people of the world.[99]

The success of that endeavour depended upon the satisfaction of two conditions: the maintenance of peace and the extension of scientific and democratic procedures into a wider society. Yet those who opposed planned science and scientific planning were likewise determined to disturb international relations by (wrongly) vilifying the internal and external policies of the U.S.S.R. Here Bernal attempted to turn his opponents' argument back on itself in order to show how they were already laying the groundwork for a Cold War that could still be avoided.

The real danger (of war) does not come from the Soviet Union, or the atom bomb, or from the inherent wickedness of man, or from our intrinsic inability to cooperate in building a new world based on common effort for common good. It comes from those who do not want this kind of world; those who talk of wars and rumours of war; those who have discovered the special values of 'Western Civilization', the defence of which we can now take up from the defeated Germans. These are the enemies of promise; these are the real heirs of the Nazis. Unless we can stop them splitting the world into two camps in men's minds, the fatal division will grow and war will be inevitable.[100]

Needless to say, one group that was unlikely to find much fault with the Soviets was the Communist Party of Great Britain, which was simultaneously excelling itself as the champion of a truly scientific socialism. But no one could make more of a fetish of science than the party's leading scientists. Now Haldane, when asked: 'Can't you apply your scientific method to these moral and political problems?' would reply: 'Yes, we can; and the man who showed us how to do it was old Karl Marx.'[101] That meant a Marxist party had, by definition, to be a party of scientists. Such was Hyman Levy's claim, as he summed up the Communist answer to the challenge of our time. 'The Communist Party', he proclaimed, 'is realist and scientific, concerned to discover the truth about social events and social processes, and, like any scientific body, bound to accept the truth when it is found.'[102] At this moment the wisdom uncovered by the party was that the celebration of science was essential to the defence of socialist achievements, in Britain as well as in the U.S.S.R.

3. The Lysenko Affair

That strategy worked reasonably well until the winter of 1947–8, when the Cold War began in earnest. An important facet of this global confrontation was how swiftly the methods, theories and technologies conventionally deemed scientific in the West were turned against the Soviet Union, the international Communist movement and, not least, anyone who claimed that only socialism could make the world safe for science. Now it was the turn of anti-communists to press a variety of scientific means into the service of their own political ends. Science, pure and applied, was used in military and diplomatic offensives designed to contain the spread of communism in Europe and elsewhere. Likewise leading academic scientists were made accomplices of that strategy either as state advisers on defence or as the designers of research projects supposedly of long-term benefit to the armed services. But science also began to be used increasingly as a cultural weapon by the West's defenders. Negatively, they would be provided with new evidence that the Soviet Union was suffering as much from the retrogression of its technology as the repression of its scientific workers. Positively, the Cold Warriors would begin to evolve a new history, philosophy and sociology of science that ran counter to the Bernalist literature in these areas. While some of them would subsequently argue that the practice of science could be studied without reference to its wider social context and others that normal scientific life could only take place in a liberal democracy, they all believed that a Marxist perspective prevented one from correctly understanding and successfully producing modern science. On all of these fronts the scientific Left fought back as best it could; opposing the arms race, defending the U.S.S.R. and developing its own approach to the social relations of science. The difference between this new phase of the cultural Cold War and the earlier one was that, this time, Bernal and his associates lost the sympathy of their liberal allies and perhaps as well the confidence of a new generation of scientific workers. The radical science movement had at last been stymied.

More than anything else, it was Stalin's sudden decision in July 1948 to put T. D. Lysenko in charge of Soviet biology that served to catalyse the decline of the scientific Left. By common consent Lysenko's victory was and continues to be seen as a fateful challenge to the customary ways in which scientific theories were supposed to be produced and applied in the modern (capitalist) world. From our earlier discussion of the Lysenkoists, we know that they had earlier criticized the theoretical and practical adequacy of formal genetics, invoked ideological criteria to settle various scientific disputes and attacked the élitist pretensions of bourgeois geneticists. Yet it was not until well after the Cold War's onset that Lysenko was permitted full sway over the agrobiological aspects of the 'Great Stalin Plan for the Transformation of Nature'. Now Lysenko's followers were able to bring the 'two camps' mentality deep into the scientific arena by playing off the practical and democratic orientation of their socialist science against the sterile and racist nostrums of capitalist pseudo-science. Whatever progressive aspects may have been involved in Lysenko's seizure of scientific power,* they were rather overshadowed at the time: by Stalin's momentary denial of the right of researchers to settle intellectual scores in their own way and by the cavalier dismissal of a number of well-known geneticists from their posts. The reason why these points were emphasized is that they ran counter to the deepest beliefs of *both* pro- and anti-communist scientists in the West as to how science ought to have been practised. Is it then any wonder that when the U.S.S.R. – the lynchpin of the left-wing scientists' arguments in favour of socialism – systematically contravened their received wisdom, they would be obliged to suffer a grievous setback?

To make matters much worse, the scientific Left had set the seal on its own defeat here by publicly rejecting Lysenkoism prior to the summer of 1948. Indeed, in 1940, three years before John R. Baker's earliest attempt to publicize the Soviet genetics controversy,[103] J. B. S. Haldane had already been prepared to concede that Lysenko's 'attacks on the importance of chromosomes in heredity seem to me to be based on a misunderstanding'. 'This would be very serious', J.B.S. admitted, 'if he were dictator of Soviet genetics.'[104] Fortunately, he was not. Nor were there any signs much before 1947 that Lysenko was improving his position at the expense of orthodox geneticists. That was how Haldane read the situation.[105] And his view was simultaneously corroborated by Eric Ashby[106] and

* Since, in theory, the principal long-term aim of a socialist society is to break down social divisions between mental and manual workers, any practicable attempt to involve scientists and peasants in each other's work might be seen as a step in the right direction. It must be said that Stalin's regime was not noted for its achievements in this domain. Nor do we know the extent to which Lysenko's populist approach to agrobiology ever became translated into the everyday social relations of collective farms. Nevertheless his followers were keen to assert that their science was revolutionary not just by virtue of its theoretical message and practical intent but, more importantly, because of the way in which it was produced. That was the message conveyed in various Soviet tracts on Lysenkoism that were aimed at a mass audience. At least two of these works were translated into English at the time: Gennadi Fish's *A People's Academy* (Moscow, 1949) and Viktor Safonov's *Land in Bloom* (Moscow, 1951).

Julian Huxley,[107] both of whom saw Lysenko just after the war. Emboldened by these reports and convinced of Lysenkoism's theoretical deficiencies, the editor of the British Communist Party's theoretical journal, *Modern Quarterly*, printed three damning articles on Soviet genetics in the autumn and winter of 1947–8. The first of these, written by R. G. Davies, disputed the experimental and practical achievements of Lysenko's school. He then rejected as 'a complete abandonment of the normal scientific criteria' Lysenko's tendency to assess biological theories 'on the basis of their social and intellectual origins or their alleged political consequences'.[108] Davies was even so bold as to charge the Soviet government with 'some responsibility' for this 'intolerable' state of affairs.[109] In a separate note J. L. Fyfe urged his fellow students of heredity to read one of Lysenko's books, in order 'to satisfy themselves that Lysenko's own theories can be safely ignored. For anybody else,' he added, 'the time spent in reading and trying to understand it would be largely wasted.'[110] Among the *Quarterly*'s contributors on this subject, only Frederick LeGros Clark cared to direct attention to Lysenko's role as 'the chosen catalyst in this process of calling out the latent genius of the farms'. For, according to Clark, Lysenko 'preached not merely a somewhat perverse set of scientific theories, but the ability of the Soviet farmer to become a scientist'.[111] But like Davies, Fyfe and Haldane, Clark was glad to record that orthodox genetics was still practised widely and with distinction in the U.S.S.R. In the meantime it looked as if Lysenko's influence was waning.

Having authored a critique worthy of a Baker or a Polanyi, left-wing scientists had little room for manoeuvre when Lysenko was officially raised to power almost overnight.[112] Lysenko's victory placed Haldane, in particular, under severe emotional and intellectual strain. As the C.P.G.B.'s leading geneticist, J.B.S. could not remain silent. Yet almost any statement he made on the controversy was bound to violate his scientific and/or his political scruples. So he initially refused, in public, to take sides, notably in his contribution in November 1948 to a B.B.C. symposium on Soviet genetics.[113] That broadcast was only part of the unprecedented coverage which the mass media gave to the 'unacceptable face' of Soviet science. In this endeavour they obviously had the support of the Society for Freedom in Science. The S.F.S. was anxious to show

how the rise of Lysenkoism more than justified the society's existence.[114] Other anti-communist scientists, including C. D. Darlington and R. A. Fisher, now joined in the struggle, as did a number of progressively minded liberals like Eric Ashby, Julian Huxley and C. H. Waddington. Even previously apolitical researchers came forward to comment at least on Lysenko's experiments, while at least one non-scientist (John Langdon-Davies) wrote a popular account of how *Russia Turns Back the Clock*. It was all rather a sad and inverted outcome of the scientific Left's long-standing commitment to stimulate the public's awareness of a nexus between science, socialism and the U.S.S.R.

The quickly coalescing consensus among the anti-communists was that Lysenko and his followers had used the brute force and ideological authority of a totalitarian state in order to replace scientific truths with demonstrably false views. The British critics of Lysenkoism asserted that: a number of geneticists had already been murdered; genetics would no longer be taught; and Soviet agriculture would suffer accordingly. What they disputed among themselves was why the Soviets were, in their view, waging a war against Reason, Truth and Civilization. R. A. Fisher put it all down to Lysenko's lust for power – 'power for himself, power to threaten, power to torture, power to kill'.[115] An alternative mode of explanation was to look at the U.S.S.R.'s denial of science as the corollary of its need for religion. (Somehow the pejorative connotation of 'religion' never carried over into Western discussion of the need for a spiritual revival to combat the alleged tyranny of scientific materialism and rationality in our own lives.) Why did Stalin, the architect of scientific socialism, need to foster 'religious' attitudes? Ashby replied that the Russians were, poor chaps, innately religious.[116] Langdon-Davies, on the other hand, felt it was the Marxist 'religion' itself that was at fault here. For after all, doesn't genetics tend 'to disprove certain beliefs which are demanded of all Soviet citizens, particularly by emphasizing the biological inequality of man and the fact that Nature is in many ways refractory to man-desired changes'?[117] Of all these analysts of the 'religious' functions served by Lysenkoism, only Julian Huxley attempted to relate the overnight ascendancy of this doctrine to the vicissitudes of the Cold War.[118] His general argument ran as follows:

Central to the present state of affairs is the historical fact that Soviet policy has undergone a radical change since the war, apparently with a view to preparing the people of the U.S.S.R. for a long struggle, possibly involving war, with the capitalist world in general, and the U.S.A. in particular. To effect this, the revival of patriotic feeling . . . which was deliberately fostered during the war . . . had been retained, but has been coupled with a glorification of communism and the present régime as the system under which alone the nation can successfully advance to new achievements.[119]

Though Huxley could understand why the Soviets, in turn, transformed Lysenko into a national hero, he still condemned them for their gross and short-sighted denial of free scientific discussions. From his and other analyses of Lysenkoism the two most common deductions made were that scientists should practise their vocation free from political interference and that the U.S.S.R. (and its Western supporters) could no longer be regarded as sound guides to the practice of science. Apart from those already on the Left, neither proposition prompted much opposition from inside the scientific community.*

Nor could it be said that Lysenko's rise to power was welcomed by most socialist researchers, certainly not those outside the ranks of the Communist Party of Great Britain. Lancelot Hogben was one such opponent. Even before the Second World War Hogben had begun to dissociate himself from the pro-Soviet inclinations of many within the scientific Left. A chance trip across the U.S.S.R. in the spring of 1940 further convinced him that the theories and practices evolved in that culturally and industrially backward society were irrelevant, not to say harmful to the cause of British socialism. In his Conway Memorial Lecture of 22 March 1949, Hogben was therefore able both to reaffirm his old convictions as a scientifically minded socialist and to explain why they could not be 'rationally' applied in the Soviet context. In fact, he said in referring to Lysenkoism,

* In the *New Statesman* of 25 December 1948, C. H. Waddington did try to show how one could oppose Lysenkoism without contradicting the scientific Left's general approach to the social function of science. There he asked 'scientists who demand to be left in peace' whether they could reconcile that position 'with their growing insistence on being considered worthy to contribute significantly to decisions on broad matters of policy'. Waddington thought they could not and therefore concluded: 'The Russians have an arguable (though I do not say convincing) case that the kind of actions they

It does not seem to me amazing that healthy courtship between [genetical] theory and [agricultural] practice is unrealizable in a vast territory with no long tradition of popular education, of skill in the use of modern techniques; that the Soviet Union has abandoned support for what is in such circumstances an unduly ambitious programme of research [in formal genetics] with no immediate prospect of results contributory to the mitigation of post-war impoverishment; that a charlatan such as Lysenko is thus able to gain a powerful following by raising the morale of the peasantry, nor that the language in which his supporters conduct his campaign lacks a discipline and reserve unlikely as yet to flourish in an empire in process of rescue from well-nigh universal illiteracy.[120]

To Hogben the Lysenko affair was only one of many indications that 'the Russians are just thirty years behind the times'.[121] Ideally, he would have liked the matter to have rested there. For Hogben was much more concerned about what he regarded as the regimentation of scientific thought that was currently taking hold of scientific laboratories in the West. However, any chance of a sympathetic reception to that perspective was destroyed, in his view, by British 'men of science with party affiliations' who continued to offer 'fulsome flattery of Soviet science' despite the excesses of Lysenko and his followers. Hogben doubly resented the attitude of his Communist colleagues. On the one hand their stand (wrongly) encouraged an association between socialism and intellectual repression. On the other, in the debates on Lysenkoism, it lent an unwarranted respectability to the anti-egalitarian views of 'scientific racists' like Baker and Darlington.[122] By now it should be clear that the Cold War was being fought out within as well as against the scientific Left. That rendered the position of pro-Communist researchers all the more difficult and 'unreasonable'.

'The party' placed additional pressure on its scientific members and supporters through its half-hearted campaign on behalf of Lysenkoist biology. Though its Central Committee refrained from laying down a clear and official line on this question, the C.P.G.B.'s leadership nevertheless threw its own weight behind Lysenko from 1948 onwards. The first indication of its support came in the form

---

have taken are justifiable. The strength of the arguments against Lysenko lies not in the field of general policy . . . but in the actual content of his theories and arguments.'

of an 'Educational Commentary' written for the *Daily Worker* by Ivor Montagu.[124] Then, in a series of meetings sponsored by the Engels Society in 1949 a number of full-time party officials, including the philosopher Maurice Cornforth, declared their opposition to what they defined as orthodox genetics.[125] Thereafter the C.P.'s own publishing house, Lawrence & Wishart, produced several books on Soviet biology, all of them at least sympathetic to the Lysenko school and none of them overly critical of its methods of achieving scientific consensus.[126]

But only one of these works, James Fyfe's *Lysenko is Right* (1950), completely jettisoned the theoretical baggage of orthodox genetics in favour of Lysenko's notions of heredity. This is the same biologist who had declared to *Modern Quarterly* readers in 1947 that they could 'safely ignore' the whole of Lysenkoist biology. Fyfe's change of heart stemmed from his faith in the U.S.S.R.'s commitment to truly scientific theories and practices. He therefore could not believe that the reorientation of Soviet biology represented anything other than the rightful and definitive supersession of Mendelism by Lysenkoism. To think otherwise, he noted, we would 'have to accept the view that the Soviet Union is governed by half-wits who cannot foresee the disastrous consequences of their own dictatorial policy'.[127] That proposition struck Fyfe as so ludicrous that he was constrained to revalue his whole approach to biology and become the perfect Lysenkoite. He similarly asked each of his peers 'to decide [in advance] on which side we stand and evaluate the contribution of both sides accordingly. Until this has been done it is extremely difficult to approach the factual and experimental results in anything like a scientific spirit.'[128] While no one could deny Fyfe's epistemological daring, his grounds for preferring 'the forces of progress' – Lysenko's socialist biology – to 'the forces of reaction' – 'capitalist' genetics – assumed the existence of a verifiable body of experimental data and field results. The only additional criterion he adduced in favour of Lysenkoism was a social one; namely that under Lysenko's inspiration 'the scientists went out to the farms and the farmers became scientists'.[129] Such was the range of largely *a priori* arguments put forward in party literature to persuade the not-so-faithful that nothing was amiss in Soviet scientific circles. Rather it was the reactionary drift of Western science that had to be criticized and combated. In effect, the party was imposing on the scientific Left in Britain a highly sectarian and nationalistic outlook that had evolved in the U.S.S.R.

Whatever the intrinsic and historical merits of the Soviets' 'two camps' philosophy, its mechanical and precipitate introduction into the British political context played directly into the hands of the scientific Right. For the notion that there could be two utterly dissimilar sciences – one socialist, the other capitalist – had never been seriously debated among left-wing scientists here, let alone publicly discussed with less committed, more liberal researchers. By contrast with twenty years of stormy controversy in the Soviet Union about the nature and limitations of 'bourgeois science', the scientific Left in Britain had oriented its politics around the deeply held conviction that there was just one international science, and it could only be fully practised and humanely applied in a socialist society. Now Communists like Bernal and Haldane were being asked to abandon that position and, with it, the prospect of maintaining a scientists' Popular Front. It was difficult enough for these scientific intellectuals to adopt, in advance of any long period of reworking their ideas, an almost wholly alien world-view. What made this project virtually impossible was that it had to be launched as part of the defence of Lysenkoist biology. Yet not a single major spokesman for the scientific Left had failed prior to 1948 to express some major reservation about Lysenkoism. Now they were supposed to stuff their scientific scruples *entirely* on 'faith' and defend the Stalinist regime's latest change in ideological direction. While there were compelling historical and international reasons for British left-wingers to speak up for Soviet socialism, the uncritical application of this perspective to the scientific arena seriously weakened the political base of all left-wing scientists. Indeed what more could anti-communists desire than the spectacle of radical researchers, as it were, denying the evidence of their senses and contradicting the philosophical tradition which they had until so recently championed?

As it happened, only one progressive scientist of any professional standing or political prominence could wholly support the Soviet's 'left turn' in biology. That was J. D. Bernal. He boldly attributed the rise of Lysenkoism to the intrinsic weaknesses of genetical theories and practices that had originally been designed to serve capitalist ends. Part of the problem had lain with the first generation of Soviet geneticists, bred as they had been 'in a scientific atmosphere derived from the conditions of bourgeois capitalism, one in which . . . science and practice are not integrally related to each other'.[130] But the bourgeois fault ran deeper even than that, Bernal asserted. Indeed, it extended into the deepest theoretical foundations of orthodox genetics, which would accordingly have to be rejected. Although he specifically exonerated Mendelian 'facts' from the ideological taint of their bourgeois inventors, Bernal did wonder 'whether it is possible to graft on to this stock of science the new activities and new needs of a growing socialist society'.[131] Pending the resolution of that puzzle, he was more than satisfied that Lysenko's triumph was both practically and ideologically justified. Bernal was especially keen to identify Lysenkoism as 'a profoundly democratic movement, one which admits of no separate cultural élite'.[132] What a contrast, he told a Moscow audience in the summer of 1949, to the situation in capitalist countries where 'the direction of science is in the hands of those who hate peace, whose only aim is to despoil and torture people, so that their own profits can be assured for some years longer'.[133]* If such were the respective natures of capitalist and socialist science, Bernal had no hesitation in opting, as he always had, for the Soviet variety.

What Bernal's apologia overlooked – Lysenko's ignorance of much of modern genetics, his failure to give accurate accounts of his own work, the methods by which his side had 'won' – could not be ignored by J. B. S. Haldane.† J.B.S. was the scientist most

* This speech so incensed various members of the British Association's council that, despite Bernal's assurance that he was referring to the ruling class rather than the scientific establishment, he was not re-elected on to the B.A.'s governing body. See 'Membership of Council: Professor J. D. Bernal', *Advancement of Science*, vol. 6 (1949–50), pp. 388–9₄.

† Over the years Bernal progressively withdrew his support for Lysenko's brand of biology. (One can compare here the first (1954) and the third (1965) editions of his *Science in History*, pp. 660–73 and p. 702 respectively.) By September 1968, in a letter to the author, he was ready to concede that 'the Lysenko controversy was very largely the personal views of Lysenko, who ignored contemporary biological science. I know this well because I visited him and saw his research work and had long conversations with him. I have subsequently changed my own view in the light of the development of molecular biology and the great discoveries of Crick and Watson described in *The Double Helix*, which seems to me more materialistic and hence more Marxist than Lysenko's views.'

widely and closely identified not only with the Communist Party but with the science of genetics as well. The pressure on him to declare for or against Lysenkoism was therefore overwhelming. Outside party circles, J.B.S. was enjoined in cartoons, leading articles and books to break with the Soviet Union in the name of scientific freedom. If he did not, his morality and sanity were likely to be called into question. Already it was becoming fashionable to ferret out the neurotic sources of bourgeois intellectuals' attraction to communism. One of the more venomous exponents of such analysis-at-a-distance was J.B.S.'s ex-wife, Charlotte, herself an ex-Communist. In her autobiography of 1949, modestly entitled *Truth Will Out*, Mrs Haldane suggested that a 'middle class commie' was typically an 'aginner',

the type of person who, as the result of psychological strain and stresses, induced in childhood or adolescence, rebuts the discipline in which he has been brought up, but is compelled to seek another, still more rigorous, who has an emotional need for direction, who however eminent intellectually can find no inner peace, save on the basis of surrendering his individual moral and political judgement to democratic centralism.[134]

To the psychological strain of having been labelled a victim of 'psychological strain' was added the party's outrage at J.B.S.'s failure to respond to his 'emotional need for direction'. Haldane was himself becoming increasingly fed up with the refusal of the C.P. leadership to set out a critical but open line on the Soviet genetics controversy. At the same time he would not do anything to give direct aid and comfort to the anti-communists in and out of science. In the face of these two irreconcilable forces his subsequent actions were bound to render him a lonely, isolated figure. On the one hand, he defended modern genetics and cast doubt on the importance of Lysenko's contributions to Soviet agriculture, while he conceded the importance of some of Lysenko's experimental results. Nevertheless, J.B.S. declared in mid-1949, 'I believe that wholly unjustifiable attacks have been made on my profession, and one of the most important lessons which I have learned as a Marxist is the duty of supporting my fellow workers.'[135] That stand, however, was not accompanied by any overall vilification of Soviet communism or public denunciation of the British party. Instead J.B.S. embarked on a 'phased withdrawal' from the

C.P.G.B. that extended over a seven-year period. By the time his departure from the party was fairly well authenticated, Lysenkoism was no longer a burning political issue and intellectual Cold Warriors had moved on to new disputes.

Meanwhile the Communist Party had suffered a number of resignations from lesser known geneticists and other scientists; the scientific Popular Front had given way to a right-of-centre coalition of anti-communist intellectuals; and a new, highly apolitical generation of academic researchers was coming to the fore. That is not to say that the scientific Left had become extinct, or that the Lysenko affair was primarily responsible for arresting the further radicalization of British scientific workers. The importance of the Soviet biological dispute was that it sharply and quickly crystallized a set of anti-socialist attitudes that might otherwise have taken years to establish. Yet even in the absence of such a dramatic incident, it would have been difficult for the scientific Left to have held on to its war-born gains. For the logic of post-war developments in British science pointed to new riches, new responsibilities and new opportunities for a community that was at last to be firmly integrated into the workings of the capitalist state. As Lord Ashby has since candidly observed, this was the period 'when we decided there should be an enormous lift in the finances available for research in universities – a difference by an order of ten times. This gave the scientists a honeymoon, and of course when you're on a honeymoon you don't start political protests.'[136] Certainly that tallies with Lord Ritchie-Calder's memory of the predicament of those formerly 'left-ish' scientists who now found themselves 'in positions of authority, and it was real authority . . . having to defend a government policy like – let's be frank about it – nuclear armament'.[137] More positively, recalls Lord Zuckerman, 'the post-war years were a period of enormous scientific opportunity. The Atomic Energy Authority was established . . . There were enormous opportunities in the field of agriculture, in the field of medicine . . . And there was an enormous sense abroad, in the universities and outside, that this was going to be a great scientific age.'[138] In all of these ways scientists were becoming absorbed, cajoled or trapped into a mood of political contentment that was usually proof against any appeals made by the old scientific Left to their social consciences. And, where residual doubts remained, it had become difficult to respond readily and openly to those who had faithfully backed the enemies of the 'Free World'. As a *New Statesman* profile of Bernal would complain in 1954, 'it is their religious attitude towards Moscow that has driven from the Communist Party so many scientists and intellectuals who share Bernal's hopes of progress through science, but know they must denounce cruelty and tyranny wherever they are found'.[139] Obviously, no rational, scientific person could be expected to join the 'religious Left'. In a way, that was quite a backhanded compliment to the new rhetoric which the Bernalists had helped to introduce into British politics.

Chapter Nine

Coming in from the Cold

I should think that all those in the thirties who believed that the natural sciences could only come to their most perfect fruition in a socialist society probably still think so now. Joseph Needham, 1968[1]

Between 1949 and 1956 a number of the scientific Left's veteran campaigners from the thirties recovered their nerve, reasserted their beliefs and regrouped their forces, despite the growing strength and shrillness of various anti-communist organizations. That resurgence continued, admittedly with a few notable gains, until Khrushchev's attacks first on the 'excesses' of Stalinism, and later on the workers' uprising in Hungary. Thereafter Bernal was to remain the only one of our main figures who worked within the political framework of orthodox communism. Nor did any of them elect to participate in the new wave of radical theory and practice represented by the 'New Left' and the Campaign for Nuclear Disarmament respectively. Politically stymied in their own society, they increasingly deflected their attention to the more remote problems posed either by past civilizations or by the Third World. For as Marxists and socialists they were not prepared to sink completely into political apathy, even if the combined forces of old age and a new epoch had conspired to cut them off from many contemporary struggles. Not until the late sixties would their devotion to scientific socialism come to be recognized, rewarded and, not least, highly regarded. One of their new admirers was a young American graduate student, who decided to devote his doctoral thesis to an analysis of their story.[2] How much this sort of esteem meant to them, coming as it did twenty years after the debacle over Lysenkoism, is rather difficult to estimate.

1. Regroupment

What can be determined is how grim and tentative were the scientific Left's efforts in the early fifties to regain some of its lost political influence. Obviously its ranks had been somewhat depleted, and it no longer enjoyed the ready sympathy of many liberal scientists. The morale of those researchers who continued to identify themselves as progressives was also at a low ebb. Having derived great strength over the years from the example of Soviet science, they were now obliged by the anti-communists to defend not only the Stalinist regime but their own personal integrity as well. Sometimes the attacks made on them were slight and silly.* Yet their combined weight seriously limited the ideological sway of the leaders and institutions of the radical scientists' movement. Nowhere was this more evident than in the Association of Scientific Workers. Indeed, under pressure from the T.U.C.'s General Council and, more importantly, from the sudden fall in its own membership, the A.Sc.W. was obliged to censor the activities of its more active (i.e. left-wing) supporters. Such was the message conveyed to its Annual Council in 1949 by the Executive Committee, which was

convinced that the association must not indulge in activities or make pronouncements on political matters which would have the effect of narrowing its appeal and of rendering it less able to represent the wide range of views to be found in its ranks at present. There is need for the exercise of a full sense of responsibility by sections of the association at all levels. Particularly is this the case in regard to public pronouncements, resolutions to bodies with which the A.Sc.W. has relations and communications to the press. All those who speak in the name of the association in the branches, areas, committees and Executive Committee should feel this sense of responsibility and exercise due circumspection in their activities and utterances.[3]

The need for self-restraint was manifested within a matter of months, when the E.C.'s Presiding Officer, J. D. Bernal, found himself censured by the British Association. In a period of such

* For example, when the World Peace Congress was convened in Paris in 1949, a local right-wing newspaper drew its readers' attention to some of the desperados among the delegates, not least 'the English "scientist" Bernal, unknown in scientific circles but well known to the police'. Bernal's close friend, the Soviet novelist Ilya Ehrenburg, quotes this nice bit of nonsense in the sixth volume of his Memoirs, *Men. Years – Life; Post-War Years 1945–54* (London, 1966), p. 136.

confusion and retrogression it was therefore understandable that some socialists like Hogben, Haldane and Needham would confine their politics to the odd speech or article on behalf of campaigns in which they themselves were not conspicuously involved. Even in the case of Bernal or Levy, both of whom managed to maintain their political momentum throughout the Cold War, a relatively greater proportion of their time had to be devoted to a reworking of their old theoretical perspectives. These were some of the main reasons why the scientific Left momentarily stumbled in the practice of its beliefs.

Nevertheless it was not long before a fair number of left-wing scientists had reactivated themselves. Their rallying point had been defined as early as the autumn of 1950 by Bernal. He argued that the 'paramount need of the world today' was neither the liberation of the Third World nor the strengthening of the European and American labour movements. Rather it was 'the securing of peace'.[4] That issue had the virtue of serving simultaneously as an antidote to the hawkish anti-Soviet mood that was coming to prevail in the West, and as an appeal to liberal, humanitarian fears of a world-wide nuclear holocaust. It also revived the old Bernalist emphasis on how the capitalist system frustrated science by applying it to ignoble ends. Such was the basis on which a new British organiza-tion, Science for Peace, was founded in January 1952. A number of veterans from the old Cambridge Scientists' Anti-war Group, including Bill and 'Tony' Pirie and of course Bernal, sat on its national committee. Over the next five years this group would remain the principal platform for the old scientific Left. In addition to its sponsorship of a number of conferences and a quarterly *Bulletin*, Science for Peace actively joined in the debate over the hazards of nuclear radiation. But for our purpose the most interest-ing thing about the S.F.P. was that it based itself explicitly upon a liberal ideology of science. In its 'Statement of Principles' scien-tific knowledge is seen as morally neutral – it can be used for good or evil purposes. Furthermore, 'as scientists we hold that a common appeal to reason and objective fact must be used to resolve the differences between the nations'. Finally, they implicitly repudiated the notion of a socialist science qualitatively distinct from its capitalist counterpart.

We assert the permanently international character of science. It is a world-wide republic of the mind. The scientists of all countries form one fraternity united in a common effort to understand nature; they could be united in a common concern for human betterment. We must seek to maintain everywhere the civil rights of scientists; and it is our duty to strive for the removal of all barriers that restrict or embarrass the free intercourse of scientists and the free interchange of scientific information throughout the world.

Four years after the triumph of Lysenkoism, the scientific Left was at last able to reaffirm unconditionally its underlying faith in the inherently progressive essence of its science. That faith was also coming to inform more openly the discussions between Soviet academicians and British left-wing researchers inside the World Federation of Scientific Workers. Indeed a liberalization of scientific life in the U.S.S.R. had already been under way for about two years. In addition to its gentle encouragement of that trend, the federation strongly associated itself with the initiatives taken by the Communist-controlled World Peace Council. As one of the most active members of both the council and the federation, Bernal's influence was inevitably very great. One of his initiatives, in May 1952, was to organize 'a world-wide meeting of scientists of such repute that governments would pay attention to their conclusions' on nuclear warfare and other subjects.[5] Partly as a result of his efforts, the now famous Pugwash Conference on Science and World Affairs was initiated four years later.[6] Such then were the national and international dimensions of the scientific Left's revival in the early fifties.

Impressive though this comeback was, it rested upon rather narrow theoretical and practical foundations. For a start the links between the scientists' new bodies and working-class politics were purely formal and highly attenuated. The margin for socialist gains among scientific workers was further restricted by the scientific Left's orthodox conception of the social relations of science. As early as 1949, Bernal was floating the notion that a second industrial revolution, in which science took the lead in formulating and solving the technical *and* organizational problems of industry, was upon us.[7] While admitting that the United States had so far taken the lead in transferring scientific knowledge into an ideology-free 'force of production', he refused to believe that such a revolution could be successfully prosecuted for long in a capitalist society. For it implied, according to Bernal, a fully integrated and planned economy which ultimately negated that system. But Hyman Levy, for one, was not sure how valid such orthodox Marxism had become in the post-war world of monopoly capitalism. Perhaps the ruling class was at last in a position to use scientific planning to secure its medium-term survival. Certainly in 1950 he observed:

It is to science that they look for salvation and to the potentialities of the general population and not to a restricted class that they must turn for recruiting the human material necessary for peopling their laboratories and their design offices and for acting as their executive officers. The crisis in capitalism, the struggle for its rehabilitation is reflected in a drastic shift in the balance of studies within the universities and in the social composition of the student class.[8]

Even if Levy were proved wrong in the long run, the immediate prospect of transforming scientists into socialists was doubtful. Bernal himself was the first to admit that the financial and ideological inducements now given to the typical researcher probably 'left him outside his science rather more timid and conventional than any other kind of intellectual worker'.[9] Still more alarming were the recent moves to place more of the burden of national defence on to scientific workers, 'who through coming to accept this as a matter of course tend to lose all sense of social responsibility and moral values'.[10] How in these circumstances the scientific Left could expect to radicalize new recruits through an appeal to their experiences and outlook as scientists was not at all clear.

2. Retirement

In fact older left-wingers were themselves finding it difficult to retain their political balance, especially after Nikita Khrushchev's widely publicized attack in 1956 upon some of the evils associated with the 'cult of the individual' under Stalin. The British Communist Party acknowledged these 'socialist illegalities' with the greatest reluctance and only after a lot of rank-and-file agitation had made itself felt.[11] Hyman Levy found himself in the forefront of these protests. A party member for over twenty-five years,

Levy's loyalties were hardly in doubt. But he could not stomach
a batch of anti-Stalinist revelations that carried with it the authority
of the Soviet state. Levy was especially shocked by the admission
of a widespread persecution of Soviet Jewry between 1948 and
1952. Leaving aside his own Jewish origins, he took this crime
personally to heart because of the many times he had mounted a
Communist platform to attack anti-semitism in Nazi Germany and
deny its existence in the U.S.S.R. Levy made his feelings known
to the British party's leadership, who in turn authorized him to
investigate these charges as part of a wider inquiry into the cult of
the individual. In the autumn of 1956 Levy and other delegates
travelled to the Soviet Union and issued a report of their findings
the following January. They acknowledged, among other things,
'the discovery from private conversation by Comrade Levy with
Jews that the years 1948–1952 were known among them as "The
Black Years", the period during which many Jews were dismissed
from their posts, Jewish poets and writers were arrested and charged
with treason and executed'.[12] A summary of the report appeared in
the C.P.'s weekly *World News and Views*, complete with Levy's
signature. Justice would appear to have been done: he was still in
the party.

Actually Levy was in complete despair about the C.P.G.B. and
his own future in it. A thinly fictionalized account of his trauma
can be found in Doris Lessing's novel *The Golden Notebook*, the
finest account we possess of what it meant to be a 'Red' intellectual
at this time. Lessing was herself a contributor to the discussions of
1956, one of which concerned 'the Jewish question'.

About three weeks ago I went to a political meeting. This one was
informal at Molly's house. Comrade Harry, one of the top academics in
the C.P., recently went to Russia to find out, as a Jew, what happened to
the Jews in the 'black years' before Stalin died. He fought the Communist
brass to go at all; they tried to stop him. He used threats: if they would not
let him go, would not help him, he would publicize the fact. He went;
came back with terrible information; they did not want any of it made
known. His argument, the usual one from the 'intellectuals' of this time:
just for once the Communist Party should admit and explain what everyone knew to be true. Their argument, the old argument of the Communist
bureaucracy – solidarity with the Soviet Union at all costs, which means
admitting as little as possible. They agreed to publish a limited report,

leaving out the worst of the horrors. He had been conducting a series of meetings for Communists and ex-Communists in which he had been speaking about what he discovered. Now the brass are serious, and are threatening him with expulsion; threatening members who go to his meetings with expulsion. He is going to resign.[13]

Here Lessing has summarized Levy's political odyssey between 1956 and the beginning of 1958. All that has been left out is the event that probably decided Levy to mount his own one-man oppositional struggle within the party. This was the reception he was given at the C.P.G.B.'s acrimonious congress in the spring of 1957. Another eye-witness account, that of the historian John Saville, needs to be quoted at length here.

The debates . . . exhibited a roughness and sectarianism which was the product of the political agony that everyone – Stalinists and anti-Stalinists – had experienced in the previous twelve months. When Professor Hymie Levy made an impassioned speech at the congress attacking the leadership for having so misled the members of the party about the real situation in the Soviet Union, he was answered next morning by a speech of great vituperation in which the parallel was made with the Bolshevik Party around 1905 who also lost many members: 'The Russians, too, were confused by the backboneless, spineless intellectuals who were turned in on their own emotions instead of using their capabilities for rallying the party'. The Daily Worker headlined this stirring stuff as 'Revisionist Views Smashed'.[14]

Levy's rupture with the leadership was now almost complete.

Nevertheless for nearly a year after the congress Levy attempted to use every means at his disposal to stimulate a more open and exhaustive intra-party debate. In addition to the staging of his own meetings, he joined hands with other dissident Communists and contributed to their informal journal The New Reasoner. Then early in 1958 Levy took the fateful step of presenting his case to a wider, non-party audience, in the form of a book on Jews and the National Question. His overt intention in all of these contributions was to offer a Marxist explanation as to how a 'cult of the individual' could come to flourish in a socialist society. For example:

During the latter years of Stalin's life, if his name was mentioned at a party meeting, the members stood up in silent reverence for a minute. To brush this off as the 'cult of the individual' and to regard it as an intrusion from *outside* into Soviet society is to miss its significance. It is the residue of the Occult . . . from the past, *within* a society which already has an economically socialist basis. It is evidence of a gap between basis and superstructure. For leading members to have an outlook into which this form of behaviour can be naturally fitted implies a society that is far removed from socialistic coherence.[15]

But why the gap; why was that incoherence allowed to persist? Levy tentatively concluded: because the C.P.S.U. and its officials, in the absence of stronger institutions supportive of socialist democracy and self-criticism, had been able to place their needs ahead of those of the Soviet people.[16] The sting in the tail of Levy's argument for his British comrades was that, if they did not heed the lessons emerging from the Soviet experience, their own party would find itself the victim of a cult of officialdom.

Needless to say, the leadership of the British party was not amused. On 8 March 1958, R. Palme Dutt, the Communists' leading theoretician, denied the substance of Levy's main charges in *Jews and the National Question*. More ominously he declared that 'with this book Levy finally parts company with Marxism'.[17] His victim did not have to be told in detail what Dutt meant. Indeed Levy saved his critics the effort by announcing to the *New Statesman*'s readers in April that 'the official journal of the British C.P., horrified that I presume to criticize the Soviet Union in any way at all, devoted seven columns to what is in effect personal vilification and misrepresentation of my views. My expulsion follows inevitably.'[18] Even at this late date Levy tried to impress on those of his comrades who remained within the party the importance of the basic right of criticism.

A political party that professes to be scientific in its approach to social issues must exercise the same principle, and insist on safeguarding it for its individual members if it is to retain its scientific structure. There is of course a time and a place for such criticisms to be expressed but the opportunity must be there and it must be otherwise unrestricted. But there is something more. The members of such a body must be provided with the fullest information available. The leadership must share its special information with the rank and file, if the latter is to be in a position to exercise its critical power to the fullest advantage. For example if the leadership of any of the Communist Parties was aware of what had been happening in the Soviet Union during the latter years of Stalin's life, and if they maintained silence before their members then, by that very action they were striking a blow at the scientific understanding of their members and at its entitlement to call itself scientific.[19]

Over half his adult life had been spent inside the party. Now he was forced to leave it. The poignancy of this moment was that Levy was about to be condemned to the political wilderness. Yet, in my own view, his development from a union organizer at the National Physical Laboratory to his last hurrah as a Communist hell-raiser had rendered him the politically most interesting and admirable member of our left-wing coterie. Now all that experience was about to be lavished on an occasional speaking engagement for the A.Sc.W., the odd letter to *The Times* and a book attacking the 'purity' of Cambridge mathematicians that somehow never got written. More sadly still, Levy was always ready to return to the C.P. fold, if only the party were prepared to offer a few public apologies.[20] But so long as his old nemesis Dutt was around, such amends could never be made. Unfortunately for Levy (and the C.P.?), Dutt did not die until a few months after Levy's own death in February 1975, at the age of eighty-five.

Levy was not the only left-wing scientist for whom the events of 1956 had a special political and personal significance. In April of that year J. B. S. Haldane officially and privately left the Communist Party[21] – just a few days after the Soviet Academy of Agricultural Sciences had decided not only to republish the works of the late geneticist N. I. Vavilov but to accept the resignation of its President T. D. Lysenko as well. Though J.B.S. had already absented himself from party affairs for nearly six years, this last gesture of regretful disapproval was significant. For it suggested that politically, as well as socially and professionally, he had grown irrevocably estranged from his own society. He no longer seemed to fit in anywhere. Neither, given his experience, was he allowed to disappear from the public's view. In these circumstances Haldane had only two options. Stay in Britain and become a crank, eccentric or jester. Such was the role which well-meaning and condescending sympathizers wanted to thrust upon him (and to which he could bring his unrivalled gifts as a pundit and popularizer). Alternatively, he could remove himself altogether to an environment where his past would be an asset rather than a hindrance to him and his wife,

Helen Spurway. With few regrets J.B.S. opted for the second course and fixed upon India as his new home.

Haldane announced his decision to leave Britain during the Suez crisis. As a fillip to the cause of anti-imperialism, he asserted to the press that he was forsaking his country because of its criminal attack upon Egypt. In fact, Haldane and Spurway had already negotiated jobs for themselves at the Indian Statistical Institute in Calcutta. And quite apart from their antipathy to the affluent, 'you-never-had-it-so-good' mood in the U.K. at this time, they were positively drawn to India's people, climate and culture. J.B.S. also approved of its government's 'neutralist' Third World perspective in politics and believed moreover that Prime Minister Jawharlal Nehru had already proved himself to be an enlightened patron of science. For Indians active in scientific and political affairs Haldane's initiative was warmly welcomed. The pre-conditions for a better life had been duly fulfilled. J.B.S. and Helen flew to Calcutta on 24 July 1957.

Despite a variety of controversies and disputes over the organization of Haldane's and Spurway's scientific enterprises J.B.S.'s sojourn in India had to be judged a genuine success. Both he and his wife quickly adapted themselves to the routines, rhythms and styles of Indian life. Their assimilation consisted of more than the adoption of local clothing and customs. Though J.B.S. did not become a Hindu himself, he did open himself out to Hinduism's cosomology and ethics. In his relations with animals, for example, he began to adopt a consistently non-violent posture. This extended beyond the practice of an increasingly strict vegetarianism to the encouragement of non-violence in the scientific study of all living creatures. More generally, J.B.S. found time for the type of philosophical speculation in which he had not indulged since the twenties. All of these developments earned for him the reputation of a wise and honoured sage. Such respect had never been so widely proffered to Haldane in his own society, and it seemed to have the effect of mellowing and enlarging his already expansive personality. One sign of J.B.S.'s new inner peace were his nightly observations of the stars from the top of his flat-roofed home in Calcutta. There he gave himself over to a characteristic mixture of scientific precision laced with metaphysical reveries. Thus:

'It is only fair to warn you that you should probably avoid being on the roof with me at night,' he wrote to the young fiancée of his secretary who was coming to stay at the flat. 'This is not for the reason which you might guess, for I am sixty-five years old and love my wife; but because I am liable to start talking about the stars, and many people find this very boring. I personally think it most exciting that Vega is a main sequence star of Type A and only about 10 persecs distant. But most people are unwilling to learn the very simple ideas involved . . .'[22]

However, while in India, Haldane did not become so absorbed in 'soft' science that he neglected in any way either his own genetical investigations or the training of an indigenous corps of research workers. In all these respects the compact he had made with his new society had been more than justified.

Then, in November 1963, en route to India from a scientific conference in the United States, J.B.S. stopped off in London for a medical opinion about the rectal bleeding from which he had been recently suffering. He was diagnosed as having cancer of the rectum. But following an operation Haldane was given some hope of recovery. During his incarceration at University College Hospital J.B.S. took two opportunities to make his views and presence felt in Britain. The first of these was the publication in the *New Statesman* of a new Haldane poem called 'Cancer's a Funny Thing'. Here's an extract.

> The microscope returned the answer
> That I had certainly got cancer.
> So I was wheeled into the theatre
> Where holes were made to make me better.
> One set is in my perineum
> Where I can feel but can't yet see 'em.
> Another made me like a kipper
> Or female prey of Jack the Ripper.
> Through this incision, I don't doubt,
> The neoplasm was taken out,
> Along with colon and lymph nodes
> Where cancer cells might find abodes.
> A third much smaller hole is meant
> To function as a ventral vent:
> So now I am like two-faced Janus
> The only god who sees his anus.[23]

These stanzas were variously described as 'courageous' or 'obscene'. What this frankness was intended to achieve was a greater awareness of the suffering that could be avoided by early diagnosis and less bodily self-disgust. Perhaps more shocking than this poem was Haldane's transformation of a proposed B.B.C. documentary on his scientific work into an audacious self-obituary. From his hospital bed J.B.S. was allowed to tell his life story, popularize his chosen science, settle a few political accounts and sum up his own world-view as a scientific socialist. (In this programme he referred to Lysenko as 'a very fine biologist, and some of his ideas are right';[24] nevertheless Haldane closely adhered to his original defence of genetics.) After this long and unexpected stop-over, he returned to India, wondering whether the cancer had been fully arrested. Some months later it was clear that his operation had not been successful. J.B.S. died shortly after his seventy-second birthday in December 1964.

Long before Haldane had booked his passage to India, Joseph Needham had immersed himself in the historical development and contemporary problems of another Asian civilization, namely China. Unlike J.B.S., Needham was able to remain in England without suffering the fate of becoming either a 'character' or a communist 'dupe'. Part of his tranquillity had been gained at the expense of his involvement in some of the more important skirmishes of the cultural Cold War. It is true that in 1952 Needham was a member of the self-selected scientific commission that charged the Americans with resorting to bacteriological warfare during the Korean 'police incident'.[25] But that controversy aside, his most significant political commitment in the post-war period has been his presidency, first of the British–China Friendship Association and later of the Society for Anglo-Chinese Understanding. Because of the 'cultural' orientation of these organizations (and the growing anti-Soviet outlook of Chinese policy after Stalin's death), Needham was able to steer clear of any deeper public entanglement in politics. Such disputes as he encountered were largely between Maoists and orthodox Communists inside the B.C.F.A.[26]

If Needham's gentle and sustained support of revolutionary China did not render him a dupe, neither did his obsession with the history of ancient China qualify him as an eccentric. Perhaps such a label was rather irrelevant in the case of someone who had already combined in his life a unique and continuing attachment to science and religion, communism and Anglo-Catholicism, and who more-over insisted on jumbling up these 'opposites'. What has really rescued Needham from crankishness, however, has been the serious-ness, scale and success of his now world-famous series on *Science and Civilization in China*.[27] It is a work of prodigious scholarship, possibly, in the words of one reviewer, 'the greatest single act of historical synthesis and intercultural communication ever attempted by one man'.[28] When the first volume appeared in 1954, it was greeted by Arnold Toynbee as 'a Western act of "recognition" on a higher plane than the diplomatic one'.[29] Indeed, Needham's project was intended from the start to bring together and vindicate all the various strands of his world-view, not least his abhorrence of the racialism that persists in the attitude of Europeans to coloured people all over the world. He has been especially critical of our historians who speak of 'our' science and 'our' modern culture.

Surely it would be better to admit that men of the Asian cultures also helped to lay the foundations of mathematics and all the sciences in their medieval forms, and hence to set the stage for the decisive breakthrough which came about in the favourable social and economic milieu of the Renaissance. Surely it would be better to give more attention to the history and values of these non-European civilizations in actual fact no less exalted and inspiring than our own. Then let us give up that intellectual pride which boasts that 'we are the people, and wisdom was born with us'. Let us take pride enough in the historical fact that *modern* science was born in Europe and only in Europe, but let us not claim thereby perpetual patent thereon. For what was born in the time of Galileo was a universal palladium, the salutary enlightenment of all men without distinction of race, colour, faith or homeland, wherein all can qualify and participate. Modern universal science, yes; Western science, no![30]

Such faith in modern science, as a force that transcends all cultures and modes of production (capitalism and socialism included), was as characteristic of Needham and the scientific Left as it was of their less radical peers. Given that degree of community between them, it is only slightly remarkable that in 1965 Needham the Maoist was elected Master of one of Cambridge's most powerful colleges. Even now in 1977 Needham is still very much alive, still a Fellow of Caius College, still working on his Chinese investigation; still a socialist.

The functional equivalent of 'India' and 'China' for J. D. Bernal has always been the Soviet Union. Ever since his first visit there in the summer of 1931, Bernal's enthusiasm for the U.S.S.R., its leaders and its peoples, had been immense. After 1945 his relationship with Soviet communism became still more intimate through his indefatigable work for the World Peace Council and the World Federation of Scientific Workers. The Soviets came to rely upon Bernal to speak out on their behalf even during the darkest moments of the Cold War. He did not fail them up to and beyond Khrushchev's secret speech to the Twentieth Congress of the C.P.S.U. in 1956. Three years earlier, on the occasion of Stalin's death, for example, Bernal was moved to assert of the Soviet dictator that he had 'combined as no man had before his time, a deep theoretical understanding with unfailing mastery of practice'. This was 'no accident', Bernal continued. For 'the true greatness of Stalin as a leader was his wonderful combination of a deeply scientific approach to all problems with his capacity for feeling and expressing himself in simple and direct human terms'.[31] In view of his work for the W.P.C. and his defence of the U.S.S.R.'s regime (including the cult of the individual), it was 'no accident' that Bernal soon achieved the status of both a national hero inside the Soviet Union and an international celebrity in the world communist movement. One measure of his stature here was the Soviet government's award to him in 1953 of its highest honour, the Stalin Peace Prize.

Bernal treasured his association with the U.S.S.R. and accepted the sacrifices that came with it. In his own country he suffered quite a bit of abuse for his pro-Soviet views. And even when in Moscow his unwavering allegiance to the East was not without its drawbacks. As Bernal complained to Ilya Ehrenburg in a note written early one September morning in 1954, he didn't like being a hero.

I have been given a room in a far too luxurious hotel ... A programme has been worked out for the few days I can spend in Moscow: a ride in the Metro, Gorky Street and on Sunday to see the architecture of the agriculture exhibition. This is my eighth visit to Moscow. I know a dozen clever, interesting people in this city, but instead of giving me the opportunity to talk to them, when there are so many engrossing things happening in the world, I am being treated like a sacred cow.[32]

Nevertheless being an object of admiration could have its rewards if the subject had some criticisms of his admirers that he wanted them to take seriously. Bernal did, not least with regard to restrictions on the civil liberties of Soviet intellectuals. In that endeavour he undoubtedly had the support of most of the U.S.S.R.'s scientific élite, whom he regularly met under the auspices of the World Federation of Scientific Workers. They were in a position to cite the highly regarded Bernal's 'liberal' views on the theory and practice of science. These were embedded in the principles of the W.F.S.W. and Science for Peace. More strikingly, they were theoretically justified in Bernal's *Science in History*, a Russian edition of which was published in 1956. This text was in fact a key document in the drive towards liberalization within the Soviet scientific community. For the essence of Bernal's argument was that science had become an ideologically neutral force of production and, as such, it now possessed an internal logic whose workings were best understood by scientists. The implications of *Science in History* were discussed more fully in November 1957 – one month after the launching of Sputnik I – at a conference in Moscow devoted entirely to that work. Bernal was its guest of honour.[33] Some might say that these developments more than justified the overwhelmingly uncritical defence of Stalinism that Bernal tended to serve up to Western audiences. But this is not a domain where it is easy to reckon up any moral accounts. Indeed one of the ironies of Bernal's writings was that they helped to introduce into Soviet political and intellectual life a perspective on science which Bukharin had brought over to Britain twenty-five years earlier. With Bukharin's subsequent disgrace and execution went a rejection of his work on the scientific aspects of socialism. Now the prestige of a man who had for many years defended the policies of Bukharin's chief tormentor (Stalin) was being used to put Bukharin's theories back on the Soviet agenda. Yet to this day Bukharin's name is unmentionable in the U.S.S.R. That is a tale that emphasizes not so much the cunning of history as its perplexity.

But then Bernal was himself, after all, a very complex man. Back in Britain he remained throughout the rest of his life as closely identified with orthodox communism as any intellectual of his generation. Yet probably his single most important political act at home in the fifties was his continuing participation in a ginger group of scientists bent on changing the Labour Party's perspective on science and technology.[34] Their meetings were regularly attended by Hugh Gaitskell, James Callaghan, Alf (later Lord) Robens and, eventually, Harold Wilson and Richard Crossman. Out of these discussions arose a new commitment on the part of Labour to modernize its own political image and fight the 1964 General Election on the basis of its ability to bring a 'white-hot' technological revolution to Britain. Wilson was particularly keen on this line, as was clear in 1961 from his preface to the party document *Science and the Future of Britain*.

The central feature of our post-war capitalist society is the scientific revolution. Both its pace and its extent are beyond the dreams of previous generations . . . The central issue of politics throughout the world today is not merely how the riches shall be distributed within and between nations but – just as important – how the new powers and energies now released by science shall be controlled. In Britain the critical difference between the Labour Party and its rivals had always been that it had believed that man-power and resources must be planned intelligently if they were to serve the common good . . . (But) in the modern world such planning would be meaningless without the full planning and mobilization of scientific resources.[35]

Here was a future Prime Minister, who would later attempt to put British capitalism onto a more scientific and managerial basis, subscribing to Bernalism pure and simple. How Bernal's words ended up in Wilson's mouth had less do do with 'Sage's' attendance of these meetings than with the influence he had earlier cast over other participants like P. M. S. Blackett, Ritchie Calder and C. P. Snow. Certainly more than one observer has noted a number of similarities between the Labour Party's science policy of this era and the programme outlined after the war by the Association of Scientific Workers in its *Science and the Nation*.[36] What was less easy to explain was how this development could be reconciled with Bernal's unswerving belief that a fully scientific capitalism was a contradiction in terms, and in reality.

Bernal alone might have been able to resolve that issue had his health not deteriorated so rapidly in the early sixties. From that time to his death in 1971, he was largely confined to a wheelchair, the victim of a series of strokes. Given the exhausting pace of

Bernal's tumultuous life, it is surprising that he had not succumbed earlier. The most tragic feature of his illness was that he virtually lost the power to speak, though his prodigious mental abilities were otherwise unimpaired. That only served to intensify the psychological duress that accompanied his often severe physical pain. Nevertheless, with the considerable aid of his wife, secretary, personal assistant and a large number of friends, Bernal somehow managed to go on revising old books and publishing new ones. (He even found time to answer a long list of questions about his life and thought which I sent to him in the summer of 1968.) Such loyalty quietly testified to the inspirational effect which Bernal regularly seemed to exercise on all those who encountered him as co-workers, comrades and friends. The sources of his charisma were varied, but they most certainly included an intensity of dedication to the extension of socialist theory and practice that was not approached by any of his contemporaries.

Lancelot Hogben, by contrast, ended his days in 1975 as a recluse, politically isolated, bereft of family and far removed from his old, too often estranged friends. For many years Hogben had been a man of the Left outside the Popular Front, a socialist without a party. His idiosyncratic politics owed something to the non-conformist religion in which he had been raised. He reserved the right to bear witness at all times to his own values, beliefs and interpretations, and such a stance, however personally uplifting and at times politically necessary, tended to remove him from mainstream left-wing activities. But Hogben's temperament did not, by itself, produce his isolation. For he was also highly critical of the orthodox Left's conception of socialism, as implied by its ecstacies over Soviet industrialism. Denied the comforts of political fellowship, it was all the more essential for Hogben to find support of a more personal or professional nature. Yet his perennially defensive and 'unmatey' outlook too often succeeded in throwing up a challenge that finally turned one against him. Incredibly enough, after forty years of companionship, this corrosive process finally ate away the remaining bonds between Hogben and Enid Charles. They divorced in 1957. (Shortly thereafter he married one Sarah Jane Evans, a resident of the valley in North Wales where Hogben spent the last decade of his life.) Four years later he retired from his Chair at Birmingham University. But rather than give up work altogether he embarked on a short but tempestuous career as the first Vice-Chancellor of the University of Guyana.[37] Upon his return to Britain Hogben continued to produce more of the popularized accounts of science, past and present, for which he had become justly famous.[38] Yet his contacts with fellow biologists had virtually ceased, principally because even in retirement he could not resist renewing old controversies, especially in the areas of statistics and eugenics.[39]

In Hogben's later years probably his greatest solace was the social and natural setting of his home in the Glyn Valley, North Wales. It was, in his terms, a bio-aesthetic paradise which he could cultivate in novel and fruitful ways. Moreover there seems to have been a good deal of affection that had grown up between him and the villagers and farmers dotted about the valley floor. (At least this was my impression after talking to a dozen or so local people in a pub, before and after I had interviewed 'the Professor' in the summer of 1968.) Despite that goodwill Hogben remained, as always, a reserved, solitary and rather brooding figure. Fortunately his second wife proved to be a good friend. But when she died in April of 1975 not even Hogben's stubborn stoicism seemed able to absorb the blow. He died four months later, just short of his eightieth birthday.

In the telling of this particular story old age has come quickly upon us. The reason for this abrupt denouement is not that the last fifteen years or so of these men's lives were 'uninteresting'; far from it. Rather ours has been a narrative in which politics has, so to speak, been in command. And on that basis it must be said that, after 1956, Bernal and the others ceased to have a significant and direct impact on the conduct of British political and cultural life. One of the problems they could not overcome was the steady erosion of their political base within the scientific community. The Association of Scientific Workers was no longer in a healthy state and, in any event, most of its energies were now directed towards technicians employed mainly outside the universities. The British Association finally jettisoned its Division for the Social and International Relations of Science in 1959.[40] Nor was it at all evident from where Bernal's and Haldane's successors might be recruited. Indeed at a meeting of scientists at University College, London, in 1958, Lancelot Hogben found himself in the bizarre position of urging young scientific workers to emulate, in however small a way, the radicalism of their sixty-year-old colleagues on the platform.[41] His plea would not be heard for at least a further ten years.

A more positive reading of the scientific Left's position was that it had largely fulfilled its self-defined mission and had nowhere else to go. First, the Left as a whole had grown more scientific or Bernalist in its orientation. That orientation continues to come through most strongly in the Communist Party's official programme *The British Road to Socialism*. Here the rationale for overthrowing capitalism has come to rest almost entirely on its inability to use modern science wisely and efficiently. In the *British Road*'s opening paragraph we are told that

We live in an age of great scientific and technological advance. Never before in history have there been such opportunities to lighten work and enrich life, abolish poverty and squalor, wipe out disease.

But in Britain, as in other capitalist countries, a deep-seated crisis of the whole economic, political and social system affects adversely every aspect of life . . .

It has never been so clear that capitalism is an outdated system, unable to use the vast scientific advances to benefit the people. The new techniques and discoveries which could in the right hands end insecurity and poverty for all time, are misused to increase private profits and to prepare ever more devastating wars.

The Communist Party believes that if our people are to enjoy a life of opportunity and prosperity and Britain play a progressive role in the world a new social system is needed, for the present one is increasingly failing. The working people will have to make a revolutionary change, end capitalism and build a socialist society. Only then, when the people own the means of production and decide their own destiny, will the miracles of modern science perform miracles for the welfare of the great majority.

It is with the conviction that Britain must take such a new path that we put forward our programme *The British Road to Socialism*.[42]

Other groupings to the left of the C.P., whether Trotskyist or not, have since managed to disagree with the party as to how a socialist transformation can be achieved without challenging its definition of what socialism is about and why its absence impoverishes us all.[43] To the Communists' Right has stood the Labour Party whose conversion to Bernalism has already been described. The new and pivotal role of the 'scientific and technological revolution' in a socialist society was shortly to be taken for granted in the work of Soviet Marxists.[44] In that respect their understanding of the 'logic of industrialism' differed little from that of conventional American sociologists who obviously felt that the capitalist system had been and would be able to sustain the onward march of science.[45] By the end of the fifties this scientific consensus had become so widespread that some writers had begun to speak of 'the end of ideology'[46] and the convergence of socialist and capitalist societies under the sway of scientific domination.[47] This was also the logic of Bernalism, albeit stood on its head.

In fact the scientism of the thirties' movement of left-wing scientists had become so widely assimilated into the rhetorics of anti-capitalist and anti-communist politics that it was gradually accepted as something natural and 'above' society, even by the thinkers and activists of the New Left. At first their priorities and methods were seen to depart quite substantially from those of the old, Communist-dominated Left. On the one hand the Campaign for Nuclear Disarmament rejected the Cold War mentality of a world divided into socialist and capitalist camps, settling instead for the less ideological view of the dangers posed by a struggle between two rather similar superpowers.[48] On the other, the two rather different coteries who successively ran the *New Left Review* were not disposed to challenging the scientific basis of Bernalist socialism. In the case of its earlier Editorial Board, that was because of a desire to shift the locus of left-wing thinking from one area – science – that had been rather thoroughly explored to another – culture, ideology, consciousness – where much more work needed to be done. The group that succeeded it, led by Perry Anderson, likewise took the scientific aspects of socialism as largely unproblematic, on the grounds that it was interested in 'social' as opposed to 'natural' concepts.[49] Hence in their own domain the members of the old scientific Left went largely unchallenged. And where they still wanted to intervene politically as cultural Cold Warriors was no longer a terrain that interested the newest crop of radicals.*

* However, within C.N.D., a Scientists' Group was established and it included among its active supporters Bill and 'Tony' Pirie. The Piries of course were members of the pre-war Cambridge Scientists' Anti-war Group and, later, Science for Peace. But S.F.P. was torn apart in 1957–8 because of the

Nevertheless Bernal and the others continued to defend the East from within the Soviet-funded World Federation of Scientific Workers, while Michael Polanyi and his associates used the C.I.A.-financed Congress for Cultural Freedom to advance the cause of Western culture. In truth this was a battle of ideas whose interest was becoming largely restricted to its most immediate protagonists. The big news, for our purposes, was that at this stage the substance of Bernal's *Social Function of Science* had largely become a political commonplace.

Obviously that pleased Bernal, who remained forever confident that one day the incompatibility between the advancement of science and the maintenance of capitalism would be conclusively demonstrated. Needham too was persuaded in 1968 that 'all those in the thirties who believed that the natural sciences could only come to their most perfect fruition in a socialist society probably still think so now'. To both men it was therefore an encouraging sign that, during the Vietnam War, more and more protests were being made about the penchant of American capitalism to direct its vast scientific resources to destructive ends. Towards the close of the sixties these complaints were systematized and generalized at a Conference on Chemical–Biological Warfare held at the Bernal Peace Library in London. Apart from the publication of its proceedings,[50] the most important result of this gathering was to inspire a group of young 'leftish' scientists to establish a British Society for Social Responsibility in Science.[51] With the active cooperation of a number of veterans from the old scientific Left, the society launched itself in April 1969 with a one-day meeting at the Royal Society. A few researchers who had been politically active in earlier decades were notable by their absence. But among its founding members were proudly listed the names of Bernal, Hogben, Levy and Needham – the four surviving subjects of this book. Now at last they had a reasonable hope that their work would be carried on and extended by a new generation of socialists.

Communist members' opposition to C.N.D.'s commitment to unilateral disarmament. As stalwarts of the Labour Left, the Piries had no hesitation in switching over to the new organization. See P. Duff, *Left, Left, Left; A Personal Account of Six Protest Campaigns, 1945–65* (London, 1971), pp. 152–9.

Afterword

It is a tragedy of the . . . Left that (its) experience has fallen between two stools. The Old Left (with some exceptions), prone to nostalgic revels in the glories of (its) heyday and understandably bent on ensuring the historical credits that are its due, has not come to grips, critically or analytically, with its experience. And the 'New Left', for the most part, has been too obsessed with negative aspects of the experience to confront it with critical objectivity. Scattered efforts made by the 'New Left' have not avoided the pitfall of hindsight which may be described as a failure of historical empathy, an inability to apprehend people and events in their historical context with its particular imperatives.   Al Richmond, 1973[1]

After reading someone else's book I want to record as quickly as I can the lessons I have drawn from it. If the work has prompted me to reassess an important aspect of my life, I sometimes write to the author and thank him or her for inspiring that reaction. Needless to say, I hope that my own narrative will elicit from some of my readers at least one of those two responses. Meanwhile here are what I regard as the politically most significant dimensions of this story.

As the 1970s come to an end we find most sections of the labour movement still officially committed to the creation of a socialist Britain. How the transition to socialism is to be made is a matter of some dispute, not least between social democrats and revolutionaries. But with the exception of a few relatively insignificant anarchist, feminist and libertarian groups, there is surprisingly little disagreement about a number of essential points; including why one should be a socialist, what forms of struggle are (not) essential for the achievement of socialism and how the new society will differ from the old one. Capitalism is condemned principally because its ruling class can neither efficiently develop Britain's productive resources nor equitably distribute what the country produces. However, despite its injustice and irrationality, this social system will not automatically give way to its social opponents. So they must fight hard, inside and outside Parliament, to secure their long-term political objectives. The undisputed subject and object of this struggle is the working class, the archetypical member of which is assumed to be a (male) manual worker employed in an industrial enterprise. The twin loci of his battle with the bosses will always be the 'point of production' and the capitalist state. Once the people, through their political agents, have taken over both of these domains it will at last be possible to bring about socialism. Only then can the 'wonders' of modern science and technology be fully employed to lighten toil and level up the nation's standard of living. Such, very broadly and briefly, are the beliefs that guide the action of most socialist organizations today – just as they did forty years ago during the heyday of the old scientific Left.

Indeed, of the many continuities that can be traced out between Bernal's generation of socialists and my own, perhaps the most striking is our shared conception of science and its social functions. We still tend to look upon science as a value-free 'force of production' and, as such, have placed it at the centre of our plans for building socialism in this country. The main difference between the new society and its predecessor is that technical/scientific resources would be greatly expanded and applied to new ends. But scientists and engineers would not find themselves working in radically new ways. Nor would we expect them to turn out theories, experiments and techniques qualitatively different from those they currently produce. For our criticism of capitalism here has been not that it has produced a 'bad' science but that it has manipulated a 'good' science for 'bad' purposes. In all of these respects most of us would still count ourselves as scientific socialists, if not Bernalists. Yet few of my contemporaries have ever heard of Bernal and his comrades, let alone dug down to the historical roots of their (and our) ruling thoughts. *The Visible College* has been written to encourage this process of self-discovery.

What we have discovered to date is that Bernalism was not only a theory or world-view but a set of practices as well. Indeed the outlook and activities of the scientific Left cannot be properly evaluated until we juxtapose them both against each other and against the historical context in which they first appeared. Thus Bernalism-as-theory, with its emphasis upon the material advantages to be gained from a socialism that was truly scientific, was in part very much a response to the depressed condition of British capitalism between the wars. Then it was at least a debatable question whether the existing 'mode of production' could satisfy anything more than the minimum material requirements of its industrial proletariat. Furthermore, given the anti-scientific inclinations of its ruling class and dominant culture, it was not at all clear where the will to modernize this system was going to originate. In these circumstances the Left would have been daft not to have served up socialism as a kind of scientific medicine designed to remedy Britain's social and industrial ailments. Bernalism-as-theory provided the intellectual underpinnings for that programme.

But it was simultaneously serving another function, which was to entice 'intellectuals' and, more particularly, scientific workers into liberal causes and, ultimately, socialist politics. Bernalism-as-practice, with its stress upon the capitalist frustrations of scientific progress, operated at two levels. On the one hand, it offered a non-political rationale for the establishment of pressure groups to protest against either the 'abuse' of their profession (say, for warlike purposes) or the failure to use their skills for humanitarian ends (like improving the diet of slum children). The innocence of these enclaves was often enhanced by the presence of some of the scientific establishment's more benevolent members, who willingly served as figureheads. In fact such organizations were more often than not 'fronts' used by Communists and 'fellow-travellers' to bring out the liberalism that was thought to be latent in certain professions. Naturally the Left elements hoped that, in time, the social consciousness of the previously apolitical would not simply be raised but radicalized; perhaps to the point of joining the Communist Party.

At this stage Bernalism-as-practice grew more complex. For the party's leadership could never reconcile its need for and distrust of intellectuals who chose to be Communists. Of course writers and researchers were required to organize their peers and build up the C.P.'s cultural resources. But their class position also predisposed them, it was thought, either to ultra-leftist antics such as giving up their jobs to live like proletarians or, far more commonly, to bouts of 'petty-bourgeois individualism', in which party discipline was openly flaunted in the name of one's personal integrity. Neither stance answered the Communists' need for politically reliable and professionally esteemed members. So what had to be fostered here was a close identification with their various professions on the part of both intellectuals *and* the party itself. That was why, very early on in the thirties, the C.P.G.B. began to emphasize that 'the first duty of [for example] a Communist scientist was to be a "good" [i.e. successful] scientist'. By making professional advancement as much into a political duty as a personal aspiration, a radicalized intellectual was given plenty of space to get on with the rest of his existence. (The party never put the family life of its members on to its political agenda.) In the case of scientific workers their loyalties to their party and profession were further reinforced by the Communists' unabashed faith in science as a way of knowing, changing and improving the world. From Bernalism-as-practice we return to Bernalism-as-theory.

Both aspects of Bernalism are still to be found at work in the British Left today. This would make sense if that body of theory and practice had consistently helped socialists to make gains at least commensurate with the amount of opposition they were meeting at any one time. In fact the historical record has been considerably patchier than we might have expected. Between the late thirties and late forties, admittedly with the assistance of an eminently scientific 'people's war', Bernal's brand of politics did appeal to many factory workers, as well as to an unprecedentedly large (though numerically still small) number of scientists and technicians. Then Bernalism began to lose ground, first in the fifties as a set of political practices aimed at scientists and, much later, as a rationale for socialism directed toward the working class. Both setbacks have long been acknowledged by leading socialist organizations, including the Communist Party. But neither of them has been seen as an occasion for reviewing and possibly revising either the Left's programme or its relationship to those of its adherents who do not work in a factory. For, in general, left-wing groups contend that it has been the strength of the ruling class rather than the shortcomings of their own politics that has been responsible for their failure to build a mass following. There is of course the possibility that both propositions might be true. That much seems clear to me from the decline of the old scientific

Left in the fifties. If we can then agree that Bernalism-as-practice needs to be reconsidered, we shall also have to re-evaluate Bernalism-as-theory.

Between 1948 and 1957 the scientists' Popular Front collapsed, and many more scientific workers left the Communist Party than entered it. How can we account for the declining fortunes of Bernalist politics in this period? One way is to point to the changing circumstances both of scientists, who were no longer quite so 'frustrated' as they had been a decade earlier, and of Communist intellectuals, who for the first time found themselves under severe pressure from liberal anti-communists, as well as party officials, to tell them two very different 'truths' about the Soviet Union. Yet why, if the C.P. is to be believed, did proportionately more mental than manual workers desert the party during the Cold War? Orthodox sociologists would reply that the radicalism of middle-class men and women generally lasts only so long as they remain 'marginal' to their chosen vocation. The more successful they become, the more they tend to be co-opted away from their youthful 'flirtations' with revolutionary politics. Somewhat surprisingly, this gloss on our conventional wisdom has also been taken seriously inside the Communist Party. At its twenty-sixth congress in 1959 the literary scholar Arnold Kettle took it upon himself to explain the difficulties in recruiting and retaining people like himself.

It is difficult not only because there are always certain obvious problems in winning over middle-class people to the side of the working class, but also because, as everyone knows, in the difficult days our party went through in 1956–57, it was the intellectuals in the party who were, as a section, the most influenced by revisionist ideas.

We should not, as Marxists, be surprised by this. It is due basically to the class and social position of professional workers and to the fatal separation of theory and practice which class society has brought about.

It would be very foolish for us to believe that most of the ex-party revisionists are wicked or insincere people.

Their principal trouble is a persistent desire to have the best of both worlds, to have their cake and eat it – to retain the privileges of their position in bourgeois society while at the same time attacking bourgeois society and associating themselves with the socialist movement.

Our job is to convince them – through experience and argument – that socialism is indeed the answer to their problems, their frustrations and their hopes . . .[2]

At the end of his analysis Kettle concedes that the Left has a responsibility to change the outlook of intellectuals through 'experience' and 'argument'. Yet for more than twenty years the Communist Party had been steeping its recruits in a certain tradition of experience and argument, which had evidently failed to achieve the desired effect. Perhaps something after all was amiss with its own programme of re-education.

In fact when Communist writers and scientists were placed under real duress as in the Cold War, it was hardly surprising that many of them began to act like 'bourgeois intellectuals'. For that is what the party had insisted they become. We already know why this strategy had been adopted and how successful it proved for a time. But the notion that a Communist scientist's ultimate loyalties lay with his/her science rather than his/her socialism carried with it some unacknowledged difficulties. What it implied, above all, was that the personal and professional undertakings of such an individual did not stand in need of reform. On the contrary, they were viewed as exemplary pursuits which a socialist society would do its utmost to encourage. Hence the struggle for socialism was primarily seen as a struggle to change society – not one's own situation – on behalf of others – not one's self. No one conveyed this position more succinctly than J. B. S. Haldane: 'I am a socialist because I want to see my fellow men and women enjoying the advantages which I enjoy myself.'[3] What is being affirmed here is a form of politics so 'external' to the rest of one's life that it necessarily had the following twofold effect. On the one hand, it raised the possibility, in theory, of a clash between one's own immediate interests as a bourgeois intellectual and the long-term aspirations of the working class. On the other, it compartmentalized one's life into three distinct and potentially competing spheres: the 'personal', the 'professional' and the 'political'. The Communist Party was able to contain both types of conflicts only so long as it could demonstrate, in theory and practice, that socialism valued and nurtured bourgeois cultural pursuits, especially the natural sciences, far more highly than bourgeois society itself. When in the period 1948–56 that difference became less than clear-cut, many Communist intellectuals naturally experienced a 'personal' crisis born of this antagonism between their professional interests and political ideals. Indeed, paradoxical as it may sound, those party scientists who left the C.P. at this time could be said to have been its most loyal and logical followers. For if the first duty of Communist researchers was to do well in their research, and the party line really compromised their professional standing, then their most politically consistent act ought to have been what it turned out to be: mass resignations. Likewise it was the party officials calling on their middle-class members to renounce their bourgeois outlook who were the real revisionists in this encounter.

Yet how could the Communist Party – leaders and rank and file – have modified their policies here so as to have retained during the fifties at least the gains they had made in the thirties? There is no simple answer to that question. But had its programme for intellectual members led them, however slowly and painstakingly, to bring their politics more directly to bear on their 'personal' aspirations and professional circumstances, then they might have found the will and the energy to have sustained and extended their socialist militancy. For the struggle for socialism would have become, in the process, a struggle to change themselves as well as their society, on behalf of themselves as well as the working class. The difference between this posture and the one they actually assumed has been defined, in the words of one American left-winger, as the difference between 'liberal' and 'revolutionary' consciousness.

> Liberal consciousness is conscience translated into action for others . . . Radical or revolutionary consciousness . . . is the perception of *oneself* as unfree, as oppressed, and finally it is the discovery of oneself as one of the oppressed who must unite to transfigure the objective conditions of their existence in order to resolve the contradiction between potentiality and actuality. Revolutionary consciousness leads to the struggle for one's own freedom in unity with others who share the burden of oppression . . .[4]

Despite its ahistorical smugness and abstract view of 'oppression', this statement does provide the basis for an alliance between manual and mental workers that in the long run might have been more durable and compelling than the one that was actually fashioned in the 1930s. Admittedly this alternative form of politics would have made heavier demands upon Communist intellectuals, who would have been expected eventually to confront, criticize and alter their own practices as members of families and professions shot through with bourgeois social relationships. That is a lot to demand of anyone, whatever their social class. Even more difficult to accept would have been the notion that the development of revolutionary consciousness had to be meshed with the liberal or reformists tasks which still had to be undertaken, and for which Bernalism remained an effective set of practices. In short we have a dilemma which no political formula could ever resolve. On the one hand, the Communist Party was obviously wise to recognize the short-sighted futility of attempting to transform at a stroke its bourgeois adherents into proletarian revolutionaries. On the other, the original terms of its relationships with intellectuals tied it too closely to the norms and values of *their* world. Thus from the thirties onwards the party never found the theoretical room that would have allowed it to say: 'the first duty of a Communist scientist is to bring his communism to bear on his (or her) own situation as a scientist'. Nor has any socialist organization of any consequence subsequently improved upon the C.P.'s record in this area. Bernalism-as-practice still rules and it is not, in itself, 'O.K.'

Likewise Bernalism-as-theory is still very much in evidence on the Left. One reason for its retention must be the tacit belief of a large number of socialists that this rationale for socialism, evolved at a time when British capitalism could not have been more unmodernized, still has a lot of appeal for working men and women. I wonder. Today much of the programme of modernization advocated by Bernal and other socialists in the 1930s has at last been initiated, albeit slowly and unevenly, within a capitalist framework. Of course the economic aspirations of the working class have been accordingly raised and are at the moment being seriously frustrated. Indeed the number of officially defined 'poor' families has significantly increased in the last decade. But in general it would appear that the gap between what the great mass of workers have at the moment and what they imagine they could have under socialism has not been sufficiently great to inspire widespread political activity on their part. In fact, barring a truly catastrophic collapse of the economy, is it really plausible to imagine large numbers of men and women workers placing their hard-won leisure time and possibily their living standards at risk, in order to establish a socialist order whose chief virtue is that it will give them a bit more of what they already enjoy under capitalism? Even in the depressed thirties Lancelot Hogben and George Orwell could not take that scenario seriously. Why then do we on the eve of Britain's first oil boom?

Why, in short, does the Left continue to adhere to a form of theory and practice that advances its cause only so far, and then only under very special circumstances? Perhaps the simplest answer is that socialists cannot see any alternative to Bernalism, because they regard this doctrine as 'right' and 'true'. One implication of such a position is that any utopian vision of socialism as a way of life qualitatively different *in every respect* from that of capitalism has momentarily and largely been eclipsed, at least in Britain. Few of us think and act these days as if things could 'really' be changed for the better. Nor could we believe otherwise, if, as the Bernalists have claimed, socialism would have to base itself upon the same sort of productive forces as are found in a capitalist society. That is a sobering, even a bleak and pessimistic prospect.

By contrast, the theoretical and practical alternatives to such 'socialist realism' are not only very much in the making but quite often far removed from the lives of working-class men and women as well. These new initiatives range from highly abstract critiques of left-wing scientism to local campaigns in the sphere of social reproduction, and on through to various forms of sexual politics. Whether such departures ultimately coalesce into an irresistible challenge to the Left's traditional outlook and practices is not at all clear, especially given recent trends in the British labour movement. Nevertheless, in the absence of that confrontation, I find it hard to imagine how a sufficient number of us are to find the energy and inspiration to create new socialist societies and regenerate old ones. On the other hand, should this political reorientation take place, I have no doubt that we shall continue to learn a great deal from the strengths as well as the weaknesses of our comrades and predecessors – not least those who made the Old Left more scientific.

Appendix

Appendix: The Scientific Left at Cambridge

A great deal can be deduced about the scientific Left at Cambridge from an analysis of those who signed the Cambridge Scientists' Anti-war Group's letter that appeared in the *Cambridge Review* of 1 June 1934 (vol. 56, p. 451). (See above, pp. 219–23.)

The letter, which was supported by seventy-nine faculty, research workers and post-graduate students based in the natural sciences, protested against the government's introduction of the Incitement to Disaffection Bill, which, it was said, might restrict the civil liberties of scientists and coerce them into doing research for the military. Though such issues were at this stage a focal point for left-wing agitation, they were fundamentally liberal and pacifist in nature. Thus we must assume that the radical nucleus of Cambridge's scientific community was smaller than the support for this correspondence would indicate. With that proviso in mind, we can use the data on Cambridge science referred to above in Chapter Seven (ref. 8) and find out whether the Anti-war Group's social profile differed significantly from that of the Cambridge community as a whole.

Excluding agricultural scientists and senior research workers, we are left with fifty faculty members and post-graduate students working in pure science who signed the letter.* They constituted only 11.8 per cent of the 423 staff and students engaged in basic research. Though a higher proportion of life scientists than physical scientists were signatories (16.6 per cent versus 10.6 per cent), this difference was not statistically significant.

Table One

Pure scientists; post-graduates compared with faculty

Status	Total	Signatories	%	X^2†	p†
Faculty	235	18	7.7	9.2	0.01
Post-graduates	188	32	17.0		
All	423	50	11.8		

* 'Faculty members' denotes those who held full-time university teaching posts and/or college fellowships, and sat on the Faculty Boards for their

Table One, however, shows that post-graduates were far more likely to support the anti-war cause than their elders. (It should also be noted that no professor publicly backed this initiative.)

Table Two
Pure scientists; men compared with women
(post-graduates and faculty only)

Sex	Total	Signatories	%	X^2	p
Men	392	38	9.7	17.5	0.001
Women	31	12	38.7		
	—	—			
All	423	50	11.8		

In Table Two a still more striking discrepancy is registered in the ratio of support offered by male and female scientific workers. At the very least

---

subjects. 'Senior research workers' refers to all other post-doctoral researchers. They have been excluded from the statistical analysis below, because the university kept no overall count of them. From the records that are available, however, I would estimate that there must have been about fifty such individuals in Cambridge at this time. Of these, eighteen signed the letter, a very high percentage indeed. (Compare with Table One below.)

The agricultural scientists – eleven of them – have been eliminated on the grounds of consistency and, I must admit, ignorance. They were the only group of applied scientists who signed the letter, in contrast to the total absence of medical and engineering personnel. (The absence of Cambridge engineers is not surprising: 30 per cent of them were army officers. See "Archimedes", 'Cambridge University Engineering Department: A Critical Study', *Cambridge Left*, vol. 2 (Autumn, 1934), pp. 19–28.) Hence I decided to restrict my sample to those engaged in High Science.

Nevertheless, the agriculturalists were obviously keen on this subject, but why I cannot tell. I do know that at least two of them, Arthur Walton and P. S. Hudson, wrote sympathetically about Soviet science in general and the Lysenko controversy in particular. (See Walton's article on Soviet agriculture in J. Needham and J. Sykes-Davies (eds.), *Science in Soviet Russia* (London, 1942), pp. 29–36. Apart from the articles Hudson co-authored with E. Richens on 'vernalization', there is his 'Vernalization in Agricultural Practice', *Journal of the Ministry of Agriculture*, vol. 43 (September 1936) pp. 536–43.) Otherwise I can only say that on the basis of this evidence it would be worth someone's while to look more closely at agricultural scientists in Cambridge during the 1930s.

† X^2 = Chi-Square test result of statistical probability. P = .01 means that there was less than one chance in a hundred that the distribution of signatories between faculty and post-graduates could have been achieved randomly. It is a convention of statisticians that any result below .05 is 'statistically significant'.

this result indicates that women were far more concerned about the approach of war than men.

Table Three
Pure scientists; Cavendish* and Dunn Labs compared with other labs
(post-graduates, faculty and senior research workers)

Lab	Total	Signatories	%	X^2	p
Cavendish/Dunn	86	33	38.3		
Other labs	387	35	9.0	(obviously significant!)	
All	473	68	14.4		

Also of interest is the effect which membership in particular laboratories had on the overall result. As Table Three suggests, those who worked in the two largest scientific centres in Cambridge – the Cavendish Laboratory for experimental physics and the Dunn Biochemical Institute – were disproportionately represented among the letter's backers. Indeed between them they nearly equalled the number of signatories generated from all other departments put together.

Table Four
Nuclear physicists; experimental vs. theoretical
(post-graduates, faculty and senior research workers)

Approach	Total	Signatories	%	X^2	p
Experimental	53	19	36.4	4.147	0.05
Theoretical	29	2	7.2		
All	82	21	25.6		

The importance of participation in a lab community is underscored when, as in Table Four, we compare the Cavendish's particle physicists with the mathematical/theoretical physicists, who had no such comparably unifying institutional base, or more simply, a 'home'.

Table Five
Cavendish nuclear physicists; faculty compared with senior research workers and post-graduates

Status	Total	Signatories	%	X^2	p
Faculty	14	1	7.1	4.815	0.05
Non-Faculty	39	18	46.2		
All	53	19	35.8		

* Excluded here are all X-ray crystallographers who were then working at the Cavendish.

One futher point about laboratory structure relates to the question of hierarchies. Thus among Rutherford's physicists we can, to judge from Table Five, detect a definite political cleavage between the Cavendish's teaching and non-teaching staffs. By contrast, faculty, senior research workers and post-graduates in Hopkin's biochemical lab spoke out in support of the Anti-war Group in roughly similar numbers.

Finally, the decision to sign the group's letter appears to have been unaffected either by one's collegiate affiliation or by previous attendance as an undergraduate. Put another way: there was not a statistically significant number of Trinity or King's men who were signatories.

References

Foreword

1. R. Boyle, *Works*, vol. 1 (London, 1744), ed. T. Birch, p. 20; as quoted in M. Purver, *The Royal Society; Concept and Creation* (London, 1967), p. 195.

Chapter One: High Science and Low Politics

1. B. Russell, *The Scientific Outlook* (London, 1931), p. 99.
2. N. Pirie, letter to the author, 17 June 1974.
3. A. Parry (ed.), *Peter Kapitsa on Life and Science* (New York, 1968), p. 118.
4. G. Hardy, 'Today and Tomorrow', *Scientific Worker*, vol. 5 (March, 1925), p. 117.
5. L. Whyte, *Focus and Diversions* (London, 1963), p. 57.
6. C. P. Snow, 'Chemistry', in H. Wright (ed.), *Cambridge University Studies, 1933* (London, 1933), p. 103.
7. J. Bell, as quoted in P. Stansky and W. Abrahams, *Journey to the Frontier* (London, 1966), p. 46.
8. See B. Woolf, 'The Biochemistry of History', *Brighter Biochemistry*, no. 8 (1931), pp. 25–6.
9. See C. P. Snow, *The Two Cultures; and a Second Look* (New York, 1963), p. 11.
10. G. Searle, *The Quest for National Efficiency* (London, 1971).
11. B. Semmell, *Imperialism and Social Reform* (London, 1960).
12. G. Werskey, '*Nature* and Politics between the Wars', *Nature*, vol. 224 (1 November 1969), pp. 462–72.
13. R. Brightman, 'The Scientific Outlook', *Nature*, vol. 130 (26 November 1932), p. 791.
14. R. Gregory, *Discovery, or the Spirit and Service of Science* (London, 1916), p. 284.
15. F. Soddy, 'Labour and the Higher Values', *Nature*, vol. 103 (7 August 1919), p. 447.
16. R. Gregory, 'Science in Civilization', *Nature*, vol. 112 (22 December 1923), p. 890.
17. R. Gregory, 'Science and Labour', *Nature*, vol. 106 (9 September 1920), p. 38.
18. W. Inge, 'Social Degeneration', *Nature*, vol. 107 (9 June 1921), p. 453.

344 Chapter One: High Science and Low Politics

19. R. Gregory, letter of c. 1903 to H. G. Wells, as quoted in W. Armytage, *Sir Richard Gregory, His Life and Work* (London, 1957), p. 56.
20. See A. Newsholme, 'Causes of Fluctuations in the Birth-rate', *Nature*, vol. 108 (22 September 1921), pp. 105–6.
21. F. Crew, 'Differential Fertility and Family Allowances', *Nature*, vol. 130 (20 August 1932), pp. 253–5.
22. E. MacBride, 'Social Biology and Birth Control', *Nature*, vol. 113 (31 May 1924), p. 774.
23. E. MacBride, 'Birth Control and Human Biology', *Nature*, vol. 127 (4 April 1931), p. 511.
24. F. Crew, 'Sterilization and Mental Deficiency', *Nature*, vol. 128 (25 July 1931), pp. 129–31.
25. T. Jones, 'Eugenic Sterilization', *Nature*, vol. 126 (30 August 1930), p. 302.
26. E. MacBride, 'Cultivation of the Unfit', *Nature*, vol. 137 (11 January 1936), p. 45 (my emphasis).
27. E. MacBride, 'Birth Control and Human Biology', p. 511.
28. R. Brightman, 'Industrial and Business Administration', *Nature*, vol. 130 (6 August 1932), pp. 181–3.
29. R. Brightman, 'Scientific Research and Industry', *Nature*, vol. 137 (22 February 1936), p. 291.
30. R. Brightman, 'Industrial and Business Administration', p. 182.
31. A. Church, 'The Significance of Imperial Chemical Industries', *Nature*, vol. 121 (23 June 1928), p. 975.
32. R. Brightman, 'Scientific Aspects of the Unemployment Problem', *Nature*, vol. 128 (22 August 1931), p. 282.
33. R. Brightman, 'Safety Work in Chemical Industries', *Nature*, vol. 128 (4 July 1931), p. 47
34. R. Gregory, 'British Chemical Industry', *Nature*, vol. 128 (11 July 1931), p. 47.
35. A. Church, 'The Significance of Imperial Chemical Industries', p. 974.
36. W. H. Bragg, as quoted in T. Humberstone, 'Science in Industry', *Nature*, vol. 117 (15 May 1926), p. 681.
37. T. Humberstone, 'Science and Labour', *Nature*, vol. 113 (24 May 1924), p. 738.
38. R. Gregory, 'Science and the Empire', *Nature*, vol. 110, (16 December 1922), p. 798.
39. E. MacBride, 'The Social Implications of Biology', *Nature*, vol. 118 (4 September 1926), p. 328.
40. W. Linn Cass, 'Unemployment and Hope', *Nature*, vol. 125 (15 February 1930), p. 225.
41. R. MacLeod, quoting an article from *Nature*, vol. 104 (6 November 1919), p. 257, in his 'Resources of Science in Victorian England: The Endowment of Science Movement, 1868–1900', in P. Mathias (ed.), *Science and Society, 1600–1900* (Cambridge, 1972), p. 162.
42. R. Gregory, *Discovery*, p. 50.
43. ibid., p. 257.

44. G. Jacks, 'Coordinating Agricultural Research', *Nature*, vol. 135 (12 January 1935), p. 46.

45. R. Gregory, 'Industrial Research', *Nature*, vol. 133 (20 January 1934), p. 78.

46. R. MacLeod and K. Andrews, 'The Committee of Civil Research: Scientific Advice for Economic Development, 1925–30', *Minerva*, vol. 7 (summer 1969), pp. 680–705.

47. E. Hutchinson, 'Government Laboratories and the Influence of Organized Scientists', *Science Studies*, vol. 1 (October, 1971), pp. 331–56.

48. W. Pope *et al.*, *The Organisation of Scientific Research* (Cambridge, n.d. [1919]).

49. 'Outline of the History and Policy of the National Union of Scientific Workers', *Scientific Worker*, vol. 7 (February 1926), p. 20.

50. As quoted in 'The A.S.W. – Twenty Years' History', *Scientific Worker*, vol. 12 (autumn 1939), p. 68.

51. A. Church, 'A Representative Body for Science in Great Britain', *Nature*, vol. 119 (5 March 1927), pp. 341–8.

52. For the list of the appeal's supporters, see 'The Association of Scientific Workers: Ten Years' Work', *Scientific Worker*, vol. 9 (October 1928), p. 116.

53. J. Huxley, *The Stream of Life* (London, 1926), p. 41.

54. J. Huxley, *What Dare I Think?* (London, 1931), p. 109.

55. ibid., p. 88.

Chapter Two: Worker, Warrior, Citizen, Socialist

1. L. Hogben, interview with the author 26 July 1968.

2. H. Levy, *Social Thinking* (London, 1945), p. 5.

3. H. Levy, 'From Myth to Rational Action', in B. Dixon (ed.), *Journey in Belief* (London, 1968), p. 164ff.

4. Levy, *Social Thinking*, p. 8.

5. H. Levy, interview with the author, 23 March 1972.

6. H. Levy, letter to the author, 17 June 1974.

7. H. Levy, *Social Thinking*, pp. 7–8.

8. H. Levy, letter of 17 June 1974.

9. H. Levy, interview with the author, 12 May 1968.

10. W. Cowley and H. Levy, *Aeronautics in Theory and Experiment*, 2nd ed. (London, 1920), p. iii.

11. H. Levy, interview of 12 May 1968.

12. From the verbatim account of Hyman Levy's talk to the London Area Science Policy Conference organized by the Association of Scientific Workers in November 1959. I am grateful to Professor and Mrs J. H. Fremlin for the extended loan of their manuscript.

13. E. Hutchinson, 'Scientists as an Inferior Class', *Minerva*, vol. 8 (July 1970), p. 401.

14. These and other quotations attributed to the young J.B.S. have been

drawn from his school diaries, which his sister, Naomi Mitchison, has kindly allowed me to use.

15. N. Mitchison, 'Beginnings', in K. Dronamraju (ed.), *Haldane and Modern Biology* (Baltimore, 1968), p. 301.

16. L. Farrall, *The Origins and Growth of the English Eugenics Movement, 1865–1925*, unpublished Ph.D. thesis (Indiana University, 1970), p. 213.

17. J. Huxley, *Memories* (London, 1970), p. 137.

18. Quoted in N. Mitchison, *Small Talk . . .: Memories of an Edwardian Childhood* (London, 1973), p. 77.

19. J. B. S. Haldane, 'The Scientific Work of J. S. Haldane (1860–1936)', *Nature*, vol. 187 (9 July 1960), p. 103.

20. J. B. S. Haldane, *The Inequality of Man and Other Essays* (Harmondsworth, 1938), p. 202.

21. N. Mitchison, 'Beginnings', p. 301.

22. L. Hogben, *Author in Transit* (New York, 1940), p. 161.

23. L. Hogben, *The Nature of Living Matter* (London, 1930), p. 6.

24. L. Hogben, *Author in Transit*, pp. 175–6.

25. J. M'Culloch, 'Brethren (Plymouth)', *Encyclopaedia of Religion and Ethics*, vol. 2 (Edinburgh, 1909), p. 847.

26. L. Hogben, *The Nature of Living Matter*, p. 6.

27. L. Hogben, interview of 26 July 1968.

28. ibid.

29. ibid.

30. I. Montagu, *The Youngest Son* (London, 1970), p. 317.

31. L. Hogben, *Exiles of the Snow, and Other Poems* (London, 1918), p. 45.

32. ibid., p. 23.

33. J. Needham [Henry Holorenshaw, pseud.], 'The Making of an Honorary Taoist', in M. Teich and R. Young (eds.), *Changing Perspectives in the History of Science* (London, 1973), p. 2.

34. C. P. Snow, 'J. D. Bernal, a Personal Portrait', in M. Goldsmith and A. MacKay (eds.), *Society and Science* (New York, 1964), p. 20.

35. Information on Oundle's and Bedford's war records can be found in: *Sanderson of Oundle* (London, 1923), pp. 70–71; and J. Sargeaunt, *A History of Bedford School* (London, 1925), ed. E. Hockliffe, pp. 221ff.

36. J. Bernal, letter to the author, September 1968.

37. J. Bernal, 'Verantwortung und Verbflichtung der Wissenschaft', in E. Kern (ed.), *Wegweisser in der Zeitwende: Selbstzeugnisse bedeutender Menschen lesansgeleben* (Munich/Basel, 1955); hereafter referred to as 'Autobiography'.

38. F. W. Sanderson, as quoted in *Sanderson of Oundle*, p. 114.

39. J. Bernal, 'Autobiography'.

40. J. Needham, as quoted in G. Werskey, 'Understanding Needham', in Needham's *Moulds of Understanding: A Pattern of Natural Philosophy* (London, 1975), p. 15.

41. J. Needham, interview with the author, 21 May 1968.

42. I am grateful to Dr Needham for showing me this schoolboy memento.

Chapter Three: Cambridge Men

1. J. Bernal, 'Autobiography'; see above, Chapter Two, ref. 37.
2. This essay first appeared in Needham's *History is on Our Side* (London, 1946), pp. 62–94, and has since been reprinted in J. Needham, *Moulds of Understanding* (London, 1976), ed. G. Werskey, pp. 31–53.
3. J. Needham, *Chemical Embryology*, 3 vols (Cambridge, 1931).
4. 'Henry Holorenshaw', pseud., 'The Making of An Honorary Taoist', in M. Teich and R. Young (eds.), *Changing Perspectives in the History of Science* (London, 1973), p. 7.
5. See J. Needham, *The Sceptical Biologist* (London, 1929); his *The Great Amphibium* (London, 1931); and *Moulds of Understanding*, pp. 57–128, where three of the essays from these early books are reprinted.
6. J. Bernal, 'Autobiography'.
7. J. Bernal, 'My Time at the Royal Institution, 1932–1927', in P. Ewald (ed.), *Fifty Years of X-ray Diffraction* (Utrecht, 1962), p. 525.
8. C. P. Snow, 'J. D. Bernal, a Personal Portrait', in M. Goldsmith and A. MacKay (eds.), *Society and Science* (New York, 1964), pp. 22–3.
9. M. Perutz, *Acta Crystallographica*, vol. 26 (1970), p. 184.
10. C. P. Snow, 'J. D. Bernal', p. 24.
11. Confirmed by Lord Snow in an interview with the author, 20 May 1968.
12. As quoted in J. Needham, 'Desmond Bernal: A Personal Recollection', *Cambridge Review*, vol. 93 19 November 1971), p. 34.
13. I. Montagu, *The Youngest Son* (London, 1970), p. 234.
14. J. B. S. Haldane, *Daedalus, or Science and the Future* (London, 1923), p. 69.
15. See J. B. S. Haldane, *Possible Worlds, and Other Essays* (London, 1927), pp. 107–19.
16. See J. Bernal, *The Origin of Life* (London, 1967), which includes Haldane's original essay on pp. 242–9.
17. J. B. S. Haldane, *Possible Worlds*, p. 298.
18. J. B. S. Haldane, *The Inequality of Man and Other Essays* (London, 1932; Harmondsworth, 1938), p. 39.
19. I. Berlin in J. Huxley (ed.), *Aldous Huxley, 1894–1963: A Memorial Volume* (London, 1965), p. 144.
20. B. Russell, *Icarus or the Future of Science* (London, 1924); and R. Graves, *Another Future of Poetry* (London, 1926).
21. As quoted in R. Clark, *J.B.S.: The Life and Times of J. B. S. Haldane* (London, 1968), p. 86.
22. J. Bernal, 'Autobiography', p. 8.
23. J. B. S. Haldane, *The Inequality of Man*, pp. 144–5.
24. J. Needham, *The Great Amphibium*, p. 18.
25. J. B. S. Haldane, *The Inequality of Man*, p. 33.
26. J. Needham, *The Sceptical Biologist*, p. 251.
27. J. B. S. Haldane, *The Causes of Evolution* (London, 1932), p. 170.
28. J. Bernal, *The Freedom of Necessity* (London, 1949), p. 101.
29. J. B. S. Haldane, *The Inequality of Man*, p. 139.
30. J. B. S. Haldane, *Daedalus*, p. 87.

31. ibid., p. 89.
32. ibid., pp. 92–3.
33. R. Fraser, *The Flying Draper* (London, 1924), p. 207.
34. J. B. S. Haldane, *Daedalus*, p. 79.
35. J. Bernal, *The World, the Flesh and the Devil: An Inquiry into the Future of the Three Enemies of the Rational Soul* (London, 1929), pp. 81–2.
36. ibid., p. 90.
37. ibid., pp. 92–3.
38. ibid., p. 57.
39. J. Needham, *The Great Amphibium*, p. 16.
40. ibid., p. 18.
41. M. Dobb, interview with the author, 6 April 1972.
42. C. P. Snow, 'Rutherford and the Cavendish', in J. Raymond (ed.), *The Baldwin Age* (London, 1960), p. 247.
43. J. Bernal, letter to the author, September 1968.
44. J. B. S. Haldane, *Possible Words*, p. 192.
45. ibid., p. 197.
46. J. B. S. Haldane, *Science and Ethics*, (London, 1928).
47. J. B. S. Haldane, *The Inequality of Man*, p. 39.
48. ibid., p. 123.
49. ibid., p. 20.
50. J. B. S. Haldane, *Callinicus, a Defence of Chemical Warfare*, 2nd ed. (London, 1925), p. 4.
51. ibid., p. 46.
52. ibid., p. 38.
53. ibid., pp. 80–81.
54. ibid., p. 82.
55. ibid., pp. 18–19.
56. J. B. S. Haldane, *Possible Worlds*, p. 200.
57. J. B. S. Haldane, *The Inequality of Man*, p. 91.
58. J. B. S. Haldane, *Possible Worlds*, p. 203.
59. ibid., p. 206.
60. ibid., p. 91.
61. ibid., p. 206.
62. J. B. S. Haldane, *The Inequality of Man*, p. 205.
63. ibid., p. 211.
64. J. B. S. Haldane, *Daedalus*, pp. 6–7.
65. J. B. S. Haldane, *The Inequality of Man*, p. 125.
66. R. Clark, *J.B.S.: The Life and Times of J. B. S. Haldane*, p. 86.
67. J. B. S. Haldane, *Daedalus*, p. 6.
68. J. Bernal, *The World, the Flesh and the Devil*, pp. 70–71.
69. J. B. S. Haldane, *Daedalus*, p. 25.
70. J. Needham, *The Great Amphibium*, pp. 31–32.

Chapter Four: The Outsiders

1. H. Levy, letter to the author, 17 June 1974.
2. L. Hogben, *Author in Transit* (New York, 1940), p. 70.
3. L. Hogben, interview with the author, 26 July 1968.
4. See L. Hogben, 'The Origins of the Society', in the pamphlet *The Origins and History of the Society for Experimental Biology*, eds. M. Sleigh and J. Sutcliffe (London, 1966), esp. pp. 7–8.
5. See I. Montagu, *The Youngest Son* (London, 1970), p. 140.
6. L. Hogben, letter to the author, 21 January 1974.
7. L. Hogben, 'Modern Heredity and Social Science', *Socialist Review*, vol. 16 (1918), pp. 147–56.
8. L. Hogben, *Dangerous Thoughts* (London, 1939), pp. 47–8.
9. J. Kerr, 'Biology and the Race', *Nature*, vol. 120 (10 September 1927), p. 354.
10. L. Hogben, interview of 26 July 1968.
11. L. Hogben, *The Nature of Living Matter* (London, 1930), p. 213.
12. ibid., p. 210.
13. L. Hogben, *Nature and Nurture* (London, 1933), p. 14.
14. N. Pastore, *The Nature–Nurture Controversy* (New York, 1949), p. 163.
15. L. Hogben, *Dangerous Thoughts*, p. 47.
16. L. Hogben, *The Nature of Living Matter*, pp. 207–8.
17. L. Hogben, *Genetic Principles in Medicine and Social Science* (London, 1931), p. 210.
18. L. Hogben, *The Nature of Living Matter*, p. 214.
19. L. Hogben, *Genetic Principles*, p. 219.
20. L. Hogben, 'The Foundations of Social Biology', *Economica*, vol. 11 (February 1931), p. 10.
21. L. Hogben, *The Nature of Living Matter*, p. 243.
22. ibid., pp. 243–4.
23. ibid., p. 266.
24. L. Hogben, *Genetic Principles*, p. 201.
25. L. Hogben, *The Nature of Living Matter*, pp. 315–16.
26. ibid., p. 243.
27. ibid., p. 266.
28. J. Huxley, 'Mr Julian Huxley Replies', *Scientific Worker*, vol. 4 (November 1923), p. 17.
29. W. McDougall, *World Chaos: The Responsibility of Science* (London, 1932), pp. 17–18.
30. L. Hogben, *The Nature of Living Matter*, p. 26.
31. J. Needham in *Science, Religion and Reality* (London, 1925), ed. J. Needham, p. 250.
32. J. Needham, *The Sceptical Biologist* (London, 1929), p. 65.
33. J. Needham, *The Great Amphibium* (London, 1931), p. 57.
34. R. Glazebrook, 'Science and Service', in T. Humberstone (ed.), *Science and Labour* (London, 1924), p. 22.
35. H. Levy, interview with the author, 10 May 1968.

36. H. Levy, letter to the author, 10 June 1974.
37. H. Levy, interview of 10 May 1968.
38. E. Bernal, letter to J. Needham, 8 October 1943.
39. H. Levy, 'Scientific Workers and the Control of Their Working Conditions', *Scientific Worker*, vol. 2 (April 1921), p. 47.
40. H. Levy, 'Environment and Efficiency in Scientific Work', *Scientific Worker*, vol. 3 (March 1922), p. 5.
41. H. Levy, 'Science and Labour', *Nature*, vol. 114 (13 December 1924), p. 850.
42. ibid.
43. H. Levy, interview of 10 May 1968.
44. 'The Association of Scientific Workers', *Scientific Worker* (October 1928), p. 116.
45. H. Levy, interview with the author, 13 March 1972.
46. H. Levy, *Modern Science* (London, 1939), p. 96.
47. W. W. Craik, *The Central Labour College, 1909–1929: A Chapter in the History of Adult Working-class Education* (London, 1964), pp. 169–71.
48. H. Levy, interview of 10 May 1968.
49. H. Levy, letter of 10 June 1974.
50. H. Levy, *Social Thinking* (London, 1945), pp. 9–10.
51. H. Levy, interview of 10 May 1968.
52. "X-ray", 'The Great Poison-gas Plot', *The Communist*, vol. 1, nos. 3–5 (April–June 1927), pp. 113–20, 173–80 and 225–32; see also "X-Ray", 'The Unmasking of the D.S.I.R.', vol. 3, nos. 5–6 (May–June 1928), pp. 281–6 and 339–45.
53. See C. Haldane, *Truth Will Out* (London, 1949), p. 49ff.
54. J. Needham, *Time: The Refreshing River* (London, 1943), pp. 12–13.
55. T. L. Humberstone, 'Science and the Public', *Nature*, vol. 122 (1 December 1928), p. 834.
56. J. B. S. Haldane, *The Inequality of Man and Other Essays* (Harmondsworth, 1938), p. 136.
57. J. Bernal, *The World, the Flesh and the Devil* (London, 1929) pp. 93–4.
58. J. Needham, *History is on Our Side* (London, 1946), p. 74; also p. 95.

Chapter Five: Increased Visibility

1. J. Needham, *Time: The Refreshing River* (London, 1943), p. 11.
2. J. Strachey, *The Coming Struggle for Power* (London, 1932).
3. J. Jupp, 'The Left in Britain, 1931 to 1941', unpublished M.Sc. (Econ.) thesis (University of London, 1956), p. 555.
4. [J. Crowther], 'A Congress of Scientists', *Manchester Guardian,* 30 June 1931, p. 8.
5. S. and B. Webb, *Soviet Communism: A New Civilization* (London, 1937), pp. 555–6.
6. J. Crowther, *Fifty Years with Science* (London, 1970), p. 77.
7. *The Times*, 1 July 1931, p. 16.
8. J. Needham, interview with the author, 21 May 1968.

9. B. Zavadovsky, in N. Bukharin *et al.*, *Science at the Cross Roads*, 2nd ed. (London, 1971), p. 70.
10. ibid., p. 80.
11. ibid., p. 171.
12. ibid., p. 210.
13. ibid., p. 212.
14. ibid., p. 24.
15. ibid., p. 31.
16. ibid., p. 43.
17. See H. Levy, 'The Mathematician in the Struggle', in C. Haden Guest (ed.), *David Guest: A Scientist Fights for Freedom* (London, 1939), pp. 152–3.
18. [J. Crowther], 'The Soviet Embassy Reception', *Manchester Guardian*, 7 July 1931, p. 8.
19. D. Singer, letter to J. Needham, 10 August 1943.
20. J. Bernal, 'Science and Society', *The Spectator*, 11 July 1931, reprinted in J. Bernal, *The Freedom of Necessity* (London, 1949), p. 338.
21. T. Greenwood, 'The Third [sic] International Congress of the History of Science and Technology', *Nature*, vol. 128 (11 July 1931), p. 78.
22. F. Marvin, 'Soviet Science', *Nature*, vol. 128 (1 August 1931), pp. 170–71.
23. 'Science', *Times Literary Supplement*, 10 September 1931, p. 687.
24. J. Bernal, *The Freedom of Necessity*, p. 335.
25. J. Needham, *Time*, p. 244.
26. L. Hogben, interview with the author, 26 July 1968; also Hogben's 'Contemporary Philosophy in Soviet Russia', *Psyche*, vol. 12 (October 1931), pp. 13–16.
27. H. Levy, *Science in Perspective: An Essay Introductory to Twenty-four Talks* (London, 1931), p. 47.
28. J. Needham, *A History of Embryology* (Cambridge, 1934), p. xvi.
29. J. Bernal, *The Social Function of Science* (London, 1939), p. 406.
30. H. Levy, *Modern Science* (London, 1939), p. 97.
31. J. Bernal, *The Freedom of Necessity*, p. 339.
32. J. Bernal, 'Autobiography'; see above, Chapter Two, ref. 37.
33. N. Pirie, interview with the author, 10 April 1969.
34. J. Crowther, *Fifty Years with Science*, p. 87.
35. J. Crowther, letter to the author, 25 July 1968.
36. M. Dobb, 'Labour Research', *Labour Monthly*, vol. 7 (December 1925), pp. 749–54.
37. [J. Bernal], ' "X-ray", The Unmasking of the D.I.S.R.', *The Communist*, vol. 3 (1928), pp. 281–6 and 339–45.
38. C.P.G.B., *Report of the Central Committee: 1st Party Congress* (London, 1938), p. 43; as cited in S. Samuel, 'English Intellectuals and Politics in the 1930s', in P. Rieff (ed.), *On Intellectuals: Theoretical Studies, Case Studies* (Garden City, 1969), p. 239.
39. J. Crowther, *The Social Relations of Science* (New York, 1941), p. 648.
40. J. Crowther, 'The Social Responsibility of Scientists', *The Scientific Worker*, vol. 9 (October 1936), p. 82.

41. ibid.
42. ibid., p. 89.
43. ibid., p. 82.
44. L. Hogben, *Science for the Citizen* (London, 1938), p. 10.
45. A. Hill, 'The International Status and Obligations of Science', *Nature*, vol. 132 (23 December 1933), p. 952.
46. A. Hill, 'The International Status and Obligations of Science', as reprinted in A. Hill, *The Ethical Dilemma of Science* (New York, 1960), p. 221.
47. L. Hogben, *Science in Authority* (London, 1963), p. 117.
48. J. Bernal, *The Social Function of Science*, p. xv.
49. J. Bernal, 'Autobiography'.
50. C. P. Snow, *Variety of Men* (Harmondsworth, 1970), p. 147.
51. R. Clark, *J.B.S.: The Life and Times of J. B. S. Haldane* (London, 1968), p. 95.
52. J. Needham and D. Needham, 'A Crystallographic "Arrowsmith"', *Nature*, vol. 134 (8 December 1934), p. 890.
53. N. Pirie, 'John Burdon Sanderson Haldane, 1892–1964', *Biographical Memoirs of Fellows of the Royal Society*, vol. 12 (November 1966), p. 221.
54. R. Clark, *J.B.S.*, pp. 115–19.
55. J. B. S. Haldane, as quoted in N. Wood, *Communism and British Intellectuals* (New York, 1959), p. 54.
56. R. Clark, *J.B.S.*, p. 121.
57. J. B. S. Haldane, *The Marxist Philosophy and the Sciences* (London, 1938).
58. J. B. S. Haldane, *Keeping Cool, and Other Essays* (London, 1940), p. 207.
59. S. Spender, *Forward from Liberalism* (London, 1937).
60. P. Berger, *Invitation to Sociology* (Harmondsworth, 1966), pp. 77–8.
61. G. Werskey, 'Haldane and Huxley: The First Appraisals', *Journal of the History of Biology*, vol. 4 (April 1971), pp. 171–83.
62. N. Mitchison, interview with the author, 19 May 1972.
63. J. B. S. Haldane, *Keeping Cool*, p. 277.
64. H. Levy, letter to the author, 10 June 1974.
65. L. Hogben, interview of 26 July 1968.
66. L. Hogben, *Lancelot Hogben's Dangerous Thoughts* (London, 1939), p. 65.
67. L. Hogben, 'Contemporary Philosophy', p. 13.
68. L. Hogben, *Author in Transit* (New York, 1940), pp. 156–7.
69. L. Hogben, interview of 26 July 1968.
70. J. Bernal, letter to the author, September 1968.
71. [J. Bernal], 'Science and Education', in *Britain without Capitalists* (London, 1936), pp. 407–68; authorship confirmed in Bernal letter.
72. C. P. Snow, in an interview with the author, 20 May 1968.
73. N. Pirie, interview of 10 April 1969.
74. B. Pimlott, 'The Socialist League: Intellectuals and the Labour Left in the 1930s', *Journal of Contemporary History*, vol. 6 (1971), pp. 12–38.
75. J. Lewis et al., *Christianity and the Social Revolution* (London, 1935), esp. pp. 416–41.
76. J. Needham, 'The Common Ground', *Spectator*, 30 October 1936, pp. 740–41.

77. J. Needham, interview with the author, 20 August 1968.
78. J. Needham, 'Cultivation of the Unfit', *Nature*, vol. 137 (1 February 1936), p. 188.
79. L. Hogben, letter to J. Needham, 10 February 1936.
80. J. Needham, interview with the author, 21 May 1968.
81. M. Adams (ed.), *Science in a Changing World* (London, 1933).
82. H. Levy, *The Web of Thought and Action* (London, 1934), p. v.
83. H. Levy, interview with the author, 10 April 1968.
84. Frontispiece to H. Levy, *The Web of Thought and Action*.
85. H. Levy, interview of 10 April 1968.
86. J. Lewis, *The Left Book Club: A Historical Record* (London, 1970), p. 51.
87. L. Hogben, *Mathematics for the Million* (London, 1936), p. 9.
88. G. Hardy, *A Mathematician's Apology* (Cambridge, 1940), pp. 25–6ff.
89. L. Hogben, *Dangerous Thoughts*, pp. 155–6.
90. See S. Raybould, *The W.E.A. – The Next Phase* (London, 1949), *passim*.
91. J. B. S. Haldane, *A Banned Broadcast, and Other Essays* (London, 1946), p. 5.
92. P. Phillips, *Prof. J. B. S. Haldane, F.R.S.* (London, n.d. [c. 1943]), p. 7.

Chapter Six: Theory

1. J. Bernal, *The Social Function of Science*, (Cambridge, Mass., 1967 ed.), p. 415.
2. ibid., p. xvii (my emphasis).
3. J. Strachey, *The Menace of Fascism* (London, 1933), pp. 11–18.
4. S. Webb and B. Webb, *Soviet Communism: A New Civilization*, 2nd ed. (London, 1937), pp. 1132–3.
5. M. Lang, 'The Growth of the Student Movement', in C. Haden Guest (ed.), *David Guest: A Scientist Fights for Freedom* (London, 1939), p. 93.
6. D. Caute, *The Fellow-travellers* (London, 1973), *passim*.
7. D. Brower, *The New Jacobins: The French Communist Party and the Popular Front* (Ithaca, 1968); and A. Richmond, *A Long View from the Left: Memoirs of an American Revolutionary* (Boston, 1973).
8. P. Gay, *The Enlightenment: An Interpretation*, 2 vols. (New York, 1966, 1969), and G. Daniels, *Science in American Society: A Social History* (New York, 1971).
9. R. Williams, *Culture and Society, 1780–1950* (New York, 1966).
10. G. Lukács, *Political Writings, 1919–1929* (London, 1972), esp, pp. 134–42; and A. Gramsci, *The Modern Prince, and Other Writings* (New York, 1957), esp. pp. 90–117.
11. K. Marx, *Early Writings* (London, 1963), trans. T. Bottomore.
12. R. Groves, *The Balham Group: The Origins of British Trotskyism* (London, 1974).
13. W. Kendall, *The Revolutionary Movement in Britain, 1900–1921* (London, 1969).
14. J. Stalin, *Leninism*, vol. 2 (London, 1938), p. 425 (my italics).
15. M. Dobb, *Russia Today and Tomorrow* (London, 1930), p. 43.

16. L. Graham, *Science and Philosophy in the Soviet Union* (New York, 1972), p. 430.
17. H. Levy, 'A Scientific Worker Looks at Dialectical Materialism', in *Aspects of Dialectical Materialism* (London, 1934), p. 21.
18. C. Dutt, 'Dialectical Materialism and Natural Science', *Labour Monthly*, vol. 15 (February 1933), p. 93.
19. J. B. S. Haldane, *The Marxist Philosophy and the Sciences* (London, 1938).
20. J. Needham, *Time: The Refreshing River* (London, 1943), esp. pp. 233-77.
21. H. Levy, *Modern Science* (London, 1939).
22. H. Levy, *A Philosophy for a Modern Man* (London, 1938).
23. J. Bernal, in *Aspects of Dialectical Materialism*, p. 89.
24. L. Hogben, *Lancelot Hogben's Dangerous Thoughts* (London, 1939), pp. 269-70.
25. C. Dutt, 'The Hesitant Materialist', *Labour Monthly*, vol. 14 (October 1932), p. 651.
26. J. Bernal, *The Physical Basis of Life* (London, 1951); and J. Needham, *Order and Life* (New Haven, 1935).
27. J. Bernal, in *Aspects of Dialectical Materialism*, p. 89 (my italics).
28. J. Needham, Introduction to M. Prenant, *Biology and Marxism* (London, 1938), p. vii.
29. J. Bernal, *Science and History* (London, 1954), pp. 5-6.
30. J. Bernal, *The Social Function of Science*, pp. 6 and 94.
31. J. Bernal, *The Freedom of Necessity* (London, 1949), pp. 340-41.
32. ibid., pp. 77 and 417; and J. Bernal, *The Social Function of Science*, pp. 4-5.
33. J. Bernal, *Science in History*, pp. 25-26.
34. J. Bernal, *The Social Function of Science*, p. 410.
35. ibid., pp. 382-3.
36. ibid., p. 91.
37. ibid., pp. 321-2.
38. ibid., p. 323.
39. ibid., p. 416.
40. J. Bernal, *The Freedom of Necessity*, p. 58.
41. ibid., p. 9.
42. J. Bernal, 'Science and Industry', in A. Hall *et al.*, *The Frustration of Science* (London, 1935), p. 69.
43. J. Bernal, *The Social Function of Science*, p. xiii.
44. ibid., pp. 63-4. Cf. J. Huxley, *Scientific Research and Social Needs* (London, 1934), pp. 255-6.
45. S. Zuckerman, *Scientists and War* (New York, 1966), p. 145.
46. J. Bernal, *The Social Function of Science*, p. 57.
47. [J. Bernal], 'Science and Education', in *Britain without Capitalists* (London, 1936), esp. pp. 427-31.
48. J. Bernal, *The Social Function of Science*, pp. 60-83.
49. ibid., pp. 38-44; and J. Bernal, 'D.S.I.R. Annual Reports, 1933-34 and 1934-35', *Scientific Worker*, vol. 9 (March 1936), pp. 37-42.
50. J. Bernal, *The Social Function of Science*, p. 391.
51. J. Bernal, 'Science and Industry', p. 54.

52. J. Bernal, *The Social Function of Science*, p. xv, and *The Freedom of Necessity*, p. ix.
53. J. Bernal, *The Social Function of Science*, pp. 210–21.
54. ibid., p. xiv.
55. ibid., p. 62; and J. Bernal, 'Science and Industry', p. 44.
56. J. Bernal, *The Social Function of Science*, p. 173.
57. J. Bernal, 'Science and National Service', *Nature*, vol. 142 (15 October 1938), p. 685.
58. J. Bernal, *The Social Function of Science*, p. 186.
59. ibid., p. 222.
60. M. Ruhemann, 'Note on Science in the U.S.S.R.', Appendix VII, in J. Bernal, *The Social Function of Science*, pp. 443–9.
61. J. Crowther, *Soviet Science* (London, 1936), esp. pp. 94–111.
62. M. Ruhemann, 'Industrial Research and Development in the Soviet Union', in J. Needham and J. Sykes-Davies (eds.), *Science in Soviet Russia* (London, 1942), p. 18 (my italics).
63. M. Ruhemann, 'Note on Science in the U.S.S.R.', p. 447.
64. J. Bernal, *The Social Function of Science*, p. 224.
65. ibid.
66. ibid., p. 158.
67. J. Bernal, *The Freedom of Necessity*, p. 414.
68. ibid., p. 411.
69. ibid., p. 386.
70. ibid., p. 414.
71. ibid., p. ix; also p. 70.
72. ibid., p. 57.
73. ibid., p. 9.
74. ibid., p. 62.
75. ibid., p. 20.
76. ibid., p. 77.
77. ibid., p. 425.
78. ibid., p. 120.
79. ibid., p. 128.
80. J. Bernal, *The Social Function of Science*, p. 310ff.
81. ibid., p. 261ff.
82. ibid., p. 352.
83. J. Bernal, *The Freedom of Necessity*, pp. viii, 1, 258, 310 and 427.
84. J. Bernal, *The Social Function of Science*, pp. 89, 246 and 411–12.
85. ibid., p. 409.
86. ibid., p. 382.
87. J. Bernal, *The Freedom of Necessity*, pp. 58–9.
88. L. Hogben, *Science for the Citizen* (London, 1938), p. 624.
89. L. Hogben, *The Retreat from Reason* (New York, 1937), p. 42.
90. L. Hogben, 'Planning for Human Survival', in G. Cole *et al.*, *What is Ahead of Us?* (London, 1937), p. 182.
91. E. Charles, *The Twilight of Parenthood* (London, 1934).
92. L. Hogben, 'Planning for Human Survival', p. 183.

93. L. Hogben, *The Retreat from Reason*, pp. 45 and 70–72.
94. L. Hogben, *Dangerous Thoughts*, p. 14.
95. ibid., p. 202.
96. L. Hogben, *Author in Transit* (New York, 1940), pp. 156–7.
97. ibid., p. 158.
98. ibid.
99. L. Hogben, 'Planning for Human Survival', pp. 186–7.
100. L. Hogben, *Dangerous Thoughts*, p. 15.
101. L. Hogben, *Author in Transit*, p. 272.
102. L. Hogben, *The Retreat from Reason*, p. 38.
103. L. Hogben, *Dangerous Thoughts*, pp. 207–8.
104. L. Hogben, *The Retreat from Reason*, pp. 41 and 66–7.
105. L. Hogben, *Dangerous Thoughts*, p. 16.
106. L. Hogben, *The Retreat from Reason*, p. 43; and *Author in Transit*, pp. 158–9.
107. L. Hogben, *Science for the Citizen*, p. 1086.
108. L. Hogben, *Author in Transit*, p. 272.
109. L. Hogben, *Science for the Citizen*, p. 1088.
110. J. Needham, *Time*, p. 70.
111. ibid., pp. 65–6.
112. ibid., pp. 58–9.
113. ibid., p. 120.
114. J. Needham, 'Desmond Bernal: A Personal Recollection', *Cambridge Review*, vol. 93 (19 December 1971), pp. 33–6.
115. J. Needham, 'Science, Religion and Socialism', in J. Lewis *et al.*, *Christianity and the Social Revolution* (London, 1935), p. 428.
116. J. Needham, *Time*, p. 41.
117. J. Needham, interview with the author, 21 May 1968.
118. E. Ashby, *et al.*, 'Genetics in the Universities', *Nature*, vol. 138 (5 December 1936), pp. 972–3.
119. J. B. S. Haldane, *Keeping Cool, and Other Essays* (London, 1940), p. 107; and L. Hogben, *Science for the Citizen*, p. 891.
120. P. Hudson, 'Vernalization in Agricultural Practice', *Journal of the Ministry of Agriculture*, vol. 43 (September 1936), pp. 536–43; J. B. S. Haldane, 'Lysenko and Genetics', *Science and Society*, vol. 4 (1940), pp. 433–7; and C. H. Waddington, unpublished talk on Lysenkoism delivered to the Theoretical Biology Club sometime in 1938.
121. B. Uvarov, 'Genetics and Plant Breeding in the U.S.S.R.', *Nature*, vol. 140 (21 August 1937), p. 297.
122. C. H. Waddington. 'Twenty-five Years of Biology', *Discovery*, (May 1935), p. 135.
123. J. Needham, 'Organizer Phenomena after Four Decades: A Retrospect and Prospect', in K. Dronamraju (ed.), *Haldane and Modern Biology* (Baltimore, 1968), pp. 285–99.
124. C. H. Waddington, 'That's Life', *New York Review of Books*, vol. 10 (29 February 1968), pp. 19–22.
125. J. Bernal, *The Social Function of Science*, p. 237, ref. 26.

126. [J. B. S. Haldane], 'Genetics in the U.S.S.R.', *University Forward*, no. 6 (1941), p. 19.
127. Helix and Helianthus, 'Genetics in the U.S.S.R.', *Modern Quarterly*, vol. 2 (1939), p. 373.
128. J. Needham, in *Biology and Marxism*, p. x.
129. J. Needham, in *Science in Soviet Russia*, p. 27.
130. J. Needham, in *Biology and Marxism*, pp. x–xi.
131. J. B. S. Haldane, 'Genetics in the U.S.S.R.', p. 21.
132. N. Grant, *Soviet Education* (Harmondsworth, 1964), p. 46.
133. J. B. S. Haldane, *Science and Everyday Life* (London, 1939), p. 243.
134. J. B. S. Haldane, *Heredity and Politics* (London, 1938), p. 126.
135. J. B. S. Haldane, *Keeping Cool*, p. 176.
136. ibid., p. 165.

Chapter Seven: Practice

1. R. Calder, *The Birth of the Future* (London, 1934), p. 276.
2. N. Wood, *Communism and British Intellectuals* (London, 1959), p. 121 (my emphasis).
3. N. Branson and M. Heinemann, *Britain in the Nineteen Thirties* (London, 1971), p. 259.
4. J. Bernal, 'The Scientist and the World Today', *Cambridge Left*, vol. 1 (winter 1933), pp. 36–45; as reprinted in J. Bernal, *The Freedom of Necessity* (London, 1949), pp. 340–41.
5. J. Bernal, *The Social Function of Science* (London, 1939), p. 10.
6. [J. Bernal], 'Science and Education', in *Britain without Capitalists* (London, 1936), pp. 412–18.
7. See the University Grants Committee's *Returns from the Universities* from 1920 to 1939.
8. This estimate is based on information from the *Cambridge University Reporter* for: 6 November 1933, pp. 245–52; 16 February 1934, pp. 621–6; 16 April 1934, pp. 822–8; 22 May 1934, pp. 1021–32; and 21 May 1935, pp. 983–95. See also the *Yearbook of the Universities of the Empire 1935* (London, 1935), pp. 39–68.
9. C. P. Snow, 'Rutherford and the Cavendish', in J. Raymond (ed.), *The Baldwin Age* (London, 1960), p. 235.
10. ibid.
11. ibid., p. 243.
12. S. Samuels, 'English Intellectuals and Politics in the 1930s', in P. Rieff (ed.), *On Intellectuals; Theoretical Studies, Case Studies* (Garden City, 1969), pp. 196–247; and P. Stansky and W. Abrahams, *Journey to the Frontier* (London, 1966), esp. pp. 106–8, and 209–13.
13. R. Pascal, interview with the author, 17 April 1972.
14. M. Dobb, interview with the author, 6 April 1972.
15. R. Nahum, in 'Socialist Students in My Time', *University Forward*, vol. 6 (1941), p. 30.
16. J. Needham, interview with the author, 20 August 1968.

17. E. Burshop, interview with the author, 12 April 1972.
18. R. Nahum, 'Socialist Students in My Time', p. 31.
19. *Left News*, no. 8 (December 1936), p. 169.
20. C. H. Waddington, interview with the author, 16 March 1972.
21. E. Burhop, interview of 12 April 1972. Cf. C. P. Snow, 'Rutherford and the Cavendish', p. 247.
22. N. Pirie, interview with the author, 17 April 1972.
23. Cambridge Scientists' Anti-war Group, *The Protection of the Public from Aerial Attack* (London, 1937), p. 9; and W. Wooster, interview with the author, 6 April 1972. Cf. E. Burhop, 'Scientists and Public Affairs', in M. Goldsmith and A. Mackay (eds.), *Society and Science* (New York, 1964), p. 34.
24. W. Wooster, interview of 6 April 1972.
25. E. Burhop, 'Scientists and Public Affairs', p. 34.
26. Unpublished cyclostyled text of C.S.A.W.G.'s discussions during May Term, 1936.
27. 'Judgement against Chief Constable', *Cambridge Daily News*, 20 December 1935, p. 5.
28. C. Bamford *et al.*, 'Scientific Workers and War', *Nature*, vol. 137 (16 May 1936), pp. 829–30.
29. A. Taylor, 'Confusion on the Left', in J. Raymond, *The Baldwin Age*, pp. 66–79.
30. Cambridge Socialist League and Cambridge Scientists' Anti-war Group, 'Why Are They Fighting in Spain?' (Cambridge, n.d.).
31. E. Hodsoll to W. Francis, 16 September 1936: Public Records Office Folio H.O. 45/17598/701010/12.
32. C. Foulkes, *'Gas!' The Story of the Special Brigade* (Edinburgh and London, 1934).
33. J. Pratt, *Gas Defence* (London, 1935).
34. J. Kendall, *Breathe Freely! The Truth about Poison Gas* (London, 1938), p. 89.
35. ibid., p. 116.
36. ibid., p. 76.
37. ibid., esp. p. xi.
38. Union for Democratic Control, *Poison Gas* (London, 1935), p. 59.
39. Socialist Medical Association, *Gas Attacks – Is There Any Protection?* (London, 1936), p. 27.
40. B. Russell, *Which Way to Peace?* (London, 1936).
41. A. Huxley, *The Encyclopaedia of Pacifism*, as quoted in G. Fay, 'Unrest', in J. Raymond, *The Baldwin Age*, pp. 135–6.
42. Ten Cambridge Scientists, 'Air Raid Protection: The Facts', *Fact*, no. 13 (April 1938), p. 20.
43. N. Wooster, interview with the author, 6 April 1972.
44. J. Fremlin, interview with the author, 17 April 1972.
45. Cambridge Scientists' Anti-war Group, *The Protection of the Public from Aerial Attack* (London, 1937), pp. 70–71.
46. T. O'Brien, *Civil Defence* (London, 1955), p. 81.

47. J. Kendall, *Breathe Freely!*, p. 115.
48. B. Holman, 'Anti-gas Research', *Scientific Worker*, vol. 10 (April 1937), pp. 150–52.
49. J. B. S. Haldane, *A.R.P.* (London, 1938), pp. 89–98.
50. C. Foulkes, 'Air Raid Precautions', *Nature*, vol. 139 (10 April 1937), p. 608.
51. ibid., p. 607.
52. J. D. Bernal *et al.*, 'Air Raid Precautions', *Nature*, vol. 139 (1 May 1937), p. 760.
53. Ten Cambridge Scientists', 'Air Raid Protection', p. 88.
54. W. Wooster interview.
55. Haldane, *A.R.P.*, p. 139.
56. ibid., pp. 9–10.
57. S. Hoare to J. Simon, 26 October 1938: H.O. 45/700281/240.
58. T. O'Brien, *Civil Defence*, p. 170.
59. 'Professor J. D. Bernal: An Outstanding Physicist', *The Times* (16 September 1971), p. 16.
60. Danielli, 'Haldane on A.R.P.', *Scientific Worker*, vol. 12 (February 1932), p. 12.
61. Letters received by J. Fremlin between 1937 and 1938.
62. J. Bernal, 'Science and Peace', in National Peace Council, *Peace Year Book* (London, 1937), pp. 88–91.
63. 'The A.S.W. – Twenty Years History', *Scientific Worker*, vol. 12 (autumn 1939), p. 72.
64. 'Association News', *Progress and the Scientific Worker*, vol. 8 (January–February 1935), p. 19.
65. 'The Policy of the Association of Scientific Workers', *Scientific Worker*, vol. 8 (December 1935), pp. 1–7.
66. J. Kuczynski, *British Trade Unionism: A Short Study Course for Scientific Workers* (London, 1943), p. 41.
67. R. Fremlin, interview with the author, 17 March 1972.
68. 'The A.S.W. and the Finance of Research', *Scientific Worker*, vol. 11 (November–December 1938), pp. 110–52.
69. ibid., esp. p. 148.
70. 'The A.S.W. – Twenty Years', p. 72.
71. J. Kuczynski, *British Trade Unionism*, p. 41.
72. *Left News*: no. 15 (July 1937), p. 432; no. 17 (September 1937), p. 498; and no. 22 (February 1938), p. 700.
73. J. Lewis, *The Left Book Club – A Historial Record* (London, 1970, pp. 83–4.
74. *Left News*, no. 16 (August 1937), pp. 477–8.
75. D. Henry, 'Manchester Scientists' Peace Association', *Nature*, vol. 140 (December 1937), p. 1055.
76. W. Armytage, *Sir Richard Gregory, His Life and Work* (London, 1957), p. 152.
77. A. Marwick, 'Middle Opinion in the Thirties: Planning, Progress and Political Agreement', *English Historical Review*, vol. 79 (1964), pp. 285–98.

78. R. Brightman, 'The Civil Population and Air Attack', *Nature*, vol. 139 (6 March 1937), pp. 382–9.

79. J. Williamson, 'Research and Industry', *Nature*, vol. 140 (11 September 1937), pp. 437–8.

80. R. Brightman, 'Science in the Modern World', *Nature*, vol. 143 (18 February 1939), pp. 262–3.

81. R. Brightman, 'University Training in Relation to Industry', *Nature*, vol. 128 (19 December 1931), pp. 1017–19; F. Marvin, 'Science and Society', *Nature*, vol. 129 (5 March 1932), pp. 329–31; and B. Uvarov, 'Genetics and Plant Breeding in the U.S.S.R.', *Nature*, vol. 140 (21 August 1937), pp. 296–7.

82. R. Rudmose Brown, 'The Scientific Values of Expeditions', *Nature*, vol. 141 (26 February 1938), pp. 345–6.

83. G. Werskey, '*Nature* and Politics between the Wars', *Nature*, vol. 224 (1 November 1969), pp. 462–72.

84. J. Crowther, *Fifty Years with Science* (London, 1970).

85. J. Huxley, *A Scientist among the Soviets* (London, 1932), p. 2.

86. ibid., p. 52.

87. ibid., p. 110.

88. C. Blacker, interview with the author, 7 August 1969; and L. Hogben, interview with the author, 26 July 1968.

89. 'Notes of the Quarter', *Eugenics Review*, vol. 35 (1943–4), pp. 54–6.

90. J. Huxley, *The Uniqueness of Man* (London, 1941), p. 69.

91. F. Crew *et al.*, 'Social Biology and Population Improvement', *Nature*, vol. 144 (16 September 1939), p. 521.

92. ibid., p. 522.

93. J. Huxley, *Scientific Research and Social Needs* (London, 1934), pp. 15–16.

94. H. Levy, in ibid., p. 16.

95. ibid., p. 20.

96. ibid., p. 252.

97. ibid., p. 279.

98. J. Huxley, letter to the author, 20 August 1969.

99. F. Crew, 'Eugenics and Society', *Nature*, vol. 137 (11 April 1936), p. 593.

100. R. Brightman, 'The Planning of Research', *Nature*, vol. 134 (28 July 1934), p. 119.

101. N. Wood, *Communism and British Intellectuals*, p. 142.

102. A. Hill, interview with the author, 6 April 1972.

103. A. Beveridge, *A Defence of Free Learning* (London, 1959).

104. J. Orr, *As I Recall* (London, 1966), esp. pp. 114–20.

105. W. Armytage, *Sir Richard Gregory*, pp. 141–4; and L. Hogben, letter to the author, 21 January 1974.

106. Association of Scientific Workers, minutes of the Annual Council meeting of 26 February 1938, p. 1.

107. R. Brightman, 'Social Responsibilities of Science', *Nature*, vol. 139 (24 April 1937), p. 689.

108. H. Levy, *Modern Science* (London, 1939), p. 197.

109. G. Werskey, 'British Scientists and "Outsider" Politics, 1931–45', *Science Studies*, vol. 1 (1971), pp. 77–80.
110. A. Gale, 'Social and International Relations of Science', *Nature*, vol. 142 (27 August 1938), p. 380.
111. S. Chapman *et al.*, 'Social Relations of Science', *Nature*, vol. 141 (23 April 1938), pp. 723–42.
112. W. Wooster, 'Social Relations of Science', *Nature*, vol. 141 (14 May 1938), p. 879.
113. J. Crowther, 'A Notable British Association Meeting', *Manchester Guardian*, 25 August 1938, p. 13.
114. It was Bernal: J. Crowther, *Fifty Years with Science*, pp. 201–2; and J. Lewis, *The Left Book Club*, p. 83.
115. J. Crowther, *Fifty Years with Science*, pp. 200–201.
116. J. Bernal, as quoted in C. Madge and T. Harrison, *Britain by Mass-observation* (Harmondsworth, 1939), pp. 13–14.
117. J. Crowther, *The Social Relations of Science* (New York, 1941), p. 632.
118. H. Levy, *Modern Science*, p. 101.
119. H. Levy, 'The Social Relations of Science: A Study in Method', *Memoirs and Proceedings of the Manchester Literary and Philosophical Society*, vol. 84 (1938–9), pp. 129–52.
120. A. Sc.W., 'The Scientific Worker – An Enquiry into Scientific Research', cyclostyled memorandum distributed to the British Association's Divisional Committee in 1939.
121. C. P. Snow, *Science and Government* (New York, 1962).
122. J. Bernal, 'Scientists and National Service', *Nature*, vol. 142, (15 October 1938), p. 685.
123. C. H. Waddington, interview of 16 March 1972.
124. A. Hutt, 'Science and Society', *Labour Monthly*, vol. 21 (June 1939), pp. 319–20.
125. B. Farrington, interview with the author, 17 April 1972.
126. ibid.
127. B. Farrington, *Head and Hand in Ancient Greece* (London, 1938); and B. Farrington, *Francis Bacon – Philosopher of Industrial Science* (London, 1951).
128. *Modern Quarterly*, vol. 1 (January 1938), p. 3.
129. C. Dutt, 'Dialectical Materialism and Natural Science', *Labour Monthly*. vol. 15 (February 1933), p. 95.
130. C. Caudwell, *Illusion and Reality* (London, 1946 ed.), p. 282.
131. ibid., pp. 285–6.
132. ibid., p. 276.
133. ibid.
134. ibid., pp. 286–7.
135. *Left News*, no. 20 (December 1937), pp. 620–21.
136. E. Ashby, interview with the author, 6 April 1972.
137. P. Phillips, *Prof. J. B. S. Haldane, F.R.S.* (London, n.d. [c. 1943]).

Chapter Eight: Two Cultures, Two Camps
 1. E. Upward, *The Rotten Elements* (Harmondsworth, 1972), p. 192.
 2. J. B. S. Haldane, *The Inequality of Man, and Other Essays* (Harmondsworth, 1938), p. 136.
 3. 'The A.S.W. and the War', n.d. [c. October, 1939].
 4. J. Huxley, 'Science in War', *Nature*, vol. 146 (22 July 1940), pp. 112–13.
 5. J. Crowther 'The War and Science', *Manchester Guardian*, 4 October 1940, p. 4.
 6. S. Zuckerman, *Scientists and War: Impact of Science on Military and Civil Affairs* (New York, 1967), pp. 147–8; and J. Crowther, *Fifty Years with Science* (London, 1970), pp. 210–22.
 7. *Science in War* (Harmondsworth, 1940), p. 1.
 8. A. Calder, *The People's War; Britain, 1939–1945* (London, 1971), pp. 280–284.
 9. H. Levy, 'France and the Communists', *New Statesman*, vol. 20, n.s. (22 July 1940), pp. 89–90.
 10. V. Gollancz, 'France and the Communists', *New Statesman*, vol. 20, n.s. (3 August 1940), p. 112.
 11. Haldane's manuscript can be found in the personal papers of C. D. Darlington.
 12. R. Clark, *J.B.S.: The Life and Work of J. B. S. Haldane* (London, 1968), pp. 162–3.
 13. 'Professor Lancelot Hogben', *The Times*, 23 August 1975, p. 14.
 14. R. Clark, *J.B.S.*, pp. 115–52.
 15. J. Needham and D. Needham (eds.), *Science Outpost: Papers of the Sino-British Science Co-operation Office, 1942–46* (London, 1948).
 16. J. Crowther, 'John Desmond Bernal – An Appreciation', *New Scientist*, vol. 51 (23 September 1971), p. 666.
 17. 'Professor J. D. Bernal', *The Times*, 16 September 1971, p. 18.
 18. P. Addison, *The Road to 1945: British Politics and the Second World War* (London, 1975); A. Calder, *The People's War*; and A. Marwick, *Britain in the Century of Total War* (Harmondsworth, 1970).
 19. N. Vig, *Science and Technology in British Politics* (London, 1968), p. 16.
 20. E. Blair, letter to J. Needham, 31 March 1942.
 21. J. Needham, *Time: The Refreshing River* (London, 1943), *History is on Our Side* (London, 1946).
 22. J. B. S. Haldane, *Keeping Cool and Other Essays* (London, 1940); Forces Edition (London, 1942).
 23. H. Levy, *Social Thinking* (London, 1945), and *Peace and the Atom* (London, 1945).
 24. J. B. S. Haldane, *Science Advances* (London, 1947).
 25. 'The Scientist's Need for a Professional Association', A.Sc.W. pamphlet (n.d., [c. 1947]), pp. 1–2.
 26. R. Dutt, in *Unity and Victory: Report of the 16th Congress of the Communist Party* (London, 1943), p. 31; as quoted in N. Wood, *Communism and British Intellectuals* (London, 1959), p. 150, n. 1.
 27. Minutes of the Divisional Committee meeting of 17 July 1941.

28. 'Science and World Order', *The Advancement of Science*, vol. 4 (January 1942), pp. 1–116.
29. J. Crowther, O. Howarth and D. Riley (eds.), *Science and World Order* (Harmondsworth, 1942).
30. J. Lawrie, 'The British Association', *Chemistry and Industry*, vol. 60 (18 October 1941), p. 753.
31. R. Clark, *The Rise of the Boffins* (London, 1962).
32. Federation of British Industry, *Industry and Research: Report of the F.B.I. Industrial Research Committee* (London, 1943).
33. Reports of the Parliamentary and Scientific Committee (1943–6).
34. Nuffield College, *Problems of Scientific and Industrial Research* (London, 1944).
35. H. and S. Rose, *Science and Society* (London, 1969), esp. pp. 67–71.
36. A. Calder, *The People's War*, pp. 541–7.
37. S. Walkland, 'Science and Parliament: The Origins and Influence of the Parliamentary and Scientific Committee', *Parliamentary Affairs*, vol. 17 (summer 1964), p. 311.
38. J. Crowther and R. Whiddington, *Science at War* (London, 1947), pp. 119–20.
39. 'Social Relations of Science – Sir W. Bragg's Tribute to the "Newer Generation"', *Manchester Guardian*, 2 December 1940, p. 8.
40. J. Bernal, 'Autobiography', see above, Chapter Two, ref. 37.
41. ibid.
42. J. Bernal, *The Freedom of Necessity* (London, 1949), p. 311.
43. ibid., pp. 311–12.
44. A. Marwick, 'Middle Opinion in the Thirties: Planning Progress and Political Agreement', *English Historical Review*, vol. 79 (1964), pp. 285–98.
45. As quoted in S. Walkland, 'Science and Parliament', p. 319.
46. H. Morrison, 'Science and Us', in *Science and Human Welfare* (London, 1946), p. 4.
47. ibid., p. 5.
48. ibid.
49. G. Thomson, 'Science and the Labour Movement', in ibid., p. 8.
50. R. Clark, *J.B.S.*, pp. 169–70.
51. J. Needham, *Science and International Relations* (Oxford, 1949), pp. 19–21.
52. J. Needham, letter to J. H. Woodger, 25 May 1946.
53. J. Needham, *Science and Civilisation in China*, 7 vols in 13 parts (Cambridge, 1954—   ).
54. 'Professor J. D. Bernal', ref. 17 above.
55. W. Wooster, 'Bernal and the W.F.S.W.', *Scientific World*, vol. 16 (1972), pp. 10–11.
56. R. Miliband, *Parliamentary Socialism*, 2nd ed. (London, 1975), pp. 272–317.
57. I. Birchall, 'The British Communist Party: 1945–64', *International Socialism*, no. 50 (January–March 1972), pp. 24–8.
58. E. P. Thompson, 'Outside the Whale', in E. Thompson (ed.), *Out of Apathy* (London, 1960), pp 141–94.

59. G. Bain, *The Growth of White-collar Unionism* (London, 1972), Table 3A1, pp. 201–2.
60. N. Vig, *Science and Technology*, p. 131.
61. J. Poole and K. Andrews (eds.), *The Government of Science in Britain* (London, 1972), pp. 159–67.
62. G. Payne, *Britain's Scientific and Technological Manpower* (Stanford, 1960), esp. Chapters 2 and 9.
63. 'The Objects of the Society for Freedom in Science', 2nd ed. (Oxford, 1946), p. 3.
64. H. Dale, letter to C. Darlington, 28 September 1948.
65. 'The Objects of the Society for Freedom in Science' (Oxford, 1944), p. 5.
66. J. Baker, 'Counter-blast to Bernalism', *New Statesman*, vol. 18 (29 July 1939), p. 174.
67. M. Polanyi, *The Contempt of Freedom: The Russian Experiment and After* (London, 1940), p. 21.
68. M. Polanyi, *The Logic of Liberty* (Chicago, 1951); and M. Polanyi, 'The Republic of Science: Its Political and Economic Theory', *Minerva*, vol. 1 (autumn 1962), pp. 54–73.
69. J. Baker, *Science and the Planned State* (London, 1945), p. 104.
70. ibid., pp. 104–5.
71. J. Baker, letter to J. Needham, 26 June 1942.
72. H. Dale, in *Bulletin of the Society for Freedom in Science*, no. 11 (March 1951), pp. 6–7.
73. E. Ashby, *Scientist in Russia* (Harmondsworth, 1947).
74. *Bulletin of the Society for Freedom in Science*, no. 3 (July 1947), p. 1.
75. S. Zuckerman, *Scientists and War: The Impact of Science on Military and Civil Affairs* (London, 1966), p. 144.
76. J. Bernal, *The Freedom of Necessity*, p. 69.
77. ibid., p. 70.
78. ibid., p. 73.
79. ibid., p. 71.
80. ibid., p. 82.
81. ibid., p. 84.
82. G. Orwell, letter to A. Koestler, 31 March 1946; in S. Orwell and I. Angus (eds.), *The Collected Essays, Journalism and Letters of George Orwell*, vol. 4 (Harmondsworth, 1970), p. 155.
83. ibid., pp. 28–9.
84. G. Orwell, *1984* (New York, 1961), esp. Part Two, Chapter 9.
85. G. Orwell, *The Road to Wigan Pier* (Harmondsworth, 1962), Chapter 12.
86. As quoted in *Polemic*, no. 3 (May 1946); reprinted in S. Orwell and I. Angus, *Collected Essays*, vol. 4, p. 185.
87. ibid., p. 187.
88. G. Wyndham-Goldie, in *The Challenge of our Time* (London, 1948), p. 12.
89. E. Forster, in ibid., p. 35.
90. M. Polanyi, in ibid., p. 41.
91. A. Koestler, in ibid., p. 18.
92. A. Lindsay, in ibid., p. 70.

93. ibid., p. 35.
94. ibid.
95. ibid., p. 18.
96. ibid., pp. 26–7.
97. ibid., p. 49.
98. J. Bernal, in *The Communist Answer to the Challenge of Our Time* (London, 1947), p. 30.
99. *The Challenge of Our Time*, p. 25.
100. ibid., p. 29.
101. ibid., p. 50.
102. H. Levy, in *The Communist Answer*, p. 75.
103. J. Baker, *Science and the Planned State*, pp. 75–6.
104. J. B. S. Haldane, *Science in Peace and War* (London, 1940), p. 83.
105. J. B. S. Haldane, *Science Advances* (London, 1947), pp. 220–26.
106. E. Ashby, letter to C. Darlington, 10 December 1947.
107. J. Huxley, 'A Scientist Goes to Russia', *New Republic*, 30 July 1945, p. 126.
108. R. J. Davies, 'Genetics in the U.S.S.R.', *Modern Quarterly*, vol. 2 (autumn, 1947), p. 348.
109. ibid., pp. 345–6.
110. J. L. Fyfe, 'The Soviet Genetics Controversy', *Modern Quarterly*, vol. 2 (autumn 1947), p. 348.
111. F. LeGros Clark, 'On Soviet Genetics', *Modern Quarterly*, vol. 3 (winter 1947–8), p. 93.
112. D. Joravsky, *The Lysenko Affair* (Cambridge, Mass., 1970), pp. 130–43.
113. J. B. S. Haldane, 'The Lysenko Controversy', *The Listener*, 9 December 1948, p. 875.
114. Society for Freedom in Science, *Papers on the Soviet Genetics Controversy*, Occasional Pamphlet no. 9 (January 1949).
115. R. Fisher, 'The Lysenko Controversy', *The Listener*, 9 December 1948, p. 875.
116. E. Ashby, *Scientist in Russia*, pp. 114–15.
117. J. Langdon-Davies, *Russia Puts Back the Clock; A Study of Soviet Science and Some British Scientists* (London, 1949), p. 137.
118. J. Huxley, *Soviet Genetics and World Science: Lysenko and the Meaning of Heredity* (London, 1949), pp. 53–4.
119. L. Hogben, *Author in Transit* (London, 1940), *passim*.
120. L. Hogben, *The New Authoritarianism* (London, 1949), pp. 5–6.
121. ibid., p. 6.
122. ibid., pp. 6–11.
123. M. Cornforth, interview with the author, 28 March 1972.
124. I. Montagu, *The Youngest Son* (London, 1970), pp. 238–9.
125. G. Almond, *The Appeals of Communism* (Princeton, 1954), pp. 314–18.
126. S. Manton, *The Soviet Union Today: A Scientist's Impression* (London, 1952), pp. 97–116; and A. Morton, *Soviet Genetics* (London, 1951).
127. J. Fyfe, *Lysenko is Right* (London, 1950), p. 62.
128. ibid., p. 53.
129. ibid., p. 31.

130. J. Bernal, 'The Biological Controversy in the Soviet Union, and Its Implications', *Modern Quarterly*, vol. 4 (summer 1949), p. 209.
131. ibid., p. 213.
132. ibid., p. 214.
133. J. Bernal, as quoted in 'Old Chrysanthemum', *New Statesman Profiles* (London, 1958), p. 50.
134. C. Haldane, *Truth Will Out* (London, 1949), p. 298.
135. J. B. S. Haldane, 'In Defence of Genetics', *Modern Quarterly*, vol. 4 (summer 1949), p. 202.
136. Lord Ashby, interview with the author, 6 April 1972.
137. Lord Ritchie-Calder, interview with the author, 19 May 1972.
138. Lord Zuckerman, interview with the author, 28 March 1972.
139. 'Old Chrysanthemum', *New Statesman Profiles*, p. 51.

Chapter Nine: Coming in from the Cold
1. J. Needham, interview with the author, 21 May 1968.
2. G. Werskey, 'The Visible College: A Study of British Left-wing Scientists, 1918–1939', unpublished Ph.D. thesis, Harvard University, 1974.
3. 'The A.Sc.W. and Politics', Supplementary Report no 1. of the Executive Committee to the Annual Council (1949) of the Association of Scientific Workers.
4. J. Bernal, 'Peace or War?', *Modern Quarterly*, vol. 5 (autumn 1950), p. 291.
5. W. Wooster, 'Bernal and the W.F.S.W.', *Scientific World*, vol. 16 (1972), p. 10.
6. E. Burhop, 'Scientists and Public Affairs', in M. Goldsmith and A. Mackay (eds.), *Society and Science* (New York, 1965), pp. 38–44.
7. J. Bernal, 'Science against War', in J. Bernal and M. Cornforth, *Science for Peace and Socialism* (London, n.d. [1949]), pp. 3–14.
8. H. Levy, 'The Crisis in the Universities', *Modern Quarterly*, vol. 5 (spring 1950), p. 157.
9. J. Bernal, 'Science against War', p. 46.
10. ibid., p. 33.
11. '1956 and After', in R. Miliband and J. Saville (eds.), *Socialist Register 1976* (London, 1976), pp. 1–57.
12. *World News and Views*, 12 January 1957; as quoted in R. Black, *Stalinism in Britain* (London, 1970), p. 427.
13. D. Lessing, *The Golden Notebook* (London, 1973), p. 466.
14. J. Saville, 'The Twentieth Congress and the British Communist Party', in *Socialist Register 1976*, p. 16.
15. H. Levy, 'Soviet Socialism', *New Reasoner*, no. 1 (summer 1957); as abridged in British and Irish Communist Organization, *The Cult of the Individual: The Controversy within British Communism, 1956–58* (Belfast, 1975), p. 39.
16. H. Levy, *Jews and the National Question*, rev. American ed. (New York, 1958), pp. 86–7.

17. R. Dutt, *World News and Views*, 8 March 1958; as cited in H. Levy, *Jews and the National Question*, p. 96.
18. As quoted in 'Professor Hyman Levy', *The Times*, 1 March 1975, p. 16.
19. H. Levy, *Jews and the National Question*, p. 12.
20. H. Levy, letter to the author, 17 June 1974.
21. M. MacEwen, 'The Day the Party Had to Stop', *Socialist Register 1976*, p. 24.
22. R. Clark, *J.B.S.; The Life and Work of J. B. S. Haldane* (London, 1968), p. 214.
23. As quoted in ibid., p. 257.
24. As quoted in N. Pirie, 'John Burdon Sanderson Haldane (1892–1964)', *Biographical Memoirs of Fellows of the Royal Society*, vol. 12 (1966), p. 222.
25. 'Bacteriological Warfare in Korea and China', *Science for Peace Bulletin*, no 5 (December 1952), pp. 4–6.
26. J. Needham, unpublished Presidential Address, delivered on 9 May 1964 to the A.G.M. of the British-China Friendship Association.
27. J. Needham, *Science and Civilisation in China*, 7 vols in 13 parts (Cambridge, 1954—   ).
28. L. Picken, as quoted on the dustjacket of the 1965 reprint of *Science and Civilisation*, vol. 1.
29. ibid.
30. J. Needham, *The Grand Titration: Science and Society in East and West* (London, 1969), p. 133.
31. J. Bernal, 'Stalin as Scientist', *Modern Quarterly*, vol. 8 (summer 1953), p. 133.
32. I. Ehrenburg, *Men, Years – Life*, vol. 6 (London, 1966), p. 215.
33. *Voprosy istorie estestvoznaniya i tekhniki (VIET)*, 1958, Vyp. 6; as cited in J. Cooper, *The Concept of the Scientific and Technical Revolution in Soviet Theory*, University of Birmingham, CREES Discussion Paper no. 9, 1973, pp. 5–7.
34. B. Lovell, 'Patrick Maynard Stuart Blackett', *Biographical Memoirs of Fellows of the Royal Society*, vol. 21 (1975), pp. 76–8.
35. As quoted by J. Crowther, *Science in Modern Society*, (London, 1967), p. 84.
36. N. Vig, *Science and Technology in British Politics* (London, 1968), pp. 26 and 30.
37. L. Hogben, 'A University in a Changing Society', *International Journal of Educational Science*, vol. 3 (1969).
38. L. Hogben, *The Vocabulary of Science* (London, 1969), and *Astronomer, Priest and Ancient Mariner* (London, 1972).
39. L. Hogben, *Science in Authority*, (London, 1963).
40. 'Council's Report to the General Committee', vol. 16 (1959–60), pp. 263–4.
41. L. Hogben, *Science in Authority*, pp. 113–21.
42. *The British Road to Socialism: Programme of the Communist Party*, 4th ed. (London, 1968), pp. 5–6.
43. E.g., P. Foot, *Why You Should be a Socialist* (London, 1976).

44. A. Zvorykin, 'Science as a Direct Productive Force', *Impact of Science on Society*, vol. 13 (1963), pp. 49–60.
45. D. Bell, *The Comming of Post-industrial Society* (London, 1975).
46. D. Bell, *The End of Ideology* (Glencoe, 1960).
47. C. Kerr, *Industrialism and Industrial Man* (Cambridge, Mass., 1960); and H. Marcuse, *One-dimensional Man* (Boston, 1964).
48. P. Anderson, 'The Left in the Fifties', *New Left Review*, no. 29 (January–February 1965), pp. 12–13.
49. P. Anderson, 'Components of the National Culture', in A. Cockburn and R. Blackburn (eds.), *Student Power* (Harmondsworth, 1969), pp. 216–217.
50. S. Rose (ed.), *Chemical and Biological Warfare* (London, 1968).
51. H. and S. Rose, 'Knowledge and Power', *New Scientist*, vol. 42 (17 April 1969), p. 108.

Afterword

1. A. Richmond, *A Long View from the Left: Memoirs of an American Revolutionary* (Boston, 1973), p. 245.
2. A. Kettle, as quoted in J. Saville, 'The Twentieth Congress and the British Communist Party', *Socialist Register 1976* (London, 1976), p. 22.
3. J. B. S. Haldane, *Keeping Cool, and Other Essays* (London, 1940), p. 279.
4. G. Calvert, as quoted in K. Sale, *S.D.S.* (New York, 1973), p. 318.

Index